The Illustrated Directory of

CLASSIC CARS

Graham Robson

PUBLISHED BY
SALAMANDER BOOKS LIMITED
LONDON

A Salamander Book

Published by Salamander Books Ltd.,
8 Blenheim Court,
Brewery Road,
London N7 9NT

A member of the Chrysalis Group plc

ISBN 1 84065 243 8

Credits

Project Manager: Ray Bonds
Designed by: Interprep Ltd.
Color reproduction by: Studio Technology
Printed in: Hong Kong

The Author

Graham Robson has been fascinated by cars – classic, modern, road, and sporting – for many years, in a career which began as an Engineering Graduate at Jaguar Cars in 1957. Along the way he also found time to compete in rallies all over Europe, to become Competitions Manager of Standard-Triumph in the 1960s, to join *AUTOCAR* magazine's technical staff, then to run the experimental and road proving departments at Chrysler UK Ltd. – before finally becoming an independent writer, historian, author, and broadcaster in the 1970s. As one of the most prolific of all British motoring writers, he is a recognized authority on many classic marques, contributes to motoring publications around the world, can often be seen commentating at major classic and sporting events around the UK, and has now written over 100 books, including several standard works on classic cars.

Acknowledgments

The publishers wish to thank the automobile manufacturers who have scoured their archives in order to provide photographs for this book, as well as many private photographers and collectors, in particular Mirco De Cet, Andrew Morland, and Keith Anderson.

Additional captions

Front cover: top, Hispano-Suiza V12; center, Auburn Straight-Eight; bottom, Derby-built Bentley.
Back cover: Ferrari F40.
Page 1: Aston Martin Vanquish V12.
Pages 2-3: Squire.
Pages 4-5: Ford Mustang.

Contents

AC Ace

Ace, Aceca, Ace-Bristol, Ace-Zephyr and Greyhound (data for Ace-Bristol)
Built by: AC Cars Ltd., Britain.
Engine: Six cylinders, in line, in four-bearing, cast-iron block. Bore and stroke 66mm by 96mm, 1,971cc (2.60 × 3.78in, 120.3cu.in). BMW-inspired pushrod overhead valve operation, two valves per cylinder, operated by pushrod and rocker, exhaust valve by pushrod, pivot, cross pushrod and rocker. Single side-mounted camshaft. Aluminium cylinder head with downdraught siamesed inlet ports and three Solex carburettors. In standard tune, maximum power 105bhp. In further-modified form, 128bhp at 5,750rpm, and maximum torque 122lb.ft at 4,500rpm.
Transmission: Single-dry-plate clutch and four-speed synchromesh gearbox (with non-synchronised first gear) in unit with back engine. Open propeller shaft to chassis-mounted hypoid final drive. Exposed universally jointed drive shafts to rear wheels.
Chassis: Separate multi-tubular frame, relying on two main tubes for beam and torsional stiffness. Fully independent front and rear suspension, by traverse leaf springs and wishbones. Bishop cam steering. Coil spring suspension, plus rack-and-pinion steering on Greyhound. Telescopic dampers. Drum brakes on all wheels at first, but Girling front discs from 1957.
Light-alloy coachwork on framework of light tubes – open two-seat (Ace), closed two-seat (Aceca), or closed 2+2 seater (Greyhound).
Dimensions: Wheelbase 7ft 6in (229), tracks 4ft 2in (127cm). Overall length Ace 12ft 8in (386cm), Aceca 13ft 4in (406cm), Greyhound 14ft 7in (444cm). Unladen weight Ace-Bristol sports car 1,850lb (838kg).
History: After years of making nothing but the 2-litre saloon design, AC

Right: Even prettier than the Ace two-seater was the Aceca coupé – sold with the light-alloy AC, or with the 2-litre six-cylinder Bristol engine. The styling was all-British, but looked Italian – a compliment to AC's car. Each car was hand-built around a twin-tube steel chassis, with transverse leaf spring all-independent springing. Maximum speed was up to 120mph.

surprised the world by announcing their new Ace sports car in 1953. Although the Ace retained the distinguished old 1,991cc engine, by now tuned to give 85bhp, the chassis and coachwork were startlingly modern. Inspiration was from John Tojeiro's Bristol-engined sports-racing car which raced in Britain in the early 1950s. Tojeiro, introduced to AC, was asked to productionise this chassis and specify the AC engine. With this superb Ferrari-like styling, the Ace went on sale in 1954. This chassis was rudimentary but strong with two main tubular longerons suitably attached to transverse leaf springs and lower wishbones. So low were the weight and the centre of gravity, that anti-roll bars were not needed to ensure good handling. Maximum speed was about 105mph in original form.

The very pretty fastback Aceca soon followed the Ace, and final work on the 40-year-old engine design produced a 105bhp power output. Demands from customers who wanted to race or rally their cars resulted in the BMW-based six-cylinder Bristol engine being offered. This could (and often was) urged to produce more than 140bhp, and made the Ace very fast indeed. In 128bhp production form a 120mph maximum speed was usual, and roadholding was as well balanced as ever. The AC engine was offered right up to the death of the Ace in the mid-1960s, but the Bristol unit was dropped in 1961, after which a few of the tuned 2.6-litre Ford Zephyr units were offered instead.

An interesting but unsuccessful diversion at Thames Ditton was that a long-wheelbase 'almost four seater' car, the Greyhound, was sold, but it was both too expensive and too unrefined to be a success. Before time finally caught up with the Ace it was transformed into the Cobra by the transplant of an American V8 engine. Sales of Cobras were so high that AC found they could fill their workshops with no difficulty, and the Ace models had to be discontinued in 1964.

AC Cobra

AC Cobra 260, AC Cobra 289, AC Cobra 427, AC Daytona Cobra (data for Cobra 289)

Built by: AC Cars Ltd., Britain, and Shelby American Inc., USA.

Engine: Eight cylinders, in 90-degree vee-formation, in five-bearing cast-iron block. Bore and stroke 101.6mm by 72.9mm, 4,727cc (4.00 × 2.87in, 289cu.in). cast-iron cylinder heads. Two overhead valves per cylinder, operated by pushrods and rockers from a single camshaft positioned in the vee of the cylinder block. Single carburettor. Maximum power 195bhp (gross) at 4,400rpm in standard form. Maximum torque 282lb.ft at 2,400rpm. Shelby-modified Mustang-type engines with up to 271bhp (gross) available to special order. Engine based on mass-production Ford of Detroit 4.2/4.7-litre unit.

Transmission: Single-dry-plate clutch, and four-speed all-synchromesh manual gearbox in unit with engine. Open propeller shaft to chassis-mounted Salisbury limited-slip final drive, with 3.45:1 ratio. Universally jointed exposed drive shafts to rear wheels.

Chassis: Tubular chassis frame, with two main longitudinal tubes and front and rear subframes supporting suspensions. Independent front and rear suspension by transverse leaf springs and lower wishbones (from 1965 by coil springs and unequal length wishbones). Steering by rack and pinion (by worm and sector on first 125 cars built in 1962). Girling disc brakes to all four wheels. Wire wheels with 185 × 15in tyres.

Dimensions: Wheelbase 7ft 6in (229cm), track (front) 4ft 7in (140cm), track (rear) 4ft 6in (137cm). Overall length 13ft (396cm). Unladen weight 2,282lb (1,035kg).

History: American racing driver Carroll Shelby first approached AC Cars Ltd of Thames Ditton in autumn 1961, proposing that they should supply Ace body-chassis assemblies, for his Los Angeles based company to insert Ford V8

engines and transmissions. A prototype was completed early in 1962, and production of the first 100 cars began later in the year. Compared with that of the Ace, the chassis was much strengthened, as were the suspension components, and a more robust 4HA Salisbury back axle was fitted. These cars were shipped from Britain to California for American-sourced parts to be fitted. The first 75 cars were equipped with 4.2-litre (260cu.in) engines, and the first 125 with Ace-type worm-and sector steering. From the beginning of 1963 the 4.7-litre (289cu.in) V8 engine, and rack-and-pinion steering became normal.

Shelby raced Cobras with great success, evolving for 1964 the brutal but sensationally fast 'Daytona' coupé body. Thus equipped, the team won the 1964 World GT Championship. There were important changes in 1965. First, a major suspension redesign replaced the transverse leaf springing by a coal-spring and double-wishbone layout. Second, and more important, from mid 1965, all Shelby supplied cars had been fitted with the much bulkier 6.989cc Ford Galaxie-based V8 engine, with 345 bhp (gross) at 4,600rpm. At the same time, AC re-designated the smaller version an 'AC 289' and were allowed to sell these cars on the British and other markets. There was always confusion over names. AC insisted that the car was an AC, but Shelby badged it, and marketed it, as a Shelby American Cobra (and it was homologated in sporting form with that name). Later, and even more confusing, the cars became known as Ford Cobras.

Production of Cobras was suspended in 1968, after which AC produced a long-wheelbase chassis version called the AC428, which was equipped with stylish and expensive Frua coachwork. The last of those cars was produced in 1973, but was not the end of the story. Under new management, the Cobra was re-introduced in 1983, as a 5-litre V8-engined Mark IV. Tiny numbers, re-creations of the original type, really, were then produced until the end of the century, along with a 355bhp supercharged version known as 'Superblower'.

Left and below: By fitting a massive Ford vee-8 engine, fat wheels, and racing equipment, Shelby turned the stylish Cobra into a brutally efficient racing car. Re-bodied versions were 'Daytonas'.

AC 'Six' 2-litre

Ace, Acedes, Aceca, Magna, Aero and other versions, built from 1919 to 1956 (data for 1927 Acedes)

Built by: Autocarriers Ltd., then (from 1922) AC Cars Ltd., Britain.

Engine: Six cylinders, in line, in five-bearing, wet-liner, cast-alloy block. Bore and stroke 65mm by 100mm, 1,991cc (2.56 × 3.94in, 121.5cu.in). Cast-iron cylinder head. Two overhead valves per cylinder, operated by single overhead camshaft. Single carburettor. Maximum power about 40bhp.

Transmission: AC plate clutch at rear of engine, cast-aluminium torque tube to gearbox, in unit with back axle. Three forward speeds, without synchromesh, ratios 4.5, 7.00 and 13.2 to 1. Alternative ratios on request. Right-hand gearchange. Overhead-worm-drive back axle.

Chassis: Pressed-steel channel-section side members, with tubular cross members. Front axle suspended on forward-facing quarter-elliptic cantilever leaf springs. Quarter-elliptic leaf springs at rear. Friction-type dampers at front only. Snubbers above back axle. Four-wheel brakes, 12in by 1¾in drums all round. Several variations in coachwork – two/three seat tourer, coachbuilt saloon, or fabric saloon.

Dimensions: Wheelbase 9ft 3in or 9ft 9in (282 or 297cm), tracks (front and rear) 3ft 9in (114cm). Overall length, from 13ft 9in (358cm) – depending on coachwork. Unladen weight, 232lb (1052kg).

History: The AC 'Six' was not a single, long-lived model, but a progressively improved family of cars. Its engine, in particular, established a record in Great Britain, by being in active production from 1919 until 1963, when it was last used by AC in the Ace sports car. AC cars were first made in 1913, although there had been tricars before that. Their first car was a four-cylinder two-seater (the engine being by Fivet, from France) and it had features like the gearbox in unit with the back axle, something which was to be an AC characteristic for so long. There was even an axle disc brake.

The legendary 'Six' was designed by John Weller during World War I, was announced in 1919, and went on sale in 1920. It was quite remarkably advanced by the standards of the day and still looked reasonably up-to-date when being sold in the 1960s. The aluminium-alloy block/crankcase combined with spigoted wet liners, was unusual, as was the fact that a cast-iron cylinder head was specified.

Right: The six-cylinder ACs had an enormously long and successful run, though only the engine was a constant feature. This was a 1925 tourer with disc wheels and the obligatory dickey seat of the 1920s. AC was guided by Selwyn Edge in the 1920s.

Ex-Napier chief Selwyn Edge joined AC in 1921 and became Governing Director in 1922, whereupon the company's founders, John Weller and John Portwine walked out. Edge then changed the company's name to AC Cars Ltd., by which it is known today.

Success in competition was thought necessary to prove the vehicle, and AC often competed for distance records at the nearby Brooklands track. The Hon. Victor Bruce won the Monte Carlo Rally in 1926 (the first win by a Briton).

The 'Six' put on weight later in the 1920s, as bodies became heavier and equipment became more complex. AC countered this by tuning up their splendid engine and for 1928 the Acedes was given a 56bhp. Half-elliptic front springs and hydraulic brakes appeared before the end of the 1920s, by which time an AC saloon might weigh up to 2,700lb (12,224kg).

When Edge retired in 1929 the company was placed in voluntary liquidation, but it was revived by the Hurlock brothers in 1931. They produced a new design, still relying heavily on the alloy 'six', but with a new chassis, a Moss four-speed gearbox in unit with the engine and a central, remote-control gearshift.

The first 'Ace', perhaps better known in its 1950s guise, appeared in 1935 and was a pretty and light little sports two-seater, ideal for rallies and trials. Acceleration from rest to 60mph in about 18seconds was fast by any standards and the handling offered by the half-elliptic leaf springs all round was very sporting.

Synchromesh gears, or the option of the British Wilson pre-selector box, came in at about the same time. 80bhp was talked of from the 1,991cc engine, but this was almost certainly optimistic. At one stage, at the end of the 1930s, an Arnott supercharger could be ordered as an extra, and automatic chassis lubrication was standardised in 1937.

After World War II, the existing designs were dropped, and replaced by a single new model, the 2-litre. This was a two-door saloon at first, but a more expensive drop-head convertible also became available. The chassis, although all-new, retained a rigid front axle and half-elliptic springs all round. Engine power was now up to a guaranteed 76bhp at 4,500rpm, but needed a triple SU carburettor installation to guarantee this. The 2-litre was not updated and eventually went out of production in 1956.

Alfa Romeo 6C Series

6C1500, 6C1750, 6C1900 models, built 1927-1933 (data for 6C1750 Super Sport)

Built by: SA Italiana Nicola Romeo & C., Italy.

Engine: Six cylinders, in line, in cast-iron block, on separate four-bearing light-alloy crankcase. Bore and stroke 65mm by 88mm, 1,752cc (2.56in × 3.46in, 107.0cu in). Detachable cast-iron cylinder head. Two overhead valves per cylinder, operated directly via screwed-in tappets from twin overhead camshafts in cylinder head. Single horizontal carburettor with Roots-type supercharger at nose of crankshaft, or single updraught carburettor without supercharger. Maximum power (supercharged) 85bhp (gross) at 4,500rpm. Maximum power (unsupercharged) 64bhp (gross) at 4,500rpm.

Transmission: Dry multi-plate clutch and four-speed manual gearbox without synchromesh, all in unit with front-mounted engine. Direct control central gearchange. Propeller shaft enclosed in torque tube, connected to spiral bevel 'live' rear axle.

Chassis: Separate steel chassis frame, with pressed and tubular cross-bracings, and channel section side members. Tubular front axle beam. Front suspension by semi-elliptic leaf springs. Rear suspension by semi-elliptic leaf springs and torque tube. Friction-type dampers. Four-wheel drum brakes, shaft and rod operated. Centre lock wire spoke wheels. 27 x 4.5in tyres. Coachbuilt two-seater open sports car body style, mostly by Zagato – light-alloy panels on wooden framing.

Dimensions: Wheelbase 9ft 0in (274.5cm), tracks (front and rear) 4ft 6.3in (138cm). Overall length 13ft 4in (406cm). Unladen weight (unsupercharged/ supercharged) 1,985/2,030lb (900/920kg).

History: The triumphs of the Alfa Romeo P2 were still fresh in the minds of Alfa-Romeo directors when they asked Vittorio Jano to develop a new, much lighter car than the RL range. The brilliant Jano, whose fame at Milan had only really just begun, laid down a conventional chassis, but graced it with the first of a series of six-cylinder engines. Between 1927, when the first 6C1500 was actually delivered, and 1933, when it was finally overtaken by the even more noteworthy 8C series, this engine family was built in many guises, with single and twin overhead camshaft cylinder heads, with or without superchargers.

The 6C1500, which founded the range, originally had big six-seater bodywork, and its unsupercharged single-cam engine could produce a top speed of 70mph. The next step was to reveal the 6C1500 Sport, complete with twin-cam detachable cylinder head, and in 1929 this was further developed into the 6C1500 Super Sport, where light-alloy bodies were specified, and where the option of a supercharged engine made top speeds of 87mph with 76bhp.

All this, however, paled into insignificance when the beautiful 6C1750 models arrived, in which the same basic engines had larger cylinder bores and longer strokes, but were outwardly much the same as before. The Gran Sport and Super Sport models had outstandingly rakish two-seater short-chassis bodies by Zagato or Touring: the supercharged Super Sport, with 85bhp, could reach more than 90mph.

The 'works' team drivers had the pick of the factory's expertise, which included providing them with engines having non-detachable cylinder heads cast in unit with the cylinder blocks, a ruse which allowed the supercharging to be boosted, and the maximum power to be raised to more than 100bhp (and top speed to about 106mph). Thus equipped, Tazio Nuvolari won the 1930 Mille Miglia in great style. Achille Varzi won the Targa Florio, and Nuvolari

Above: Vittorio Jano designed a brand-new six-cylinder car for Alfa Romeo in the 1920s, and the 6C cars were built in Milan for seven years. This was the 1928 6C 1500 Super Sport (twin-camshaft) model.

then went on to win the Tourist trophy race, which was held in Northern Ireland at the time.

Development of competition cars, however, was rapid, and from 1931 the 6C1750 model was supplanted by the even more exciting 8C2300 sports cars, but there was still a close connection, for these eight-cylinder engined cars had many engine components in common with the 6C1750 units. Jano having been instructed to lay down the new engine on just that basis.

In fairness, one should mention that unsupercharged, long-wheelbase, mildly tuned versions of this chassis and power train were always available, but somehow it was the very fast sports cars which always stole the headlines. Certainly the twin-cam cylinder heads, with valves opposed at 90 degrees, and with classically simple valve operation, set the standard followed by many other designers in the 1930s, and the basic design was used on all *eight*-cylinder Alfas built until the outbreak of war in 1939 as well. The 6C1750 Super Sport, of course, became so famous in Italy that in the 1960s *Quattroroute* (the Italian motoring magazine) sponsored the deign of a modern 'look-alike' car using current-model Alfa Romeo mechanical equipment. It says much for the 1920s type of Alfa Romeo that the modern car was not even thought to have as much character and appeal.

Even after the 8C2300 had been designed, introduced, and taken precedence over the 6C1750 cars, that was not quite the end of the story. Alfa Romeo realised that the 8Cs were too costly, and too esoteric, to appeal to every sportsman, and in 1933 they produced a series of 197 6C1900 GT cars, in which the famous six-cylinder engine was bored out to a capacity of 1917cc, and had a light-alloy twin-cam cylinder head, which was a material innovation for the type. It is not without significance that the bore and stroke of this engine was the same as that of the current 8C2600 Monza, for the policy of commonisation of moving parts was well developed at Alfa Romeo at this time.

The last 6C car of all was built in 1933, after which its place was taken by the new 6C2300, which had an entirely different twin-cam engine.

Alfa Romeo 8C Series

8C models built from 1931 to 1939 (data for 8C2300 or 1931 – Spider Corsa version)
Built by: SA Alfa Romeo, Italy.
Engine: Eight cylinders, in line, in two four-cylinder light-alloy blocks bolted up to a ten-bearing light-alloy crankcase. Bore and stroke 65mm by 88mm, 2,336cc (2.56in × 3.46in, 142.5cu in). Two detachable light-alloy cylinder heads. Two overhead valves per cylinder opposed to each other at 90 degrees and operated by twin overhead camshafts and tappets screwed on to the valve stems. Single downdraught carburettor and Roots-type supercharger. Dry-sump lubrication. Maximum power 155bhp at 5.200rpm (165/180bhp at 5,400 in 1932/43).
Transmission: Multiple-dry-plate clutch, and four-speed manual gearbox (without synchromesh), all in unit with front-mounted engine. Direct action central gearchange. Propeller shaft enclosed in torque tube to spiral-bevel 'live' rear axle.
Chassis: Separate pressed-steel chassis frame, with tubular and sheet-metal cross-bracing, and channel-section side members. Tubular front axle beam. Front and rear suspension by half-elliptic leaf springs and friction-type dampers. Four-wheel drum brakes, shaft and cable operated. 18in centre-lock wire wheels 29 × 5.50 tyres.
Dimensions: Wheelbase 9ft 0.2in (275cm), front track 4ft 6.3in (138cm), rear track 4ft 6.3in (138cm). Overall length 13ft 5in (409cm). Unladen weight 2,205lb (1,00kg).

History: Vittorio Jano joined Alfa Romeo in 1923, and immediately began a design programme which led to the famous P2 Grand Prix cars, and to the use of twin-cam engines in the 6C1500 and 6C1750 series of cars. By the end of the 1920s Alfa's sports and racing cars were pre-eminent. To ensure continued domination, Jano then designed the legendary straight-eight twin-cam engine, which was to power the 8C cars throughout the 1930s and (in developed form) Alfa's Grand Prix cars for a number of years.

The engine was a constructional masterpiece, with two four-cylinder blocks and two cylinder heads on a common crank and crankcase, with camshaft drive by a train of gears up the centre of the unit. 8C2300 cars were tremendously successful sports cars in the early 1930s, and were speedily developed into the 8C2600 Monza sports-racing machines by the Scuderia Ferrari. The 2300 Monza and B-Type single-seaters had much in common, and the 8C2900 range (with the same basic engine, enlarged and made more powerful – up to 220bhp) kept the government-controlled Milan producers competitive. Production was always low, almost handbuilt, but Mussolini intended the cars as prestige machines, and not profit-makers and if every modern-day schoolboy yearns after a Ferrari, in the 1920s and 1930s he would have wanted an Alfa Romeo. A car needs no better epitaph than that.

Below: This famous 8C Alfa Romeo is a Monza, the ultra-special racing derivative, as driven by Tazio Nuvolari in the early 1930s. In this period Enzo Ferrari prepared the 'works' cars.

Alfa Romeo Giulietta Series

Giulietta, built from 1954 to 1964 (data for 1956 Sprint Veloce)
Built by: Alfa Romeo SpA., Italy.
Engine: Four cylinders, in line, in five-bearing light-alloy block/crankcase. Bore and stroke 74mm by 75mm, 1,290cc (2.91in × 2.97in, 78.7cu.in). detachable light-alloy cylinder head. Two overhead valves per cylinder, opposed to each other at 90 degrees in part-spherical combustion chamber and operated by inverted-bucket tappets from twin overhead camshafts. Two horizontal twin-choke Weber carburettors. Maximum power 90bhp at 6,500rpm. Maximum torque 87lb.ft at 4,500rpm.
Transmission: Single-dry-plate clutch and four-speed synchromesh manual gearbox, both in unit with front-mounted engine. Remote control central gearchange. Two-piece open propeller shaft to hypoid-bevel 'live' rear axle.
Chassis: Unitary-construction pressed-steel body/chassis unit, in two-door four-seat coupé style by Bertone. Independent front suspension by coil springs, wishbones and anti-roll bar. Repeat suspension by coil springs, radius arms and A-bracket. Telescopic dampers. Worm-and-roller steering. Four-wheel, hydraulically operated drum brakes. 15in pressed-steel bolt-on wheels. 155 × 15in tyres.
Dimensions: Wheelbase 7 ft 10in (239cm), track (front) 4ft 2.9in (129cm), track (rear) 4ft 2in (127in). Overall length 12ft 10.5in (393cm). Unladen weight 1,973lb (895kg).
History: The Giulietta series, born in 1954, was really Alfa's first attempt at mass-production, although the 1900 model had paved the way to this a few years previously. It was laid down specifically to be produced in many versions – four-door saloon, two-door coupé, and open Spider, and each and every one of the cars had a splendid and all-new twin-cam light-alloy engine. Until then, only Jaguar had put a twin-cam into true quantity production, but by the start of the 1960s Alfa Romeo had overtaken their figures. The 1,290cc engine was only the first of a magnificent pedigree and family of units – since expanded through 1600, 1800 to 2-litre versions, and forming the backbone of middle-class Alfa private car production. The Sprint came about as a result of a *muletto* car built by Bertone, and speedily adopted by Alfa Romeo. For years it was known as the most beautiful of all small GT cars, and was only surpassed by the bigger-engined Giulia GT which followed in the 1960s. Well over 150,000 Giuliettas of all types were built in ten years, which included some really fierce Zagato-bodied competition cars and more than 25,000 Sprint GTs and Veloces. The Giulietta was the car which changed Alfa's public image – before this they had made a few expensive cars, and after it they were to make a lot of middle-class thoroughbreds with world-wide appeal.

Right: The Giulietta Spider, as styled by Pininfarina, was one of the purest and most classic sporting two-seater shapes yet seen. For the final years the cars gained a 1.6-litre engine, and a bonnet scoop.

6 FLE

Alfa Romeo Montreal

Montreal model built 1970 to 1976
Built by: Alfa Romeo, Italy.
Engine: Eight cylinders, in 90-degree vee-formation, in five-bearing light-alloy combined block/crankcase. Bore and stroke 80mm by 64.5mm, 2,593cc (3.15 × 2.54in, 158.2cu in). Two detachable light-alloy cylinder heads. Two overhead valves per cylinder, inclined to each other and operated by twin overhead camshafts through inverted bucket-type tappets. Spica fuel injection and dry-sump lubrication. Maximum power 200bhp (DIN) at 6,500rpm. Maximum torque 173lb.ft at 4,750rpm. The engine is a de-tuned and developed version of the Alfa Type 33 racing sports car unit of the late 1960s, raced in 2-litre, 2½-litre and 3-litre form.
Transmission: Single-dry-plate clutch, and five-speed all-synchromesh manual gearbox, all in unit with front-mounted engine. Remote-control central gearchange. Open propeller shaft to hypoid-bevel 'live' rear axle with limited-slip differential.
Chassis: Unitary-construction, pressed-steel, two-door, closed-coupé body shell, based on modern 1750/2000 floor pan. Front suspension by coil springs, wishbones and anti-roll bar. Rear suspension of live axle by coil springs, radius arms and anti-roll bar. Telescopic dampers. Rack-and-pinion steering. Four-wheel ventilated disc

Right: The Montreal was a car which started life as a special Motor Show exhibit, but public interest led it to be put into production. The chassis was that of the Alfa 1750 touring car, and the 2.6-litre vee-8 engine was a de-tuned version of the Type 33 racing car unit. Styling was by Bertone, and all those built had left hand drive. The headlamps are partly hidden by slats. Without any doubt this was the fastest production Alfa Romeo so far built, and the racing type of engine was remarkably docile.

brakes with servo assistance. 14in cast-alloy road wheels, 195/70 × 14in tyres.
Dimensions: Wheelbase 7ft 8.5in (235cm), track (front) 4ft 6in (137cm), track (rear), 4 ft 3.5in (131cm). Overall length 13ft 0in (422cm). Unladen weight 2,800lb (1,270kg).
History: Alfa Romeo showed a sleek 'styling exercise' at Expo 1967 in Montreal, which nobody took very seriously. The world was much more impressed in 1970 when the same car re-appeared in production from and powered by nothing less than a de-tuned version of the Type 33 racing two-seater's twin-cam V8 engine. The rest of the chassis was fairly ordinary (it was based on the floor pan and suspensions of the 1750/2000 saloon), but the performance was very impressive, with maximum speeds of between 130 and 140mph. Styling was by Bertone, some of whose finest work has been with Alfa Romeo, and the car was called 'Montreal' after its initial public appearance. It made no concessions to habitability and was a two-seater closed car, pure and simple. A feature was the headlamp positioning, with slatted covers making the lights almost invisible by day, although they were effective in use. The engine had been carefully detuned to take all the temperament out of it, with fuel injection to ensure good behaviour at all times. Never a high-production car, the Montreal was the 'flagship' of the Milan company's range.

Alfa Romeo SZ

Alfa Romeo SZ sports coupé. Along with RZ open version, built from 1989 to 1993

Built by: Alfa-Lancia Industriale S.p.A., Italy.

Engine: Eight cylinders in 90-deg vee, five-bearing cast alloy cylinder block. Bore and stroke 93 × 72.6mm, 2,959cc (3.66 × 2.86in, 180.6cu.in). Two light alloy cylinder heads. Two valves per cylinder, operation by single overhead camshaft per head. Bosch/Alfa electronic fuel injection. Maximum power 210bhp (DIN) at 6,200rpm. Maximum torque 181lb.ft at 4,500rpm.

Transmission: Rear-wheel-drive, single dry plate diaphragm spring clutch and five-speed all-synchromesh manual gearbox, all in unit with front-mounted engine. Remote-control, central gearchange.

Chassis: Unitary-construction pressed-steel body-chassis unit skinned in ICI methacrylic composite skin panels. Independent front suspension by coil springs, wishbones, telescopic dampers and anti-roll bar. De Dion rear suspension by coil springs, angled radius locating arms, Watts linkage and telescopic dampers. Rack-and-pinion steering, with hydraulic power assistance. Four-wheel disc brakes. Cast alloy 16in wheels, 205/55-16in (front) and 225/55-16in (rear) tyres.

Dimensions: Wheelbase 8ft 2.8in (250.9cm), front track 4ft 9.6in (146.4cm), rear track 4ft 8.1in (142.6cm). Overall length 13ft 3.8in (405.9cm). Unladen weight 2,778lb (1,260kg).

History: For Zagato, the specialist body-building concern which manufactured the body shell of the astonishing SZ sports coupé, this was a project made in heaven. Blessed by Alfa Romeo, who needed a short-run headline raiser at this stage of its history, there was no commercial risk and, in a way, the more outrageous the car looked, the better. Conceived in 1987 as a statement of its character, of its engineering genius, and its love for all things automotive, the new car was based on existing Alfa Romeo underpinnings – the 75 saloon – but had an entirely fresh steel body shell.

Not meant to be practical, not meant to be timeless, but meant to be a fun car for those who could afford it, the SZ was always placarded as a limited-

Above right and below: No-one ever called the Zagato-constructed Alfa Romeo SZ classically beautiful, but it was certainly brutal, unmistakeable, and appealing. Later cars were also available with a convertible style.

production machine. Starting in 1989, only 1,000 of the coupés would be produced and, although we did not know it at the time, when that run had been completed and sold, they would be followed by a convertible derivative, of which only 800 were built.

The style was, and always will be, controversial, for it flew in the face of almost everything Alfa Romeo was doing at the time. Built up on a short (98.8in/251cm) wheelbase platform, the new car had a bluff nose, a waistline which rose consistently towards the tail, slab sides and a fastback cabin profile. Not only that, but the details were, in many ways, bizarre – six small rectangular headlamps, no visible door handles and a freestanding rear aerofoil. The facia/instrument panel, at least, was conventional, well-equipped, and stylish.

Some loved it, some hated it, but when questioned Zagato merely replied politely that it was an Alfa project for which they had been hired to build production machinery. They were ideal for this task, they said, because the shell itself was a low-volume unit, and many of the skin panels were in high-tech composites, which needed a specialist to make, fettle and fit them together.

Under the arresting skin, the running gear was closely based on that of the 75 saloon, with the same pressed-steel platform. Like the highest-performance version of that car, there was a silky, high-revving and very effective V6 engine up front, while the five-speed transmission was at the rear, in unit with the final drive. As with several existing Alfa Romeos, there was De Dion rear suspension, which meant that the wheels were linked by a stout tube, but that the transaxle was mounted to the floorpan.

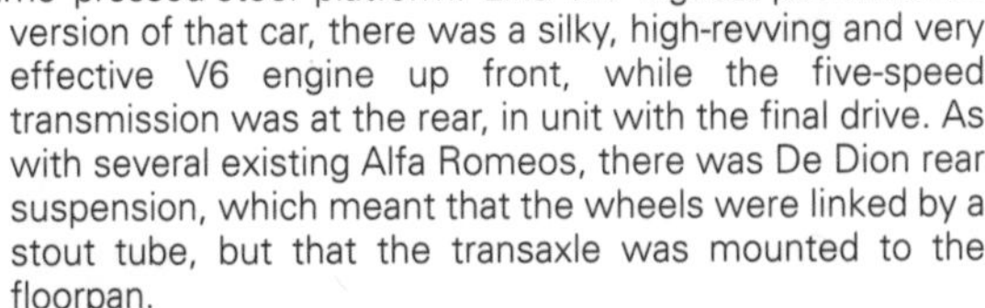

But, forget the looks for a moment, and consider how the SZ performed. Fast in a straight line (in spite of the unpromising-looking body shape it could beat 150mph), it was a true driver's car, with awesome grip, and a great feel. Much of the chassis development, after all, had been influenced by Alfa's current 75 racing saloons, so this was expected.

The mark of a great car is not what is the immediate public reaction, but what reputation it acquires over the years. The SZ, and the convertible RZ, therefore, seem to be safe, for they are now highly prized machines.

Alfa Romeo Type RL

Alfa Romeo RLN, RLS, RLSS and RLT, built from 1923 to 1927 (data for RLSS)

Engine: Six cylinders, in line, in cast-iron block with detachable four-bearing light-alloy crankcase. Bore and stroke 76mm by 110mm, 2,994cc (3.0in × 4.33in, 182-7cu.in). Two overhead valves per cylinder, operated by pushrods and rockers by side-mounted camshaft. Cast-iron detachable cylinder head. Dry-sump lubrication, one pressure and one scavenge pump. Twin updraught Solex or Zenity carburettors. Maximum power 83bhp at 3,600rpm.

Transmission: Dry multi-plate clutch, and four-speed manual gearbox, with centre or right-hand gearchange, in units with engine. Open propeller shaft to spiral bevel 'live' rear axle.

Chassis: Separate steel chassis frame, with channel-section side members, and steel cross braces. Half-elliptic leaf springs front and rear. Forged front axle beam. Mechanically operated footbrake on all four wheels, handbrake on transmission-sited drum. Friction-type dampers. Worm-and-wheel steering. Light-alloy coachwork, various coachbuilders.

Dimensions: Wheelbase 10ft 3in (312cm), tracks (front and rear) 4ft 9.5in (146cm). Overall length (depending on coachwork) about 15ft 0in (457cm). Unladen weight 3,600lb (1.633kg).

History: The RL Series (RL means 'Romeo Series L') stemmed from the design of a car, laid down in 1920, meant to comply with the 3-litre Grand Prix formula. When that formula was changed to a 2-litre limit, for 1922, the project was dropped. The detuned and productionised versions were first shown in Milan in October 1921, but did not properly get into production

until 1923. From then until 1927 the various marks of RL Alfas were a mainstay of the Italian company's activities. At first there were two series – the RLN touring car chassis with its 2.916cc engine, and the RLS with a 2,996cc engine. The capacity difference was simply achieved with a one millimetre different cylinder bore.

The 'S' chassis was a foot shorter than the 'N' at 10ft 3in, and the enlarged engine had twin carburettors instead of a single unit. Early cars had rear-wheel brakes only, but a four-wheel system was installed from late 1923. The RLN became the RLT in 1925 and the RLS the RLSS, but the cars continued on with minor improvements only. The engine, with its conventional pushrod overhead valve gear, was soon to be made Alfa's twin ohc units, but of its day it was very powerful; the SS model even had dry sump lubrication.

Racing versions of the S, with shortened (9ft 3in) wheelbases were made and were most successful. Enzo Ferrari, then employed by Alfa, was the team's star driver. Sivocci won the 1923 Targa Florio, and Antonion Ascari failed to repeat this in 1924 only when his engine seized 50 yards from the finish! It was in 1924 that Ferrari won the Coppa Acerbo in a 3.6-litre version, the largest possible in that cylinder block.

Although the chassis was entirely conventional, performance was always high, and the body styles striking. The RLs were dropped not because they had become obsolete, but because Vittorio Jano had become Chief Designer and wanted to see his own ideas put on sale. The famous 6C and 8C models were the result of that resolve. About 2,500 RL Alfas were built, but fewer than 20 survive today.

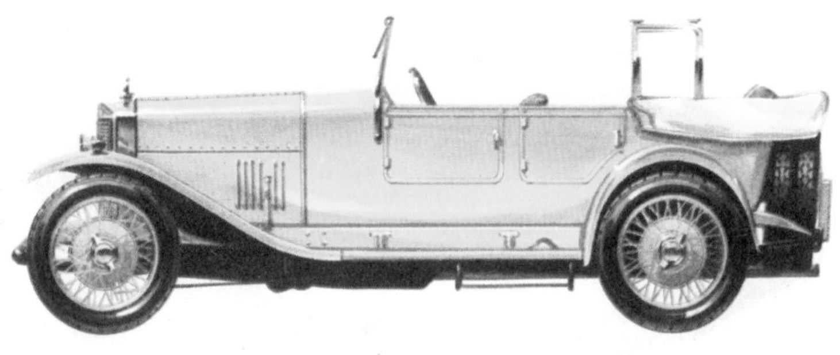

Above left and above: As with many vintage cars, the RL Alfas could be supplied with many bodies. This 1926 tourer had four doors, a separate windscreen for rear seat passengers, and twin spare wheels. The engine had overhead valves and produced about 83bhp (SS).

Left: The Alfa RLSS, here seen as a 1926 model with Weymann 'torpedo' body, was an efficient 3-litre car. Enzo Ferrari raced the cars with success, before turning to team management.

Alvis 12/50

12/50 SA to TJ, built from 1923 to 1932 (data for SA type of 1923)
Built by: Alvis Car and Engineering Co. Ltd., Britain.
Engine: Four cylinders, in line, in three-bearing cast-iron block. Bore and stroke 68mm by 103mm, 1,496cc (2.68 4.06in, 913cu.in). cast-iron cylinder head. Two overhead valves per cylinder, operated by pushrods and rockers from single, side-mounted camshaft. 5.35:1 compression ratio. One Solex carburettor. Engine originally derived from the first side-valve Alvis power unit, introduced in 1920. Power output about 50bhp minimum (each engine power tested before fitting). SC type had 1,598cc (97.5cu.in) engine. TE, TG and TJ types had 1,645cc (100.4cu.in) engine. All other types retained basic engine.
Transmission: Four-speed manual gearbox, without synchromesh, separated from engine by short shaft. Right-hand gearchange. Live spiral-bevel axle, fully floating type.
Chassis: Simple separate chassis, with pressed-steel channel-section members, and pressed cross members. Half-elliptic front and rear springs. No dampers. Ribbed drum brakes, mounted only on rear wheels. Worm-and-wheel steering with adjustable steering column. Dash-mounted petrol tank, gravity feed to engine. Two-seat lightweight sports bodywork normal. Many other options available (including saloon coachwork on later models).
Dimensions: Wheelbase 9ft 0.5in (275cm), track (front and rear) 4ft 2in (127cm). Overall length 12ft 9in (389cm).
History: The Alvis car was inspired by T. G. John, who set up his own company

in Coventry in 1919. The very first Alvis was dubbed a 10/30 model – which meant 10 British RAC-rating horsepower, and about 30 developed horsepower. Deliveries of this simple, but well-engineered, side-valve car, with its 1,460cc engine, began in 1920. Development, mainly through races and trials, was swift. The 10/30 soon became the 11/40, then the 12/40, and briefly the overhead-valve 10/30hp Super Sports.

The 12/50 Alvis, the first of a famous line of light sporting cars, arrived in 1923 to replace the Super Sports 10/30. Its power unit was a shorter-stroke/larger-bore version of that engine, aimed at giving more power and higher-revving capabilities. The pedigree of this model stretches from 1923 to 1932, when it was finally superseded by more modern designs. Although the chassis received little development in that time, the engine was persistently updated and made more powerful. Cars in factory-sponsored and private hands achieved great success in motor racing of the period.

Over the years there were at least eight basic body types, of which the most famous was undoubtedly the 'duck's back' shell with polished aluminium panelling. In 1931/32 the 12/50 was joined by the 12/60 type, basically the same car but having a more powerful engine with twin SU carburettors, close ratio gears, and more comprehensive equipment.

Below: Everybody loved the duck's back Alvis 12/50s, which were typical of the best in vintage sports cars.

Amilcar C-Series

C-Series cars, built from 1920 to 1929 (data for CGSS model)
Built by: Sté Nouvelle pour l'Automobile Amilcar, France.
Engine: Four cylinders, in line, in two-bearing cast-iron, block/crankcase. Bore and stroke 60mm by 95mm, 1,074cc (2.36in × 3.74in, 65.5cu.in). detachable light-alloy cylinder head. Two side valves per cylinder, operated by single side-mounted camshaft, via finger placed between stem and camshaft. One updraught Solex carburettor. Maximum power up to 35bhp at 4,500rpm. Optional supercharged version, with 40bhp at 4,500rpm.
Transmission: Multi-plate clutch, running in oil, and three-speed manual gearbox (without synchromesh) all in unit with engine. (Four-speed gearbox on last few built.) direct-acting central gearchange. Propeller shaft in torque tube to spiral-bevel 'live' rear axle.
Chassis: Separate pressed-steel chassis frame, with channel-section side members, fabricated and tubular cross-bracing. Forged front axle beam. Front suspension by half-elliptic leaf springs. Rear suspension by quarter-elliptic leaf springs. Friction-type dampers. Four-wheel drum brakes, rod and steel-strip operated. 27in centre-lock wire wheels. 27 × 4.00in tyres.
Dimensions: Wheelbase 7ft 7in (231cm), track (front and rear) 3ft 7in (109cm). Overall length 12ft (366cm). Unladen weight 1,200lb (544kg).
History: The Amilcar was a typical post-war French *voiturette*, or 'light car', in that it combined a tiny engine with minimal chassis and body weight to provide economical and amusing transport for the new motorists who could not afford anything bigger. Many such firms bought all their components from proprietary manufacturers, but Amilcar at least managed to design and build their own four-cylinder water-cooled engines.

The company was set up by Emil Akar and Joseph Lamy, and it is interesting to conjecture how the near-anagram of Amilcar's name evolved from those two people.

Below: Looking quaint with hood up, the 1926 Amilcar Italiana.

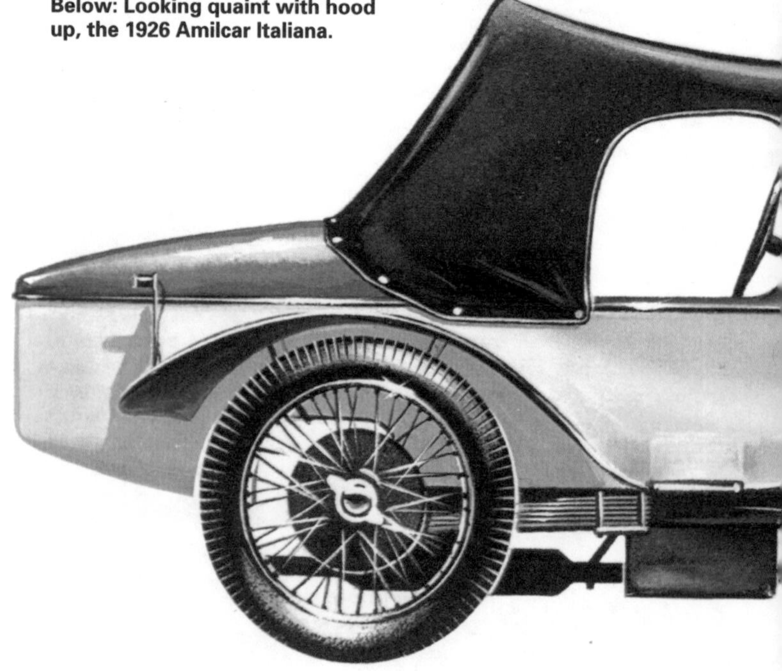

Above: A typically-detailed example of the Amilcar of the 1920s, with its light and functional wings, and the spare wheel fixed to the bonnet side.

Design was in the hands of Edmond Moyet, and André Morel worked, tested, and raced for the new firm. Amilcar was really founded from the ruins of the pre-war Le Zèbre firm, for whom Morel and Moyet had worked, and the cars were made in the old factory, near Paris.

The original product, first seen in 1920, was the Type CC, the basis for all four-cylinder cars to come in the 1920s. Its engine was small (903cc) and side-valve, while its rudimentary chassis had quarter-elliptic leaf springs at front and rear. The original car was so simple that in true 'cycle car' guise it had a straight-bevel final ▶

drive, without even a differential; this was later amended. The CC was normally a two-seater and strictly a touring car, weighing not more than 950lb (431kg) complete. From 1922 the range began to expand.

First along was the C4, with a longer chassis and enlarged 1,004cc engine, which could take four-seater bodies, while the CS was a rather more sporting version of the CC, with 985cc. The CS3, on the other hand, was a three-seater, where the third passenger could be accommodated in a dickey seat hanging over the tail. Most cars were built with the Petit Sport body – a narrow two-seat open shell, with a pointed tail and cycle type or combined wings with the running boards.

By 1924 a more sporting Amilcar still had evolved, directly as a result of the events contested by the factory in preceding years. The CGS (GS meaning 'Grand Sport') was a direct development of the CS, but had a bored-out 1,074cc engine, much improved brakes, a strengthened and lengthened chassis, and half-elliptic front springs. Ricardo had redesigned the head, which was now made of aluminium, and even though the CGS was quite a lot heavier than previous Amilcars it could still reach 75mph. Pressure lubrication was a great engine advance (splash lubrication had been normal up to then).

The CGS was good and sold well, but Moyet had even more exciting developments in mind. For 1926 he revealed the CGSS – the 'Surbaissé' model, so named because it had a lowered chassis frame and radiator. The power output had again been increased – to between 30 and 35bhp, and before the end of the model's run it was even given a four-speed gearbox. A few of the cars were built with Cozette superchargers, and such a model won the 1927 Monte Carlo Rally outright. Amilcar's problem, as with most of the other 'light car' builders, was that they were not sufficiently capitalised to change and update their cars frequently. By the end of the 1920s, whatever the increase in performance that had been achieved, they were still very much of an early-vintage design, and indeed a survivor of the 'light car' age which seems to have all but disappeared. Competition from quantity-production builders (like Citroën, in France, for instance) intensified, and their prices were much

Right and below: The CGSS model was a more sporting type of Amilcar, which raced and rallied with great success. The engine was small but the car was light. It was nippy and handled well.

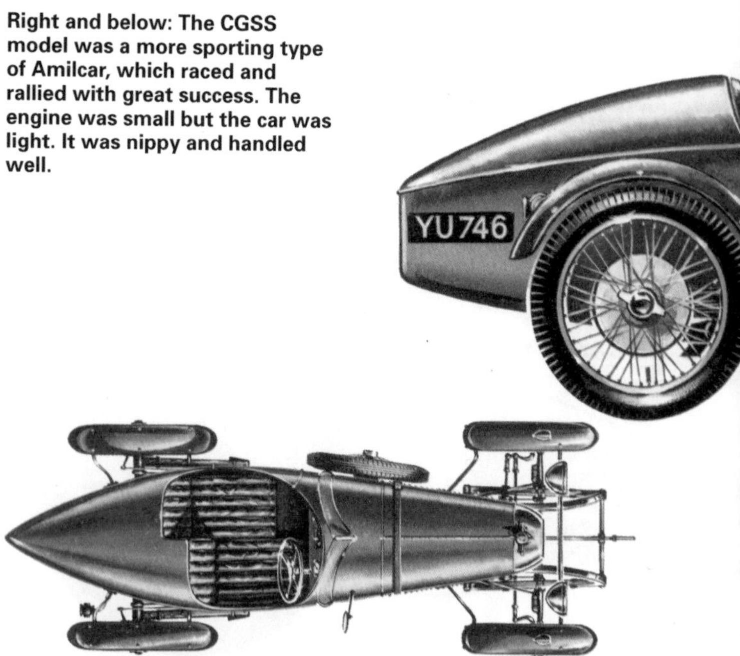

Above: The 1920s Amilcar C4 inspired many other sporting styles in the 1930s.

lower than Amilcar could manage.

Although their days as *voiturette*-manufacturers were over in 1929, they had already introduced parallel touring-car models. Between 1923 and the mid 1930s, a series of touring cars – the Type Es, Js, Ls, Gs (almost an alphabet of models) were on offer, some of them with six-cylinder models. Even so, nearly 4,700 of the CGS/CGSS sports cars were built in only five years, and rather more than 6,000 of the touring C-Series four-cylinder cars.

Armstrong Siddeley Special

Armstrong Siddeleys, built from 1919 to 1960 (data for 1933 Siddeley Special)
Built by: Armstrong Siddeley Motors, Ltd., Britain.
Engine: Six cylinders, in line, in seven-bearing light-alloy block/crankcase, with cast-iron wet liners pushed in on assembly. Bore and stroke 88.9mm by 133.4mm, 4,960cc (3.5in × 5.25in, 302.6cu.in). detachable alight-alloy cylinder head. Two in-line overhead valves per cylinder, operated by pushrods and rockers from single side-mounted camshaft. Single downdraught Claudel-Hobson carburettor.
Transmission: Armstrong Siddeley 'Wilson-type' preselector four-speed gearbox (with 'clutch' take up, and gear engagement by friction brake bands on appropriate gear trains), in unit with front-mounted engine. No clutch. Pre-selector lever on steering column, under steering wheel. Enclosed torque-tube propeller shaft to spiral-bevel 'live' rear axle.
Chassis: Separate pressed-steel chassis frame, with channel-section side members, pressed, fabricated and tubular cross bracing. Forged front axle beam. Front suspension by half-elliptic leaf springs. Rear suspension by half-elliptic leaf springs, torque tube and radius arms. Hydraulic dampers. Worm-and-nut steering. Four-wheel drum brakes, hydraulically operated (vacuum servo assistance on later models). 19in bolt on wire wheels or steel disc wheels to choice. 6.5 × 19in tyres. Open or closed coachwork to order, from Armstrong Siddeley or from specialists.
Dimensions: Wheelbase 11ft (335cm), track (front) 4ft 8in (142cm), track (rear) 4ft 10in (147cm). Overall length from 16ft 0in (488cm). Unladen weight (depending on body) from 5,000lb (2,268kg).
History: The firm came together by the fusion of Armstrong-Whitworth's car-making activities and Siddeley-Deasy of Coventry, and the cars were henceforth

built alongside the planes and aero-engines which were Armstrong's principal products. From 1919 to 1939 the company concentrated on solidly built, upper-middle-class family vehicles, but for comfort, ease of driving and high quality rather than performance. The massive vee-profiled radiators and the Sphinx mascots were recognition points, along with the refusal to put styling before interior passenger space.

This readily accepted tradition made the arrival of the beautifully engineered 5-litre Siddeley Special of 1932 a delightful surprise. For the first time the company used its aero-engine knowledge to great effect, for the new six-cylinder unit used hiduminium alloy castings for block/crankcase and cylinder head, and many construction details (for instance the multitude of bolts 'stitching' one casting to its neighbour, and the use of Claudel-Hobson carburettors) were similar. This car had a robust if conventionally engineered chassis, which allowed speeds of well over 80mph even in limousine form, and more than 90mph if open touring coachwork was ordered.

Armstrong Siddeley are famous for introducing the Wilson-type epicyclic self-change gearbox in 1928, and developing the pre-selector facility. The box was heavy, but as it did away with the clutch this nullified the loss, and in the days when the fully automatic gearbox was still a dream the Wilson-change was startlingly modern. It was taken up by many other car-makers, supplied direct to some, and licence-built by the others.

The Siddeley Special was high-priced – £1,050 bought a good four-seater sports saloon – and only about 140 of these cars were built in four years. There were models for most tastes, and in many engine sizes, and the company's reputation was secure in the 1930s. After the war, times were harder, and in spite of the fine Sapphire model demand dropped and the last car was built in 1960.

Left: Armstrong Siddeley's Special was their finest and most sporting car. Under the impressive coachwork was a powerful 4,960cc straight six-cylinder engine designed up to aero-engined standards. Gears were pre-selected.

Aston Martin DB2

DB2 models built 1950 to 1953, succeeded by DB 2/4 from 1953 to 1957 and DB3 from 1957 to 1959.
Built by: Aston Martin Ltd., Britain.
Engine: Six cylinders, in line, in four-bearing cast-iron block/crankcase. Bore and stroke 78mm by 90mm, 2,580cc (3.07in × 3.54in, 157.5cu.in). detachable light-alloy cylinder head. Two overhead valves per cylinder, inclined to each other at 30 degrees, operated by twin overhead camshafts, through inverted bucket-type tappets. Twin horizontal constant-vacuum SU carburettors. Maximum power 105bhp (net) at 5,000rpm. Maximum torque 125lb.ft at 3,000rpm.
Transmission: Single-dry-plate clutch and four-speed synchromesh manual gearbox (no synchromesh on first gear) both in unit with engine. Steering column or remote-control central gearchange to choice (column control soon dropped from specification). Open propeller shaft to hypoind-bevel 'live' rear axle.
Chassis: Separate fabricated multi-tube (square-section tubing) chassis frame, with cross and diagonal bracings. Independent front suspension by coil springs, trailing arms and anti-roll bar. Rear suspension by coil springs and twin trailing arms with Panhard rod location. Piston-type hydraulic dampers. Worm-and-roller steering. Four-wheel hydraulically operated drum brakes of 12in diameter. 16in centre lock wire wheels. 6.00 × 16in tyres. Light-alloy two-door coupé coachwork by Tickford (like Aston Martin, owned by David Brown Industries).
Dimensions: Wheelbase 8ft 3.0in (251.5cm), track (front and rear) 4ft 6in (137cm). Overall length 13ft 6.5in (412.8cm). Unladen weight 2,500lb (1,134kg).
History: Aston Martin proved their post-war design in the classic manner, by first building prototypes, and subjecting them to the public ordeal of long-distance sports car racing. The DB2 prototypes distinguished themselves in 1949 at the Le Mans and Spa 24-hour events and went into production in 1950. In more and more developed form the cars were then made until 1959 when they were finally supplanted by the DB4s. The cars were really a very clever amalgam of Aston Martin's post-war multi-tube chassis and Lagonda's Bentley-designed twin-cam engine – industrialist David Brown buying up both firms soon after World War II.

The DB2, too, had sleek good looks and impeccable road behaviour, all allied to an effortless 100mph-plus performance. One feature of the body was that the entire bonnet/wings/nose panel hinged ahead of the wheels and gave unrivalled access to the engine bay. The multi-tube chassis frame was expensive to make and repair, but as the company only made a handful of cars every week they were prepared for complication. It was, after all, very rigid. Perhaps the best version of this car was the DB2/4, which followed in 1953, with a large opening back window and – eventually – considerably more power, plus a tiny occasional rear seat.

Top right: The DB2 series arrived in 1949, was raced, and went into production in the form shown. The DB2/4 had an opening rear door/window, and later 3-litres. The DB Mk 3 evolved from it.

Centre: From 1953 the DB2 was modified, and made more practical, as the DB2/4. Not only were the lines smoothed out, and the interior made more civilised, but within a year a larger and more powerful, 2.9-litre, engine was standardised.

Right: The DB2/4, and later the DB Mk III, were built with a smart and practical hatchback body style, the first ever such fitted to a high-performance car.

CSV 451

MCA 183

VGD
929

Aston Martin DB4, DB5 and DB6

DB4, DB5, DB6, including DB4GT, built from 1958 to 1971 (data for DB4, 1959 model)

Built by: Aston Martin Lagonda Ltd., Britain.

Engine: Six cylinders, in line, in seven-bearing light-alloy block. Bore and stroke 92mm by 92mm, 3,670cc (3.62in × 3.63in, 223.9cu.in). light-alloy cylinder head. Two overhead valves per cylinder, inclined to each other, in part-spherical combustion chambers and operated by twin overhead camshaft, through inverted bucket-type tappet. Twin horizontal constant-vacuum SU carburettors. Maximum power 240bhp (net) at 5,500rpm. Maximum torque 240lb.ft at 4,250rpm.

Transmission: Single-dry-plate clutch and four-speed all-synchromesh manual gearbox, both in unit with front mounted engine. Remote control central gearchange. Open propeller shaft to hypoid-bevel 'live' rear axle.

Chassis: Fabricated steel platform-type chassis frame, with lightweight bodyshell of 'Superleggera' construction welded to it after assembly. Body has many lightweight forming tubes, light-alloy skin panels and bracing members. Independent front suspension by coil springs, wishbones and anti-roll bar. Rear suspension by coil springs, twin radius arms and Watts linkage. Telescopic dampers. Rack-and-pinion steering. Four-wheel disc brakes, with vacuum servo assistance. 16in centre-lock wire wheels. 6.00 × 16in tyres.

Dimensions: Wheelbase 8ft 2in (249cm), track (front) 4ft 6in (137cm), track (rear) 4ft 5.5in (136cm). Overall length 14ft 8.4in (448cm). Unladen weight 2,900lb (1,315kg).

History: During the 1950s, Aston Martin continued to race their sports cars with great success. In 1957 they produced brand new DBR1 and DBR2 models, both sharing the same basic multi-tube chassis, but whereas the DBR1 had an engine ▸

Below: The DB4 carried over many well-loved Aston Martin 'trade marks' including the grille shape, and the fast-back theme. Even the mildest versions could nudge 140mph, and the lightweight DB4GTs which followed were race winners when bodied by Zagato.

Above: The DB4 had exposed headlamps, all later versions having cowls.

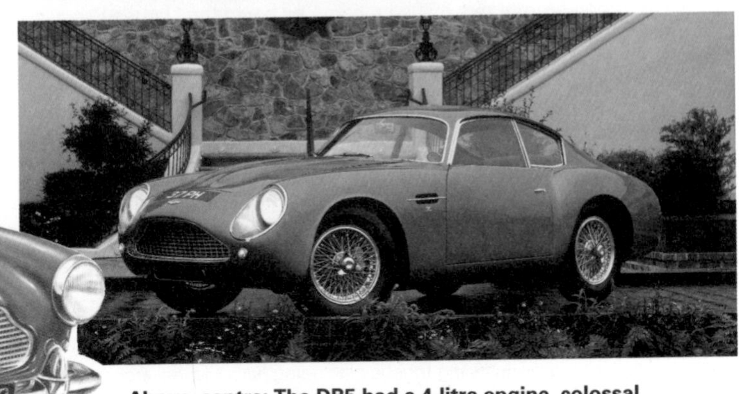

Above, centre: The DB5 had a 4-litre engine, colossal performance, and a great reputation.

Above: The short-wheelbase, lightweight bodied, DB4GT Zagato was a very rare, 150mph version of the original design.

developed from that of the old DB2/DB3 series, the DBR2 used a new and much bulkier 3.7-litre twin-cam unit. It was therefore no real surprise when, in September 1958, a new road car was announced, fitted with a detuned version of this engine. This was the DB4, and it was the first of a family of models which was to carry Aston Martin forward to the end of the 1960s. It was not a direct replacement for the DB2 and 2/4 cars, as it was much larger, heavier and faster, and of rather different construction, but it was not long before it took over the whole of the Newport Pagnell factory. In fact it was the first 'nearly four-seat' Aston Martin for some years, although of course the W.O. Bentley-inspired Lagondas had fulfilled that role for some years in the 1940s and 1950s. The new car was unashamedly styled on Italian lines, by Touring of Milan, and used that firm's patented lightweight method of body construction. The chassis was a complete innovation for Aston Martin, being fabricated, platform style, from sheet steel. The suspension design was also new – with wishbone independent front suspension replacing the trailing-arm layout of the DB2 family, although the well-located beam rear axle method was retained. Aston Martin found their gearbox within the David Brown organisation. Even in original guise, with an easy 240bhp developed, the DB4 was a very quick car, much better built than some so-called Italian masterpieces, but it was very expensive to build, virtually by hand, for all that.

The first DB4 was sold at the beginning of 1959 and the last of that family – a DB6 Mark II, was delivered early in 1971. In those twelve years the basic shape of the car remained unchanged, but there was a persistent updating which led to more and more performance and better and better fittings and equipment. Within months, the prototype DB4GT – a short-chassis version of the DB4, with faired headlamps and rather more power – had been raced successfully by Stirling Moss at Silverstone, and the production version with 314bhp and three twin-choke Weber carburettors was in production by the end of 1959. That led to an even more exciting and very low production version (only 25 were made), with stubby bodies by Zagato of Italy, in which the maximum speed was more than 150mph – and this at a time when anything higher was definitely a racing speed for huge sports cars. More than 1,100 DB4s were made between 1959 and 1963, in standard and Vantage-engine form, before the DB5 appeared. This combined the long wheelbase DB4 bodyshell with the DB4GT's faired nose, had a full 4-litre engine and was also to be sold as a smart drop-head convertible. Unlike any other 'DB' Aston Martin, this made its name by being the 'James Bond' car in the film Goldfinger, although Aston Martin resisted all attempts to have them make lethal replicas!

Convertibles became Volantes and the DB5 also became the DB6 in October 1965. This was a more involved change than at first appeared, because the car's wheelbase was slightly lengthened to give more rear seat space, and along with a spoiler on the boot lid the car's looks had been altered substantially. By now, too, a five-speed ZF gearbox was standard, or a Borg-Warner automatic gearbox was available at no extra cost.

Aston Martin now turned their attention to a new model, the DBS, which although based on the DB6's basic engineering, was longer and wider and ready to receive a new four-cam V8 engine they were developing. This car was released in October 1967 and meant that the DB6's days were numbered. The DB6 was so popular, however, that it carried on, latterly in upgraded Mk II guise, until the spring of 1971, by which time it was offered for a time with AE fuel injection, and with various styling touches including flared wheel arches. Even a handful of three-door estate cars were built on the basis of the DB6, but these were even more handbuilt than the usual Aston Martin. It is a sad commentary on the DB4s/5s/6s that although they were beautiful, fast and very roadworthy, they were never really profitable to their makers – a trait common to many other Supercars in Europe in the 1960s.

Above: The DB6, announced in 1965, was a developed version of the DB5, with a bigger cabin and a restyled rear.

Below, centre: The DB5, complete with cowled headlamps, sloping tail and small fins, was instantly recognisable, especially after it became famous in James Bond movies.

Bottom: The DB6 had a longer wheelbase, more cabin space, and a rear spoiler as standard.

Aston Martin DB7

Aston Martin DB7 family, introduced in 1994 (data for original model)
Built by: Aston Martin Lagonda Ltd., Britain
Engine: Six cylinders, in line, in seven-main-bearing alloy cylinder block. Bore and stroke 91 × 83mm, 3,239cc (3.58 × 3.27in, 197.7cu.in). Light-alloy cylinder head. Four valves per cylinder, operation by twin overhead camshafts and inverted bucket tappets. Zytec fuel injection with Eaton Supercharger. Maximum power 335bhp (DIN) at 5,500rpm. Maximum torque 360lb.ft at 3,000rpm.
Transmission: Rear-wheel-drive, single-dry-plate diaphragm spring clutch and five-speed all-synchromesh manual gearbox, all in unit with front engine. Remote-control, central gearchange. Optional automatic transmission.
Chassis: Unitary-construction pressed-steel body-chassis unit in 2+2 sports coupé or convertible style. Independent front suspension by coil springs, wishbones, telescopic dampers and anti-roll bar. Independent rear suspension by coil springs, wishbones and fixed-length drive shaft links, telescopic dampers, and anti-roll bar. Rack-and-pinion steering with hydraulic power assistance. Four-wheel disc brakes with ABS. Cast alloy 18in wheels, and 245/40-18in tyres.
Dimensions: Wheelbase 8ft 6in (259.1cm), front track 5ft 0in (152.4cm), rear track 5ft 0.2in (153.0cm). Overall length 15ft 2.3in (463.1cm). Unladen weight 3,859lb (1,750kg).
History: If Ford had not bought Aston Martin in 1987, the company might very well have had to close down. Yet even if it had survived under Victor Gauntlett's chairmanship, it could never have generated the capital to fund major new models. Ford, though, bought the latter company for what a whimsical director later described as 'petty cash' (Aston Martin was building 200 cars a year, while Ford-UK was building 400,000), took time to study what it had purchased, and eventually started the modernisation process.

Below: Not only was the DB7 Volante a rare and desirable car - but the 'Neiman Marcus' Vantage version was a specially equipped 'Limited Edition.'

Above: Aston Martin designer Ian Callum was encouraged to shape the new DB7 with reference to the company's famous heritage. Much of the chassis was borrowed from Jaguar, as well as a supercharged 6-cylinder

Ford intended to expand Aston Martin, and to evolve a larger range of models, but all this would take time. First of all, it commissioned the big V8-engined Virage range (which started to reach its customers in 1989), a car which replaced the venerable V8 and V8 Vantage types, but these were never likely to sell in large numbers.

What was needed was a smaller and relatively cheaper model, quite unrelated to the Virage, a car which would appeal to more customers because they could, perhaps, afford it. Victor Gauntlett had talked wistfully, and regularly, about such a car in the 1980s, but little actual design work had ever been done.

Three years after the takeover, Ford acted decisively. Gauntlett moved out, Ford's legendary one-time PR man Walter Hayes was pulled out of retirement to become the new chairman, and things became more purposeful. Although Hayes was a dynamic character who showered Ian Callum of his styling staff with pictures of earlier classic Aston Martins, telling him: 'Like that please, but modern', he could still not find anywhere to build the cars, because the existing Newport Pagnell plant was small and quaint.The opportunity came in 1992, in a typically complex Ford manner. Ford had owned Jaguar since 1989, Jaguarsport had developed a new factory at Bloxham (near Banbury) to produce the Jaguar XJ220 supercar, and production of that car was scheduled to end in 1994. Jaguarsport was part-owned by Tom Walkinshaw, who had been dabbling with a restyled Jaguar XJS but needed money to produce it.

It was a complicated situation, but it was typical of Hayes that he cut through the corporate jungle. As approved by Ford, he would co-operate with Walkinshaw in completely re-engineering the new car, Ian Callum would shape it, Walkinshaw would have a role (this did not last long, in fact), ▶

Aston Martin would take over the Bloxham factory, and the new car would be built there.

Although Aston Martin's publicists were delightfully vague about its origins, the definitive machine, to be titled DB7, was based on a modernised derivative of the Jaguar XJS (we now know that it was really that of the Jaguar XK8, which would not be announced until 1996), and that car's all-independent suspension chassis.

The straight-six engine, while recognisably developed from that of the 3.2-litre Jaguar AJ26, was equipped with an Eaton supercharger (this was the first-ever supercharged Aston Martin production car), and produced a mighty 335bhp. Getrag (manual) and ZF (automatic) transmissions were both available, the chassis naturally coming with power-assisted steering and anti-lock brakes as standard.

It was, however, the shape of the new DB7 which caused so much discussion – and attracted heaps of enthusiastic comment. Ian Callum, aided and encouraged by Hayes, had been inspired by the best of previous Aston Martins, and had seen what Jaguar had already schemed up (and discarded) for XJS replacements, and what they were already considering for the XK8 of 1996. The result, which nodded to all of them, but which was totally individualistic, was a stunning fastback 2+2 seater where there were no straight lines, no bumps, gouges or out-of-place lines, and where there was definite front-end evidence of an Aston Martin heritage. And this was only the beginning, for Aston Martin let it be known that convertible ('Volante') versions would eventually follow, and they were also considering monstrous alternative engines too.

Prototypes were shown in 1993, but series production did not begin until mid-1994 (after Jaguar XJ220 assembly had ended at Bloxham). After building just 150 cars in 1994, the company then settled to producing more than 600 cars a year at Bloxham, the limit of its craftsman-building capacity. From the beginning, there was a queue to buy, the company easily shrugging off ill-informed comments about the 'Jaguarness' of the general layout.

The DB7, after all, was a remarkable achievement. As an independent

Above: Whatever the angle from which it was viewed, the DB7 Vantage was beautifully proportioned, with carefully integrated details such as lights and air intakes.

concern, Aston Martin could never have built it at all, but under Ford's control they now had a super-coupé, costing £78,500 (a bargain at this performance and equipment level), which was very fast – 157mph flat out, and 0–100mph in a mere 14.4 seconds put that record straight – extremely well and sumptuously equipped, and handled like a real thoroughbred.

When the Jaguar XKR appeared in 1996, criticis thought that the two cars looked so similar as to be suspicious, but Aston Martin knew that every skin panel, and the interior, on their car, were unique, and would remain so. Not only that, but the range continued to expand, and demand always exceeded supply. First of all, for 1996 the long-expected cabriolet version, which carried the company's traditional 'Volante' title, had appeared. Then, in the spring of 1999, came the amazing DB7 Vantage, based on the same structure and style, but equipped with a mighty 420bhp 6-litre V12 engine which yet another Ford associate – Cosworth – had developed from a Ford-USA design. Here was a new car with truly colossal performance – a 185mph top speed, and 0–100mph in 11.8 seconds – and one which could face down any other supercar in the world, Ferrari inclusive.

This meant that the Bloxham factory (once, incidentally, a flour mill, though completely transformed by Ford money during the 1990s) was guaranteed to be bursting at the seams for years to come. With production nudging upwards towards the 800/year mark (something which had *never* before been achieved by this marque), with a Virage replacement going on sale in 2001, and with a third (lower-priced) range also promised a few years down the road, the British company's future was well and truly underpinned.

Left: The DB7 Vantage was available from 1999, with the new Cosworth-developed Ford 420bhp 6-litre V12 engine - and a 185mph top speed.

Aston Martin Vanquish V12

Aston Martin Vanquish, introduced in 2000
Built by: Aston Martin Lagonda Ltd., Britain.
Engine: Twelve cylinders in 60-degree vee, seven-bearing cast alloy cylinder block. Bore and stroke 89 x 79.5mm, 5,935cc (3.50 x 3.13in, 362cu.in). Two light alloy cylinder heads. Four valves per cylinder, operated directly by twin overhead camshafts per bank, and inverted bucket tappets. Maximum power 450bhp (DIN) at 6,500rpm. Maximum torque 410lb.ft at 5,000rpm.
Transmission: Rear-wheel-drive, single-plate diaphragm spring clutch and six-speed all-synchromesh manual gearbox, all in unit with engine. Remote-control, paddle-shift gearchange, and alternative 'automatic mode' sesttings.
Chassis: Semi-monocoque extruded aluminium chassis platform, reinforced with carbon fibre composite mouldings, and attachments to aluminium body skin panels. Independent front suspension by coil springs, wishbones, telescopic dampers and anti-roll bar. Independent rear suspension by coil springs, wishbones, telescopic dampers, and anti-roll bar. Rack-and-pinion steering with hydraulic power assistance. Front and rear disc brakes with power-assistance and ABS. 19in wheels, 225/40-19in (front) and 285/40-19in (rear) tyres.
Dimensions: Wheelbase 8ft 10in (269cm). Overall length 15ft 3.6in (466.5cm). Unladen weight 4,013lb (1,820kg).
History: It took 31 years, and several changes of ownership, before the 'Class-of-'69' V8-engined models were finally replaced. For 2001 Ford finally provided a great deal of up-front finance to see the all-new Vanquish (surely a car which James Bond would find himself using in future films?) onto the market.

Although existing Aston Martin DNA – the looks, the character, and the made-to-measure manufacturing process – was retained, here was a car which was new from end to end. Except that the brawny V12 engine was a developed and enlarged version of that already introduced for the DB7 Vantage, it had new running gear, a new type of chassis and, above all, a new style.

Because Ian Callum had inspired the shape of both cars, it was easy to see a few family resemblances to the DB7, but there seemed to be no relationship with the old, and much loved Virage types. Although only slightly larger than the DB7, the Vanquish rode on a four-inch longer wheelbase, and its lack of free-standing front or rear bumpers made it look altogether more bulky, and

Below: The all-new Vanquish was expected to rival Ferrari in every respect.

Above: The Vanquish was set to transform Aston Martin's prospects in the 2000s.

purposeful. With close-coupled four-seater accomodation, wall-to-wall leather, thick carpets and wood trim, this was the sort of car which every traditional Aston Martin customer understood – even though they would have to get used to a new F1-type 'paddle-change' for the six-speed transmission.

Under the skin there was a new aluminium chassis/platform/semi-monocoque, technically of the same type as used in the late-1990s Lotus Elise (Lotus had done much work in developing this car), its performance, rigidity and general worth being emphasised by the use of carbon fibre mouldings around the door frames, the transmission tunnel, and the windscreen pillars.

The claimed top speed was 190mph, which guaranteed that the chassis, all-independent suspension, brawny disc brakes, fat tyres (larger at the rear than the front) and the speed-sensitive power-steering would all be of the very highest standard.

The engine, of course, matched up to all that, being a 450bhp version of the Ford-based/Cosworth-redeveloped 6-litre V12 which had first been seen in the DB7 Vantage of 1999, and it was this which made the Vanquish so special, and so obviously a match for anything being produced by rivals such as Ferrari. While the previous Aston Martin V8 had been powerful, well-proven and characterful, when the time came to develop its successor there was really no argument against a V12, for such engines have always given out spine-chilling noises and vast power outputs.

The arrival of Vanquish, however, did more than merely signal that a formidable new-generation Aston Martin Supercar was finally here. It also signalled that Ford was serious about its 1987 purchase, that it was intent not only on modernising the quaint old Newport Pagnell factory, but that it wanted to confront Ferrari, face-to-face. The message was clear – whatever Fiat had achieved with Ferrari, then Ford could match it with Aston Martin. The battle for 2000s Supercar sales was going to be fascinating.

Auburn Straight-Eight

Straight-Eights built from 1925 to 1936 (data for 1935 851 Supercharged)
Built by: Auburn Automobile Company Inc., United States.
Engine: Lycoming Type GG. Eight cylinders, in line, in five-bearing cast-iron block. Bore and stroke 77.8mm by 120.6mm, 4,587cc (3.06in × 4.75in, 279.9cu.in). aluminium cylinder head. Two valves per cylinder operated by single side-mounted camshaft. Stromberg carburettor, in association with Schwitzer-Cummins centrifugal supercharger. Maximum power 150bhp (gross) at 4,000rpm.
Transmission: Single-dry-plate clutch and three-speed manual gearbox without synchromesh, with direct-acting central gearchange. Open propeller shaft to two-speed Columbia 'live' rear axle (ratios 5.00 or 3.47:1), axle speed control by hand lever on steering column, engine-vacuum assisted.
Chassis: Separate steel chassis, with channel-section side members. Pressed-steel front and rear cross members and cruciform bracing under the passenger floor. Half-elliptic springs front and rear. Forged axle beam at front. Hydraulic piston-

type dampers. Four-wheel hydraulically operated drum brakes. 16in wire wheels with conventional disc wheel type fastening nuts. 6.50 × 16in tyres. Two-seater 'Speedster' coachwork, with outside flexible stainless steel exhaust pipes. Fold down hood. No running boards. No rumble seat.

Dimensions: Wheelbase 10ft 7in (323cm), track (front) 4ft 11in (150cm), track (rear) 5ft 2in (157cm). Overall length 16ft 2.4in (494cm). Unladen weight 3,360lb (1,524kg).

History: Auburn's Straight-Eight series of cars, made in steadily developed form between 1925 and 1936, were inspired by the arrival of E. L. Cord as the company's General Manager in 1942. Before Cord, Auburns had been rather ordinary cars; ▶

Below: Straight-Eight Auburns were built from 1925 to 1936, in many styles. This car was one of the last – a 1935 Type 851 Supercharger with a phaeton body. In this tune the 4.6-litre straight-eight engine produced 150bhp.

after he arrived they took on considerable style. The chassis of the Straight-Eight was always particularly rigid, and the basic engineering very solid. The engines were always bought from Lycoming in Pennsylvania. Among earlier features were Bijur central chassis lubrication, striking and prolific body options and a great deal of performance. From 1932, the dual-ratio Columbia rear axle was a great feature, but in 1935 and 1936 the much-revised engines were offered with superchargers.

The 851 Speedster was given lines by Gordon Buehrig, who had also shaped the Model 810 Cord, and it made no concessions to the big 127-inch wheelbase. There were only two seats, a vision-restricting hood, and vast shining external exhaust pipes through the side of the bonnet. Ab Jenkins proved that there was performance to go with those looks. At Utah in 1935 his Speedster covered more than 100 miles in each of twelve consecutive hours – a United States stock-car record. For 1936 the 851 was followed by the 852, but by then the American public had turned away from such machines. The last of all Auburns was made in that year; in fact only 500 were made in 1935 and 1936.

Right: In 1929 the boat-tail Speedster was one of the most dramatic shapes around. It made no effort to provide more than two seats – not even a dickey. The engines were supplied by Lycoming (who also made aero-engines) and the cars were inspired by E. L. Cord, who ran the Auburn Group. The Speedster of the early 1930s was popular but expensive. By 1932 it had a dual-ratio rear axle, and visibility from the driving seat was very restricted.

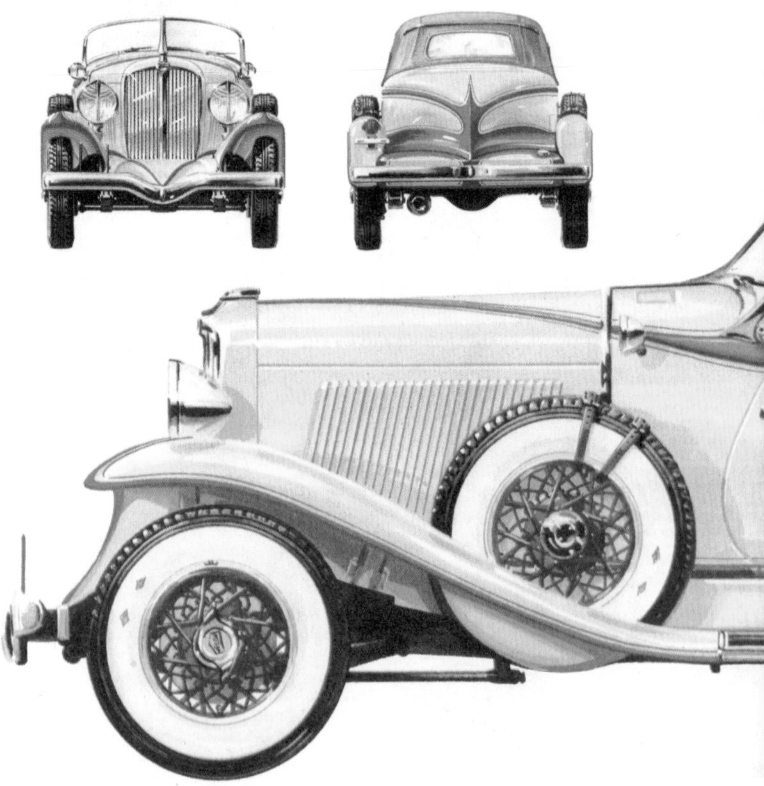

Left and below: The Auburn Speedster could only be an American design. By this time the rounded body lines were way ahead of the rest of the world's styling fashions. This is Auburn's 8-100A speedster, as sold in 1932 with its Lycoming engine.

Audi Quattro (1980-1989)

Audi Quattro sports coupé, built from 1980 to 1989
Built by: Audi AG, Germany.
Engine: Five cylinders, in line, in six-main-bearing cast-iron cylinder block/crankcase. Bore and stroke 79.5 x 86.4mm, 2,145cc (3.13 x 3.40in, 130.9 cu.in). Light-alloy cylinder head. Two valves per cylinder, in line, operation by single overhead camshaft and inverted bucket-type tappets. Bosch fuel injection and KKk turbocharger. Maximum power 200bhp (DIN) at 5,500rpm. Maximum torque 210lb.ft at 3,500rpm.
Transmission: Four-wheel-drive, single-dry-plate diaphragm spring clutch and five-speed all-synchromesh manual gearbox, all in unit with front-mounted engine. Remote-control, central gearchange.
Chassis: Unitary-construction pressed-steel body-chassis unit, in two-door four-seater style, with front-mounted engine. Independent front suspension by MacPherson struts, coil springs, lower wishbones, telescopic dampers, anti-roll bar. Independent rear suspension by MacPherson struts, coil springs, lower wishbones, telescopic dampers, anti-roll bar. Rack-and-pinion steering with power-assistance. Four-wheel disc brakes, with vacuum-servo power assistance (ABS on later models). Cast-alloy 15in road wheels, and 205/60-15in tyres.
Dimensions: Wheelbase 8ft 3.4in (252.4cm), front track 4ft 9.7in (146.5cm), rear track 4ft 11.1in (150cm). Overall length 14ft 5.4in (440.4cm). Unladen weight 2,838lb (1,290kg).
History: Everyone remembers the Quattro for the way that it transformed world-class rallying. Before the 1980s, rallies had been won by raucous, two-wheel-drive machines, which always fought for grip on loose surfaces and ice. After 1980, with new regulations to favour them, the four-wheel-drive turbocharged Quattros swept all before them for years.

Audi's Quattro was not only the company's first four-wheel-drive private car, but the first of an entirely new generation of four-wheel-driven models from all round the world. Until then, four-wheel-drive had been crude, and unrefined, but

Below: The Quattro S1, produced only in 1985, was a 20-off rally special, a version of the Sport Quattro with at least 500bhp.

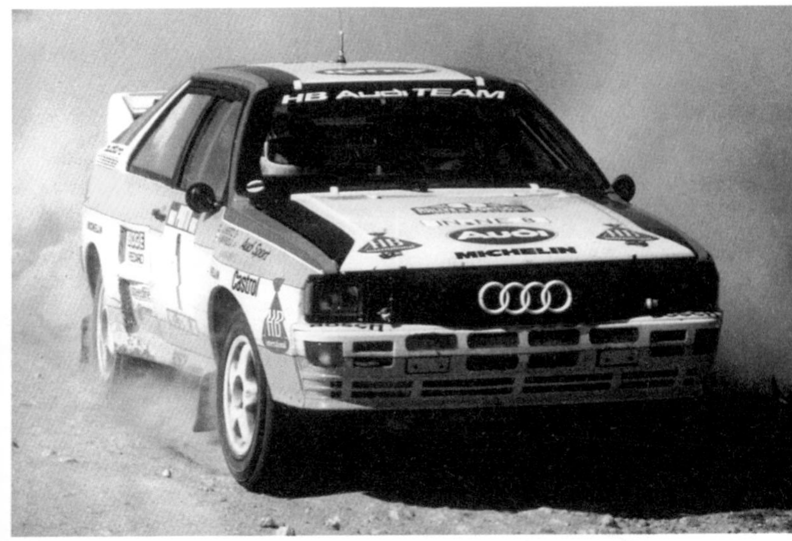

Above: The Quattro was a successful four-wheel-drive road car, and a stunning rally car too. This 'works' car was on the Rally of Portugal in 1985.

the Quattro was the first of a new and civilised breed.

Conceived in the late 1970s, if not by accident, but certainly by stealth, by combining the running gear of the VW Iltis cross-country vehicle (Audi was a subsidiary of VW), with the modified structure of a new front-wheel-drive Audi Coupé model, the original Quattro Turbo Coupé was meant to be a 'rally special' – but once testers' opinions of the road version were broadcast, that all changed. Only 400 were to have been built, but in the end no fewer than 10,629 such cars would be built in a decade.

The Quattro's secret was not in its performance, but in its elegant four-wheel-drive solution, for in its general layout it was more of a converted front-wheel-drive car which just happened to have found a way to get the rear wheels driven too. The engine was up front, ahead of the line of the front wheels, the main gearbox was behind that line, and there was a grapefruit-sized centre diff mounted in that transmission to split the torque between front and rear wheels.

The original ('Ur', as it was always known in German) Quattro had a 200bhp turbocharged straight-five cylinder engine, which guaranteed a 138mph top speed, but it was the traction and the balance which was so astonishing. By later standards, no doubt, the car's turbo lag, and understeering tendencies, could be criticised, but in 1980 this was a massive leap forward.

Not only was the Quattro an effective rally machine – in the next few years drivers like Hannu Mikkola, Michele Mouton and Stig Blomqvist proved that point, time and time again – but it was a great commercial success. ABS brakes eventually arrived, the front-end was restyled, digital instruments were adopted, but the basic 2+2 seating was not changed until the late 1980s.

Before long, Audi had applied the same four-wheel-drive system to all its other models, as an option, and though only about five per cent of Audis had this layout, it still made a massive commercial impact.

The 306bhp short-wheelbase Sport Quattro followed in 1983 (only 200 were built), and the 'Ur' eventually inherited a 220bhp/20-valve 2.25-litre engine, but even after the original style had been made obsolete, the Audi four-wheel-drive system continued on cars built into the 21st Century.

Austin-Healey 3000

3000 models BN7, BT7, BJ7 and BJ8, 1959 to 1967, also 100-6 models BN4 and BN6, 1956 to 1959 (data for BJ8)

Built by: British Motor Corporation Ltd., Britain.

Engine: Six cylinders, in line, in four-bearing cast-iron block. Bore and stroke 83.3mm by 88.9mm, 2,912cc (3.28in × 3.5in, 177.7cu.in). Cast-iron cylinder head (aluminium on competition cars). Two overhead valves per cylinder, operated by pushrod and rocker from side-mounted camshaft. Two SU carburettors. Maximum power 148bhp (net) at 5,200rpm. Maximum torque 165lb.ft at 3,000rpm.

Transmission: Single-dry-plate clutch, and four-speed synchromesh manual gearbox (without synchromesh on first gear), remote control central gearchange. Optional overdrive on top and third gears. Open propeller shaft to hypoid-bevel 'live' rear axle.

Chassis: Separate steel chassis frame, with box-section side members, box and pressed cross brace and cruciform members. Welded to steel body after manufacture. Independent front suspension by coil springs, wishbones and anti-roll bar. Rear suspension by half-elliptic leaf springs and radius arms. Piston-type hydraulic dampers. Cam-and-peg steering. Disc front brakes and drum rear brakes, hydraulically operated 15in steel disc or optional centre-lock wire spoke wheels. 5.90 × 15in tyres. Steel sports car body style, with tiny 'plus 2' seats behind front bucket seats. Optional hardtop. Body/chassis units built by Jensen.

Dimensions: Wheelbase 7ft 7.7in (233cm), track (front) 4ft 0.7in (124cm), track (rear) 4ft 2in (127cm). Overall length 13ft 1.5in (400cm). Unladen weight 2,460lb (1,116kg).

History: Donald Healey's Healey 100 was the result of an unofficial competition set up by Sir Leonard Lord in 1952. The rules were that mainly BMC components should be used; BMC would sponsor the winner. MG and Jensen were losers. The first Austin Healeys had four-cylinder 2.6-litre engines, and these were made between 1953 and 1956. Chassis and bodywork were designed by Geoffrey Healey and his father Donald. The car was a great export success, and racing versions (the 100S – 'S' for Sebring) achieved great things in 1954/5. When supplies of the old 'four' ran out, the car was re-engined as a 'six' with the new BMC 'C' series 2.6-litre unit.

Three years later, in 1959, the engine was enlarged to 2.9-litres, and the Austin-Healey 3000 was born. In the next eight years there were four distinct types of 3000 but illogically enough the last one, with its wind-up windows, walnut facia and most powerful engine, was called the Mk III! If the 3000 had faults they were that it was too low-slung, too coarse and too cramped to be totally successful. It was, however, a real man's sports car and in final tune was capable of over 120mph. The 'big Healey', as it was always affectionately known, was a formidable rally car, winning Alpine and Liège-Sofia-Liège rallies, and it dominated the GT categories for many years. As a racing car it was too standard to be an outright winner, but properly prepared, it was just about unbreakable. Nearly 43,000 '3000s' were built, and the car was forced off the market at the end of 1967 by United States legislation rendering continued production uneconomic.

A car like the 3000 could never have been planned, but merely evolved, as those who loved it, and conceived it, thought of more and more enhancements. By the late 1960s, no doubt, it badly needed better ventilation, more performance, and a serious re-style, but its character could not be improved.

Replicas, or re-creations, were attempted in the 1980s and 1990s, though designer Geoff Healey would not sanctify them with his approval. Although they looked similar, and had bigger, more powerful, engines, the essential character was missing.

Now, as earlier, there was no substitute for the real thing.

Above: In the 1950s and 1960s the most exciting of all Austin-Healey 3000s were the 'works' team competition cars, prepared at the MG works at Abingdon. They had light-alloy bodies and powerful (210bhp) tuned engines. They were equally at home in the roughest of rallies or in long-distance road races (above: Paul Hawkins/Timo Makinen in the Targa Florio). Brute strength and noise were features.

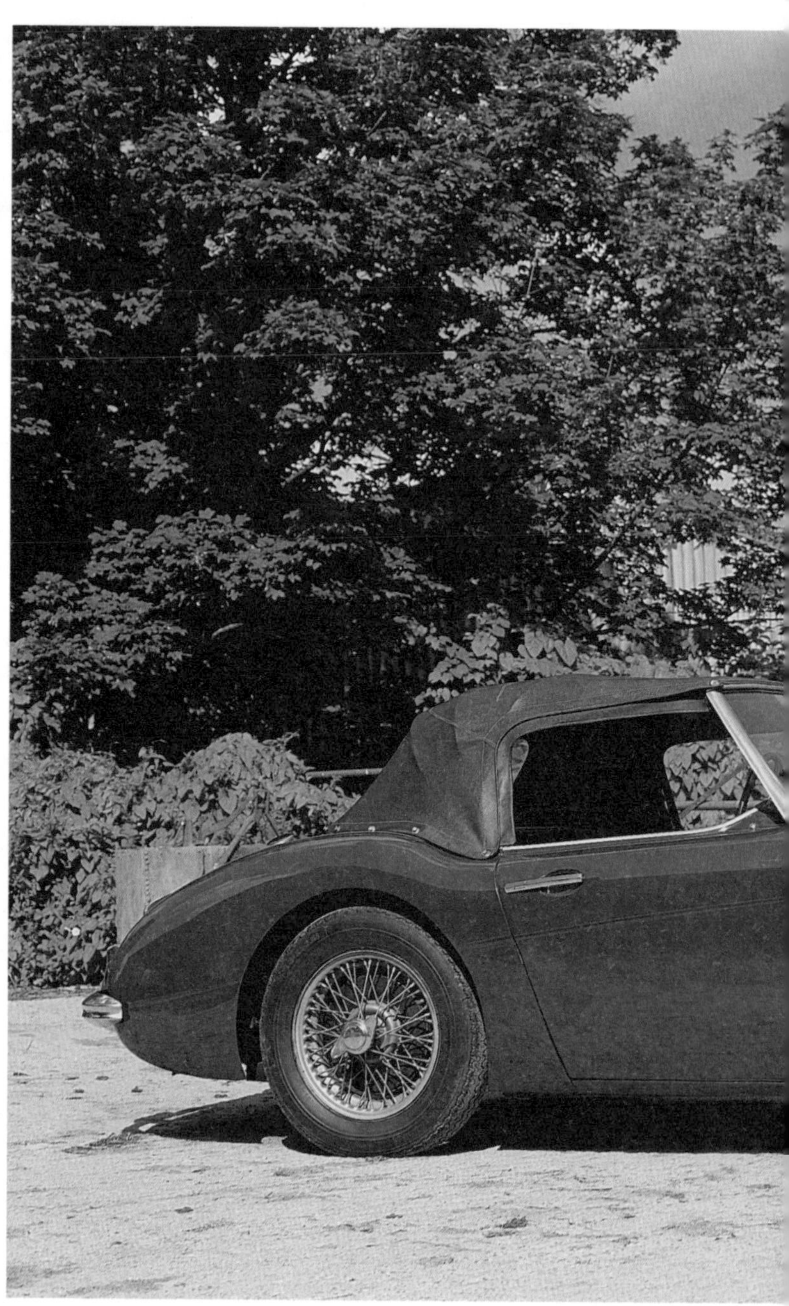

Above: When Donald Healey's team conceived the lines of the original 'Healey 100' of 1952, they cannot have known that this car would still be so well-liked for so many years. The six-cylinder cars

were modified versions of the original 100/4s, complete with a slightly longer wheelbase and exterior door handles. This is a 3000 Mk I of 1959/1961.

Austin Seven

Austin Seven, all models, and Big Seven, 1923 to 1939 (data for 1923 model)

Built by: Austin Motor Co. Ltd., Britain.

Engine: Four cylinders, in line, in two-bearing cast-iron block. Bore and stroke 56mm by 76.2mm, 747cc (2.2in × 3.0in, 45.6cu.in). Cast-iron cylinder head. Two side valves per cylinder, directly operated by block-mounted camshaft. Single updraught carburettor. Maximum power 10.5bhp at 2,400rpm.

Transmission: Single-dry-plate clutch and three-speed manual gearbox, with direct-acting central gearchange. Forward ratios 4.9, 9.0 and 16.0:1. open

propeller shaft to centre bearing, then torque tube to spiral-bevel 'live' rear axle. **Chassis:** Simple separate steel chassis frame, with channel-section side ▶

Below: The little 747cc Austin Seven was a familiar part of the motoring scene between the wars. It was born in 1921/22 to fill a big gap in the Austin range, and designed by Sir Herbert Austin and one young draughtsman. It was simple, rugged, versatile, tiny, light, and very easy to drive. It was Britain's cheapest car for years, and in 16 years about a quarter-million were sold. This is a 1927 Chummy Tourer.

members and minor cross bracing. Front suspension by transverse leaf spring to forged front axle and splayed radius arms. Rear suspension by cantilever splayed quarter-elliptic leaf springs. Worm-and-sector steering. Small four-wheel drum brakes, with handbrake operating on front wheels. No dampers. Initially only two-door tourer coachwork, but speedily followed by fabric-covered two-door saloons. In later years, every possible variation including vans and two-seater sports cars.

Dimensions: Wheelbase 6ft 3in (190cm), track (front and rear) 3ft 4in (102cm). Overall length 8ft 10in (269cm). Unladen weight 800lb (363kg).

History: The Austin Seven was born because of a financial crisis and it made a financial fortune. After World War I, Sir Herbert Austin settled on a 'one-model' policy at Longbridge, but he chose the wrong model – an expensive and stodgy 'Twenty'. With losses mounting up, Austin took one design draughtsman with him to his home and spent months on the all-new 'baby' Austin. Called a 'Seven' because of British fiscal rules, it nonetheless went into production as a 7.8hp car. Its engine, even if it *was* all-new, could only produce about 10 to 11bhp. Fortunately for the customers, the cars' all-up weights were rarely over 800lb (363kg). The Seven, when announced in autumn 1922, was not yet ready for production, and was shown with a 696cc engine even less powerful than the one which went into production the following year. It was, in all respects, tiny and, although four seats were provided, there was really no way that an 800lb car could support and carry the same weight in passengers.

The original asking price in March 1923 was £165, and over the years the cheapest versions of the cars (tourers with minimum equipment) were cheapened further. In the mid 1930s a magic £100 car was briefly sold, but a more normal price level in the 1930s was £120-£135. The car was an immediate and heartening success, and by 1924 there was little doubt that Austin's future was assured. Even though the little car was very crude and small (it soon became the butt of dozens of music-hall jokes) and slow (45mph was a very good maximum speed at first), it was also very reliable – and it was *much* cheaper than almost anything else on the British market, a notable exception being Ford's heavily taxed Model T. Among the car's early vagaries were four wheel brakes which were a bit of a joke, an 'in-out' clutch that was no joke, and fittings which bordered on the primitive. On the other hand, the two-bearing, side-valve engine seemed to stand every abuse and the car itself was small enough and light enough to be taken almost anywhere.

Not only was the Austin Seven a car of its decade, but of the next decade too. In terms of numbers sold it was most popular in the mid 1930s and it only came to a rapid and rather sad end in 1939 when Austin at least began to produce something approaching modern body styling. In all those years the basic chassis and mechanical layout remained unchanged, although the rudimentary frame was stiffened and lengthened and the engine was eventually given a centre crankshaft bearing. Even so, the story of the Austin Seven is one of continuous development within the narrow limits of its layout. The things that should have been changed, if logic had prevailed – like the front and rear suspensions which put axle location and ride comfort at the back of the development queue – were never touched. However, an electric starter motor was added in 1924, coil ignition in 1927, a stronger crankshaft in 1930, a four-speed gearbox in 1933, synchromesh for that box a year later, second gear synchromesh two years later still and a three-bearing engine in 1937. In the meantime the engine power had been pushed steadily up – to 12bhp at 2,600rpm in 1933, 13.5bhp at 3,000rpm in 1934, and 17bhp at 3,800rpm a couple of years later. Body variations were legion. Specialist body makers like Swallow (William Lyons) and Gordon England made their names by courtesy of the little Austin chassis. Austin themselves offered anything from a stark little two-seat sports car to the 'Top Hat' metal panelled saloon. There were tiny commercial vans and the British Army bought some tourers affectionately called 'prams'. The car was built under licence in Germany as a BMW Dixi, in the United States as a Bantam, and in France as a Rosengart and it was illegally copied in Japan as a Datsun.

Austin's son-in-law Arthur Waite raced special-bodied Austin Sevens with great success and the engine proved to be so astonishingly tuneable that he sanctioned the building of special single-seater racing cars with supercharged 747cc engines installed. Even when the engine was obsolete at Longbridge, Reliant continued to make and sell replicas for their three-wheelers, and the 750 racing formula insists on engine and basic chassis being used in cars built to its rules.

Production lasted for 16 years, and about a quarter-million of all types were sold. Austin have never made as cheap or as relatively popular a car, before or since. They attempted to revive the name with the A30 and then with the Mini but there could only be one proper Austin Seven.

Below: One of the earliest of all Austin Sevens was this 1923 Tourer, which sold for £165, and weighed just 800lb. Its maximum speed was 45mph.

Ballot RH Series Eight

RH Eights built 1927 to 1932 – 2.6, 2.8 and 3.0-litre versions (data for 3.0-litre RH3)
Built by: Etablissements Ballot, France.
Engine: Eight cylinders, in line, in cast-iron block, with detachable nine-bearing aluminium crankcase. Bore and stroke 68mm by 105mm, 3,050cc (2.68in × 4.13in, 186cu.in). Light-alloy cylinder head. Two valves per cylinder, operated by single overhead camshaft, drive by skew gears and shaft at rear of engine. Vertical valves in flat faced cylinder head. Single updraught Zenith twin-choke carburettor.
Transmission: Twin-plate clutch in unit with engine. Four-speed manual gearbox without synchromesh, also fixed to engine. Sliding gears at first, constant mesh gears on last batch of cars built. Direct action central gearchange. Open propeller shaft to spiral-bevel 'live' rear axle.
Chassis: Separate steel chassis frame, with channel-section main side members and tubular and pressed cross bracing. Half-elliptic leaf springs at front and rear. Forged front axle. Hydraulic lever arm dampers. Worm-and-nut steering. Rod-operated four-wheel drum brakes, with vacuum-servo assistance. 31in centre-lock wire wheels, fitted with 31 × 5.25in tyres. Several coachwork versions to choice, from Belgian/European specialists.
Dimensions: Wheelbase 10ft 10.5in or 11ft 10in (331cm or 261cm). Tracks (front and rear) 4ft 5in (135cm). Overall length depending on coachwork. Unladen weight (chassis only) 2,520lb (1,143kg).
History: Before 1914, Ballot in Paris specialised in the manufacture of car and stationary engines. From 1918, Edouard Ballot decided to extend his company's prestige by making and selling complete cars. First he engaged Ernest Henry (of 1913/1914 Peugeot fame) to design eight-cylinder and four-cylinder racing cars. The first Ballot road car was the 2LS, really a slightly civilised racing two-seater, and this was followed in 1923 by the 2LT type. The 2LT introduced Ballot's particular and notable engine/cylinder layout, where the overhead-cam operated in-line valves operated in a flat head with Heron-type bowl-in-piston combustion chambers. The 2LT was supplemented by the 2LTS in 1925, which had more conventional combustion chamber arrangements and rather more performance in 1927, however, Ballot decided to push up their offerings even more – in specification, performance and price.

Although they catalogued a 2-litre 'six' at the beginning of 1927 this car never went into production. In its place, at the Paris show of 1927, came the eight-cylinder, 2.6-litre Model RH Ballot. Its chassis followed the 2LT's lines closely, although the wheelbase was considerably lengthened. The engine, more closely

Above: A feature of the RH Eights was its magnificent eight-cylinder engine, with 'Heron' combustion chambers and an overhead camshaft. The long wheelbase encouraged splendid and elegant bodies.

related to the Heron-headed 2LT 'four' than to the 2LTS 'four', initially had a cylinder bore of 63mm, and a capacity of 2,618cc, but to improve the performance when heavy coachwork was fitted this was twice increased – to 66mm in 1928 and to 68mm for 1930. The RH had a beautifully and flexibly tuned engine, which made the car an aristocrat among French machines, with a rather flexible chassis which sometimes caused grievous harm to the none-too-rigid bodies of the day.

In 1932, like so many other makers of exclusive cars, Ballot ran into financial difficulties, and were soon taken over by Hispano-Suiza. That was really the end of Ballot cars as we know them. A new model produced in Paris and badged as a Ballot HS26 was, in fact, a 4.6-litre small-scale replica of Spanish Hispano models. Even this car reverted to type and became a Hispano-badged machine before long.

Below: Striking in style and advanced in engineering, the Ballot Type 2LT was a fine vintage car. This body was by Legache-Glaszmann of France. The car preceded the legendary 'Eights'.

Bentley 3-litre

3-litre models built 1921 to 1928 (data for short-wheelbase 'Standard')
Built by: Bentley Motors Ltd., Britain.
Engine: Four cylinders, in line, in five-bearing cast-iron block and light-alloy crankcase. Bore and stroke 80mm by 149mm, 2,996cc (3.15in × 5.87in, 183cu.in). non-detachable cast-iron cylinder head. Four valves per cylinder, operated by rockers from a single overhead camshaft. Camshaft driven by vertical shaft and gears from nose of crankshaft. Two SU carburettors after 1924, single Smith carburettor up to that date. Maximum power 80 to 85bhp, depending on time.
Transmission: Single-dry-plate, inverted cone clutch, slightly separated from four-speed unsynchronised gearbox. Remote control right-hand gearchange. Open propeller shaft to spiral-bevel 'live' rear axle.
Chassis: Separate steel chassis frame, with channel-section side members and angled and tubular cross bracing. Half-elliptic leaf springs for front and rear suspension. Forged front axle beam. Hartford-type friction dampers. Worm-and-wheel steering. Rear-wheel drum brakes (up to 1923), four-wheel drum brakes (after 1923), without servo assistance. Centre-lock wire wheels, several size changes between 1921 and 1928. Initial tyre fitments 820 by 120 type. Coachwork to choice; cars supplied from Bentley Motors as rolling chassis – sports, touring or saloon styles.
Dimensions: Wheelbase 9ft 9.5in (298cm), tracks (front and rear) 4ft 8in (142cm). Overall length 13ft 3in (404cm). Unladen weight (depending on coachwork) from 2,800lb (1,270kg).
History: W. O. Bentley had already made his name as an importer of French DFP sports cars before World War I, and for his BR air-cooled rotary aero-engine designs during it, when he decided in 1919 to make a car of his own design. The 3-litre, first seen at the 1919 Olympia Motor Show, and first sold in 1921, was the first of his legendary strain. Indeed, it is true to say that the 4½, 6½ and 8-litre cars (if not the unsuccessful 4-litre) are all recognisably descended from the

3-litre. Chassis engineering was conventional in every way. Interest, and praise, was always reserved for the engine. Massively built, tall and elegant in the Edwardian style, it was near-unique in having four-valves per cylinder and gave the bulky cars a sparkling performance.

Even though the firm was always under-capitalised (it was close to bankruptcy at least three times in the 1920s), Bentley himself eventually agreed to a Le Mans racing programme, to speed development and to provide publicity. The three-litre in 'lightweight' open guise won the race in 1924 and 1927. Cars also raced with distinction in the Tourist Trophy Race (second in 1922) and at the Indianapolis 500 Miles Race (where Hawkes's car averaged 81mph).

Bentley was so confident of his engineering that a five-year guarantee was given on the mechanical items in the car. Three-litres were in production for seven years, in several basic guises and in three wheelbase lengths. The Speed Model, with tuned-up engines, arrived in 1924, and following the development of the 4½-litre Bentley (the engine being an amalgam of 3-litre and 6½-litre 'six' design thought) a number of common parts were specified. There were three distinct sets of gearbox ratios. Chassis price, at first, was £1,100 (usually raised to about £1,400, depending on the coachwork chosen), but by 1924 the long-wheelbase 'Standard' chassis had been reduced to £895. This long-wheelbase chassis was the most popular – 765 being sold – while 513 of the Speed Model were produced. In total, 1,619 3-litre Bentley's were built. The car was finally replaced by the 4½-litre.

Below: W. O. Bentley's 3-litre was the first of the famous Cricklewood-built cars, many having sports bodywork. 'Old No. 7' was raced by the factory at Le Mans in 1926, then went on to win that event in 1927 after all three team cars were involved in a crash at White House. 'Sammy' Davis and Dr. Benjafield were its drivers. The 4½-litre followed.

Bentley 3½- and 4¼-litre

3½-litre and 4¼-litre models. 1933 to 1939 (data for 4¼-litre)
Built by: Rolls-Royce Ltd., Britain.
Engine: Six cylinders, in line, in seven-bearing cast-iron cylinder block. Bore and stroke 89.9mm by 114.3mm, 4,257cc (3.5in × 4.5in, 260cu.in). Cast-iron cylinder head. Two overhead valves per cylinder, operated by pushrods and rockers from side-mounted camshaft. Twin SU carburettors. Power output never officially stated by Rolls-Royce, probably about 125bhp.
Transmission: Single-dry-plate clutch and four-speed manual transmission (synchromesh on top and third gears), in unit with engine. Right-hand gearchange. Open propeller shaft to spiral-bevel 'live' rear axle. 1938 and 1939 models had 'overdrive' gear ratios – in which third gear was direct, and fourth was a geared-up ratio.
Chassis: Separate steel chassis, with channel-section side members and pressed-steel and tubular cross members. Half-elliptic leaf springs at front and rear. Forged front axle beam. Hydraulic Rolls-Royce dampers, additional ride control governing hydraulic pressure, aided by gearbox-driven pump. Rod-operated drum brakes, boosted by gearbox-driven mechanical servo motor. Worm-and-sector steering. Car normally sold as rolling chassis. Wide choice of saloon, coupé and cabriolet coachwork from approved coachbuilders.
Dimensions: Wheelbase 10ft 6in (320cm), tracks (front and rear) 4ft 8in (142cm). Overall length (varied slightly depending on coach-builder) 14ft 6in (442cm). Unladen weight chassis only, 2,560lb (1,161kg). Typical weight with saloon body, 3,920lb (1,778kg).
History: Bentley Motors ran into financial trouble at the start of the 1930s, and were finally bankrupted in 1931. The company's trade marks and assets were taken over by Rolls-Royce soon afterwards and manufacture of 'W.O.' cars ▶

Above: The lightest 'Derbys' were the early 3½-litre models; later cars put on weight. This is a beautiful 1935 saloon, which combined 90mph pace with the best quality coachwork.

Right and below: In everything other than name the 3½-litre and 4¼-litre Bentleys were sporting Rolls-Royces. Dubbed the 'Silent Sports Car', they brought high performance to Rolls-Royce, and a new refinement to fast motoring. There was no connection with previous Bentleys.

ceased at once. Although Bentley himself worked for Rolls-Royce until 1935, he had little to do with new designs. Rolls-Royce decided to make a new model called a Bentley, even though they had no intention of using existing components. Even the famous radiator design would be modified. Only the badging would be carried forward. Their first intention was to productionise their 'Peregrine' experimental car, which had a 2.3-litre six-cylinder engine, and to supercharge that engine, as they saw no need to make the 'Bentley' as quiet and dignified as existing Rolls-Royce cars. Development was difficult and at the end of 1932 it was decided to substitute a much-modified Rolls-Royce 20/25 six-cylinder engine for the 'Peregrine' unit. Thus a new concept of Bentley, the 'Silent Sports Car' as adverts would call it, was born. Public release was in October 1933, and deliveries began during the winter.

As originally launched, the car had a 3,669cc engine, with twin SU carburettors. In their usual way, Rolls-Royce never released any maximum power figures, but the engine was thought to produce about 110bhp. The gearbox and right-hand gearchange were based on those of the Rolls-Royce 20/25 models. The car used a beam front axle with half-elliptic leaf springs, no less than was normal in those days. By 1939, though, other makes had begun to fit independent front suspension, which left the Bentley's ride and handling at a competitive disadvantage. The mechanically operated brakes and the gearbox-driven servo motor were Rolls-Royce idiosyncrasies which worked very well, though they did not represent modern thinking. The cars were always sold from Derby as complete rolling chassis with the restyled and very distinctive radiator shell in place. Usually the customer had specified a coachbuilder and body style required, and cars took up to three months to be completed. Park Ward, on the other hand, were very close to Rolls-Royce, and offered what amounted to standard styles, which cut down the waiting period considerably.

The problem with most quality British cars of the period was that they carried

Below: Every Derby-built Bentley had a coachbuilt body – saloon, sporting or touring. The green racing version is that raced by Eddie Hall in the TTs – unofficially backed by Rolls-Royce.

heavy bodywork, as a chassis price of £1,100 and a typical all-up price of £1,460 indicate. Maximum speeds of over 90mph were common, but year by year acceleration and fuel consumption suffered as weights continued to creep up. Rolls-Royce's solution was to enlarge the engine from 3,669cc to 4,257cc, without any other major change. Slightly more power and considerably more torque did the trick.

In 1938, which meant that the cars would only be available for two selling seasons, the 4¼-litre car was given 'overdrive' gearing, a misnomer in that no separate overdrive was fitted. In fact the axle was slightly changed and third gear in the box became the direct drive, while fourth was a geared-up cruising ratio. The effect was to make the car more long-legged and even more refined. An increase in tyre section helped this transformation.

The 'Derby' Bentleys, as the cars were soon nicknamed, soon made themselves an excellent reputation and they were in truth much better all-round performers than the old 'W.O.' models had been. Between 1933 and 1940, nearly 2,500 examples were built, slightly more than half of them being 4¼-litre cars; 200 of these were 'overdrive' models. But for the outbreak of war Rolls-Royce would probably have replaced the car for 1940 with the new Mark V Bentley, with a new chassis frame plus coil-sprung independent front suspension. Existing engine, gearbox and other transmission parts would have been specified – as usual – all bodies would be supplied by outside coachbuilding specialists. In the event, eleven such Mark Vs were completed, of 19 chassis laid down, before the start of hostilities, and several survive. The Mark V, with its 4¼-litre engine, was a precursor of the post-war Bentley (the Mark VI) – although this later car was to have the inlet-over-exhaust cylinder head layout. That engine, a final derivation of the Rolls-Royce 20/25 layout, was last used in 1959, by which time it had grown to 4,887cc. All post-war Bentleys have been built at Crewe, while Derby has concentrated on aero-engine manufacture.

Bentley 6½-litre 'Speed Six'

Speed Six built 1928 to 1930
Built by: Bentley Motors Ltd., Britain.
Engine: Six cylinders, in line, in light-alloy block with non-detachable cylinder head. Bore and stroke 100mm by 140mm, 6,597cc (3.94in × 5.51in, 402.5cu.in). Four valves per cylinder, operated by bifurcated rocker (inlet valves) or individual rockers (exhaust side) from single overhead camshaft. Three-throw coupling-rod drive and gear from nose of crankshaft. Twin plugs, one each side of cylinder head, under the manifolding; ignition by twin magnetos (coil and magneto supply in tandem later fitted). Twin horizontal SU carburettors. Compression ratio 5.3:1. Maximum power 180bhp at 3,500rpm with 'single port' block.
Transmission: Single shaft-operated dry-plate clutch. Four-speed unsynchronised gearbox, separately mounted, with right-hand gearchange. Open Hardy Spicer propeller shaft to spiral-bevel rear axle, of optional 3.54 or 3.85:1 ratio. Either 'C' Type or straight-cut gear 'D' Type gearboxes fitted.
Chassis: Channel-section side members in steel, liberally cross braced, conventionally over-slung at rear. Half-elliptic leaf springs front and rear, with worm-and-sector steering. Cable-operated self-wrapping drum brakes. Outside handbrake, sports car bodies only. Coachwork to choice – saloon, coupé, or open sports.
Dimensions: Wheelbase 11ft 8.5in (357cm), 12ft 8.5in (387cm), or 11ft (335cm) to choice (short wheelbase on Le Mans version only). Front and rear track 4ft 8in (142cm). Overall length 15ft 1in to 16ft 7in (460cm to 505cm) depending on wheelbase length and coachwork. Unladen weight between 4,480lb and 5,040lb (2,031 and 2,286kg).

Below: Built in 1929, this Speed Six had a touring body by Vanden Plas, who used to build Le Mans coachwork for the Bentley factory. This car had four separate doors, and a windscreen for the rear seat passengers, which could still be used with the hood erect.

Above: Ettore Bugatti might have christened the vintage Bentley as the 'fastest Lorry in the World', but this was pure jealousy. Heavy, high-geared, with a rumbling exhaust note, the Speed Six was a superb sports car of its day, with a natural cruising speed of at least 80mph.

History: The 'Speed Six' is probably the most famous of all W. O.'s Bentleys. In factory drivers' hands, these cars won twice at Le Mans (in 1929 and 1930) – with Chairman Woolf Barnato in the winning car on each occasion, at Brooklands and in minor races elsewhere. Their domination of sports car racing was so complete that entries from other teams declined sharply.

Bentley's advanced six-cylinder engine, developed from but by no means the same as the original 'four' in design, was conceived in 1924, and the standard 6½-litre Bentley was put on sale at the end of 1925. Originally it had been a 4½-litre 'six', but it was found to be lacking in power and torque.

The 'Speed Six', with a chassis intended for sporting use if necessary, followed in 1928, and was produced until 1930, when it was replaced by the magnificent Bentley 8-litre. In all 545 6½-litre cars were built of which an exclusive 182 were 'Speed Sixes'.

Like others of the period, the car was massively strong and heavy. Even with the 180bhp engine, the Speed Six's normal maximum speed was no more than 92-95mph.

The engine's overhead camshaft drive was complex and unique, with triple eccentric coupling rod operation, thought by 'W. O.' to be more reliable than either chain or gear-drive systems. The cylinder head, as with all such Bentleys, was non-detachable and in unit with the cylinder block.

Built almost regardless of cost (the new car price, depending on coachwork, was between £2,300 and £2,500), the engineering was painstakingly thorough. There was a vast petrol tank (up to 43 gallons – 195 litres – on the race cars), and even the electron alloy oil sump held more than five gallons.

Although the car was magnificent in build and in durable performance, the company which made it was always financially insecure. Perhaps Bentley had the worst of bad luck when they chose the depths of the depression to upgrade the car to the very exclusive 8-litre; within a year of this launch the company was in liquidation.

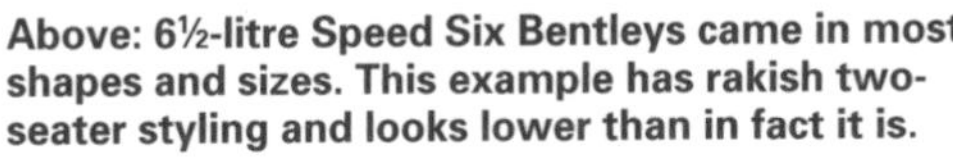

Above: 6½-litre Speed Six Bentleys came in most shapes and sizes. This example has rakish two-seater styling and looks lower than in fact it is.

Left and below left: Two entirely different and attractive ways of bodying a Speed Six Bentley chassis. At the top is a 1930 fixed-head coupe by H. J. Mulliner, and the 'fast-back' saloon was built for Captain Woolf Barnato by Gurney Nutting in 1930, as low as possible.

Bentley Continental R, T and Azure

Bentley Continental family, introduced in 1991
Built by: Bentley Motors Ltd. (a subsidiary of Rolls-Royce Motor Cars Ltd.), Britain.
Engine: Eight cylinders, in 90-deg. vee, five-main-bearing light-alloy cylinder block. Bore and stroke 104.1 × 99.1mm, 6,750cc (4.09 × 3.90in, 411.7cu.in). Two light alloy cylinder heads. Two valves per cylinder, overhead, in line, operation by pushrods, rockers and hydraulic tappets from camshaft in vee of cylinder block. Bosch Motronic fuel injection and Garrett AiResearch turbocharger. Maximum power 360bhp (DIN) at 4,200rpm. Maximum torque 553lb.ft at 2,000rpm.
Transmission: Rear-wheel-drive, torque convertor and GM four-speed automatic transmission, all in unit with engine. Remote-control gearchange on steering column.
Chassis: Unitary-construction pressed-steel body-chassis unit in two-door four-seater style (Azure derivative had drop-head coupe style). Independent front suspension by coil springs, wishbones, telescopic dampers, anti-roll bar, and automatic variable ride control. Independent rear suspension by coil springs, semi-trailing arms, telescopic dampers and automatic variable ride control. Rack-and-pinion steering with hydraulic power asssistance. Four-wheel disc brakes with ABS. Cast alloy 16in wheels, 255/60-16in tyres.
Dimensions: Wheelbase 10ft 0.25in (306.1cm), front track 5ft 1.0in (155cm), rear track 5ft 1.0in (155cm). Overall length 17ft 6.3in (534.2cm). Unladen weight 5,340lb (2,420kg).
History: For the 1980s, Rolls-Royce produced a successor to the long-running Silver Shadow/Bentley T-Series models. Based on the same, but developed, V8-engined floorpan, these mechanically identical cars were called Rolls-Royce Silver Spirit and Bentley Mulsanne, respectively.

Although there would be no newly-developed coupés and convertibles for many years, the old-type Corniches (the Bentley version was later re-badged 'Continental') carried on, and the chassis was continually updated. By the end of

Below: The Continental SC was an appealing evolution of the Continental R, with a removable glass panel above the front seats.

Above: From front to rear, variations on a V8-engined Bentley theme - Azure, Continental SC, Continental T and Continental R, The Continental T had a shorter wheelbase than other types.

the 1980s there were hugely powerful turbocharged versions, the roadholding of the saloons had been much improved, and Bentley's image began to come back from the shadows.

The time was therefore ripe to introduce new-style coupés and convertibles, this process duly beginning in 1991, with the launch of a sleek but bulky four-seater coupe called the Continental R. The verbal reference to the old-type R-Type Continental of the 1950s was intentional, for Bentley wanted to re-emphasise their high-performance and speciality image, this new car certainly delivering all such characteristics.

Built up on the latest 120in wheelbase floorpan of the Bentley Turbo R (complete with a 360bhp turbocharged version of the legendary 6.75-litre V8 engine), the Continental R had a craftsman-built steel body shell (with aluminium closing panels), in the shape of a full four-seater cabin, but with only two passenger doors.

At once solidly traditional, yet obviously in the Supercar category, here was a big, rock-solid, new Bentley coupe, complete with the established radiator style, and all the fixtures and fittings expected by the clientele. Because it was so heavy (5,340lb) and unaerodynamic in shape, the measured top speed of about 150mph was a surprise, though the usual fuel consumption of not better than 13mpg was not.

Hidden away, of course, this was a car which melded the very best of high quality materials – the highest-grade wood for furnishing, the best-quality leather for seating, thick carpets, and hundreds of hours of careful fitting-out – with what was an extremely mechanically advanced chassis.

The engine, though venerable in concept, produced more torque than any other engine in the world, had fuel injection and every electronic control, the automatic transmission was the latest GM-supplied four-speeder, and the manners were impeccable. Suspension, all-independent and still soft, now had electronically monitored ride controls, high-pressure braking was effortless, and steering was light and quite unobtrusive – the effect being that of driving a drawing room rather than a motor car.

To some observers, the Continental R was everything that they considered to be obscene about a motor car – to them, high performance, weight, and heavy fuel consumption were quite unjustified – but neither Bentley nor its customers took too much notice of this. The demand, however limited, was for the best high-performance coupé which could possibly be produced at a 1992 price in the ▶

UK of £160,000, and Bentley was in the market of doing that. By producing six cars a week, no more, from its factories (Park Street Metal, of Coventry, supplied the body shells), there was profitable business to be done.

The Continental R, in any case, was only the start. Four years down the road, in 1995, the company introduced the Azure, another magnificently-equipped convertible, which was to all intents and purposes a direct soft-top development of the Continental R coupé. The Azure, as expected, was still a four-seater, and had a massive power-operated soft top which could turn free-as-air driving into closed comfort in a matter of seconds.

In basic chassis specification and almost in performance, the Azure was a Continental R 'with free air'. Amazingly, its open-top shell was torsionally much stiffer than that of the ousted Bentley Continental/Rolls-Royce Corniche had ever been, yet it made no concessions to comfort.

Production was a complex affair, for Park Street Metal provided partly completed shells to Pininfarina of Italy, who completed them, painted them, added the folding soft-top, then returned them to Crewe for final assembly to take place. As it had 385bhp (the Continental R was updated at the same time), it was seen to be reasonable value for £215,000in 1995, and soon 200 cars a year were being produced. Even though Rolls-Royce was introducing a new

Below: The short-wheelbase Continental T had 420bhp, and a top speed of at least 170mph. It was quite the fiercest of all Bentleys.

family of BMW-engined cars, this never put the continuing career of the two-door Bentleys in danger.

The third model in this family was the Continental T, launched in 1996, as a shorter-wheelbase (by four inches) version of the Continental R, with 400bhp, flared wheelarches, brutal five-spoke wide-rim alloy wheels – and a price tag of £220,000. This car, for sure, was the indulgence to end all indulgences: much more expensive than the Continental R, it had rather less interior cabin space, a more abrupt, but still comforting, character, and more on-the-road 'presence'.

Even after VW took control of the company in 1998, evolution continued, with engines being upgraded (the 1999 model Continental T had 420bhp), with limited-edition types launched, and with the Continental SC (like the Continental R but with a removable glass roof panel) also going on sale. A customer could choose from a bewilderingly wide range of body and trim colours and optional equipment, so there was really no such thing as a 'standard' Bentley of this type.

Cosworth started building these V8 engines from 1996, late model Continental Ts could reach 170mph (though with horrifyingly high fuel consumption), and even though the cars were known to be obsolescent, they continued to sell at the start of the 21st Century. By the summer of 2000, special Mulliner-trimmed SCs cost more than £257,000.

There was something so monstrously indomitable, so solid, so majestic, and so supreme about these machines that Mr Toad, if transplanted to this age, would no doubt be an owner.

Benz 1880s Tricycle

¾hp model, built from 1885, replicas sold up to 1890
Built by: Benz and Co., Germany.
Engine: Single cylinder, horizontally mounted fore-and-aft in frame, with exposed vertical crankshaft and flywheel. Water cooled. Bore and stroke 116mm by 160mm, 1,691cc (4.56in × 6.30in, 103.2cu.in). Two valves, single cam operating exhaust valve by rockers and levers and offset pin in cam end face operating inlet slide valve. Benz surface carburettor. Maximum power about 1.5bhp at 250/300rpm.
Transmission: Belt drive from flywheel to differential and cross-shaft all in unit with engine. Final drive to rear wheels by chain. Release of direct drive (no step-down gears provided) by pulling belt-control arm to neutral position. Engine mounted behind seats and in front of driven rear axle.
Chassis: Separate tubular chassis frame. Three wheels, single front wheel mounted and controlled bicycle fashion. Cog-and-twin-rack steering, between vertical steering posts of front wheel and vertical steering column, via drag links. Front wheel suspended by full-elliptic spring and radius arms. Rear suspension by full-elliptic leaf springs. No dampers. Rear wheel transmission brakes, operated by belt-control lever. Centre lock wire wheels and solid tyres.
Dimensions: Wheelbase 4ft 9.1in (145cm). Unladen weight 585lb (265kg).
History: Lenoir's early gas engine inspired Nikolaus Otto to develop the first practical four-stroke petrol engine. His applications for patents on the very principle of four-stroke internal combustion were turned down, which left the two pioneers – Gottlieb Daimler and Karl Benz – to race towards the building of the first petrol powered car. Benz had been operating a machine shop in Mannheim since 1871 and had had his first two-stroke engine running in 1879; he started to build a four-stroke machine in 1884 as soon as the patent-application was thrown out. The Benz tricycle which ran in 1885 was the very first practical car – even though it beat Daimler's invention

Right: A historic machine – the very first petrol-driven 'car' to be used on the road – by Karl Benz in 1885.

only by a matter of months. It was a tricycle because Benz could not solve the problems of lightweight twin steered front wheels, and it had a tubular chassis frame because bicycles were built like that. The engine produced only 1½bhp at not more than 250rpm and it was very crude with an exposed crankshaft; nevertheless it was a practical and neat little mechanical package of which several replicas were sold in the next few years. A good cruising speed was 10mph, but seven or eight mph was thought to be satisfactory. Benz was nevertheless *the* pioneer, and legendary for all that.

BMW Six-cylinder Coupés

BMW 2800CS, 3.0CS, 3.0CSi and 3.0CSL (data for 3.0CSL, 1973 model)
Built by: Bayerische Motoren Werke AG., Germany.
Engine: Six cylinders, in line, in seven-bearing cast-iron block. Bore and stroke 89.25mm by 80mm, 3,003cc (3.51in × 3.15in, 183cu.in). Light alloy cylinder head. Two overhead valves per cylinder, inclined to each other in poly-spherical combustion chambers and operated by rockers from single overhead Bosch fuel injection, with nozzles in inlet ports. Maximum power 200bhp (DIN) at 5,500. Maximum torque 200lb.ft at 4,300rpm.
Transmission: Single-dry-plate clutch and four-speed synchromesh manual gearbox, in unit with front-mounted engine. Open propeller shaft to chassis-mounted hypoid-bevel final-drive unit, with optional limited-slip differential. Exposed universally jointed drive shafts to rear wheels.
Chassis: Unitary-construction pressed-steel body/chassis unit, in two-door 2+2 coupé layout. Light-alloy skin panels (some 1974 models fitted with large boot lid aerofoil spoiler, and scoop at rear of roof). All independent suspension, front by coil springs, MacPherson struts and anti-roll bar, rear by coil springs, semi-trailing wishbones and anti-roll bar. Telescopic dampers. Ball-and-nut steering, optionally power assisted. Four-wheel servo-assisted disc brakes. 14in bolt-on cast-alloy road wheels. 195.70VR14 tyres.

Below: With a shape like this, wasn't it inevitable that the be-finned 3.0 CSLs should be called 'Batmobiles'? The wing, the rear roof slot, and the front wing strakes, were all to make the racing versions more stable. It worked so well in 1974 that other cars withdrew in disgust, unable to match their performance. Underneath the engine, transmission and chassis are all based on a production coupe.

Above: Compare the original 3.0CSL with the 'Batmobile' (below) which was developed from it – as a road car the Karmann-styled car is very handsome with the extra wind-cheating aids. 140mph performance is matched by all-independent suspension, four seats, and a silky overhead cam 3-litre six-cylinder engine. In spite of the many weight-saving features, the CSL was still a reliable and totally civilised sports coupé.

Dimensions: Wheelbase 8ft 7.3in (262cm), track (front) 4ft 8.9in (144cm), track (rear) 4ft 7.1in (140cm). Overall length 15ft 3.4in (466cm). Unladen weight 2,600lb (1,180kg).

History: In spite of producing fine post-war cars, BMW were in financial trouble by the end of the 1950s. Not even sales of the little Isetta 'bubble' cars, or the nice little 700cc car could help. The firm was revived very rapidly at the start of the 1960s by the first of an entire series of modern designs, all of which have used the same family of overhead-camshaft engines. At first there was merely a 'four', originally of 1500cc, then 1600cc, then 1800cc and finally 2000cc. The car which rescued BMW was the 1600 and 1800 saloon (which was later enlarged to become the 2000).

In 1965, however, BMW also announced a sleek two-door coupé, styled and engineered by Karmann, fitted with the 2000's mechanicals. This, the 2000CS coupé, in fuel-injection form, was the first of a very successful line. This car had distinctive styling with vast and wide headlamps.

In 1968, with BMW well and truly in the forefront of executive and sporting car productions, the first of the six-cylinder cars was shown. This had all-new structures, but the engine was really a six-cylinder version of the established overhead-cam 'four' and shared many common components. At the same time, by a rather drastic piece of mechanical surgery, the new six-cylinder engine was also persuaded to fit the Karmann-built coupé shell. This had a revised nose, with twin circular headlamps, and was called the 2800CS.

By 1971, with the largest of the six-cylinder engines enlarged from 2.8-litre to 3.0-litre, the coupé was thoroughly re-engineered under the skin, to have the backward-sloping MacPherson strut front suspension of the big saloons. It was also given the full 3-litre engine and became the 3.0CS. a year later, with fuel injection at least offered on the big 'six', the coupé became the 3.0CSi, and had 140mph performance to match its very impressive looks. The car then carried on until 1975 unchanged, but eventually in two versions – a carburettor-engined car, with automatic transmission as standard, and the injection-engined car available only with the four-speed manual gearbox.

By 1972, however, BMW's interest in racing had intensified. Up to then they had been happy to enter four-cylinder BMW's (sometimes in turbocharged form) in touring-car events, and often succeeded in winning outright. Now they turned their attention to the big six-cylinder coupés, which could be homologated as 'touring cars'. Even with their normal engines, they could be super-tuned to give more than 300bhp, but the Karmann-styled car had certain aerodynamic deficiencies. Thus it was that BMW announced a lightweight car. The 3.0CSL (the 'L' standing for 'Lightweight' in most languages!) was effectively a 3.0CSi,

Above: The very first coupé from which the classic line was developed was the 2000CS of 1965, but this became the 2800CS (illustrated here) at the end of 1968. The basic lines were not changed, but six-cylinder cars had twinned headlamps, a revised interior, air outlets behind the front wheels, and other visual details.

but with drastically lightened trim and furnishings, light-alloy skin panels and doors and an engine marginally bored out to take it over the 3-litre class limit. The factory CSLs, therefore were often entered as 3½-litre cars, and had more than 350bhp, especially after the 24-valve cylinder heads had been developed. The aerodynamic stability problems were solved a year later, in the autumn of 1973, when the CSL was modified to include a slim air-flow aligning wing across the top of the rear window, tiny strakes on the front wings and a vast inverted aerofoil section fixed to the boot lid. Thus equipped, and immediately nicknamed the 'Batmobiles', the factory cars could match anything Ford, with the Capris, could field, but the cars were so specialised and costly that they killed all opposition except Ford, and the racing series for which they were evolved died because of lack of entries! There was great controversy over these less-than-practical road cars, and the aerodynamic fittings were actually banned from road use in West Germany, but the cars were sensationally fast.

Private owners could have their cars without the special fittings, and even – if they insisted – with steel instead of light-alloy panelling. The CSL managed to overshadow the more mundane, but still very desirable CSAs and CSis, which continued to sell well until 1975, when they were all withdrawn in favour of the new 633CSi coupés. No more outrageously shaped nor dramatic 'saloon' car has yet been seen on the world's tracks. Turbo-charged versions were raced by the factory in later years.

Left: It is difficult to look at the BMW 3-litre coupé and see that it is based on more mundane saloon car engineering. The floor pan, and all the chassis items, however, are shared with the 3-litre four-door saloons. The neat and integrated coupés are the shortest of the family, which also includes long-wheelbase limousines.

BMW 328

BMW 328 and Frazer Nash-BMW (data applies to both cars)
Built by: Bayerische Motoren Werke AG., Germany.
Engine: Six cylinders, in line, in four-bearing cast-iron block. Bore and stroke 66mm by 96mm, 1,971cc (2.60in × 3.78in, 120.3cu.in). Two overhead valves per cylinder, with inclined operation in part-spherical combustion chambers. Unique pushrod valve operation: inlet valve directly operated by pushrod and rocker, exhaust valve by pushrod, pivot, cross pushrod and rocker. Single side mounted camshaft. Aluminium cylinder head with downdraught siamesed inlet ports and three Solex carburettors. Maximum power 80bhp (DIN) at 4,500rpm.
Transmission: Single-dry-plate clutch and four-speed manual gearbox (synchromesh on top and third gears), with direct control gearchange. Open propeller shaft to spiral-bevel 'live' rear axle.
Chassis: Separate frame, of ladder-type construction, main members of steel tubing, and cross members of box or tubular sections, independent front suspension by transverse leaf spring and lower wishbones. Rear suspension by half-elliptic leaf springs. Hydraulic dampers all round. Rack-and-pinion steering. Four-wheel hydraulically operated drum brakes. 16in pressed-steel disc brakes, with four-pin drive and centre-lock fixings. 5.50 × 16in tyres. Two-seat sports bodywork of alloy panelling on ash frame in nearly every case. Cabriolet version, with fold-down hood, also available.
Dimensions: Wheelbase 7ft 10.5in (240cm), track (front) 3ft 9.4in (115cm), track (rear) 4ft (122cm). Overall length 12ft 9.5in (390cm). Unladen weight (sports body) 1,700lb (771kg).
History: The BMW 328 was the final flowering of a series of designs initiated in 1933. Kernel of the family of cars was a splendidly detailed six-cylinder engine (which was later fitted with unusual valve gear), a rigid tubular chassis, quite unlike most European designs of the 1930s, and independent front suspension, at a time when this was considered expensive and unpredictable. The engine first appeared as a 1¼-litre unit,

Above: Three of these beautiful, special-bodied 328s were prepared for the Mille Miglia race of 1940, taking third, fifth and sixth places.

Below left: The original BMW 328 started a revolution in sports car style and engineering, which would surely have progressed further if war had not intervened. The engine had a clever form of valve gear invented by Dr. Fiedler, and was later used in post-war Bristol and Frazer Nash cars.

then in the Type 315 and 319 cars in 1½-litre form.

The Type 328 was a sports car pure and simple, designed to be smooth, look smooth, and have impeccable road manners – this, at a time when sports cars were normally harsh, crudely equipped and rather spartan. Body styling included faired-in headlamps and flowing integrated lines, which were all ahead of their time. BMW developments from this car undoubtedly inspired William Lyon's thinking on car shapes for his Jaguars of the 1940s.

The Type 328 was announced in 1936, and was distinguished by its unique cylinder head and valve gear. A part-spherical combustion chamber and good breathing were considered essential, but Dr. Fiedler, the designer, was ordered to stick with one side-mounted camshaft. He solved the restriction brilliantly by inventing the extra cross-pushrod arrangement to operate the inclined exhaust valves, and he arranged for the inlet port to enter the cylinder head from the top of the engine, with the carburettors atop that. The only disadvantage was that the engine, in total, was quite tall. BMW styling, however, could easily accommodate this.

Apart from its striking styling, the car was also equipped with a full undertray to improve aero-dynamics. Original cars had a hidden spare wheel, but most have the familiar part-recessed spare on the tail panel. The British BMW concessionaires AFN Ltd., imported the car as the Frazer Nash-BMW, and proved its worth with a 101 miles in a one-hour run at Brooklands in 1937. The last production cars were built in 1940, before German war production caused all private car building to cease. In all, 461 328s were built and the engine was adopted in post-war years by Bristol for their 400 and 406 models.

BMW 507

507 model, built from 1956 to 1959
Built by: Bayerische Motoren Werke AG., Germany.
Engine: Eight cylinders, in line, in 90-degree vee-formation, in five-bearing light-alloy block. Bore and stroke 82mm by 75mm, 3,168cc (3.23in × 2.95in, 193.3cu.in). Two detachable light alloy cylinder heads. Two overhead valves per cylinder, operated by pushrods and rockers from single camshaft mounted in centre of cylinder block 'vee'. Two down-draught twin-choke Solex carburettors. Maximum power 150bhp (net) at 4,800rpm. Maximum torque 127lb.ft at 2,500rpm.
Transmission: Single-dry-plate clutch and five-speed, synchromesh manual gearbox (without synchromesh on first gear) both in unit with front-mounted engine. Central gearchange. Open propeller shaft to hypoid-bevel 'live' rear axle, with optional limited-slip differential.
Chassis: Separate pressed-steel chassis frame, with box-section side members and tubular cross-bracing. Independent front suspension by torsion bars and wishbones. Rear suspension by torsion bars, radius arms and Panhard rod. Telescopic dampers. Pinion-and-sector steering. Four-wheel, hydraulically operated drum brakes. 16in bolt-on or centre-lock pressed-steel disc wheels. 6.00 × 16in tyres. Two-seat open sports or hardtop coachwork.
Dimensions: Wheelbase 8ft 1.5in (248cm), track (front) 4ft 8.7in (144cm), track (rear) 4ft 8in (142cm). Overall length 14ft 5in (439.4cm). Unladen weight 2,530lb (1,147kg).
History: As a logical development of their 501 saloon car series, BMW married a shortened version of that chassis with the developed 3.2-litre V8 engine, which had become optional, and clothed the result in an outstandingly attractive two-seater sports car body style. Under the skin, the separate four-speed gearbox of the saloons had given way to a new five-speed box in unit with the engine and the rear suspension was both revised and improved. Overall design

Above and below: Perhaps the loveliest of all BMWs – pre-war or post-war – was the 507 of the 1950s. It had a 3.2-litre vee-8 engine, and could reach 140mph.

is attributed to Dr. Fiedler, who takes credit for the pre-war Type 328, and apart from its high price the Type 507 was a worthy successor. Maximum speed was between 135 and 140mph, with acceleration and stability to match. Although the 507 looked ideal for use as a competition car, the factory never entered it in any events, and private owners were too impressed by its looks and its high standard of finish and equipment to abuse it in this way. Two hundred and fifty-three BMW 507s were built.

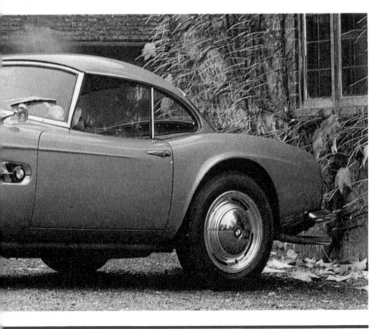

BMW M3

BMW M3 sports saloon, first generation built 1986 to 1990
Built by: BMW AG, Germany.
Engine: Four cylinders, in line, in five-main-bearing cast iron cylinder block. Bore and stroke 93.4 × 84mm, 2,302cc (3.60 × 3.30in, 140.4cu.in). Aluminium alloy cylinder head. Four valves per cylinder, in narrow vee, operation by twin overhead camshafts and inverted bucket tappets. Bosch/BMW fuel injection. Maximum power 200bhp (DIN) at 6,750rpm. Maximum torque 177lb.ft at 4,750rpm.
Transmission: Rear-wheel-drive, single plate diaphragm spring clutch and five-speed all-synchromesh manual gearbox, all in unit with front-mounted engine. Remote-control, central gearchange.
Chassis: Unitary-construction pressed-steel body-chassis unit in two-door saloon style. Independent front suspension by MacPherson struts, coil springs, lower wishbones, telescopic dampers and anti-roll bar. Independent rear suspension by coil springs, semi-trailing arms, telescopic dampers and anti-roll bar. Rack-and-pinion steering, with hydraulic power assistance. Four-wheel disc brakes with ABS. Alloy 15in road wheels, 205/55-15in tyres.
Dimensions: Wheelbase 8ft 4.9in (256.2cm), front track 4ft 8in (141.2cm), rear track 4ft 8.4in (143.3cm). Overall length 14ft 3.1in (434.5cm). Unladen weight 2,762lb (1,252kg).
History: For many years there had been a strong 'racer' streak at BMW where, in deepest Bavaria, its engineers produced a series of splendidly powerful engines, and limited-production cars to use them. In the early 1980s BMW also produced a turbocharged Formula 1 engine (Nelson Piquet became World Champion using them), which actually used the existing four-cylinder road-car cylinder block, so when they decided to re-enter saloon car racing later in the decade this was an obvious component to use.

The new M3, previewed in 1986, and starting an illustrious racing career in 1987, was the result. Starting with the two-door saloon body shell of the latest 3-Series range, which had been unveiled at the end of 1982, BMW set out to produce a race-winning 'homologation special' which would also be a great road car. Starting with the body shell, where the rear window rake was changed to improve the aeodynamics, and there was a large transverse rear spoiler to add to the rear-end grip at high speeds, BMW also added flared front and rear wheelarches (the better to cover the ultra-wide tyres to be used on race tracks).

They then chose an engine based around a big-bore 2.3-litre version of the F1-proved four-cylinder block, mating it with a 16-valve twin-cam cylinder head and fuel injection: this, in effect, was two-thirds of the six-cylinder M635CSi power unit. In road-tune it produced a lusty 200bhp, but in razor-edge race tune (when it showed that it could carry on working flat out for 24 hours) it was good for 320bhp. When backed by a five-speed Getrag gearbox, and with all the expertise that the engineers could build in to the chassis, this was indeed a remarkable race car. Outpaced on the race track, as expected, by the 500bhp Ford Sierra RS500 Cosworths, the M3s were so nimble and so reliable that they won many touring car races in the next few years.

As road cars, with 140mph top speeds and sparkling acceleration to match, they were amazingly popular. Built only in left-hand-drive, and with hard, no-compromise suspension, they were exhilarating machines to drive, especially on roads where handling, balance and response was more important than outright pace. BMW, somehow, had built in a load of character, from the urgent bark of a well-tuned engine, to the way that a driver felt, through his feet and hands – and the seat of his pants – the chassis response.

In the years that followed, there were further improvements to this pedigree, including the addition of an M3 Evolution model (1988), where 500 special versions were produced with a 220bhp engine and more obvious, more effective aerodynamics, while in 1990 the M3 Sport Evolution actually provided a

Left and below: BMW developed the M3 as a car that could be competitive in saloon car racing. In road car form it originally had 200bhp, with a very urgent character and excellent road manners.

Above: The M3 Sport Evolution of 1990 featured a 238bhp/2,467cc engine, and was made in tiny numbers for motor racing.

238bhp/2,467cc version of the same engine. The arrival of a Cabriolet version of the car, complete with a power-operated soft top, was a final bonus.

When the last of the original-generation M3s were produced in 1990, no fewer than 17,184 saloons and 786 Cabriolets had been manufactured. Even more amazing was that BMW had records of more than 300 M3s being used in saloon racing. The next-generation M3, which had a silky six-cylinder engine, was a very different animal.

BMW Z1

BMW Z1 open sports car, produced 1986 to 1990
Built by: BMW AG, Germany.
Engine: Six cylinders, in line, in cast-iron cylinder block. Bore and stroke 84 x 75mm, 2,494cc (3.31 x 2.95in, 152.2cu.in). Light alloy cylinder head. Two valves per cylinder, in narrow vee, operation by single overhead camshaft, rockers and inverted bucket tappets. Bosch/BMW fuel injection. Maximum power 170bhp (DIN) at 5,800rpm. Maximum torque 164lb.ft at 4,300rpm.
Transmission: Rear-wheel-drive, single-dry-plate diaphragm spring clutch and five-speed all-synchromesh manual gearbox, all in unit with front-mounted engine. Remote-control, central gearchange.
Chassis: Unitary-construction pressed-steel body-chassis unit, in two-door roadster style, with slide down passenger doors. Independent front suspension by MacPherson struts, coil springs, lower wishbones, telescopic dampers and anti-roll bar. Independent rear suspension by coil springs, multi-links and wishbones, telescopic dampers and anti-roll bar. Rack-and-pinion steering, with hydraulic power assistance. Four-wheel disc brakes with ABS. Cast alloy 16in wheels, 225/45-16in tyres.
Dimensions: Wheelbase 8ft 0in (243.8cm), front track 4ft 8in (142.2cm), rear track 4ft 9in (144.7cm). Overall length 12ft 10.5in (392.4cm). Unladen weight 2,948lb (1,337kg).
History: Why build a one-off testbed if you can build thousands, sell them at a profit, and part-pay for the programme? That, it seems, is what BMW thought when they decided to put the Z1 roadster on the market in 1986. It was not a big programme, and in four years only 8,000 such cars would be sold, but it made its point.

Conceived early in the 1980s, the Z1 was a two-seater roadster with unique and surprising features. Not only did it have a six-cylinder engine (when a more sporty 'four' might have been expected), but there was a novel type of rear suspension, and very novel construction features.

Below: BMW's first mass-market two-seater, the Z1, had passenger doors which, when opened, slid downwards into the sills.

Above: In many ways the Z1 was a styling forerunner of the later Z3, though this was the only BMW to adopt such a cowled-headlamp type of nose.

Starting, first, with the body, where the novelties were clear, BMW styled a neat by unexciting two-seater roadster – unexciting, that is, until one found that the doors did not open in the conventional manner, but retracted downwards, into the capacious sills, actuated by electric motors and toothed belts. The body shell itself was also equipped with an extra composite-fibre sandwich underfloor, which added to the rigidity, but while there was a familiar MacPherson strut suspension up front, this was the very first BMW to be equipped with what the company called its 'Z-axle'. 'Z' for what? – all we needed to know was that there were coil springs and an anti-roll bar, plus a complex system of upper and lower transverse and semi-trailing links to guide the movements of the wheels, and that this gave dramatically better grip, traction and roadholding than any of the semi-trailing cars which had previously come out of Munich.

Power was by the same 2.5-litre/170bhp six-cylinder engine which was already being used in 3-Series and 5-Series saloons, still with only a single overhead camshaft and two valves per cylinder in part-spherical combustion chambers. Backed by the same close-ratio five-speed gearbox also found in those cars, it was a satisfactory, if understated, way to produce a top speed of 136mph.

It was difficult to know quite what BMW intended the Z1 to achieve, for although its model name suggested that it was to be the first of a family of 'Z' cars – which it was – it was never backed up by anything as radical. Not quite as fast as expected, not quite as startlingly styled as it might have been, it was nevertheless a distinctive machine with all the right BMW credentials – the familiar kidney nose, the smooth and near-silent engine, the immaculate build quality, all backed by the huge self-confidence (don't say 'arrogance' please. . .) for which BMW was famous.

It was, above all, an ideal test bed for the new Z-axle, for this layout would soon be applied in other, mass-production, BMWs, proving conclusively that the days of tail-happy cars from Munich were over. The Z1, in other words, did its job. It never generated a huge demand, so when production ended in 1990 BMW concluded that it had all been worth it. The Z3, which followed in the 1990s, was a much more conventional car.

Bristol 400

Bristol 400 model built 1947 to 1950
Built by: Bristol Aeroplane Co. Ltd., Britain.
Engine: Six-cylinders, in line, in four-bearing cast-iron cylinder block. Bore and stroke 66mm by 96mm, 1,971cc (2.60in × 3.78in, 120.3cu.in). BMW-inspired pushrod valve operation, two overhead valves per cylinder. Inlet valve directly operated by pushrod and rocker, exhaust valve by pushrod, pivot, cross pushrod and rocker. Single side-mounted camshaft. Aluminium cylinder head with downdraught siamesed inlet ports and three Solex carburettors. Maximum power 85bhp (net) at 4,500rpm. Maximum torque 107lb.ft at 3,500rpm (very early models with three downdraught SU carburettors produced 80bhp at 4,200rpm).
Transmission: Single-dry-plate clutch and four-speed, manual synchromesh gearbox (without synchromesh on first gear), in unit with engine. Direct action central gearchange. Open propeller shaft to spiral-bevel 'live' rear axle.
Chassis: Separate steel chassis, with box-section side members, and strong box and pressed cross bracing members. Independent front suspension by transverse leaf spring and upper wishbones. Rear suspension by longitudinal torsion bars, radius arms and A-bracket. Bristol-made telescopic dampers. Rack-and-pinion steering. Four-wheel hydraulically operated 11in drum brakes, with fly-off cable handbrake. 16in disc wheels with 5.50 × 16in tyres. Steel body produced by Bristol, with aluminium skin panels.
Dimensions: Wheelbase 9ft 6in (290cm), track (front) 4ft 4in (132cm), track (rear) 4ft 6in (137cm). Overall length 15ft 3in (465cm). Unladen weight 2,537lb (1,151kg).
History: The Bristol Aeroplane Company, aided and abetted by the Aldington family (who imported BMW cars in the late 1930s) took over the obsolete designs of the BMW concern after the war had been won, amalgamated the basis of the 326 chassis frame, the high-performance 328 engine and the styling of the 327 body, to come up with the unexpectedly integrated Bristol 400 design. From that day to this, Bristol cars have been assembled at Bristol airfield (since 1960 under separate management) in small numbers, magnificently detailed and constructed, and sold at high prices.

Above and left: Showing obvious styling links with the pre-war BMW 326 and 328 models, the Bristol 400 used chassis and engines developed from the German cars. Only a close-coupled 2-door 4-seater was sold. The aerodynamics were excellent. The 400 was a good rally car, with 700 cars built from 1947 to 1950.

The BMW-inspired engine was not superseded until 1961, when the 407 model adopted a Chrysler V8, and the chassis, or rather repeated modifications of it, are still being made. The 400, of which just 700 were made in three years, was an attractive if none-too-rapid Grand Touring car and was only ever available in two-door coupé/saloon guise. Later, the 401 saloon, the 402 convertible, the 403 which evolved from the 401, the 404/405/406 replacements all followed on logically from the 400, retaining the traditions and pushing up the performance. The engine was also used by AC, and by Frazer Nash in sports cars, and proved to be surprisingly tuneable for sports car racing and Formula Two.

The early Bristols, as would be expected from an aircraft company, were aerodynamically efficient. Later Bristols have become less slippery and more like high priced flagships.

Bugatti EB110GT

Bugatti EB110GT sports coupé, built from 1992 to 1995
Built by: Bugatti Automobili, Italy.
Engine: Twelve cylinders, in 60-deg vee formation, in seven-bearing cast-alloy cylinder block/crankcase. Bore and stroke 81 × 56.6mm, 3,500cc (3.19 × 2.23in, 214cu.in). Two cast-alloy cylinder heads. Five valves per cylinder, operation by twin overhead camshafts per head. Bugatti fuel injection with four IHI turbochargers. Maximum power 560bhp (DIN) at 8,000rpm. Maximum torque 451lb.ft at 3,750rpm.
Transmission: Four-wheel-drive, multi-dry-plate clutch and six-speed all-synchromesh manual gearbox, all in unit with mid-mounted engine. Remote-control, central gearchange.
Chassis: Unitary-construction carbon fibre composite monocoque/platform, and an alloy body shell. Independent front suspension by coil springs, wishbones, telescopic dampers and an anti-roll bar. Independent rear suspension by coil springs, wishbones, telescopic dampers and an anti-roll bar. Rack-and-pinion steering with power-assistance. Four-wheel disc brakes with vacuum servo assistance and ABS. 18in cast alloy wheels, 245/40-18in (front) and 325/30-18in (rear) tyres.
Dimensions: Wheelbase 8ft 4.4in (255cm), front track 5ft 1.0in (155cm), rear track 5ft 3.7in (162cm). Overall length 14ft 5.2in (440cm). Unladen weight 3,571lb (1,620kg).
History: Overhyped and in a way over-engineered it might have been, but the short-lived Bugatti EB110GT was an archetypal example of motoring excess – excess in performance, excess in equipment, and certainly excessively expensive. But a lack of sales didn't mean that this was no classic car. Now, and in the future, it always will be.

Bugatti – the original Bugatti, that is – had stopped making cars soon after World War II, but it was not until 1986 that Italian entrepreneur Romano Artioli managed to buy the trademarks. With boundless ambition, he then set out to build a new mid-engined two-seater which would out-do anything that Ferrari, Porsche, Lamborghini and Jaguar could offer.

In his mind, the new car, which he titled EB110GT, would be more extreme than its opposition – five valves per cylinder instead of four, four turbochargers

Below: Although it carried the same name as its French ancestors, the EB 110GT was mechanically closer to Italian rivals such as Lamborghini.

Left: The EB110GT looked as startling as the performance it delivered. Marcello Gandini styled it, and used the same type of 'coleopter' doors which he had bequeathed to the Lamborghini Countach of the 1970s. Under the skin was a four-turbo V12 engine and four-wheel-drive. The top speed was more than 210mph.

instead of normal-aspiration, six-speeds instead of five, and four-wheel-drive instead of rear-wheel-drive. Not only that, but he would have it styled by Marcello Gandini (who already had the Lamborghini Miura and Countach to his credit), while the engine would be designed by a disaffected team of ex-Lamborghini engineers.

To cap it all, and in deliberate provocation of his rivals, it seemed, there would be a new factory at Campogalliano, on the outskirts of Modena. Engineering was overseen by Nicola Materazzi (who had run the Ferrari F40 programme at Ferrari), a carbon-fibre composite was chosen for the chassis (which meant that expensive autoclaves had to be installed at Campogalliano), and, well before prototypes took to the road, the hype began.

At first, however, prototype cars were built with welded/fabricated alloy chassis, and there was much to do with the engine and transmission. The engine itself was a technical masterpiece, with five valve heads (three inlet, two exhaust), and with forced induction by four small IHI turbochargers – two to each bank, each one being powered up by three cylinders and feeding high-pressure mixture to the same cylinders. The clever part was ensuring that everything worked well together – and it did.

When the four-wheel-drive was being engineered, Bugatti had obviously taken lessons from both Porsche and Lamborghini, for there was a rigid alloy tube linking the engine to the front diff, the centre power split directing only 27 per cent of engine torque to the front wheels.

Because Artioli, after all, was not superseding an old model with his new EB110GT, no secrecy was needed, so the prototype was launched in a blaze of expensive glory in Paris, more than a year before the first production cars could be delivered. When test cars were supplied, experts found that all the claimed performance – including a top speed of 213mph – was authenticated, and that the handling and traction were well-up to supercar standards.

As with the rival Jaguar XJ220, Artioli's problem was that the EB110GT became available as the European economy crashed, which caused most if not all of his probable clientele to cancel their orders. The project staggered on until 1995, then went spectacularly bankrupt, and only a handful of EB110GTs were ever delivered. In Modena, no trace of this project now remains.

Bugatti Type 13 'Brescia'

Type 13 built from 1910 to 1926 (data for 1921 Brescia)
Built by: Automobiles E. Bugatti, France.
Engine: Four cylinders, in line, in cast-iron block with three-bearing light-alloy crankcase bolted to it. Bore and stroke 69mm by 100mm, 1,496cc (2.72in × 3.94in, 91.3cu.in). Fixed cylinder head. Four overhead valves per cylinder, vertically mounted and operated by curved valve tappets from single overhead camshaft. Single Zenith updraught carburettor.
Transmission: Multi-disc clutch, running in oil in unit with engine, connected to separate four-speed manual gearbox, without synchromesh. Remote-control right-hand gearchange. Open propeller shaft to straight-bevel 'live' axle.
Chassis: Separate pressed-steel chassis frame, with channel-section side members and tubular and fabricated cross bracing. Forged front axle beam. Front suspension by half-elliptic springs. Rear suspension by reversed cantilever quarter-elliptic leaf springs and a tubular torque rod from axle to frame. Friction-type dampers. Worm-and-nut steering. Transmission foot brake and rear wheel brakes operated by handbrake. Centre-lock wire wheels. 710 × 90mm tyres. Open two-seat coachwork by Bugatti.
Dimensions: Wheelbase 6ft 7in (200cm), tracks (front and rear) 3ft 9.3in (115cm). Overall length 9ft 0in (274cm). Unladen weight 1,547lb (701kg).
History: Ettore Bugatti had been in business of designing cars since 1900 and produced one-offs for himself and contracted designs for other people in profusion. His first true 'Bugatti' production cars, by general agreement, were the Type 13 four-cylinder machines which first appeared in 1910. These, even in original form, established the Bugatti tradition of having overhead-camshaft operation and fixed cylinder heads – something which was not to waver in the next thirty years. Pre-war Type 13s had two valves per cylinder, but the post-war cars had four valves per cylinder, operated in that unique manner by banana-shaped tappets running in the cylinder head. The cars were raced with great success at Le Mans, but it was the 1921 Brescia race which gave the sports versions their now-legendary name. In the meantime the engine had grown from 1,327 to 1,486cc, by being bored out. The 100mm stroke, a Bugatti trademark along with the 88mm of several racing engines, was established on

Above and below: The 'Brescia' Bugatti was so named after the Type 13's success in the 1921 Brescia race. Like other early Bugattis, it had four valves per cylinder, operated by curved tappets from an overhead cam. Above is a young Raymond Mays in his Brescia 'Cordon Rouge', a very fast sprint car of the early 1920s.

this engine. The Type 13 also grew up into the Types 22 and 23, but there were mechanically the same cars with lengthened wheelbases and different coachwork. In one form or another they remained in production until 1926, and about 2,000 were built – just about a quarter of all Bugattis. The Brescia's looks are unmistakable, although the radiator shape had not at that stage become the classic Bugatti-horseshoe taken up by cars built to follow its success.

It typified Bugatti's approach to design, in that he paid less attention to the chassis and suspensions than to the mechanical engineering. The suspension – by half-elliptic front springs and reversed quarter-elliptic leaf rear springs, was no more than up-to-date in 1919, but it was carried over to every other Bugatti except for the front-wheel-drive racing car. Steering was precise, but not helped by a flexible frame. Coachwork, pro-filed likes the radiator, was simple but attractive, and the car's appeal was in the manner of its going. Some say it has never since been matched.

Bugatti 41 'Royale'

Type 41S, built individually between 1927 and 1933 – only six built
Built by: Automobiles E. Bugatti, France.
Engine: Eight cylinders, in line, in nine-bearing cast-iron block. Bore and stroke 125mm by 130mm, 12,763cc (4.92in × 5.2in, 778.8cu.in). Fixed cylinder head. Three overhead valves per cylinder (two inlet and one exhaust). Exhaust valve in line, inlet in line and parallel to exhaust valves. Operation by adjustable rockers from single overhead camshaft. Single updraught carburettor. Dry-sump lubrication. Maximum power about 300bhp at 2,000rpm.
Transmission: Multi-disc clutch, running in oil, connected to engine through two fabric universal joints. Open propeller shaft to three-speed manual gearbox (without synchromesh) mounted in unit with straight-bevel 'live' axle. Remote control central gearchange.
Chassis: Separate pressed-steel chassis frame, with channel-section side members and pressed and tubular cross members. Forged front axle beam, machine bored through its centre. Front suspension by half-elliptic springs. Rear suspension by two sets of quarter-elliptic leaf springs – one set cantilevered forward and in use always, another set cantilevered back and only coming into play for heavy loads. Friction-type dampers. Four-wheel cable-operated drum brakes, without servo assistance. Cast-alloy road wheels. 6.75 × 36in tyres. Individual coachwork by specialists (some cars rebodied several times).
Dimensions: Wheelbase 14ft 2in (432cm), tracks (front and rear) 5ft 3in (160cm). Overall length, depending on coachwork, from 22ft 0in (671cm). Unladen weight, depending on coachwork, from about 5,600lb (2,540kg).
History: The 'Royale' or 'Golden Bugatti' as it has also been named, was a car for kings, and that was how Bugatti himself wanted to see it sold. This vast car, with its engine intended for use (and very successful) in French aeroplanes, was the biggest, the heaviest, probably the fastest, and certainly the most expansive 'production' car in the world. It is little wonder that, although it was a real masterpiece, with a maximum speed of more than 100mph, and a three-speed gearbox in unit with the back axle (second was direct and top was very much of *Grand Routes* overdrive), only six were ever completed. Bugatti himself had always been sanguine about the car's success, and had laid down a series of 25. The prototype was built in 1926/7 with an even bigger engine,

Above and below: Two views of one of the six enormous, and very expensive Type 41 Bugatti 'Royale' cars. The engine was a 12.8-litre straight eight, and the cars could easily exceed 100mph.

of 14,726cc, than eventually was sold. It spite of its name, no 'Royale' was ever sold to any of the world's monarchs, although several visited Molsheim to inspect the prototype. Only three cars were ever sold when new – one to France, one to Germany and one to Captain Foster in Britain. Three other machines were built and run by the Bugatti family. It is quite amazing that all six cars survive to this day, all in possible running condition. One at least of these was saved from the scrap business in New York during World War II and one was reputedly hidden down a sewer in Paris during the German occupation, to ensure its survival. The car, incidentally, was so exclusive and expensive that in Britain it was listed at £5,520 for the rolling chassis at a time when a Rolls-Royce Phantom II cost a mere £1,900. A Frenchman would have had to pay half a million Francs for the pleasure. Everything was on a grand scale, including fuel consumption which could never have been better than about 6 to 8 mpg. Yet in spite of its immense size, and a traditional Bugatti radiator to suit, the proportions are so good that this is not obvious. The engines later found a good home in French high-speed railcars, which were used until the 1950s.

Bugatti Type 57

Type 57, 57C, 57S and 75SC (data for Type 57SC)
Built by: Automobiles E. Bugatti, France.
Engine: Eight cylinders, in line, in six-bearing block, with cast-alloy crankcase bolted to it. Bore and stroke 72mm by 100mm, 3,257cc (2.83in × 3.94in, 198.7cu.in). Fixed cylinder head. Two overhead valves per cylinder, opposed to each other at 90 degrees included angle in part-spherical combustion chamber and operated by finger-type rockers from twin overhead camshafts. Single updraught Zenith carburettor. Maximum power about 175bhp at 5,500rpm.
Transmission: Twin-dry-plate clutch and four-speed manual gearbox (without synchromesh) in unit with engine. Direct-acting central gearchange. Open propeller shaft to spiral-bevel 'live' rear axle.
Chassis: Separate steel chassis frame. Pressed channel-section side members, with tubular and fabricated cross bracings. Forged front axle beam, drilled through for lightness. Front suspension by half-elliptic leaf springs. Rear suspension by reversed-cantilever quarter-elliptic leaf springs and torque rod from axle to frame. Worm-and-nut steering. Friction-type dampers. Four-wheel drum brakes, rod and cable operated. Centre-lock wire wheels. 5.50 × 18in tyres (front), 6.00 × 18in (rear). Variety of Bugatti-supplied coachwork, open or closed, or from coachbuilders.
Dimensions: Wheelbase 9ft 9.5in (298.5cm), tracks (front and rear) 4ft 5in (135cm). Overall length 13ft 3in (404cm). Unladen weight (chassis only) 2,100lb (952kg).
History: There is little doubt that although the 'Royale' is the most famous of all Bugattis, the Type 57 series is the most popular. And very deservedly so. Introduced in 1934 and running through until the outbreak of war in 1939, in all its forms it sold to the tune of 710 cars. It was designed almost entirely by Jean Bugatti (son of Ettore), and was almost entirely new. Even the twin-cam engine, with bore and stroke of the single-cam Type 49, was quite unlike earlier twin-cam 'eights' (as used in the Type 50s and 51s), because its cams were driven by a train of gears at the tail of the crankshaft and cylinder block. The gearbox had constant-mesh gears, and at first it was even intended to give the front axle

Below and right: One of the most extraordinary of many exotic Bugattis was the Type 57SC Atlantic coupé. Few were made at Molsheim, and only three are now in existence. The supercharged engine produces well over 150bhp, and top speed is at least 110mph.

Above: Bugatti's Type 57 chassis, with its straight-eight twin-cam 3.3-litre engine, was probably the finest Molsheim car of all. The British drop-head coachwork contrasts sharply with the famous Bugatti radiator. The car had a very simple chassis, hard sprung.

a measure of independence between its wheels, although Ettore Bugatti himself forbade that.

There were several variations. The original Type 58 was in production until 1936, and was followed in 1937 by the Series 2 cars with engine improvements including rubber mountings. The Series 3 cars arrived at the end of 1938 with hydraulic brakes and telescopic dampers as the major changes.

The Type 57S ('S' for Sport) was announced in 1935, had a tuned engine, with dry-sump lubrication, and a modified chassis frame, lowered to allow sleeker bodywork to be offered. The 57C version had a supercharged engine producing at least 200bhp, and the combination of this engine and the 57S chassis gave rise to the 57SC the peak (in most people's opinions) of Bugatti's excellence. Cars with this engine and sports or coupé bodywork could beat 100mph by a wide margin – a good one might touch more than 120mph. Both cars were withdrawn in 1939 as they were becoming too expensive to manufacture,

although the 57 and 57C continued to sell well.

Perhaps more sensational even than the chassis was the type and nature of coachwork fitted, some Bugatti-made, and some by outside specialists. The Atlantic coupé, a true fast-back car with pronounced dorsal fin, was the most bizarre of all, and was both rare and effective. The chassis was long enough for four-door saloons to be built (almost impossible on other Bugattis) which makes the 57 chassis very versatile indeed. It was the last of all production cars from Molsheim, as production never got under way again after the war.

Below: Artists would normally argue that a vertical radiator clashed with the swooping lines of such cars - but in the case of a Corsica-bodied Bugatti Type 57 there were no such complaints. Two seats and a 110mph top speed - bliss by any standards in the late 1930s.

Cadillac Allante

Cadillac Allante models, initiated by Pininfarina, built from 1986 to 1993
Built by: Cadillac Motor Car Division of General Motors, USA, and Pininfarina Studi e Recherche S.p.A., Italy.
Engine: Eight cylinders, in 90-deg vee, in five-main-bearing aluminium alloy cylinder block. Bore and stroke 87.8 × 76.96mm, 4,082cc (3.46 × 3.03in, 249cu.in). Two cast iron cylinder heads. Two valves per cylinder, overhead, in line, operation by pushrods and rockers from single camshaft in vee of cylinder block. GM electronic fuel injection. Maximum power 172bhp (DIN) at 4,300rpm. Maximum torque 235lb.ft at 3,200rpm.
Transmission: Front-wheel-drive, torque converter and four-speed automatic transmission, all in unit with front-mounted engine. Remote-control central gearchange.
Chassis: Unitary-construction two-seater pressed-steel body-chassis unit, constructed by Pininfarina, completed at Cadillac. Independent front suspension by MacPherson struts, coil springs, wishbones, telescopic dampers, anti-roll bar. Independent rear suspension by MacPherson struts, transverse leaf spring, and lower links. Rack-and-pinion steering, with hydraulic power assistance. Four-wheel disc brakes with ABS as standard. Cast alloy 15in wheels, 225/60-15in tyres.
Dimensions: Wheelbase 8ft 3.4in (252.5cm), front track 5ft 0.5in (153.8cm), rear track 5ft 0.5in (153.8cm). Overall length 14ft 10.6in (453.7cm). Unladen weight 3,494lb (1,585kg).
History: Cadillac + Pininfarina + Allante, a simple marketing ploy with a very complicated manufacturing story behind it. It was Cadillac (the flagship company of North America's General Motors) who decided that their marque needed an image boost, and went to Italy, wallets wide open, to buy one.

The story starts with the existing front-wheel-drive Cadillac Eldorado, which in the mid-1980s was selling at the rate of 75,000 cars a year. If the platform of this car was shortened, Cadillac's planners decided, to give a 99.4in. wheelbase, and clothed in a snob-value Pininfarina convertible body style, it should be a marvellous, high-price, flagship for the late 1980s. Pininfarina would not only style the two-seater drophead body, but would build, paint and trim them in quantity.

Technically the idea was good, but it was not easy to achieve. For the 1987 model year there was to be a 170bhp version of the Eldorado platform, the highest-powered Cadillac of this period. The longest-ever production line was then set up, flying quantities of those platforms out to Turin, Italy, by 747 freighter, where Pininfarina built the bodies. The same freighters then took part-finished cars back to Detroit, where they were completed at Cadillac's Hamtramck factory.

It was a fascinating idea, and at first it looked as if three 747 round trips every week – totalling 168 bodies – would be needed to satisfy the forecast demand. With the usual raft of Cadillac options, including a smooth lift-off hardtop, to be made

Above and below: The Allante's style and body construction was by Pininfarina, but the front-wheel-drive and V8 engine was pure Cadillac: an intriguing combination.

available, US prices began at $54,700.

The Allante's looks were more startling than the engineering they hid, for the Eldorado-derived front-wheel-drive V8 package was the same as that also used in several other related General Motors cars, though the fuel-injected 4.1-litre V8 was unique to Cadillac themselves. With pushrod overhead valves and an aluminium cylinder block, it was an interesting amalgam of traditional and advanced. It revved only up to 4,750rpm, at which point the hydraulic tappets pumped up, and it was of course mated to a four-speed automatic transmission.

Allante buyers in the USA (it was never officially marketed outside North America) got a lot for their money, for in addition to the driver-friendly front-drive chassis, they also got the 'designed by Pininfarina' cachet, and a comprehensively equipped facia, plus plushily trimmed seats. The soft-top, naturally, was power operated, for Cadillac liked to make sure that there was never any effort in driving its cars. For a two-seater (there was not even an 'occasional' seat behind the front seats) this was quite a large and heavy machine: nearly 15 feet long, and weighing close to 3,500lb. Only the massive Fleet Broughams were heavier Cadillacs at the time.

Like all such American cars of the day, where engines were being hit very hard by the latest exhaust emission controls, here was a quick, but not sensationally fast, car. On American roads it could cruise in complete silence at 65mph, or whatever the State troopers would allow, and we know from published tests that it was good for 124mph, flat out.

It was not the performance, therefore, but the equipment – and the cachet – that were supposed to sell the Allante to its wealthy clientele. Leather, thick carpets, wall-to-wall power assistance and masses of electronics were all there in big numbers.

Unhappily for Cadillac, sales were slow – 3,963in the first model year, and 2,569in the next. Although there would be bigger engines from 1989, this was not enough to sell the cars which died out in 1993.

Cadillac V8

Type 51 V8, built from 1914 to – for Series 314 – 1927 (data for 1914 Type 51)
Built by: Cadillac Motor Car Co., United States.
Engine: Eight cylinders, in 90-degree vee-formation, in two four-cylinder blocks, with three-bearing light-alloy crankcase. Bore and stroke 79.4mm by 130.2mm 5,157cc (3.12in × 5.12in, 314cu.in). Fixed cylinder heads. Two side valves per cylinder, operated by fingers from single camshaft mounted in crankcase. One single up-draught Cadillac carburettor. Maximum power 70bhp (gross) at 2,400rpm.
Transmission: Multi-dry-plate clutch and three-speed manual gearbox (without synchromesh), both in unit with front-mounted engine. Direct-acting central gearchange. Open propeller shaft to spiral-bevel 'live' rear axle.
Chassis: Separate pressed-steel chassis frame, with channel-section side members and tubular and pressed cross bracing. Forged front axle beam. Front suspension by semi-elliptic leaf springs. Rear suspension by semi-elliptic leaf springs, supported on a transverse leaf spring bolted centrally to chassis frame, with torque rod from axle forward to chassis frame. No dampers. Worm-and-sector steering. Rear-wheel cable-operated drum brakes. 36in bolt-on artillery-type road wheels. 36 × 4.5in tyres.
Dimensions: Wheelbase 10ft 2in (310cm), tracks (front and rear) 4ft 8in (142cm). Overall length 15ft 5in (470cm).
History: Cadillac cars were the inspiration originally of Henry M Leland and were modest little single-cylinder machines at first, while the Model A Cadillac was very similar to the very first Fords in many ways. This car established the Cadillac tradition of interchangeability (at a time when hand-building and hand-fitting was normal). Cadillac was formed into the new General Motors group in 1909, and soon became the prestige-leader of that group of manufacturers. The V8-engined car of 1914 was a hallmark in modern American design; as it had been designed to be technically advanced and very reliable it was without any doubt, the world's first commercially successful V8. It was so good a unit that in developed form it carried on as the mainstay of Cadillac's products until 1927, when the even

more outstanding 341 unit replaced it. The engine's progenitor was D. McCall White, a Briton who had already worked for Napier and Daimler in England before joining Cadillac in 1914; its design had been laid down before then, however. Other features about the car, apart from its engine, were the high quality of its equipment, the rigidity of its chassis frame and its great attention to detail in all respects. GM make no secret of the fact that a De Dion V8 engine was purchased for study, but they were adamant that their own effort was more modern in all respects. One surprisingly backward-looking feature was the rear suspension, where the half-elliptic leaf springs on the axle were separated from the chassis by a further transverse platform spring – something found unnecessary in Europe before this, but retained by Cadillac into the 1920s. Cadillac V8 cars were used in great numbers for high-ranking staff officers' transport during World War I. The Type 51 was followed by Types 53, 55, 57, 61 and V63 before finally giving way to the Type 314 models in July 1925. More than 13,000 cars were built in the 1915 model years and more than 26,000 in the best-yet year of 1922.

Left and above: Cadillac did not make the first V8-engined car in the world, but in 1914 their car was the best one. The machines were superbly tooled, with all-interchangeable parts. At this time many cars were still hand-constructed. The tourer (left) is one of the first 1914 models, the later model (above) a 1917 example. The new V8 engine was used, in developed form, until 1927.

Cadillac V12

V12 models, built from 1930 to 1937 (data for 1930/31 model)
Built by: Cadillac Motor Car Co., United States.
Engine: Twelve cylinders, in 45-degree vee-formation, in two cast-iron blocks, with five-bearing light-alloy crankcase. Bore and stroke 79.4mm by 101.6mm 5,676cc (3.12in × 4.0in, 368cu.in). Two detachable cast-iron cylinder heads. Two overhead valves per cylinder, operated by pushrods and rockers from single camshaft mounted in centre of crankcase 'vee'. Two up-draught Cadillac carburettors. Maximum power 135bhp (gross) at 3,400rpm. Maximum torque 284lb.ft at 1,200rpm.
Transmission: Twin-dry-plate clutch and three-speed, synchromesh manual gearbox (without synchromesh on first gear), both in unit with front-mounted engine. Direct-acting central gearchange. Propeller shaft, enclosed in torque tube, driving spiral-bevel 'live' rear axle.
Chassis: Separate pressed-steel chassis frame, with channel-section side members and tubular and channel-section cross bracing. Forged front axle beam. Front and rear suspension by semi-elliptic leaf springs. Lever-arm hydraulic dampers. Worm-and-sector steering. Four-wheel, mechanically operated drum brakes with vacuum-servo assistance. 18in or 19in bolt-on wire wheels. 7.00 × 19in or 7.50 × 18in tyres.
Dimensions: Wheelbase 11ft 11in (358cm), tracks (front and rear) 4ft 11in (150cm). Overall length 17ft 10in (544cm). Unladen weight 4,400lb (1,995kg).
History: Not content merely with launching a near-unique V16 car at the beginning of 1930, Cadillac then surprised everyone by announcing a V12 car only months later, in time for the 1931 season to begin! Having, however, launched the V16 at the beginning of the year, the V12 was not so much of an effort. All chassis and

even coachwork parts were shared, and the V12 engine was a very cleverly productionised 'three-quarters' of a V16. Externally one had to count the sparking plugs to be sure which unit it was, as effectively it had merely had four cylinders chopped off from one end of the assembly. For 1931, the Cadillac range therefore included a V8, a V12 and a V16 car, along with the Cadillac-built La Salle V8, with a great deal of cross-fertilisation of parts.

The V12, like the V16, was remarkably refined, silent and reliable and gave Cadillac that 'magic carpet' performance which set them apart from all rivals for a time. The only criticism possibly aimed at the V12 was that it undoubtedly took sales away from the V16 car – and in a market where tycoons and playboys had already suffered financial shock in the Wall Street crash this was unwise. Not that Cadillac cared, as there was very little more complication in having two engines and two models sharing much of the same tooling and assembly processes. Between 1930 and 1940, indeed, total sales of all Cadillac V12 and V16 cars (including the side-valve V16 of 1937-50) were just over 15,000, of which the original V16 accounted for nearly 3,900 cars and the V12 for nearly 11,000. If we consider the level of sales achieved by any other of the 'top hat' brigade, that is a remarkable record of success for a period when the North American buyers were hardly in a buoyant mood. It emphasises just what a high reputation Cadillac held in its own market at the time and it was probably a source of relief to the rivals, world-wide, that Cadillac never seriously thought about exports.

Below: Cadillac's V12 model, built in small numbers (11,000 in eight years) was a closely related sister to the even more magnificent V16. The unit produced about 135bhp.

Cadillac V16

V16 (ohv series), built from 1930 to 1937 (data for 1930/31 model)
Built by: Cadillac Motor Car Co., United States.
Engine: 16 cylinders, in 45-degree vee-formation, in two cast-iron blocks, with five-bearing light-alloy crankcase. Bore and stroke 76.2mm by 101.6mm 7,413cc (3.0in × 4.0in, 452cu.in). Two detachable cast-iron cylinder heads. Two overhead valves per cylinder, operated by pushrods and rockers from single camshaft mounted in centre of crankcase 'vee'. Two up-draught Cadillac carburettors. 165bhp (gross) at 3,400rpm. Maximum torque 320lb.ft at 1,500rpm.
Transmission: Twin-dry-plate clutch and three-speed, synchromesh manual gearbox (without synchromesh on first gear), both in unit with front-mounted engine. Direct-acting central gearchange. Propeller shaft, enclosed in torque tube, driving spiral-bevel 'live' rear axle.
Chassis: Separate pressed-steel chassis frame, with channel-section side members and tubular and channel-section cross bracing. Forged front axle beam. Front and rear suspension by semi-elliptic leaf springs. Lever-arm hydraulic dampers. Worm-and-sector steering. Four-wheel, mechanically operated drum brakes, with vacuum-servo assistance. 19in bolt-on wire wheels. 7.50 × 19in tyres.
Dimensions: Wheelbase 12ft 4in (376cm), tracks (front and rear) 4ft 11in (150cm). Overall length 18ft 6in (564cm). Unladen weight 5,000lb (2,268kg).
History: Hindsight tells us that nearly every luxury car launched during the Depression suffered badly, but Cadillac's magnificent individualistic V16 car survived because of its own excellence, because of the resilience of Cadillac themselves and because of the huge backing from the parent, General Motors. The engine had been conceived in 1927, but took more than two years to perfect and was not leaked to the dealers until the last days of 1929. Just after

the whirlwind days of Wall Street crash had shattered the business community, Cadillac's aims were, quite simply, to produce the smoothest possible power plant which should, at the same time, upstage the products of Packard and Duesenberg, not to mention Rolls-Royce and other imported cars. They had, for years, disclaimed interest in straight-eight engines when all around were adopting them. This engine went two stages better – it had a vee-layout, with two banks of eight cylinders! In mechanical detail it was otherwise identical: it had detachable heads and cast-iron cylinder blocks on a cast-alloy crankcase, with the valve gear operated conventionally from a single camshaft in the crook of the crankcase's 'vee'. Yet in spite of its magnificent looks, it was certainly not as powerful as the Duesenberg engine and the heavy cars themselves could reach only about 90mph. Cadillac did not mind this, as they were interested in prestige rather than performance. Sales were never expected to be high and many mechanical components were in any case shared with the chassis of the V8-engined cars. Whatever the economic prospects, the Cadillac V16 and its 'smaller sister' the V12, caused rivals to react. From America (Packard, Lincoln and Pierce), from Germany (Maybach), from France (Hispano-Suiza) and from Britain (Rolls-Royce), came a phalanx of V12 units, and Marmon even produced a V16 of their own. Cadillac sold more than 3,000 V16 cars in 1930 and 1931, but less than 300 in 1932 and 125 in 1933, then only about 50 a year until 1937. This car, along with the V12, was supplanted by a new 135-degree side-valve V16 unit, which was also refined, but was somehow cheaper and nastier than the thoroughbred original.

Below: Cadillac's V16 model of 1930/37 was a true 'classic'. This two-seater (with dickey) was built in 1932. The complexity was worth it.

Caterham (Lotus) Seven

Originally Lotus Seven Series 3, from 1973 Caterham Super Seven, introduced in 1968 (data for 1980/1990s Caterham Super Seven)
Built by: Caterham Car Sales Ltd., Britain.
Engine: Large variety of four-cylinder proprietary power units – Ford, Vauxhall, Rover and others, 1,300cc – 2,000cc (79.4 cu.in to 122 cu.in). Power outputs ranging from 72bhp (DIN) to 175bhp.
Transmission: Rear-wheel-drive, single-dry-plate diaphragm spring clutch and four-speed/five-speed or six-speed all-synchromesh manual gearbox (depending on engine employed), all in unit with front-mounted engine. Remote-control, central gearchange.
Chassis: Separate multi-tubular chassis frame, with light-alloy two-seater body shell. Independent front suspension by coil springs, wishbones, telescopic dampers, anti-roll bar. De Dion rear suspension by coil springs, radius arms, transverse stabiliser, telescopic dampers. Rack-and-pinion steering. Front disc brakes, rear drum (or disc, depending on the engine specification) brakes. Pressed steel or cast alloy road wheels, 13, 14, 15 or 16in, tyres according to wheels and engine specification.
Dimensions: Wheelbase 7ft 4.6in (225cm), front track 4ft 5.9in (137cm), rear track 4ft 4in (132cm). Overall length 11ft 1.0in (338cm). Unladen weight, depending on engine and specification 1,142 – 1,383lb (518 – 627kg).
History: Colin Chapman began his motor industry career in the 1940s by buying and selling used cars, operating on the fringe of London's notorious Warren Street market place. From there he progressed to building Austin Seven-based specials, which he personally drove in sporting trials and in sports car racing. Early in the 1950s (but only as a part-time occupation) he started marketing the very first Lotus 'production' car, the Lotus 6, which had a multi-tube chassis frame, and which was sold in kit form so as not to attract British purchase tax. In 1957, with Lotus's original reputation established in sports car racing, and with a more advanced multi-purpose two-seater sports car in mind, he replaced the Lotus Six by a more advanced (but still stark) two-seater, the Lotus Seven.

Then, and later, the Seven was everything that most contemporary sports cars from larger makers were not. Because of its complex but efficient multi-tube chassis frame, it was very light. Like every Lotus, it had good roadholding and (depending on the engine chosen) it could be very rapid indeed. Because it was sold in kit form, with very few creature comforts, fixtures or fittings, it was also very cheap to buy. Within the limits of the mass-production (bought-in) items which had to be fitted to the front suspension, and the use of a proprietary back axle beam, it also rode and handled very well indeed. Those with experience suggested that it was the nearest thing to a motorcycle on four wheels that could be imagined.

Although a Seven could be, and mostly was, used on the public road, its real stamping ground was on the race track, where it could usually dominate its engine size class because of its light weight and splendid roadholding. There were even cases where the Seven was banned from certain championships, which it would otherwise have dominated.

The original Seven was a commercial success, so Lotus introduced the Seven Series 2 in 1960, this having a modified (and stiffer) chassis frame, modified bodywork and many other details, while there were more complex rear-axle location methods. Not only that, but a number of Standard and Triumph 'building blocks' were now used in the suspension, along with a Triumph Herald steering rack. Modern Ford overhead-valve engines were also used.

Above: Each and every Lotus/Caterham Seven shared the same basic style, complete with starkly-trimmed cockpit, and long flowing front wings, but a multitude of different engines was available, some as powerful as 175bhp.

Then, from 1968, the Series 3 Seven appeared, this forming the template of what would eventually become the Caterham Super Seven, and used a Ford rear axle. Blended into the mixture as before was a series of larger and more powerful Ford overhead-valve engines, these being the first Sevens which could regularly reach, and exceed, 100mph. It wasn't long, too, before Lotus's own twin-cam engine, as used in Elans and Ford Escort twin-cams of the period, became an option. The Series 3 was the definitive Seven, for it had front disc brakes as standard, better (though still minimalist) equipment, and a large, ever-growing, list of optional extras. Before long Lotus was supplying five cars every week.

From 1970 Lotus then produced the Series 4, which was different in many ways, for it had a glassfibre instead of an aluminium body shell, and was more obviously 'styled' than before. Because of this, however, traditional customers began to shy away. It was not long before Lotus (or, in particular, Colin Chapman) began to lose interest in the car – the streamlined sports-racers and the sleek little Elans and Elan Plus Twos were so much more exciting and, it seemed, easier to sell – but before the company could bring itself to discontinue the range, a saviour turned up.

Lotus dealers Caterham Cars, and their boss Graham Nearn, were so enthused about the Seven that they took over all the rights – marketing, development *and* production – and set about reviving the range. From 1973, Nearn took responsibility for the entire operation, speedily dropping the unloved Series 4, and reintroducing the Series 3, with a new name – Caterham Super Seven. Such a car, and its descendants, then remained in production, selling more and ever more readily, for the rest of the century.

By 2000 the Seven had taken on the mantle of a more advanced 'Morgan', for the pedigree had been on the market for 43 years, the visual link between ▶

1957 and 21st century types was obvious, and there was absolutely no sign of demand drying up. Along the way, assembly had been moved, first from Hethel (Norfolk) to Caterham, south of London, and eventually to Dartford in Kent, and almost every component had either been improved, changed, or superseded by something new. The style, though, was (and probably always will be) recognisably the same.

As a Caterham, the Seven gradually, but persistently, became more sophisticated, took on more engine options, and (whisper it quietly) became more practical. It was a lengthy, gradual, but seemingly logical business, with each change and improvement following on from the last.

Although four-cylinder in-line engines were always used (there being no space for other configurations to be employed in that narrow engine bay), by the 1990s the Ford engine monopoly had been lost, for Caterham not only fitted many cars with 16-valve twin-cam Vauxhall units (of the type found in Astra GT/E types), but also the light and advanced Rover K-Series engine (as used in the hottest 200s and 400s, and of course in the MG MGF sports car).

These were always matched with appropriate four-, five- or (latterly) even

six-speed transmissions, often with special clusters, or complete assemblies like those from companies such as Hewland, and the performance of 175bhp/six-speed examples can be imagined.

In the 1980s, ways were found of re-packaging the chassis tubes around the cockpit (there were no passenger doors, of course) to allow the seats to move back and provide more leg space, while a De Dion rear suspension was made available from 1984. Although the car was eventually put through the toughest of all tests – the German TUV tests – it was never necessary to change it fundamentally, which explains why production was higher than ever in the 1990s, and why the same style, the same vision – cramping soft top, and the same lack of doors persisted throughout.

A 1960s icon, and a 1970s marketing phenomenon, the Caterham Seven had become an important sports car symbol by the end of the century.

Below: This particular Seven was built in 1983, the style having been unchanged for more than 20 years - and it would still be unchanged in the 2000s.

Chadwick 'Great Six'

'Great Six' model, built from 1907 to 1916 (data for 191 model)
Built by: Chadwick Engineering Works, United States.
Engine: Six cylinders, in line, in three cast-iron blocks, with four-bearing light-alloy crankcase. Bore and stroke 127mm by 152.4mm 11,583cc (5.0in × 6.0in, 707cu.in). Non-detachable cylinder heads. Two side valves per cylinder, in T-head layout with exposed valve stems, operated by tappets from two camshafts mounted in crankcase. Single side-draught Chadwick carburettor. Maximum power 95bhp at 1,450rpm.
Transmission: Expanding drum clutch in unit with front-mounted engine. Shaft drive to separate four-speed manual gearbox (without synchromesh). Remote-control quadrant-type right-hand gearchange. Straight-bevel differential in tail of gearbox and countershaft to sprockets. Final drive to rear wheels by chain in chain case.
Chassis: Separate pressed-steel chassis frame, with channel-section side members, additional circular-section tension bars for added rigidity and pressed and tubular cross bracing. Forged front axle beam. Front suspension by semi-elliptic leaf springs. Rear suspension by semi-elliptic leaf springs, with additional transverse 'platform' leaf spring, fixed to rear of semi-elliptics, and radius arm axle location combined in chain case. Friction-type dampers. Worm-and-nut steering. Mechanically operated foot brake, by contracting band on countershaft drum, near gearbox. Hand brake operating on rear wheel drums. Artillery-style

road wheels. 36 × 4in tyres (front) and 37 × 5in tyres (rear).

Dimensions: Wheelbase 9ft 4.2in (285cm), tracks (front and rear) 4ft 8in (142cm). Unladen weight, depending on coachwork, from 4,080lb to 4,850lb (1,850kg to 2,200kg).

History: The Chadwick's claim to fame is that it was America's very first high-performance car to reach volume production. The first Chadwicks had four-cylinder engines, but from 1907 the 'Great Six' (it was 'great' in size, in performance and eventually in reputation) took over. The Type 19 engine introduced in 1911 had overhead inlet valves, but for several years (and in the 'Black Bess' competition cars of 1908 and 1909) a conventional T-head layout was used. The engine was 'classic North American' in this respect, with twin-cylinder blocks sitting atop a common crankcase and with all valve stems exposed. The cars which appeared in the 1908 Vanderbilt Cup and Savannah Grand Prix employed superchargers, the first recorded instance of a supercharger being used in a motor car, but this feature was not normally offered on production Chadwicks. The whole car was massive and impressive and for production cars the conventional semi-elliptic springs at the rear were augmented by a transverse-leaf 'platform' spring, which had been abandoned in Europe some years earlier, by all apart from Delaunay-Belleville. Chadwick's last car was built in 1916, but the name made an appearance in the 1940s on a golf trolley!

Left: Chadwick's 'Great Six' was aptly named. This 1907 tourer had an 11.6-litre engine. Supercharged cars were raced in 1908 – a world 'first'.

Chevrolet Camaro

Camaro, introduced in 1966 (data for 1967/68 350SS model)
Built by: Chevrolet Motor Co. (Division of General Motors), United States. Many different mechanical specifications, from 3.8-litre six-cylinder engine to 6.5-litre V8 engine in Camaros. The following is a typical sporting version.
Engine: Eight cylinders, in 90-degree vee-formation, in five-bearing cast-iron block. Bore and stroke 101.6mm by 88.4mm, 5,733cc (4.0in × 3.48in, 350cu.in). Two detachable cast-iron cylinder heads. Two overhead valves per cylinder, operated by pushrods and rockers from single camshaft mounted in centre of cylinder block 'vee'. One downdraught four-choke Rochester carburettor. Maximum power 300bhp (gross) at 4,800rpm. Maximum torque 380lb.ft at 3,200rpm.
Transmission: Single-dry-plate clutch and four-speed all-synchromesh manual gearbox, in unit with front-mounted engine. Direct-acting central gearchange. Open propeller shaft to hypoid-bevel 'live' rear axle with limited-slip differential. Optional transmissions include three-speed manual and three-speed fully automatic with torque converter.

Chassis: Unitary-construction, pressed-steel body/chassis structure, in two-door four-seater coupé form. Front suspension by coil springs, wishbones and anti-roll bar. Rear suspension by half-elliptic leaf springs. Telescopic dampers. Recirculating-ball steering, with optional power assistance. Four-wheel drum brakes, with vacuum-servo assistance (optional front disc brakes). 14in press-steel disc wheels. F70 × 14in tyres.
Dimensions: Wheelbase 9ft 0in (274cm), front track 4ft 11in (150cm), rear track 4ft 10.9in (150cm). Overall length 15ft 5in (470cm). Unladen weight 3,300lb (1,497kg).
History: The Camaro was conceived by General Motors for Chevrolet to sell in direct competition to Ford's successful Mustang. Not only that, but it would also be sold, with different mechanical permutations and a face-change, as the Pontiac Firebird. It was a carefully researched answer to an already-successful formula, with a two-door body shell, 'almost-four' seats and a whole variety of engines, power outputs, transmissions and optional equipment.

The Camaro could be had as a 140bhp, six-cylinder car with drum brakes and three-speed gearbox, while on the other hand it might be a 6.5-litre V8 with 330bhp, automatic transmission and power-assisted everything else. Amid all this the 350SS was the most sporting and had handling improvements to match.

Much re-styled, much modified and much-attacked by safety and pollution limits, the Camaros are still made and have been a great and lasting success for General Motors. For a period they were also very successful racing 'saloon' cars in America and in Europe.

Below: By 1972 Camaro (and its sister car, the Pontiac Firebird) had been re-styled several times. It was sold only as a four-seater coupé, with a choice of vee-8 engines. Race-tuned Camaros were very fast indeed. In shape it was most un-American.

Chevrolet Corvette

Corvettes, built from 1953 to date (data for 1963 Stingray)
Built by: Chevrolet Motor Co., United States.
Four engines – 250, 300, 340 and 360bhp versions – available for 1963. The following is typical of the 360hp tune.
Engine: Eight cylinders, in 90-degree vee-formation, in five-bearing cast-iron block/crankcase. Bore and stroke 101.6mm by 83.5mm, 5,363cc (4.0in × 3.25in, 327cu.in). Two detachable cast-iron cylinder heads. Two overhead valves per cylinder, operated by pushrods and rockers from single camshaft mounted in centre of cylinder block 'vee'. Rochester fuel injection. Maximum power 360bhp (gross) at 6,000rpm. Maximum torque 352lb.ft at 4,200rpm.
Transmission: Single-dry-plate clutch and four-speed, synchromesh manual gearbox, both in unit with front-mounted engine. Remote-control central gearchange. Open propeller shaft to hypoid-bevel final-drive unit with limited-slip differential. Exposed fixed-length drive shafts to rear wheels. Optional torque converter and three-speed Chevrolet automatic transmission.
Chassis: Separate pressed-steel chassis frame with box-section side members and boxed cross bracing. Independent front suspension by coil springs, wishbones and anti-roll bar. Independent rear suspension by transverse leaf spring. Lower wishbones and fixed length drive shafts. Telescopic dampers. Recirculating-ball steering. Four-wheel, hydraulically operated drum brakes, with vacuum-servo assistance. 15in centre-lock cast-alloy disc wheels. 7.10/7.60 15in tyres. Open or closed glassfibre bodywork.
Dimensions: Wheelbase 8ft 2in (249cm), track (front) 4ft 8.3in (143cm), track (rear) 4ft 9in (145cm). Overall length 14ft 7.3in (445cm). Unladen weight 3,250lb (1,474kg).

Above: The original Corvette style of 1953 was simple, effective, and distinctive. Note – no bumpers, and only two headlamps.

Below: First-generation Corvettes were open-top two-seaters, with a wrap-around screen and a glass-fibre body style. They soon became America's favourite.

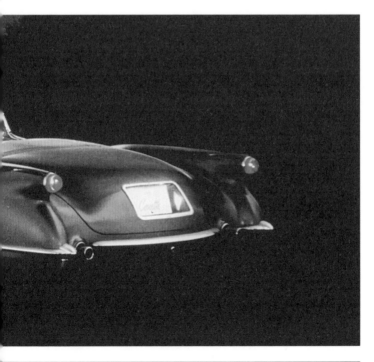

History: Chevrolet's interest in two-seater sports car motoring in modern times dates from 1951, when styling chief Harley Earl was beginning to think about such machines; the first mock-up of a new two-seater car to be called 'Corvette' was completed in 1952. General Motors rushed it into production at the beginning of 1953 and it became a cult-car, North America's only domestic two-seater sports car, except for the less rorty Thunderbirds of the mid 1950s, ever since. In 1953, apart from its short wheelbase and generally sporting looks, its only technical innovation was the glassfibre body-shell – used mainly to save time in tooling between the decision to go ahead and first deliveries. Since 1953, however, there have been four basic styles of Corvettes – including the first bulbous machines of 1953 to 1962, the Stingray machines of 1962 to 1967, and the even-more Europeanised cars of 1967 to 1984. There have been persistent rumours of a new mid-engined Corvette to replace the last of the classic front-engined cars, but this has not yet progressed beyond the status of a motor show 'special' as far as the public is concerned.

The first Corvettes had in-line six-cylinder 'Blue Flame' engines, but the first V8 engine option arrived in 1955. This was speedily followed by fuel injection in 1957, four-speed transmission and limited-slip differential and yet other engine tunes – all optional. The Stingray had a dramatically shaped fastback option, with all-independent suspension (the rear certainly inspired both by the Arkus-Duntov racing 'specials' *and* the Jaguar E-type suspension); four-wheel disc brakes were available from 1965. Bigger and better engines culminated in the 7-litre unit of 1966 (in later years the engines were enlarged and softened at the same time to look after exhaust-emission limitations). Although the latest cars have probably been the most popular, it was the Stingrays which gained most plaudits, and nearly 118,000 cars were built in its production run, rather less than half of these being the coupés. In its most powerful guise, the maximum speed was way over 150mph. Sales were rock solid throughout the 1970s, the

Above: The Stingray, launched in 1963, was the first Corvette to offer a choice between open-top roadster or fastback coupé.

pedigree then being re-defined with a new generation car in 1984. American buyers, it seemed, would always want to buy the glassfibre-bodied two seater Corvette, whose 50th anniversary was approaching in 2003.

Left: This new-generation Corvette, introduced in 1984, was so beautiful that it caused a sensation, and sales boomed. With a sturdy chassis, all-independent suspension, and high performance, it was a great performance bargain.

Chevrolet Corvette ZR-1

Chevrolet Corvette ZR-1 sports car, with Lotus-designed engine, built from 1990 to 1995

Built by: Chevrolet Division of General Motors, USA.

Engine: Eight cylinders in 90-degree vee-formation, in five-main bearing aluminium cylinder block/crankcase. Bore and stroke 99 x 93mm, 5,727cc (3.90 x 3.66in, 350cu.in). Two light-alloy cylinder heads. Four valves per cylinder, in narrow-angle vee, operation by twin overhead camshafts and inverted bucket-type tappets. GM electronic fuel injection. Maximum power 375bhp (DIN) at 5,800rpm. Maximum torque 370lb.ft at 4,800rpm.

Transmission: Rear-wheel-drive, single-dry-plate diaphragm spring clutch and six-speed all-synchromesh manual gearbox, all in unit with engine. Remote-control, central gearchange.

Chassis: Separate pressed-steel chassis frame, topped by two seater body shell in glassfibre. Independent front suspension by plastic transverse leaf spring, wishbones, adjustable telescopic dampers and anti-roll bar. Independent rear suspension by transverse plastic leaf spring, wishbones, adjustable telescopc dampers, anti-roll bar. Rack-and-pinion steering, with power-assistance. Four-wheel disc brakes with power assistance and ABS as standard. Cast-alloy 17in road wheels, 275/40-17 (front) and 315/35-17 (rear) tyres.

Dimensions: Wheelbase 8ft 0.2in (244.3cm), front track 5ft 0in (152.4cm), rear track 5ft 2.0in (157.5cm). Overall length 14ft 10.5in (453.4cm). Unladen weight 3,519lb (1,596kg).

History: First there was the Corvette, General Motors' all-American sports car of the 1950s, then there was the 1970s slump as American sports car buyers tired of the old Stingray shape, and next there was re-birth with the stunning new-generation Corvette of 1984. But for the 1990s, GM need more pizzazz, and hired Lotus to provide it.

GM had taken control of Lotus in 1986, using them to revitalise several projects. One was the Corvette, where Lotus designed a stunning, all-new V8

Below: By the 1990s all Corvettes had startlingly smooth lines, and in the case of the ZR1 they also had colossal, 170mph-plus performance.

Above: All the 1984-generation Corvette sports cars were fast and attractive, the Lotus-engined ZR1 being the very best and most powerful of all.

engine. All previous Corvette V8s had been cast-iron pushrod valve types, but here was an aluminium design with four valves per cylinder, twin-overhead camshaft cylinder heads. Although throttled back to deal with North American exhaust emission regulations, it pumped out 375bhp at 5,800rpm, with a positive avalanche of mid-range torque, and a whole chorus of bone-tingling noises to match. Other Corvettes were fast, but from 1990 the ZR-1, as it was titled, was brutal, visceral and tyre-stripping. Nowhere in the USA (or anywhere on the planet, for that matter) could a claimed top speed of 171mph be verified, and even the 0–100mph acceleration time of 13.5 seconds was rarely experienced.

The ZR-1, it seemed, had everything – the sleek good looks of the latest Corvette, the advanced engineering which only a world-class 'name' like Lotus could provide, a rock-solid ZF six-speed transmission to back it, along with all-independent suspension and four-wheel ABS-standard disc brakes to match all that. The style, of course, was miraculously smooth by most previous Corvette standards. From 1984 the latest car had been shown with a long, wide and almost flat snout, a graceful side profile ending in a sharply cut-off tail, and a no-compromise two-seater cabin, the whole being available in open top of smart coupé styles. The original ZR-1 was also given a unique tail, which featured near-rectangular tail-lamps, though these were later taken up by the rest of the Corvette range. Like all previous Corvettes, there was a separate chassis frame, the body being moulded from glassfibre, with GM making continuous improvements to build quality, fit, finish and equipment.

If there was a problem, it was that at this time North American buyers were still wedded to getting their performance from vast, simple, cheap-to-buy/cheap-to-fix engines, so they found it difficult to relate to the new 32-valve Lotus-designed LT5 unit.

The ZR-1 was, at once, much more powerful (375 against 245bhp), and much more expensive than the push-rod engined type which may explain why, after the first two years, Chevrolet found it hard to sell the 32-valve monster.

By 1995 the output of pushrod Corvette V8s had been pushed up over 300bhp, and the writing was on the wall. With an eye more to profitability than to image, GM therefore laid the ZR-1 to rest at the end of that year.

Chevrolet International Six

International Six, introduced for 1929
Built by: Chevrolet Motor Co. (Division of General Motors), United States.
Engine: Six cylinders, in line, in three-bearing cast iron block/crankcase. Bore and stroke 84.1mm by 95.25mm, 3,175cc (3.31in × 3.75in, 194cu.in). Detachable cast-iron cylinder head. Two overhead valves per cylinder, operated by pushrods and rockers from single camshaft side-mounted in cylinder block. Single up-draught Carter carburettor. Maximum power 46bhp (gross) at 2,600rpm.
Transmission: Single-dry-plate clutch, and three-speed, manual gearbox (without synchromesh), both in unit with front-mounted engine. Direct-acting central gearchange. Propeller shaft, enclosed in torque tube, driving spiral-bevel 'live' rear axle.
Chassis: Separate pressed-steel chassis frame, with channel-section side members and pressed and tubular cross bracing. Forged front axle beam. Front and rear suspension by semi-elliptic leaf springs, rear location by torque tube. Lever-arm hydraulic shock dampers. Worm-and-sector steering. Four-wheel, rod-and-shaft operated drum brakes. 20in pressed-steel-disc wheels. 4.50 20in tyres. Variety of open and closed coachwork.
Dimensions: Wheelbase 8ft 11in (272cm), tracks (front and rear) 4ft 8in (142cm). Overall length 13ft (396cm). Unladen weight 2,400lb (1,088kg).
History: Chevrolet's Classic Six was followed by a whole series of four-cylinder cars, but after the complete integration of General Motors, it was decided that Chevrolet should have a new six-cylinder engine. First thoughts on this date from 1925, but it was not until the end of 1928 that the International Six was ready for sale to the public. The new engine, which had only three crankshaft bearings, and retained cast-iron pistons at a time when almost all modern trends were towards light-alloy pistons, became known very affectionately as the 'Stovebelt Six' after its use, all over the engine, of quarter-inch bolts of a type

identical to those found in domestic appliances. Although the International was a very homely car, it was nevertheless twice as powerful as the model it replaced and was more than a match for Ford's new Model A. Chevrolet had won first place in USA car sales in 1927, when Ford Model T production closed down, and had lost it again in 1929-30, but they took back world leadership firmly thereafter, and have rarely been pipped by Ford.

The International Six, all in all, was designed to give trouble-free motoring without gimmicks and the Depression-torn American public loved it for that. It was also a much more relaxed-riding car than the deadly rival Ford, with semi-elliptic springs. The fact that it rarely achieved more than 20mpg fuel-consumption was not a sales handicap, for petrol prices in America were very cheap indeed. Internationals became Masters and Standards in 1933 and thereafter Chevrolet cars gradually but firmly began to be modernised. They were given 'knee-action independent front suspension in 1934, but it is interesting to know that a buyer could still have a beam front axle, if he insisted, right up until 1940. There were no more cabriolets after 1935. The 'Stovebolt' engine was much modified in 1937, becoming the 'Blue Flame' unit with four-bearing crank and 85bhp from 3.55-litres. The engine itself ran on and on and on – the cast-iron pistons and splash lubrication lasting until 1953, and there are still six-cylinder engines with a vague descendancy at Chevrolet today. Indeed, Chevrolet's first modern V8 engine was not introduced until 1955.

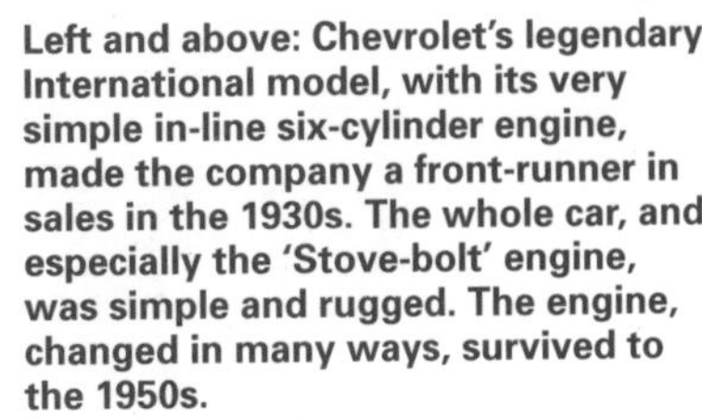

Left and above: Chevrolet's legendary International model, with its very simple in-line six-cylinder engine, made the company a front-runner in sales in the 1930s. The whole car, and especially the 'Stove-bolt' engine, was simple and rugged. The engine, changed in many ways, survived to the 1950s.

Chitty-Bang-Bang

Chittys I, II, and III (data for Chitty I).
Built by: Count Zborowski, Britain.
Engine: World War I-type Maybach aero-engine. Six cylinders, in line, (six separate cylinders on cast-iron crankcase). Four overhead valve per cylinder, operated by exposed pushrods and rockers. Bore and stroke 165mm by 180mm, 23,092cc (6.50in × 7.09in, 1,409cu.in). Compression ratio 5.95:1. originally one horizontal Maybach carburettor, later progressively modified to triple Claudel-Hobsons on separate manifolds. Dry-sump lubrication developed by Zborowski. Maximum power 305bhp at 1,500rpm. Maximum speed at least 115mph.
Transmission: Mercédès scroll clutch and four-speed gearbox, with output drive to externally mounted sprockets. Final drive to rear axle by exposed chain. Starting of engine by means of crowbar attached to nose of crankshaft.
Chassis: Lengthened 1907 Mercédès 75hp type, with straight channel-section side members. Half elliptic front and rear springs. No dampers originally, but Hartford units in final form. Chassis side members stiffened with flitch plates. Rear wheels and transmission brakes, no front brakes. Centre-lock-wire wheels. 895 × 135 tyres. Originally two-seat 'sports' type of coachwork by Blythe of Canterbury, including radiator cowl and swept 'boat tail' in Brooklands racing form. Up to 800lb (363kg) of sand carried behind driving seats to help driving wheel adhesion.
History: The three Chitty-Bang-Bang cars were all exciting and outrageous 'one-off' designs built for Count Louis Zborowski, an English/American who lived in a stately home – Higham – in Kent. His main interest was motor sport, and these cars were intended to give him the fastest and most impressive transport in the world. In each case, the theory was that a simply (even crudely) engineered

chassis, would have a vast aeroplane engine installed, would be geared up accordingly, and would have simple touring or sporting bodies appropriate to the purpose. Chitty I was purely a Brooklands racing car. Chitty II another racing four-seater which also earned its keep as a fast touring car, while Chitty III was originally intended as a racing machine, but was also used for touring. Chitty IV, a much more advanced car, was only partly-built when Zborowski was killed in a factory-owned Mercédès racing car at Monza in 1924, and was never completed. It was to have been a saloon car Chitty.

The idea of Chitty I was born due to the enormous surplus of Allied and enemy aeroplane engines immediately after World War I. Zborowski purchased a 23-litre, six-cylinder Maybach engine from the British Disposals Board (it had evidently been used in a German Gotha bomber), took it back to Higham and asked his engineering consultant Clive Gallop to build a car. The chassis frame, a lengthened 1907 75hp Mercédès type, kept its original transmission and radiator. Final drive by chain was normal for Edwardian if not Vintage cars (but the Mercédès was an Edwardian chassis). Gallop had to devise a dry-sump lubrication to get sufficient ground clearance. Blythe Bros. of Canterbury (owned by Zborowski) built the crude but brutal body, and the car first raced in Easter 1921. At Brooklands, Chitty won several races, and proved that it could approach 120mph, in spite of having poor roadholding and negligible brakes! However, ▶

Below: Count Louis Zborowski had the money and the enthusiasm to have the fastest possible Brooklands special built. There were three Chitty-Bang-Bang models, all with vast aeroplane engines used in World War I. Chitty II (shown here) had an 18.9-litre six-cylinder Benz engine producing at least 230bhp. Chitty I had a 305bhp 23-litre Maybach 'six', and Chitty III a 14.8 litre Mercédès 'six'. All had lengthened and stiffened Mercédès frames, that of this Chitty thought to be from an Edwardian Mercédès 60 model. In this guise it lapped the Brooklands oval at 108.27mph, but Chitty I was fastest of all – 113.45mph at Brooklands, and a top speed of about 125mph. Chain drive was a feature on Chitties I and II, with rear wheel brakes, and an enormous exposed exhaust system.

even before the end of 1921, the Count had decided that he wanted an improved car. Chitty I was 'retired' and Chitty II was born.

The second car was built on similar lines. The chassis, as before, was from a pre-war Mercédès, but with a rather shorter wheelbase. The engine, an aero-engine in the same philosophy, was an 18,882cc six-cylinder Benz unit with a nominal 230bhp. Chitty II was intended more as a high-speed touring car, and was given a splendid four-seat touring body by Blythe Bros. It only raced once at Brooklands, in the autumn of 1921, lapping at 108.27mph, but it did not win its race.

Chitty III, built in 1922, was a much-modified Mercédès 28/95 chassis, imported originally as a complete car with a rudimentary test body. The 7¼-litre Mercédès engine was removed and a 14,778cc six-cylinder Mercédès aero-engine, of 160 nominal horsepower, installed. The Mercédès transmission was retained, so this was the only Chitty with propeller-shaft drive to a 'live' axle. During 1924, Chitty III won races at Brooklands, and could lap at more than 112mph, almost as quickly as the original Chitty I. The first car, incidentally, raced at Brooklands again in 1922, but nearly killed Zborowski in an enormous high-speed accident when a front tyre burst on the steep banking. The car finished up in the infield, but was scarcely damaged and was eventually rebuilt.

After Zborowski's death, Chitty I was bought by the Conan-Doyle brothers, neglected for some years, finally abandoned at Brooklands and later cut up. Chitty II, which had been sold to make room for Chitty III at Higham, was sold and resold and eventually restored, and it is now in the United States. Chitty III, raced at Brooklands as recently as 1939, was sold for road use then broken up. Chitty II is therefore the only such legendary aero-engined car still in existence today.

One other car built by Gallop for Zborowski in the same period, *not* called a Chitty but unmistakably related to them, was the Higham Special Brooklands car. This car, with its 27-litre American Liberty V12 engine, was sold to Parry Thomas, renamed 'Babs' and improved. It took the World Land Speed Record, then killed its owner in a crash on Pendine Sands in Wales. It was buried there, but was exhumed in 1969, and it has now been restored by Owen Wyn Owen in North Wales.

Right: There was an obvious link with Mercédès in every Chitty – as can be seen from the radiator style fitted to Chitty-Bang-Bang II in 1922.

Above and left: Function and speed were more important than comfort in Chitty II – the hood was more for show that for weather protection.

Chrysler Airflow

Airflow models, built from 1934 to 1937 (data for 1934 8-cylinder model)
Built by: Chrysler Corporation, United States.
Engine: Eight cylinders, in line, in five-bearing cast-iron block/crankcase. Bore and stroke 82.5mm by 114.3mm, 4,893cc (3.25in × 4.5in, 298.6cu.in). Detachable cast-iron cylinder head. Two side valves per cylinder, operated directly by single camshaft mounted in cylinder block. Single down-draught carburettor. Maximum power 130bhp (gross) at 3,400rpm.
Transmission: Single-dry-plate clutch, three-speed, manual gearbox (without synchromesh) and free-wheel, all in unit with front-mounted engine. Direct-acting central gearchange. Open propeller shaft to spiral-bevel 'live' rear axle. Optional automatic overdrive from 1935.
Chassis: Pressed-steel unitary construction body/chassis unit, with boxed structural members integral with body framing. Tubular front axle beam. Front and rear suspension by semi-elliptic leaf springs. Lever-arm hydraulic dampers. Worm-and-wheel steering. Four-wheel, hydraulically operated drum brakes. 16in pressed-steel-disc wheels. 7.00 × 16in tyre. Closed four-door six-window coachwork.
Dimensions: Wheelbase 10ft 3in (312cm), track (front) 4ft 8.7in (144cm), track (rear) 4ft 9in (144.8cm). Overall length 17ft 4in (528cm). Unladen weight 4,150lb (1,882kg).
History: The streamlined, unitary-construction 'Airflow' model must go down in history as one of the great pioneering 'flops' of all time, even though it did not sell as badly as rivals would have us believe. The concept was of a conventionally engineered Detroit car, which would take advantage of the latest in unitary-construction techniques to save cost and weight and would introduce full-width styling at a time when such things were becoming fashionable. The public, while admiring Chrysler's products at the time, were not taken by the style, which was to be tackled with more sympathy by Ford (with the Lincoln Zephyr) less than two years later. Although it continued until 1937, a conventionally styled version – the Airstream – was both more cautious and more successful. The pity of it all was that, apart from its unconventional looks, the Airflow was a fine car. It was in every way a trendsetter for the future, never acknowledged by its business rivals. There was a six-cylinder version, as well as two straight-eight versions. In later models an automatically engaged overdrive was a popular fitting.

Above and left: Chrysler's Airflow concept was a brave attempt to change the shape of modern cars. North America in 1934 was not ready for the full-width styles (some say they were clumsily done), and the model failed. The advance of unit-construction body work was almost ignored at the time.

Chrysler 70-72

70 range, introduced 1924 (the original Chrysler motor car)
Built by: Chrysler Corporation, United States.
Engine: Six cylinders, in line, in seven-bearing combined block/crankcase. Bore and stroke 79.4mm by 120.6mm, 3,580cc (3.12in × 4.75in, 218cu.in). Detachable cast-iron cylinder head. Two side valves per cylinder, operated by tappets from single camshaft mounted in side of crankcase. Single up-draught Zenith carburettor. Maximum power 68bhp.
Transmission: Multiple dry-plate clutch (later changed to single-plate type) and three-speed manual gearbox (without synchromesh), both in unit with front-mounted engine. Direct-acting central gearchange. Open propeller shaft drive to spiral-bevel 'live' rear axle.
Chassis: Separate pressed-steel chassis frame, with channel-section side members and pressed and tubular cross bracing. Tubular front axle beam. Front and rear suspension by semi-elliptic leaf springs. Lever-arm hydraulic dampers. Worm-and-sector steering. Four wheel, hydraulically operated brakes. Hand brake working contracting band on transmission drum behind gearbox. Artillery-style road wheels. 30 × 5.75in tyres. Choice of coachwork, open or closed.
Dimensions: Wheelbase 9ft 4.7in (286cm), tracks (front and rear) 4ft 8in (142cm). Overall length 13ft 6.5in (413cm). Unladen weight, depending on coachwork, from 2.845lb to 3,160lb (1,290kg to 1,433kg).
History: Before Walter Chrysler sponsored his own make of car in 1924, he had already earned himself a formidable reputation (and a lot of money) as what was effectively the first well-known 'company doctor'. His efforts with General Motors (1912 onwards), Willys-Overland and Maxwell were legendary, which made a good public reception for his new six-cylinder Chrysler 70 almost certain. This was an absolutely conventional Detroit car, except that it embraced hydraulic braking (when this was a very new concept), and its engine breathing arrangements owed a lot to Ricardo ideas. 70mph it easily attained, and no fewer than 32,000 of the cars were sold in 1924 through existing Maxwell dealers (Chrysler had taken over Maxwell in 1923). Walter Chrysler capped this with 43,000 sales in 1925 and the inexorable rise of the Chrysler Corporation to a position in the 1930s where it could challenge Ford for second place (behind

Below: In the 1920s, the 'vintage' years, cars were thoroughly reliable, and a joy to drive. Even this Model 70 Chrysler, built in huge quantities, looked dashing, was smartly finished, and was a cut above the ordinary steel-bodied saloon car built in Detroit. It had a 3.6-litre engine and a three-speed 'crash' gearbox.

Above: The 70 range's engineering might have been ordinary, but some of the body styles were very dashing indeed. This tourer, registered and still used in Britain, had side-mounted spare tyre and a dickey seat behind the hood in the best USA tradition.

General Motors) was under way.

By 1927 total sales had zoomed to 200,000 a year, but this figure was helped enormously by two extra models. One was the frugal and value-for-money 58 model, which succeeded the Maxwell, but the other was the luxurious and rather faster Imperial Six. Not only that, but Chrysler was also thinking of breaking into the lower priced market (good Chevrolet territory) and was planning the De Soto. The 58 and the 70/72 models, however, were the cars on which Chrysler's fortunes were founded, and it was not until Chrysler took over Dodge in 1928 that the next great expansion could develop. The Model 70's hydraulic brakes, incidentally, were of the contracting 'band-brake' type – the more conventional (by our standards) type not being adopted until 1928 for the 1929 models.

Below: Chrysler's 70 range was very conventional, but sold in huge numbers because of Walter Chrysler's splendid reputation. His first 'own name' car was sold through existing Maxwell dealerships – Chrysler himself having taken over that company in 1923. This smart five-seater tourer was built in 1924, the first year of production, when 43,000 examples were sold.

Citroën 2CV

2CV model, built from 1948 to 1990 (data for original 375cc model)
Built by: S.A. André Citroën (Citroën S.A. since 1968), France.
Engine: Two cylinders, air-cooled, in horizontally opposed layout, in cast-iron cylinder barrels, bolted to two-piece two-bearing light-alloy crankcase. Bore and stroke 62mm by 62mm, 375cc (2.44in × 2.44in, 22.9cu.in). Light-alloy cylinder heads. Two overhead valves per cylinder, inclined to each other in part-spherical combustion chambers and operated by pushrods and rockers from camshaft mounted in the crankcase underneath the crankshaft. Single downdraught Solex carburettor. Power limited to 9bhp (DIN) at 3,500rpm. Maximum torque 17lb.ft at 1,800rpm.
Transmission: Front-wheel-drive power pack. Horizontally opposed engine ahead of the front wheel line and four-speed all-synchromesh gearbox behind that line. Single-dry-plate clutch, gearbox and transaxle all in unit with engine. Engine drives gearbox by shaft over top of final drive, gearbox is all-indirect and output shaft is directly linked to spiral-bevel final drive unit. Central, remote-control gearchange, with lever protruding through centre of facia. Exposed, universally joined drive shafts to front wheels.
Chassis: Simple pressed, welded, and fabricated platform chassis, carrying all stresses, with rudimentary and very simple body shell welded to it. All-independent suspension, front by leading arms, and rear by trailing arms, interconnected by chassis-mounted coil springs under the centre floor. Inertia dampers, on all wheels, with cast weights and coil springs inside damper body. Rack-and-pinion steering. Four-wheel drum brakes, inboard at front. Bolt-on pressed steel disc wheels. 125 × 400mm Michelin tyres.
Dimensions: Wheelbase 7ft 9.3in (237cm), tracks (front and rear) 4ft 1.6in (126cm). Overall length 12ft 4.7in (378cm). Unladen weight 1,100lb (499kg).

Above: The utilitarian 2CV was eventually taken up by city trendies, which led to special-edition types like this 'Charleston' being put on sale.

History: Preliminary work began on Citroën's new 'peoples' car' at the end of the 1930s, and prototypes were built in the final form during the German occupation of France, but the 2CV was not actually announced until 1948. It was designed by M. Boulanger, also much credited with the '*traction avant*' layout, and followed that car's philosophy of not aligning itself to any fashions. Designed specifically as a bridge between the horse-and-cart trade and the motor car business, the 2CV was meant to operate under all conditions of abuse, on and off the roads, and was deliberately underpowered to restrict the payload possibilities.

The front-drive power pack, with a simple but very strong air-cooled flat-twin engine, was the most complicated part of the car. The interconnected coil-spring suspension (both front and rear springs were housed in the same under-floor chamber and reacted against each other in certain wheel movement conditions) was simple but effective. The rest of the car was simplicity itself, with styling that owed much to French commercial vehicles (and the use of very simple steel pressings), instantly removable doors and seats, and roll-back canvas roofs and boot covers. Even the headlamps were adjustable for vertical alignment via a very simple driver-controlled linkage. Not even the 2CV, however, could resist the demands of progress. Over the years its engine size crept up – first to 425cc and finally to 602cc – as did the power, and even the standard of the fittings.

The 2CV was joined by the much more civilised but mechanically almost identical Ami 6 at the beginning of the 1960s, and by the different but similar Dyane later in that decade. The basic 2CV, however, refused to die, and the 1973/74 energy crisis gave it a boost which continued until 1990, when the last of nearly four million 2CVs was built.

Left: Prototypes of the 2CV were even plainer than the production car, the design having been conceived in the late 1930s.

Citroën DS/ID Series

Citroën DS and ID19, 12, and 23 family, built 1955 to 1975 (data for DS19)
Built by: S. A. André Citroën, France.
Engine: Four cylinders, in line, in three-bearing cast-iron cylinder block. Bore and stroke 78mm by 100mm, 1,911cc (3.07in x 3.94in, 116.6cu.in). Detachable cylinder barrels, wet liners. light-alloy cylinder head. Two overhead valves per cylinder, inclined in part-spherical combustion chamber, operated by pushrods and rockers from single side-mounted camshaft. Twin-choke downdraught Weber carburettor. Maximum power 75bhp (gross) at 4,500rpm. Maximum torque 101lb.ft at 3,000rpm.
Transmission: Front-wheel-drive power pack. Engine longitudinally mounted behind line of front wheels, gearbox ahead of it. Single-dry-plate clutch and four-speed manual synchromesh gearbox (without synchromesh on first gear). Automatic hydraulic control of clutch and gear-change. Gear lever in facia behind steering wheel. Spiral-bevel final drive. Exposed, universally jointed drive shafts to front wheels.
Chassis: Pressed-steel unitary-construction body/chassis unit, of punt-type design, with detachable skin panels. Self-levelling independent suspension all round, with high-pressure hydro-pneumatic springs; leading arms and anti-roll bar at front, trailing arms at rear. Dampers incorporated in hydro-pneumatic suspension. Power-operated rack-and-pinion steering. Power-operated brakes, disc front (inboard) and drum rear. Pressed-steel disc wheels, 165-400mm front tyres and 155-400mm rear tyres. Four-door saloon bodywork by Citroën. Later models had a long-wheelbase five-door estate car option.
Dimensions: Wheelbase 10ft 3in (312cm). Track (front) 4ft 11in (150cm). Track (rear) 4ft 3.2in (130cm). Overall length 15ft 9in (480cm). Unladen weight 2,500lb (1,134kg).
History: To replace their long running '*traction avant*' models, Citroën were

expected to produce something startling. Their DS19 model did not disappoint anyone. Styled for the 1960s, and engineered for even further ahead, it was technically very advanced, compared with any of the opposition.

The layout was much as before, but with a front-drive power pack in which the engine was behind the transaxle, but everything else was new. Everything possible was power-assisted or power-operated. The all-independent suspension had high-pressure hydro-pneumatic units, automatically self-levelling according to load, and a driver's control allowed the car to be raised even further for crossing rough ground. A wheel could be changed by putting the suspension on 'high', inserting an axle stand where appropriate, then 'lowering' the suspension, which allowed the offending wheel to lift itself into the air. The car's shape was shark-like and very sleek, with a low drag coefficient. Even with an ageing engine (rather modified from the unit of the *traction*) the DS19 had a surprisingly high maximum speed and fuel economy possibilities. Although gears were shifted manually, the gear lever merely signalled the driver's intentions to a hydraulic mechanism which looked after clutch control and gear selectors. This was only the start. The DS19 was soon followed by the mechanically simpler ID19, and shortly by the long-wheelbase 'Safari' estate cars.

Over the years the car was made faster, better equipped, and even more sophisticated. Engines were enlarged in 1965 (and redesigned) to 2.1-litres, and again in 1972 to 2.3-litres. a four-headlamp layout with lamps connected to the steering (and swivelling with the front wheels) arrived in 1967 and a fuel-injected engine option in 1970 (along with a five-speed gearbox). A fully-automatic gearbox was available after 1971. The cars were finally deposed by the transverse-engined CX models in 1975.

Below: When announced in 1955, the DS19 caused a sensation. Its layout was ultra-modern, its suspension unique, and its styling years ahead of its competition. Suspension height could be varied manually, and most mechanicals – brakes and gearchange – were powered. There was also the Safari.

Citroën SM

SM coupé, built 1970 to 1975 (data for 1970 version)
Built by: Citroën S.A., France, and latterly by Automobiles Ligier, France.
Engine: Maserati-manufactured, six cylinders, in 90-degree vee formation, in four-bearing light-alloy cylinder block. Bore and stroke 87mm by 75mm, 2,670cc (3.42in × 2.95in, 163cu.in). Two aluminium cylinder heads. Two overhead valves per cylinder, inclined in part-spherical combustion chamber, operated by two overhead camshafts per cylinder bank, via inverted bucket tappets. Three twin-chokes, downdraught Weber carburettors. Maximum power 170bhp (DIN) at 5,500rpm. Maximum torque 170lb.ft at 4,000rpm. Later models had Bosch fuel injection and 178bhp.
Transmission: Front-wheel drive power pack. Engine behind front wheel centre line and gearbox ahead of it. Single-dry-plate clutch and five-speed all-synchromesh gearbox. Remote control, central gearchange. Hypoid-bevel final drive. Exposed, universally jointed drive shafts to front wheels.
Chassis: Pressed-steel unitary-construction body/chassis unit. Self-levelling independent suspension all round, with high-pressure hydro-pneumatic springs, wishbone linkage at front, trailing arms at rear. Dampers incorporated in hydro-pneumatic suspension. Power-operated, variable-ratio rack-and-pinion steering. Power-operated brakes, all-round discs (inboard at front). 15in pressed-steel road wheels. 195/70VR15 tyres. Three-door coupé coachwork by Citroën. No alternatives.
Dimensions: Wheelbase 9ft 8in (295cm), track front) 5ft (152cm), track (rear) 4ft

Below and above right: The eccentric Citroen SM coupé is perhaps the most complex of all modern cars. Front-wheel-drive, hydro-pneumatic springing and a powerful 2.7-litre vee-6 engine are no more than expected from this French concern, but in addition the full power steering is very direct, and variable ratio. In spite of its bulk, the SM has only two doors.

4.2in (132cm). Overall length 16ft 0.6in (489cm). Unladen weight 3,200lb (1,451kg).

History: Citroën formed a liaison with Maserati at the end of the 1960s, and although it was disbanded in 1973 there was time for some joint work to be completed. The most exciting result, without doubt, was the Citroën SM coupé – although Maserati also benefited from Citroën's expertise in their Bora/Merak series. The SM was unashamedly a very fast, very expensive, prestige Citroën – larger than the DS saloons, but with rather less passenger space. It used every DS technical feature and more, and was driven by a Maserati V6 engine. The engine itself was unusual in that it used a wide, 90-degree, angle between cylinder banks, which was because it was derived from Maserati's existing V8 unit. The transaxle was by ZF, and was not fitted with Citroën hydraulic controls. The rack-and-pinion steering, completely power-operated was special in that it had a variable response ratio, to give easy parking without the usual accompaniment of vague straight-line feel. In the straight-ahead position, the steering felt very direct indeed.

Citroën never found another use for the splendid 2.7-litre V6 engine in production cars (although a few very special V6 DS saloons were made for VIPs). Maserati picked it up for their mid-engined Meraks, and Ligier for their limited-production GT cars. Fuel injection replaced the triple-carburettor installation in 1972, with a small power boost and better low-speed pick-up. Another option in France was the Borg-Warner automatic version, for which the engine was enlarged to a full 3-litres.

The SM was never meant to sell in large quantities and it was something of an embarrassment to Citroën production planners. In the last years of its life, final assembly was contracted out to Guy Ligier's little factory in Vichy, where the last SM was built in 1975. This, incidentally, was after the Citroën-Peugeot merger had been agreed, and the SM (as a loss maker) was in any case due to be dropped. Apart from the latest Rolls-Royces and the modern Mercédés-Benz executive cars, probably no more mechanically advanced car has ever been sold to the public. It was a car of which André Citroën, founder of the company, would have been proud.

Citroën Type A

Type A models, built from 1919 to 1922 (data for 1919 model)
Built by: S. A. André Citroën, France.
Engine: Four cylinders, in line, in cast-iron block, with two-bearing light-alloy crankcase. Bore and stroke 65mm by 100mm, 1,327cc (2.56in × 3.94in, 81.0cu.in). Detachable cast-iron cylinder head. Two side valves per cylinder, operated by tappets from single camshaft, mounted in cylinder block. Single Solex carburettor. Maximum power 18bhp at 2,100rpm.
Transmission: Cone clutch and three-speed manual gearbox (without synchromesh), both in unit with front-mounted engine. Direct-acting central gearchange. Open propeller shaft drive to spiral-bevel 'live' rear axle.
Chassis: Separate pressed-steel chassis frame, with channel-section side members and tubular cross bracing. Forged front axle beam. Front suspension by leading quarter-elliptic leaf springs. Rear suspension by upper and lower trailing quarter-elliptic leaf springs. No dampers. Foot brake acting on transmission drum behind gearbox. Bolt-on steel-disc wheels. 710 × 90 tyres.
Dimensions: Wheelbase 9ft 6in (290cm), tracks (front and rear) 3ft 11.1in (120cm). Overall length 13ft (396cm). Unladen weight (chassis only) 990lb (449kg).
History: André Citroën, Managing Director of Mors and the inventor of double-bevel 'herring-bone' gearing, built a factory in Paris in 1917 and in the spring of 1919 launched the first of a long line of famous Citroëns – the Type A. It was really to be the first mass-produced French car, and was completely equipped with all-weather and electrical equipment as standard. It was cheap, it was available and it was helped by a strike at the Renault factory at about the time of its launch.

Technically, the Type A was almost completely conventional, but 30,000 orders were taken before deliveries began. Sales were soon aided by a flourishing dealer network and the gimmick of taking over the Paris taxi fleet helped enormously. Within two years the side-valve Type A had been joined by the enlarged and improved Type B2 and shortly after that by an overhead-valve

Above: A 1922 model, visually the same with those characteristic disc wheels and the noteworthy radiator shape.

conversion on the same basic engine. Alongside it came the legendary 855cc 5CV, which included the three-seater 'Clover Leaf' style. The Type A had been the first quantity-built French car the public could afford and it was the best possible start for Citroën.

Left: Citroën's Type A built only for a few years, established André Citroën as a leading maker of 'people's cars' in France. Up to then, he had made his name as the chief executive of Mors, who made most costly cars, and had invented the double-bevel 'silent' gear wheel. The Type A was France's first true mass-production car, and post-war buyers queued up to take delivery. Mechanically, the Type A was very simple, and typically 'vintage', with various oddities. The cone clutch was old fashioned, but the unit gearbox advanced. More than 30,000 were ordered before deliveries began, and Citroën never looked back. Even Renault, the acknowledged leaders in France, were very worried.

Citroën 'Traction Avant'

11CV and 15CV models, built 1934 to 1955 (data for 11CV – post-war types)
Built by: S. A. André Citroën, France.
Engine: Four cylinders, in line, in three-bearing cast-iron cylinder block. Bore and stroke 78mm by 100mm, 1,911cc (3.07in × 3.94in, 116.6cu.in). Detachable cylinder barrels, wet liners. Cast-iron cylinder head. Two overhead valves per cylinder, operated by pushrods and rockers from side-mounted camshaft. Single down-draught Solex carburettor. Maximum power 56bhp (net) at 4,250rpm.
Transmission: Front-wheel-drive power pack. Engine longitudinally mounted behind line of front axle, gearbox ahead of it. Single-dry-plate clutch and three speed manual gearbox (synchromesh on top and second gears). Spiral-bevel differential. Exposed, universally jointed drive shafts to front wheels.
Chassis: Pressed-steel unitary-construction body shell, with four passenger doors. Power pack bolts on to front of shell and can be wheeled away for major maintenance. Independent front suspension by wishbones and longitudinal torsion

bars. 'Dead' rear axle beam (tubular), radius arms and transverse torsion bars. Hydraulic lever-type dampers. Rack-and-pinion steering. Four-wheel hydraulically operated drum brakes. Pressed-steel disc brakes. 185-400mm tyres.

Dimensions: Wheelbase (6-seater) 10ft 1.5in (309cm), (8-seater) 10ft 9in (328cm). Tracks (front and rear) 4ft 8in (142cm). Overall length 14ft 9.5in or 15ft 5.5in (451 or 471cm). Unladen weight 2,465lb or 2,604b (1,118kg or 1,181kg).

History: Before 1933, Citroën's cars had been relatively conventional, although they had already adopted Budd-type pressed-steel bodies. Then came their great technical breakthrough – the announcement of the all-new front-wheel-drive 7CV. ▶

Below and below left: The legendary saloon *traction avant* Citroën was built from 1934 to 1955 without a break (apart from war years). There were four-cylinder and (from 1938) six-cylinder cars. The *'traction'* now lives on in legend as a 'Maigret' police car.

This car would have been complex enough and troublesome enough to bankrupt Citroën had it not been for timely help from the Michelin (tyre) family. Not only did the new car have front-wheel drive, but a unit-construction body/chassis at a time when such things were almost unknown. The styling, although related to currently accepted standards, was low and relatively wind-cheating. The engine, although new, was of one 1,300cc and it soon became clear that it lacked power. Within a year, the bore and stroke had both been increased. The 7CV disposed of 1,628cc and the '7S' 1,911cc. With that engine size the new '11CV' car soldiered on very successfully until 1957 – more than 700,000 were built in the 24 years, which included the war-time years.

From 1938, a six-cylinder version of the car, the 15CV (or Big Six as it was known in Britain), was added to the range. Eventually there were alternative wheelbases – the long-wheelbase cars having extra occasional seats in the lengthened rear compartment, which made them very popular for taxi and hire

Right and below: One of the most attractive types of *traction avant* Citroen was the two-seater open tourer, built only in the 1930s. The mechanical features were like those of the saloons. Recognition points of all *traction avant* Citroën's included the chevron marks on the radiator grille, the long low lines quite out of the ordinary for the 1930s, the front-drive shafts seen behind the bumper, and the unmistakable shape of the front wings. Power pack layout was such that the entire engine and transmission could be unbolted from the unit-construction body shell within 90 minutes, for major repairs.

car use. In the 1930s, too, there were higher-priced convertibles (with double dickey seat) and fixed-head coupé cars, but these were not re-introduced in 1945 when production resumed following the war.

The '*traction avant*' (front-wheel drive) as it was always affectionately known among motorists, set new standards for roadholding and response, even though its performance was never startling, and its refinement not too obvious. Front-drive was most responsible for this, but the wide wheel tracks and low-slung construction must have helped. One immensely clever practical feature was that after 90 minutes of work in an agency the entire engine/transmission/front suspension power pack could be removed from the body – and this made major work easy to perform. Even when time caught up with the '*traction*' the main elements of its design were carried forward to the futuristic DS19 of 1955. The Big Six had already tested hydropneumatic suspension by then.

Cord L-29

L-29 front-wheel drive car, built from 1929 to 1932 (data for 1929 Model)
Built by: Auburn Automobile Co., United States.
Engine: Lycoming-manufactured. Eight cylinders in line, in cast-iron block, with five-bearing light-alloy crankcase. Bore and stroke 85.7mm by 114.3mm, 5,275cc (3.37in × 4.5in, 322cu.in). Detachable cast-iron cylinder head. Two side valves per cylinder, operated directly by single camshaft mounted in side of crankcase. Single twin-choke up-draught Schebler carburettor. Maximum power 125bhp (gross) at 3,600rpm.
Transmission: Single-dry-plate clutch and three-speed manual gearbox (without synchromesh), both in unit with front-mounted engine and final-drive unit. Engine mounted behind transmission and transmission behind line of front wheels. Remote-control facia-mounted gearchange. Direct connection to hypoid-bevel final drive. Exposed, universally jointed drive shafts to front wheels.
Chassis: Separate pressed-steel chassis frame, with channel-section side members, tubular and pressed cross-bracings and cruciform. De Dion front suspension, with tube ahead of transmission, by upper and lower forward-facing quarter-elliptic leaf springs. Rear suspension by forged axle beam and semi-elliptic leaf springs. Lever-arm dampers. Worm-and-roller steering. Four-wheel, hydraulically operated drum brakes. 18in centre-lock wire wheels. 7.00 × 18in tyres.
Dimensions: Wheelbase 11ft 5.5in (349cm), track (front) 4ft 10in (147cm), track (rear) 5ft (152.4cm). Overall length 17ft 1.5in (521cm). Unladen weight 4,620lb (2,095kg).
History: Errett Lobban Cord took control of Auburn in 1924, when they were a stumbling little concern in Indiana, turned round their fortunes very rapidly and decided to launch a new car bearing his own name. By 1928 he controlled assets worth more than $11 million and as the United States was in the grip of an economic boom he decided to market a car with advanced engineering features. The Cord L-29 with front-wheel drive designed by racing genius Harry Miller was the result. Cord's opinion was that the advanced engineering would sell his cars and he assumed that reliability would follow in the footsteps of his genius design. The L-29, however, was not all new – its front-drive package

Right: Errett Lobban Cord's first and quite magnificent folly was the front-wheel-drive L-29 Cord, built for only three years in the depths of the North American Depression. Cord had taken control of Auburn in 1924, and by 1928 had built it up strongly. He then wanted to sell an advanced car with radical engineering features. Racing car personality Harry Miller designed one, and the L-29 was the result. The in-line Lycoming straight-eight drove forward to the transmission through a conventional gearbox. Miller also chose to use De Dion front suspension (his racing cars used such a system), and the result was a very low car with wonderfully racy lines. A high price and the Depression killed the car.

involved taking an existing Lycoming straight-eight (Lycoming was another Cord-owned company) and a conventional three-speed gearbox, fixed directly to a hypoid-bevel differential. This, of course, had to be chassis mounted, so the L-29, perforce, had to have independent or De Dion suspension. Miller chose the latter system, as his racing cars were also built like that.

The L-29's advantage, because it had no conventional transmission, was that it could be built up to 10in (25cm) lower than its competitors, which gave it a very 'racy' look. Like some other American cars, however, the L-29 was launched by accident, at exactly the wrong time. It first went into the showrooms at the end of 1929, the launch almost coinciding with the first panics on the Wall Street financial market. Priced at more than $3,000 in 1930 (although reduced, in a panic, to $2,395 a year later) it was too expensive to attract enough custom and was therefore a real marketing albatross around Auburn's and Cord's necks. Production staggered on until the middle of 1932, by which time 5,600 cars had been built. The car itself was excitingly engineered and always looked low and sleek, but it was still unproven when launched and soon had a bad name for reliability. It was, nevertheless, *the* first American car to be quantity built with front-wheel drive. Cord was not daunted by this failure and tried again in 1934 with the Cord 810.

Cord Models 810 and 812

810 and 812 models, built from 1935 to 1937 (data for supercharged Model 812)
Built by: Auburn Automobile Co., United States.
Engine: Lycoming-manufactured. Eight cylinder in 90-degree vee-formation, in three-bearing cast-iron block. Bore and stroke 88.9mm by 92.25mm, 4,729cc (3.5in × 3.75in, 288.6cu.in). Two detachable cast-alloy cylinder heads. Two valves per cylinder, operated by rollers, with horizontally positioned intake and exhaust ports. Single down-draught carburettor, and Schwitzer-Cummins supercharger, driven by ring gear from centre bearing of camshaft. Maximum power 195bhp (gross) at 4,200rpm.
Transmission: Front-wheel-drive power pack. Engine behind line of front wheels, driving over differential to gearbox mounted ahead of front wheels. Single-dry-plate clutch, semi-automatic, in unit with engine. Four-speed synchromesh manual gearbox (no synchromesh on first gear). Gear selection by small lever and gate on right of steering column. Actual gearchanging by pressing clutch pedal, helped by electro-vacuum mechanism. Spiral-bevel differential. Exposed, ball-jointed drive shafts to driven front wheels.
Chassis: Front-wheel-drive power pack in the nose, mounted on front portion of chassis/body (including scuttle) and all bolted-up to unitary-construction pressed-steel body/chassis unit. Independent front suspension by trailing arms, and transverse leaf spring. 'Dead' rear axle beam, with half-elliptic leaf springs. Hydraulic lever arm dampers. Gemmer steering. Four-wheel drum brakes, hydraulically operated. 16in pressed-steel bolt-on disc wheels. 6.50 × 16in tyres. Cord (Auburn manufactured) coachwork in various touring and saloon styles, with hidden headlamps, two or four doors.
Dimensions: Wheelbase 10ft 5in (317cm), track (front) 4ft 8in (142cm), track (rear) 5ft 1in (155cm). Overall length 16ft 3.5in (497cm). Unladen weight 3,650lb (1,655kg).
History: The L29 Cord having died in 1932, the front-wheel-drive car was first conceived by Auburn in 1933 as a Duesenberg, then discarded. It was revived, and hurriedly revamped by Gordon Buehrig and his engineers in 1935. Not only was it remarkable for a very complex transmission, but for some really advanced and attractive styling, which put the Cord at least 10, if not 20, years ahead of its time.

Disappearing headlamps, front wing mounted, were a feature, as was the

Below: The 1937 Model 812 Sportsman and, above, the 1936 Model 810 Westchester sedan were just two of the styles sold in two years.

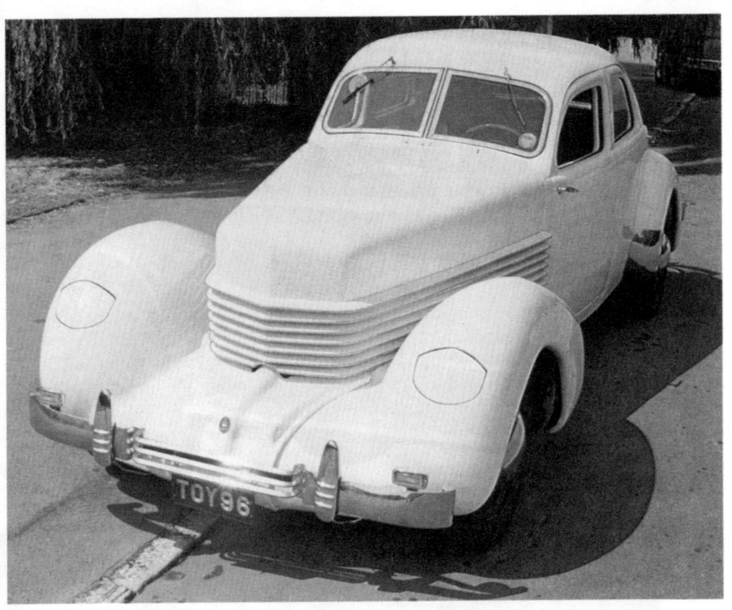

Above: Cord's splendidly individual Model 810/812 was a last desperate attempt to keep the Auburn-Duesenberg-Cord empire afloat. First conceived as a Duesenberg in 1933, it was dropped, then quickly revamped by Gordon Buehrig and his team in 1935 and announced in the same year. Under the skin was a Lycoming vee-8 engine and front-wheel-drive, but the styling was always the talking point. The later, 812, models could be had with blown engines.

instantly recognisable horizontal fluting of nose and bonnet sides. The engine was specially designed for the Cord by Lycoming, also part of the Auburn Combine. The transmission, perhaps of necessity because of its remoteness from the driver, was controlled by a combination of preselection, electro-vacuum operation and a tiny lever and gate on the steering column. The four-speed transmission had very much of an 'overdrive' top gear, although even third gear was high by comparison with almost any other contemporary North American car.

Release in the autumn of 1935 was premature, and many sales were lost because production could not immediately begin. Indeed, the first 100 of these beautiful cars were more or less handbuilt, which hit the company's finances very hard. The model 810 was expensive and unusual-looking, which partly explains the reluctance of possible buyers, and even the addition of a very powerful super-charged Model 812 for 1937 could not save the day. The late-model 812s with their external flexible exhaust pipes were striking cars, but in all only 2,320 810s and 812s were sold in two selling seasons. The last was built in August 1937, but happily a great proportion of these cars survive.

Daimler 4HP

4hp car, built from 1896 to 1903 (data for 1896 model)
Built by: Daimler Motoren-Gesellschaft, Germany, and by Daimler Motor Syndicate Ltd., Britain.
Engine: Two cylinders, in line, in cast-iron blocks, with two-bearing light-alloy crankcase. Bore and stroke 90mm by 120mm, 1,527cc (3.54in × 4.72in, 93.2cu.in). Fixed cast-iron cylinder heads. Two valves per cylinder, automatic (atmospheric) inlet valves, mounted overhead; side-mounted exhaust valves, operated by tappets from camshaft in side of crankcase. Spray-type carburettor. Max. power 4.5bhp.
Transmission: Clutch in unit with front-mounted engine and shaft to separate four-speed manual gearbox (without synchromesh), all mounted in chassis subframe. Straight-bevel differential in tail of gearbox. Countershaft from differential, with sprockets. Final drive to rear wheels by chain. Remote-control

gear-change in passenger compartment, on dashboard.
Chassis: Chassis frame of wood with steel-plate reinforcements. Forged front axle beam. Front and rear suspension by full-elliptic leaf springs. No dampers. Tiller steering (wheel steering by 1900). Foot brake by band contracting round drum on gearbox counter-shaft. Hand brake operating bands on rear-wheel drum. Third, spoon, brake on tyres, hand operated. Fixed artillery-style wheels, smaller at front than back, with solid tyres. Choice of open coachwork.
History: Gottlieb Daimler was involved in internal combustion engine research from the beginning of the 1880s and he built the world's first motor cycle in 1885 (which he never duplicated). His original car was built in 1886, having road trials in Cannstatt. Although Daimler soon became proprietary suppliers of engines, they did not make complete cars for some years. The company was set up in 1890, but Daimler left it for a while from 1893 to 1895. The first production Daimlers were built in 1896 and the Phönix (Panhard-like with its front engine) soon followed it. This 4hp twin-cylinder machine was also built in Coventry, under licence to one of Harry Lawson's companies. Ironically, the last Daimler machine in its native Germany was built in 1902, but the British marque became one of *the* most famous of all. Like other pioneering designs, the original 4hp Daimler was startlingly crude, with almost ineffective brakes, very casual cooling (the radiator was out at the back, where it could get liberally plastered with filth) and tiller steering. In those days, too, the struggle was not to make the car go well, but to keep it going at all. The Daimlers did this far better than most.

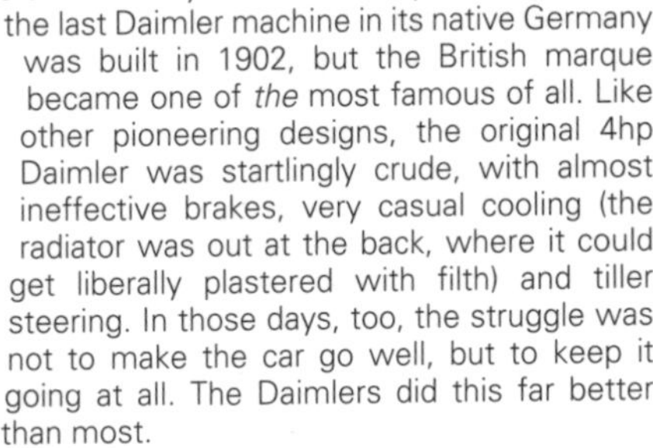

Left: The very early Daimlers were historically important, but both crude and frail. Note the method of steering, the engine under the floor, the solid tyres, and the fragile chassis.

Daimler Double-Six

Double-Six 50, 30, 4-/50 and 30/40 models, built from 1926 to 1937 (data for 50)
Built by: Daimler Motor Co. Ltd., Britain.
Engine: Twelve cylinders, in 60-degree vee-formation, based on seven-bearing light-alloy crankcase. Six cylinders per bank, in sets of three-cylinder cast-iron blocks. Bore and stroke 81.5mm by 114mm, 7,136cc (3.21in × 4.49in, 435.4cu.in). Detachable cast-iron cylinder heads. Double sleeve-valve system, with sleeves, made from steel, oscillating inside each other and inside cylinders. Sleeve valves operated by chain-driven eccentric shafts. Two Daimler carburettors (one to each cylinder bank). Maximum power 150bhp (net) at 2,480rpm.
Transmission: Single-dry-plate clutch, in unit with engine, and separate four-speed manual gearbox (without synchromesh), with direct-acting central gearchange. Open propeller shaft to underslung worm-drive rear axle.
Chassis: Separate steel chassis frame. Channel-section side members with tubular and pressed cross bracing. Forged front axle beam. Front and rear suspension by half-elliptic leaf springs. Lever-type hydraulic dampers. Worm-and-sector steering. Four-wheel, rod operated drum brakes, vacuum-servo assisted. Push-on handbrake. Centre-lock wire wheels. Tyres from 6.75×33in, depending on wheelbase and body style chosen. Coachwork by specialist builders; many styles and types.
Dimensions: Wheelbase 12ft 11.5in or 13ft 7in (365 or 414cm), tracks (front and rear) 4ft 9in or 5ft (145 or 152cm). Overall length, according to coachwork and wheelbase, from 18ft 7in (566cm). Unladen weight, according to coachwork, from 6,200lb (2,812kg).
History: Daimler's sleeve-valve engine tradition was well established before Laurence Pomeroy (senior) joined the company, but the six-cylinder cars were being left behind in the luxury field by Rolls-Royce, in spite of continual Royal patronage. Pomeroy therefore settled upon the inspired solution of providing a V12-engined Daimler motor car, while using many existing parts. His Double-Six (so named because of the layout, and because in many ways, such as carburation and ignition, it *was* a double-six) comprised, effectively, two sets of cylinder blocks and components from the six-cylinder 25/85 Daimler sleeve-valve engine, placed at 60 degrees to each other on a new light-alloy crankcase. This disposed of 7,136cc, and gave a splendid 150bhp power output and all the flexibility for which Daimler town carriages were famous. Each bank retained its own carburettor, water pump cooling and ignition system. Inlet manifolding was on the outside of the engines and exhaust manifolding neatly in the centre of the 'vee'.

The rest of the chassis, although vast and carefully detailed, was conventional. Coachwork, of course, was by specialist builders approved by Daimler themselves. A typical five-seat saloon of 1926 would cost about £2,500 – rather less than the princely sum of £2,800 or thereabouts asked for a handsome 40/50 Rolls-Royce.

To look after less affluent (relatively-speaking, that is) customers, the 50 was joined in 1928 by the 30, a similarly conceived V12, but this time using two sets of 16/55 components and having a 3.7-litre capacity. The lowered-chassis specials, produced by Thomson and Taylor at Brooklands were striking sporting versions of the 50. In 1930, the two cars were redesigned to become 40/50 and 30/40 models respectively, with the important addition of the fluid flywheel and Wilson preselector gearbox which was to be standardised on all future Daimlers.

However, with the world depression intensifying, sales of the twelve-cylinder-engined Daimlers were understandably low, and the models were dropped in favour of poppet-valve straight-eight engined cars in 1934. In 1937, for a very brief period, a hybrid 'Double-Six' was sold – having 40/50 cylinder dimensions, but poppet-valve breathing arrangements.

Above: This stately Double-Six limousine, with greater-than-normal headroom, could only be one of the Hooper-bodied Royal fleet. Radiators on King George V's car were black.

Left: Startling and sleek but quite unlike a Daimler was the low chassis 1931 Double-Six by Corsica of London.

Datsun 240Z

Datsun 240Z, 260Z and 280Z models, built from 1969 to 1978 (data for 240Z)
Built by: Nissan Motor Co. Ltd., Japan.
Engine: Six cylinders, in line, in seven-bearing cast-iron block. Bore and stroke 83mm by 73.7mm, 2,393cc (3.27in × 2.90in, 146cu.in). Cast-iron cylinder head. Two overhead valves per cylinder, operated by single overhead camshaft. Twin side-draught constant-vacuum SU carburettors. Maximum power 151bhp (gross) at 5,600rpm. Maximum torque 146lb.ft at 4,400rpm.
Transmission: Single-dry-plate clutch and five-speed all-synchromesh manual gearbox, in unit with front-mounted engine. Central, remote-control gearchange. Open propeller shaft to chassis-mounted hypoid-bevel final drive. Exposed, universally joined drive shafts to rear wheels.
Chassis: Unitary-construction pressed-steel body/chassis unit, in single fixed-head three-door body-style. Independent front suspension by MacPherson struts and an anti-roll bar. Independent rear suspension by MacPherson struts and lower wishbones. Rack-and-pinion steering. Servo-assisted brakes, front discs and rear drums. 14in pressed-steel disc wheels. 175 × 14in tyres.
Dimensions: Wheelbase 7ft 6.5in (230cm), track (front) 4ft 5.5in (136cm), track rear 4ft 5in (135cm). Overall length 13ft 7in (414cm). Unladen weight 2,300lb (1,043kg).
History: Datsun, like other Japanese car makers, have prospered mightily since 1945. With the accent firmly on export, they eventually developed a series of attractive sporting cars. The Datsun Fairlady, with its rigid back axle and MGB-

like styling, was successful enough, but in 1969 Datsun's successor to it, the 240Z, was unveiled. It combined striking good looks (reminiscent, some say, of Jaguar's E-Type), with typical Japanese-car reliability, and good performance. In a way, in American eyes it effectively replaced the Austin-Healey 3000. Whereas the big Healey had been killed by USA legislation, the 240Z was designed to meet and beat the same rules.

It began to sell well at once, being sold as a Nissan in some markets and as a Datsun in others. The factory launched it into a competition programme, and its successes included a win in the East African Safari in 1971. Later, in the modern idiom, its engine, which, incidentally was shared with other Nissan/Datsun saloons, was enlarged, and other versions were developed. The 240Z became the 260Z, and subsequently – for North America in particular – the 280Z was developed. The closed two-seater coupé was later joined by a longer wheelbase 2+2 version. Both cars sold in large numbers until 1978, when they were replaced by the 280CX, which had a new body shell and style.

Below: Datsun's 240Z sports coupé family was a long-running success story. Sold in huge numbers for nine years (in 2.8-litre form, only in the USA), the Datsuns were real muscle cars, and the engines made exciting noises. This is Tony Fall driving a Castrol-sponsored 240Z on the 1972 RAC Rally.

De Dietrich 24/28HP

24/28hp models, built from 1903 to 1905
Built by: De Dietrich et Cie, France.
Engine: Four cylinders, in line, in two pairs of cast-iron blocks with light-alloy water jackets and two-bearing light-alloy crankcase. Bore and stroke 114mm by 130mm, 5,308cc (4.49in × 5.12in, 324cu.in). Fixed cylinder head. Two overhead valves per cylinder, inlets in one line and exhausts in another, operated by pullrods and rockers, from two camshafts mounted in crankcase. Single up-draught carburettor. Maximum power about 30bhp.
Transmission: Cone clutch in unit with front-mounted engine. Separate mid-positioned four-speed manual gearbox (without synchromesh). Remote-control right-hand gearchange. Final drive by chain, from sprockets on transmission cross shaft to sprockets at rear wheel hubs. Bevel differential inside rear of transmission case.
Chassis: Separate chassis frame, with wood/steel side members (steel applied as flitch plates) and tubular cross members. Forged front axle beam. Front and rear suspension by semi-elliptic leaf springs. No dampers. Worm-and-nut steering. Foot brakes acting on drum mounted on sprocket cross shaft at side of transmission.

Hand brake by brake bands on drums at rear wheels. Bolt-on artillery-style wheels.
Dimensions: Wheelbase 7ft 8.3in (234.5cm), tracks (front and rear) 4ft (122cm). Overall length 11ft 0.3in (336cm).
History: This manufacturer of railway rolling stock first built cars in 1897 which were licence-built Bollees. From 1902 De Dietrich began to build more conventionally laid out machines, with water-cooled four-cylinder engines of Turcat-Méry design. In the same year he employed the 19-year-old Ettore Bugatti to design the well-known 24/28 De Dietrich. This car was similar in layout to the Turcat-Mérys, but had a new type of engine where the valves were all overhead and the cylinder head was integral with the block (always a Bugatti hallmark). Valve operation was by pullrods rather than by pushrods. The transmission layout – a cone clutch, a massive separate gearbox, cross-shaft final drive and chain drive sprocket to the back wheels, was absolutely typical of the period, and it needed Renault and other influences to convince the firm they should adopt shaft drive later. Bugatti left De Dietrich in 1904 and a year later the cars were renamed Lorraine-Dietrichs to emphasise their French ancestry. The last Lorraine car of all was built in 1934.

Left: Even in stripped 1903 racing guise, the De Dietrich looks massive and impressive. The car was designed by a youthful Ettore Bugatti.

De Dion Bouton 'Single Cylinder'

De Dion Boutons, 3½ to 12hp, built from 1900 to 1913 (data for 1900 3½hp)
Engine: Single cylinder, vertically mounted in chassis, water-cooled, with cast-iron cylinder block. Bore and stroke 80mm by 80mm, 402cc (3.15in × 3.15in, 24.5cu.in). Two valves. Automatic (atmospheric) inlet valve, inverted over camshaft-operated side valve, mounted below it. Splash lubrication. Replenishment through steel measuring cup needed every 20 miles. Single De Dion carburettor. About 3.5bhp at 1.500rpm.
Transmission: Two-speed constant-mesh gearbox, in unit with engine, engaged by expanding clutches, controlled from steering column. No reverse gear as standard, but epicyclic reverse train optional. Spur gear drive to differential carrier, mounted on chassis. Exposed, universally jointed drive shafts.
Chassis: Tubular chassis frame, separate from choice of bodies. Tubular front axle beam. Front suspension by half-elliptic leaf springs themselves suspended at their trailing shackles by a transverse leaf spring. Rear suspension by three-quarter elliptic leaf springs, patent De Dion axle with chassis-mounted

differential and tube connecting wheels running behind the differential/final drive housing. No dampers. Brakes (early models) operated by foot pedal contracting shoes on to the transmission. Later, handbrake on steering column operated shoes on rear wheel drums. 700-80mm tyres.

Dimensions: Wheelbase 5ft 1.5in (156cm), tracks front and rear 3ft 8in (112cm). Overall length 7ft 8in (234cm).

History: Comte Albert de Dion and Messrs Trepardoux and Bouton began building light steam-powered pleasure carriages in the 1880s. Eventually they became fascinated by the Daimler experiments and Bouton designed his first petrol engine in 1893. Trepardoux, for his part, believed only in steam and left in a huff. Single-cylinder petrol-engined tricycles went on sale in 1895, and logic made it certain that small *'voiturette'* four-wheelers would follow – which they did in 1900.

De Dion engines were of the 'high-speed' variety – 1,500rpm being normal compared with the 500rpm of the Benz – but more significant was the advanced chassis design. The engine/transmission units were rear-mounted at first, fixed up to the chassis, and drove the rear wheels through exposed drive shafts; the wheels were connected by a beam. Thus the world-famous De Dion suspension was born.

The 3½hp model was first, but was rapidly supplemented and supplanted by other 'singles' of up to 12hp, the last being built in 1913. 'Fashion' shortly took hold of De Dion and dummy bonnets were followed, in 1904, by the engines becoming front-mounted in what we now call the 'conventional' manner.

Early transmissions were splendidly detailed, with constant-mesh gears being – literally – clutched to their shafts by expanding friction clutches. Steering, at first, was by hand lever, but a wheel followed in 1904.

Left: One of the most famous and most numerous of all veteran cars – the 3½hp De Dion Bouton. This is a 1903 model.

DeLorean DMC-12

DeLorean DMC sports coupé, built only in 1981 and 1982
Built by: DeLorean Motor Company, Northern Ireland.
Engine: Renault unit, six cylinders in 90-degree vee formation, and four bearing light-alloy cylinder block. Bore and stroke 91 × 73mm, 2,849cc (3.58 × 2.87in, 174cu.in). Two light-alloy cylinder heads. Two valves per cylinder, in line, operation by single overhead camshaft per head, and inverted bucket tappets. Bosch K-Jetronic fuel injection. Maximum power 132bhp (DIN) at 5,500rpm. Maximum torque 153lb.ft at 2,750rpm.
Transmission: Rear-wheel-drive, single-dry-plate diaphragm spring clutch and five-speed all-synchromesh manual gearbox, all in unit with rear-mounted engine. Optional automatic transmission. Remote-control, central gearchange.
Chassis: Separate backbone-style pressed-steel chassis frame, topped by a glassfibre body shell with stainless-steel skin panels. Independent front suspension by coil springs, wishbones, telescopic dampers, anti-roll bar. Independent rear suspension by coil springs, semi-trailing arms and wishbones, telescopic dampers and anti-roll bar. Rack-and-pinion steering. Four-wheel disc brakes. cast-alloy wheels, 14in front, 15in rear, with 195/60-14in (front) and 235/60-15in (rear) tyres.
Dimensions: Wheelbase 7ft 11in (241.5cm), front track 5ft 2.5in (159cm), rear track 5ft 3in (160cm). Overall length 14ft 0in (426.5cm). Unladen weight 2,745lb (1,245kg).
History: In so many ways the DeLorean was a great car, but its reputation will always be tainted by the seedy organisation which built it. It was, after all, the first car to be built with stainless steel body skin panels, and the first (and so far) only series production car to have been built in Northern Ireland. The man who conceived it, though, was later convicted of multi-million pound fraud, and nothing can rescue it from that.

John DeLorean achieved great things at General Motors – he ran the entire cars and trucks divisions in the early 1970s – before being eased out. Conceiving

Below: Only Mercedes-Benz had ever before used 'gullwing' action passenger doors, which DeLorean specified as one of the selling points on the DMC-12.

Above: The DMC-12's smart, sharp-edged Giuigiaro style was so well-proportioned that the true location of the V6 engine - in the tail - was disguised.

his own specialist sports car, with a rear-engined layout and lift-up gull-wing doors, and having it styled by Giugiaro of Italy, he then spent years hawking it around the world before persuading the British government to back him, in a new enterprise, in Northern Ireland. At this point he hired Lotus to convert his bright idea into a practical two-seater.

Starting in 1978, Lotus re-designed everything, effectively developing a larger version of the Esprit's backbone chassis, where the Renault V6 engine was, by edict from DeLorean himself, in the tail, behind the line of the rear wheels. The body, its style freshened up by Giugiaro, was made by Lotus's famous VARI glassfibre process, and clad in natural finish stainless steel skin panels.

By mid-1980 the design was complete, by the end of the year the brand-new factory at Dunmurry came falteringly to life, and from 1981 sales began. At first there were heady claims, that more than 20,000 cars a year would be assembled, and that there were long waiting lists in the USA, where all original cars were sold, but these were as unsubstantial as the profits being made. Here was a car always surrounded by hype, by smokescreens which covered company finances and inter-personal feuds – in other words a difficult birth. The company's own spokesman could not generate a favourable press, and DeLorean's own arrogant (and, as it now seems, shifty) demeanour did not help.

Observers were ready to give the DMC-12 a favourable reception if its behaviour matched its original launch, and its looks, for everyone was agreed that it looked attractive, if a little sharp-edged for the styling trends of the period. Worries about the practicality of the lift-up gullwing doors were suspended (but what would happen if a car was inverted in an accident ?), though it soon became clear that maintenance of the stainless steel panelling was always going to be problematical.

There was another problem. Although the DMC-12 handled well enough (though its tail-heavy weight distribiution had to be tackled by the fitment of wider-seation rear tyres), it was at once larger and less powerful than originally hoped. Impressive to look at, it could only accelerate to 60mph in 10.5 sec, and its top speed was no more than 109mph – neither of which was a match for the Porsches which DeLorean himself aimed to displace.

By 1982 stocks of unsold cars were piling up, both in the USA and in Northern Ireland, so deliveries to other countries never began. Eighty cars a day had been built in late 1981, but by the spring of 1982 it was all over, the company was wound up soon afterwards, and various fraud cases ensued. Only 8,000 cars were ever built.

Delage Series D1 and Grand Prix Cars

D1 models, all forms, built from 1923 to 1928 (data for 1928 model)
Built by: Automobiles Delage, France.
Engine: Four cylinders, in line, in cast-iron cylinder block with five-bearing light-alloy crankcase. Bore and stroke 75mm by 120mm, 2,121cc (2,95in × 4.72in, 129.4cu.in). Detachable cast-iron cylinder head. Two overhead valves per cylinder operated by pushrods and rockers from single camshaft mounted in side of crankcase. Single up-draught Zenith carburettor. Maximum power 38bhp (gross) at 2,400rpm.
Transmission: Multi-dry-plate clutch and four-speed manual gearbox (without synchromesh), both in unit with front-mounted engine. Direct-acting central gearchange. Open propeller shaft to spiral-bevel 'live' rear axle.
Chassis: Separate pressed-steel chassis frame, with channel-section side members and tubular and pressed cross bracing. Forged front axle beam. Front and rear suspension by semi-elliptic leaf springs. Worm-and-nut steering. Four-wheel, shaft-and-cable operated drum brakes. Centre-lock wire wheels. 820 × 120mm tyres. Opening touring, sporting or saloon car coachwork to choice.
Dimensions: Wheelbase 10ft 6in (320cm), tracks (front and rear) 4ft 5in (135cm). Overall length 13ft 10in (422cm). Unladen weight 2,100lb (952kg).
History: The first Delages were runabouts with conventional shaft drive and a single cylinder 6½-horsepower engine supplied by De Dion. Delage soon became interested in motor sport and second place in the French Coupes des

Above and below: Mainstay of the Delage range in the 1920s was the versatile D1 series. The original D1 was a gentle little 2.1-litre touring car, but successive D1S and D1SS types were fiercer and more sporting. Logically enough the first 'S' was for Sports, and the second 'S' for Super. The D1SS is the car most people admire – and (above) examples are still raced in vintage events. Below: The 1924 D1SS Tourer was an impressive machine.

Voiturettes in 1906 was followed by an outright win in 1908. With the racing 'bug' well and truly established, he was to be building Grand Prix cars even before World War 1, and all-conquering machines in the 1920s. By then he had engaged the noted designer Lory to design first an impressive 2-litre V12 engine and later a very successful 1½ -litre straight eight. His cars also held the Land Speed Record for a short time.

At the beginning of the 1920s there were big six-cylinder Delages, but the company's mainstay – neither as visually exciting, nor as fast, as the luxury cars or the racing cars – was the D1 series. This car was laid out on more practical and more simple lines, but it was not made spindly or weak in the process. Indeed, a car built around the D1's frame was used in hill-climbs and sprints with nothing less than a 5.1-litre Type CO engine! The D1, as announced, was a gentle and reliable four-cylinder car, with a 2.1-litre engine and such mechanical niceties as overhead valves (side-valve layouts were still 'conventional' for cheaper machines), a four-speed gearbox and four-wheel brakes. Cruising speed might have been no more than 50mph and maximum speed between 65 and 70mph, but the cars exhibited impeccable handling, great reliability and of course used the noble radiator design which classed them as relatives (even if they were considerably cheaper) of the luxurious 'sixes', and even of the racing Delages.

Delage was quite unable to leave a production car alone if it was not sporting enough for him, so the D1S of 1924/25 evolved. The 'S' was for sporting (*'Sportif'* in French) and the cars, built near Paris, backed up this title to some extent. They were given a much shorter wheelbase (9ft 9in in place of 10ft 6in), which did wonders for the handling and the weight, centre-lock 'Rudge' wire wheels, different gearbox ratios, bigger valves and an altered camshaft for the engine and a narrow and distinctive radiator. That was still not enough for Delage, however. Next along, in 1925, was the D1SS model, with the SS in this case denoting Super Sports. This had all the D1S features, with a lowered and lightened chassis, close-ratio gears, from 1926, and other details. Even so, a look at production figures shows that the basic D1 was much the most popular, with more than 9,000 sold in five years, whereas only 983 D1S/D1SS cars were built over the same period. There were other variants too – the D1C being a

'high-chassis' device intended for 'Colonial' conditions (442 sold) – and between 1926 and 1929 there were the DM/DMS/DMN cars, all of which were based on D1 engineering and fitted with six-cylinder 3.2-litre engines, very closely related to the four used in the D1s. The D1's engine was eminently tuneable, as the 50bhp boasted by the D1SS proved, and if it had not been for Delage's predilection for ever-larger and more luxurious machines, sporting or ceremonial, that pedigree would have served the French company well into the 1930s, perhaps even ensuring survival.

THE DELAGE GRAND PRIX CARS – 1926/27

In the 1920s Albert Lory designed two wonderfully complex and successful racing Delages. The vee-12 cars of 1923/25 were a miracle of effective complication – by 1925 they were developing 195bhp at 7,000rpm, in supercharged form from two litres. The next series, built especially for the short-lived 1½-litre 'formula' had simpler, but still very powerful 1,488cc straight-eight engines. The first chassis frames were too flexible, and road-holding was not a strong point, and although the team won the 1926 British GP at Brooklands, and took second place at San Sebastian, they had one glaring fault – the hot exhaust pipe was carried past the driver's elbow and effectively 'cooked' him during a long race. For 1927 the engines were re-designed, with the exhaust system on the left, and in this guise Robert Benoist won five major events that year. With twin blowers and two Zenith carburettors, the engines produced a phenomenal 170bhp at 7,000rpm – the best yet achieved in terms of specific output. There were four of these cars, one of which was bought, developed and raced with great success by Dick Seaman in 1936. Even in the 1940s the engines were used in other racing cars.

Below: Like the D1 in spirit but entirely special in engineering were the Delage Grand Prix cars of the 1920s. There were 2-litre vee-12 cars in 1923/25, and the straight-eight 1½-litre machines (shown here) in 1926/27. They were winners, but early cars cooked their drivers – note the exhaust pipe!

Delage Series D8

D8 models, built from 1930 to 1935 (data for original 1930 model)
Built by: Automobiles Delage, France.
Engine: Eight cylinders, in line, in cast-iron block, bolted to five-bearing cast-alloy crankcase. Bore and stroke 77mm by 109mm, 4,050cc (3.03in × 4.29in, 247.1cu.in). Detachable cast-iron cylinder head. Two overhead valves per cylinder, operated by pushrods and rockers from single camshaft mounted in side of crankcase. Single Smith Barraquand five-jet carburettor. Maximum power 120bhp at 4,000rpm.
Transmission: Single-dry-plate clutch and four-speed manual gearbox (without synchromesh), both in unit with front-mounted engine. Direct-acting central gearchange. Open propeller shaft to spiral-bevel 'live' rear axle.
Chassis: Separate pressed-steel chassis frame, with channel-section side members and pressed and tubular cross bracing. Forged front axle beam. Front suspension by half-elliptic leaf springs (long torque rods added on later high-power models). Rear suspension by half-elliptic leaf springs. Friction type or hydraulic damps. Four-wheel, shaft and cable-operated drum brakes, with assistance from Clayton Dewandre vacuum-servo mounted to side of gearbox. 18in steel disc wheels. 7.00 × 18in tyres.Coachwork to choice – two-door and

Right: This is an early D8, a 1930 D8C coupé. Hidden behind the upright radiator is a straight-eight engine. Delage supplied most D8s to coach-builders for special treatment.

Below and right: Fastest of all the Delages were the D8SS models, with dropped frames and 145bhp 4-litre engines. This 1933 Sedanca had a British body style by Gurney Nutting.

HS 6322

four-door saloons, two-door coupés and open cars, usually by Figoni and Falaschi.
Dimensions: Wheelbase 10ft 10in or 11ft 11in (330cm to 363cm), tracks (front and rear) 4ft 8in (142cm). Overall length depending on body, from 16ft (488cm). Unladen weight, from 4,400lb (1,995kg).
History: If the Delage D1s were the company's mainstay in the last half of the 1920s, and the Grand Prix cars the most beautifully engineered, there is little doubt that the eight-cylinder D8 models were the most magnificent of all Delage machines. From 1930 to 1935 (when Delage sold out to their deadly rivals, Delahaye), the D8 series in all its glory was one of the most desirable high-performance cars being built in France, or perhaps in the whole of Europe. History has now blurred the originator of that famous aphorism: 'One drives, of course, an Alfa Romeo, one is driven in a Rolls, but one gives only a Delage to one's favourite mistress.'

The D8 was a very glamorous car, and it sold well to customers who wanted their friends and business acquaintances to know that they were affluent. The 1930s, for those millionaires whose fortunes were not decimated in the Depression, were halcyon days and motoring conditions, particularly in Europe, were ideal. There were still not too many cars on the roads and the high-performance of a Delage could be used repeatedly.

The D8's chassis, at first, was relatively conventional, with half-elliptic springing all round and cable-controlled brakes, but the all-new eight-cylinder engine combined the best of vintage engineering with a thoroughly up-to-date power output and an ability to turn over fast. Delage's radiator, of course, was very imposing and reminded many people of a Hispano-Suiza (which pleased Louis Delage very much, even though his design had been maturing for an equally long time) and the coachwork which was added to that imposing chassis and prow was never modest and never undramatic.

The original design was soon followed by more sporting variants like the D8 Grand Sport, Front axle location on all D8s was improved with long radius arms to isolate braking torque and to improve steering stability at high speeds. The

Below and right: All the Delage D8s were fast and very impressive, but this 1932 Grand Sport, with 2/4 seat open touring body by Letourneur et Marchand is rather special. The wheel discs were detachable. Those monstrous headlamps were powerful, to match the 100mph speeds.

Grand Sport was not quite a 100mph car, due to the bluff nose and large frontal area, but it had flashing acceleration by the standards of the day and got by on a fuel consumption of about 14mpg, but such would be of no interest to the average D8's owner. Delage himself still hankered after a motor sporting involvement, and sent a special-bodied D8 Grand Sport to attack long-distance records at Montlhéry, where the car achieved nearly 110mph for 24 hours.

Between 1932 and 1935, further D8 improvements were made and the D8S and D8SS models were introduced. These models had a chassis frame dropped by more than three inches, an engine increased in power output from 120 to 145bhp and raised overall gearing. The D8SS also was offered with a shortened, 10ft 2in (310cm), wheelbase, but these were extremely rare. Only two-seater bodies could be fitted to this chassis and the top speed was now well over 100mph. Early D8s had grouped chassis lubrication points, but the D8S and SS cars were endowed with a Rolls-Royce type of centralised chassis lubrication system. Centre-lock wire wheels were standardised, whereas the original D8 had been given steel disc wheels. It was once said that to introduce an eight-cylinder engine in Depression or post-Depression years was a sure guarantee of eventual commercial disaster and in Delage's case there was some truth in the saying.

Although the D8 was a splendid car, well-engineered, often beautifully styled and rather 'sexy' in the modern idiom, it was always an expensive car and sales were never high. Louis Delage himself was reluctant to change the face of his company to suit it more closely to economic conditions and he soon quarrelled with his director. He therefore left the company that bore his name in 1935 and the firm shortly merged with Delahaye. There had been companion four-cylinder and small six-cylinder and eight-cylinder Delages for some years. By 1935 the cars had acquired synchromesh gears and hydraulic brakes, along with transverse-leaf independent front suspension, but only the D8 120 (a Delahaye creation), with differently dimensioned engine, inherited these, along with the Cotal electro-magnetic gearbox. This, the last of the straight-eight 'Delages', died with the outbreak of war in 1939.

Delahaye Type 135 Sports/Saloon

Type 135 models, built from 1935 to 1950 (data for 1935 model)
Built by: Automobiles Delahaye, France.
Engine: Six cylinders, in line, in four-bearing cast-iron cylinder block Bore and stroke 80mm by 107mm, 3,237cc (3.15in × 4.21in, 197.5cu.in); competition model available with engine of 84mm by 107mm, 3,557cc (3.31in × 4.21in, 217cu.in). Detachable cast-iron cylinder head. Two overhead valves per cylinder, operated by pushrods and rockers from single side-mounted camshaft. Three downdraught Solex carburettors. Power output 130bhp at 3,850rpm (Superlux and Coupe des Alpes models), or 160bhp at 4,200rpm (Competition).
Transmission: Single-dry-plate clutch and four-speed synchromesh manual gearbox (no synchromesh on first gear), both in unit with front-mounted engine. Optional Cotal electromagnetic gearbox. Open propeller shaft to spiral-bevel 'live' rear axle.
Chassis: Separate pressed-steel chassis frame, with box-section side members and pressed and tubular cross bracing. Independent front suspension by transverse leaf springs and wishbones. Rear suspension by half-elliptic leaf springs. Hydraulic piston-type dampers. Four-wheel drum brakes, with Bendix mechanical servo. Centre-lock wire wheels and 6.00 × 17in tyres. Variety of coachwork: open sports, touring or saloon.
Dimensions: Wheelbase 9ft 8in (295cm), track (front) 4ft 7in (140cm), track (rear) 4ft 10in (147cm). Overall length 15ft (457cm). Unladen weight, depending on coachwork, from 2,750lb (1.247kg).
History: The origins of Delahaye lie in a company set up as long ago as 1845 to produce brick-making machinery. Emile Delahaye, was at first a railway engineer, who designed rolling stock for French and Belgian railroads, but he produced his first car of German Daimler type, in 1895, and two years later he moved his company from Tours to Paris, settling down to a variety of engineering projects.

Above and below: Different themes on the same Delahaye Type 135 chassis. The stark sports car was developed to race – Arthur Dobson winning the celebrated Brooklands 'Fastest Road Car' event in 1939. The drop head (below) was a fast road version.

The first shaft-driven cars arrived in 1907 and a V6 project (remarkably early in the history of the motor car) in 1912. During World War 1, the company produced a great variety of items for the war effort, including vast quantities of rifles, stationary engines, gun parts and aircraft components. After the war, the company settled down to build dull and dependable cars, usually of rather backward design.

It was necessary to modernise the car line in a big way and, with the current ▶

range selling rather badly, the new design was first shown in 1933 at the Paris Show. Not only did it have a light and modern chassis layout, with independent front suspension, but there was a choice of a 3.3-litre, six-cylinder engine or a related 2.1-litre 'four', backed by the Cotal electro-magnetic gearbox or a synchromesh change to choice. The short cut was made possible without enormous investment because these engines were directly developed from units already in production for the company's commercial vehicles. Not only this, but for the first time in years, the Delahaye car had coachwork with distinct eye-appeal.

The larger six-cylinder car effectively was the prototype of the famous '135' series which was to serve Delahaye so well until the end of the 1940s. This design would probably not have done the job on its own, but this is uncertain because, in 1935, Delahaye took over the financially ailing Delage concern, where there was already an established clientele. Delage's elegance was therefore handed on to Delahaye, and helped to cause a dramatic change in their fortunes. A Superluxe six-cylinder car soon went to Monthléry to take 19 world and international class records, and when the same car later won an Alpine Coupe in the rally of that name, the Coupe des Alpes variant was born.

More important, though, in 1936, was the 'Competition' Type 135, with its enlarged 3½-litre engine. This car had a rather stark two-seater open body, with cycle-type wings, and a power output of no less than 160bhp (which was already up to Jaguar XK120 standards of more than ten years later). In the French GP of that year, a sports car race, the new cars finished 2nd, 3rd, 4th and 5th behind the winning Bugatti. A 3.2-litre car had already finished 5th at Le Mans in 1935, and one of the cars won the Monte Carlo Rally in 1937. In 1938, however, came

the crowning glory of outright victory at Le Mans in the 24-hour race, which completely set the seal on the worth of the Type 135. By comparison with Delage, too, Delahaye was very much the dominant part of the business and they introduced a V12-engined car for competition use in France, which produced no less than 250bhp.

The Type 135 was not, however, solely a competition car. Many were supplied with lusciously appointed coachwork, perhaps not quite with the restrained elegance of a Hispano-Suiza or a Rolls-Royce, but certainly fit to be used (as they often were) in the smart areas of Paris and on the Riviera. They usually looked, as they were, very fast, and always seemed to offer a great deal of comfort and refinement. When the six-cylinder engine's lorry origins are considered, this is remarkable. The chassis and roadholding were advanced, especially by previous Delahaye standards and especially when compared with many of the expensive competitive limousines. The car went out of production after France joined the fighting in 1839, but after concentrating on truck production during the war (at the behest of the Germans) the company came back in 1946 with up-dated Type 135s. They were now even more expensive, relatively speaking, than before, and the market for such cars in a post-war France was small.

The Type 175S model was introduced in 1948 (with a larger seven-bearing, 4½-litre engine); the chassis included De Dion rear suspension. This car was nevertheless dropped in 1951 in favour of the Type 235, which was effectively a 1938-type 135 chassis with an up-rated, 152bhp, engine and more modern Charbonneux-styled coachwork. Delahaye were taken over by Hotchkiss in 1954, after which car production ceased in favour of trucks.

Below and left: 1938 31/2-litre Type 135M Delahaye, with Carlton Carriage Co. saloon body, reminiscent in some ways of the late-1930s SS-Jaguars.

Delaunay-Belleville 'Sixes'

Type H models, built from 1908 to 1910, and Type HB, built from 1911 to 1914 (data for Type HB)

Built by: S.A. des Automobiles Delaunay-Belleville, France.

Engine: Six cylinders, in line, on three-bearing light-alloy crankcase, topped by two pairs of three-cylinder cast-iron blocks. Bore and stroke 85mm by 130mm, 4,426cc (3.35in × 5.12in, 270cu.in). Fixed cylinder heads. Two side valves per cylinder, directly operated from single camshaft mounted in side of crankcase. Single Delaunay-Belleville carburettor. Rated at 15-20CV French taxation class. Actual power output about 30bhp.

Transmission: Leather-cone clutch attached to engine. Separate four-speed manual gearbox (without synchromesh), with remote-control right-hand gearchange. Propeller shaft with spring buffers, to relieve torque reaction, and straight-level 'live' rear axle.

Chassis: Separate pressed-steel chassis frame, with channel-section side members, channel and tubular cross bracing. Forged front axle beam. Front suspension by half-elliptic leaf springs. Rear suspension by half-elliptic leaf

Below: This magnificent 1910 Type HB may look like a cab, but Burlington Carriage built it as a town car.

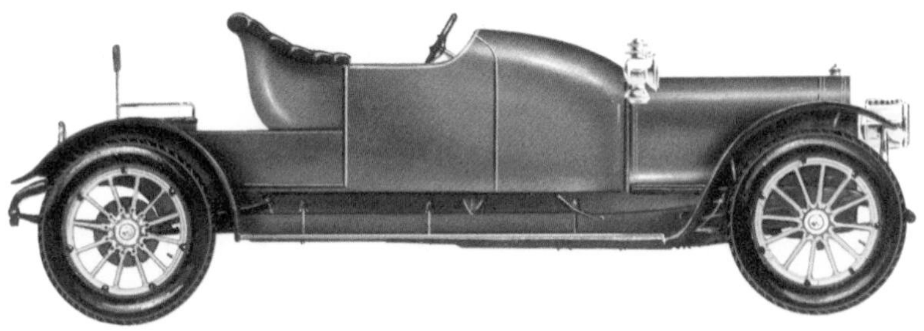

Above and below: Two contrasting body styles on Delaunay-Belleville chassis show that not every customer wanted his expensive French car for formal purposes. The red sports car was made in 1911, with a Torpedo style, fixed bucket seats, and a perch behind them for occasional (and unlucky!) extra travellers. The impressive Type HB car by the British Burlington Carriage company was obviously used by the type of person who might also buy a Napier or a Rolls-Royce. The owner travelled in enclosed comfort, with a landaulette hood to be dropped if the weather permitted. The chauffeur had to sit in the open behind a big screen. The car had a six-cylinder $4^{1}/_{2}$-litre engine.

springs, along with transverse 'helper' leaf spring. Worm-and-nut steering. Footbrake acting on transmission drum behind gearbox. Handbrake acting on drums fixed to rear wheels. Fixed artillery-style wooden wheels (detachable rums from 1913). 880 × 120mm tyres.

Dimensions: Wheelbase 10ft 6in (320cm), tracks (front and rear) 4ft 7.5in (141cm). Overall length, depending on coachwork, from 14ft 10in (452cm). Unladen weight (chassis only) 2,000lb (907kg).

History: Delaunay-Belleville made their first cars in 1904 and soon developed them into exclusive landaulettes and limousines, intended for the carriage trade and for chauffeur-driven transport. Like most other makers of the period, they started by building four-cylinder engines, but as the multi-cylinder craze spread across Europe they were not slow to join in that particular race. In many ways, Delaunay-Belleville had similar fortunes to those of Napier, although their cars were never as sporting; they soldiered on in production until 1950, but towards the end they were merely building tiny numbers of 1930s designs suitably updated.

The very first six-cylinder car from Delaunay-Belleville at St Denis, near Paris, was an 8-litre monster, with separate cylinders, but at least it had a seven-bearing crankshaft and simple 'L-head' valve gear arrangements. It was also chain-driven – another Edwardian 'standard' which was shortly to go out of fashion. All this was in 1908, by which time the Delaunay-Belleville marque was beginning to be talked of as the finest car in France, if not in the whole of Europe.

By 1909 there were no fewer than five six-cylinder models in the line-up, of which the mainstay engine was the H-series. This was built right up to the outbreak of war in 1914, as the H (or, retrospectively known, the HA) until 1910 and the HB thereafter. Like the British Napier or Rolls-Royce 'sixes', with which there were certain similarities of basic layout it had its cylinder blocks cast in groups – in this case in two groups of three cylinders each. The French car, however, did not trust the properties of existing cylinder head gaskets, and used integrally cast cylinder heads.

Valve gear, as with the pioneering Model-C 'six', used a simple 'L-head' layout,

which meant that valves had to be withdrawn through detachable compression caps in the fixed cylinder head for attention. Surprisingly enough, the crankshaft was provided with only three main bearings, even less than a normally expected four-bearing layout, which indicates how understressed and slow-revving the unit was. The rest of the car, mechanically, was conventional enough with a leather-cone clutch and a massive separate gearbox with the usual right-hand change. Delaunay-Belleville, after all, were offering comfort, reliability, and dignified grace, with the accent on smooth motoring in the finest possible coachwork. The circular radiator was an obvious D-V trademark and many of the cars were distinguished by their high and handsome coachwork. There were 'colonial' models with raised ground clearance, and 'light' models with shorter wheelbases and less passenger space.

In the period from 1908 to 1914, no fewer than 2,227 examples of the H-series cars were built and sold. In spite of this search for a 'best car' reputation, the British price of £600 or French price of 15,000 francs (both for the chassis only) were substantially under those quoted by Rolls-Royce and others. Fittings like wheels fixed to their axles (without even detachable wheel rims until 1913) would have irritated the owner-driver, but D-V expected every owner to have a chauffeur to do that sort of job for him, and to drive the car. Very few of the bodies added to the H-series chassis had completely closed bodies and a few were clothed in very racy-looking open tourers. The 'Torpedo de Luxe' had two seats behind that massively long bonnet and a swelling scuttle, and contrived to look the image of a Mercer.

Among the distinguished customers were Czar Nicholas II of Russia, who specified a Barbey compressed-air starter, which was an optional extra. The cars were so tough and reliable that they were used as staff cars and ambulances during World War 1, and such conversions as the fire engine used in Britain in the 1920s were not unexpected. As the Napier in Britain, however, Delaunay-Belleville cars did not generate their own (Rolls-Royce-type) legends, and began a long and slow decline in the 1920s from which they never really recovered. Their great days, the H-series days, were from 1910 to 1914.

Left: The big six-cylinder cars from Delaunay-Belleville were dignified, and attracted bodywork to suit. This 1911 Type HB had a Surelévé Double Berline style quite obviously related to town carriages of old. Clearly it was chauffeur driven, and gives the impression of two separate cabins.

Doble Steam Car

Four-cylinder Model E, built from 1923 to 1932 (data for 1923 model)
Built by: Doble Steam Motors Corporation, United States.
Engine: Four cylinder, double-acting, balanced-compound steam engine, with pairs of cast-iron cylinders (one high-pressure, one low-pressure) and one valve chest per block. Blocks fixed to four-bearing light-alloy crankcase, itself integral with rear axle. Bore and stroke (high-pressure cylinder) 66.7mm by 127mm (2.62in × 5.0in), and (low-pressure cylinder) 114.3mm by 127mm (4.5in × 5.0in). Total swept volume 3,494cc (213.2cu.in). Stephenson-link valve gear and piston-type valves. Seamless steel steam generator, 575.7ft (175.5m long, of forced-circulation, water-tube type.
Transmission: No clutch and no variable-transmission gearbox. Engine in horizontal position, under rear seats, pointing forward, and crankshaft directly linked to 'live' rear axle. No gearchange. Remote-control steam cut-off mechanism, on steering column.
Chassis: Separate pressed-steel chassis frame, with channel-section side members, tubular and pressed cross bracing. Forged front axle beam. Steam generator under 'bonnet', engine under rear seats. Front and rear suspension by semi-elliptic leaf springs. Lever-arm hydraulic dampers. Worm-and-wheel steering. Rear-wheel drum brakes; foot operation and hand operation (both mechanical) side by side and independent. Bolt-on steel disc or bolt-on wire wheels. 6.2in section tyres. Choice of open or closed, touring or limousine coachwork.

Below: If ever a car deserves to be called exclusive, a Doble steam car is one such. Only about 42 Dobles were built between 1923 and 1932, though Abner Doble once said he was ready to make 1,000 cars every year. This 1925 tourer emulated the Springfield-built Rolls-Royces in every way but ultimate quality, and was impressively silent.

Dimensions: Wheelbase 11ft 10in (361cm), tracks (front and rear) 4ft 9in (145cm). Unladen weight, depending on bodywork chosen, 3,900lb to 4,550lb (1,769kg to 2,063kg).
History: Abner Doble was the grandson of a Scot who arrived in San Francisco in 1850. The family fortune was made in manufacturing mining tools, but Abner Doble built his first steam car in 1905. In 1914 he drove a prototype 'condenser' Doble to Detroit and found some backing for his project. The first car, a twin-cylinder steamer was offered for sale in 1917. About 80 cars of the Doble Detroit series were sold before he returned to San Francisco, joined with his three brothers, and offered the well-developed Series E and Series F four-cylinder cars from 1923. As steam cars go, it was very advanced, raised steam very rapidly from cold and had lots of performance and dignity to match its silence, but it was very expensive. Doble modelled his Emeryville factory on the Rolls-Royce operations at Springfield and since his selling prices were between $8,000 and $11,000 few cars were made and the market was restricted to the rich, the famous and the pleasure-seeking. No less a person than Howard Hughes bought a couple of them. In spite of early claims to be ready to make 1,000 cars a year, not more than 42 of the fine four-cylinder Dobles were ever built.

The company finally collapsed in 1931, never having made a profit on its car sales. Doble himself remained faithful to steam for the rest of his life, as a consultant to many companies making non-automotive steam engines.

Dodge Viper

Dodge Viper sports car, introduced in 1992 (data for original specification)
Built by: Chrysler Corporation, USA.
Engine: Ten cylinders, in 90-degree vee formation, in six-bearing light-alloy cylinder block/crankcase. Bore and stroke 101.6 × 98.6mm, 7,997cc (4.00 × 3.88in, 488cu.in). Two light-alloy cylinder heads. Two valves per cylinder, overhead and in line, operation by pushrods and rockers from a central camshaft in the vee. Maximum power 400bhp (DIN) at 4,600rpm. Maximum torque 450lb.ft at 3,200rpm.
Transmission: Rear-wheel drive, single-plate diaphragm spring clutch and six-speed all-synchromesh manual gearbox, all in unit with the front-mounted engine. Remote-control, central gearchange.
Chassis: Separate chassis frame, with box section main members, and cross-bracing. Pressure-moulded plastic composite bodyshell. Independent front suspension by coil springs, wishbones, telescopic dampers and anti-roll bar. Independent rear suspension by coil springs, wishbones, telescopic dampers and anti-roll bar. Rack-and-pinion steering, with power-assistance. Four-wheel disc brakes with vacuum-servo assistance, but no ABS anti-lock. 17in cast-alloy wheels, 275/40-17in (front) and 335/35-17in (rear) tyres.
Dimensions: Wheelbase 8ft 0.2in (244.3cm), front track 4ft 11.6in (151.4cm), rear track 5ft 0.6in (154cm). Overall length 14ft 7.1in (445cm). Unladen weight 3,200lb (1,452kg).
History: Without the drive and enthusiasm of Bob Lutz, the legendary Viper would never have been built. Lutz, an all-time car enthusiast, and ex-Ford at the very highest level, became Chrysler's president in the late 1980s. Along with Lee Iacocca, his exuberant chairman, and with gleeful help from Carroll Shelby, he helped the Viper move from Good Idea, to concept car, to production machine and, finally, to motoring icon.

First shown in 1989, as a one-off concept, the Viper eventually went on sale in 1992, a car inspired by the career of Shelby's 1960s Cobra (which Iacocca had always loved, and which also explains the serpent's name which was chosen),

Below: AC Cobra influence, if not shared parts, was found in the Viper (hence the choice of name), which had a simple chassis, a hugely powerful engine and lightweight body construction.

Above: The Viper's sensational styling hid a 400bhp V10 engine, a six-speed gearbox, and all-independent suspension. Those side-mounted exhaust pipes meant business.

and in general layout as near to a direct descendant as possible. Like the Cobra, it combined a two-seater layout with a massively powerful engine, an outrageous character, and colossal performance. Americans had loved the Cobra in the 1960s, and a new generation loved the Viper in the 1990s.

Although the styling of the plastic-bodied two-seater shell (by Tom Gale of Chrysler's own design studios) was outrageous enough – deep skirts along the flanks, exhaust pipes poking out through them, scoops behind the front wheels to pull hot air out of the engine bay, and originally only one colour, bright red – this all hid a perfectly conventional (by USA standards) separate steel chassis frame, though this had all-independent suspension, fat tyres and the ability to hold the road well in most conditions.

The secret of the Viper's appeal was in its engine, a huge 8-litre V10, the like of which no American car lover had ever seen before. Deep down, in its origins, there was a cast iron engine intended for use in Chrysler Corporation trucks, but this was a specialised, all-aluminium, version of the same which had been evolved with the aid of Chrysler's then-associate company, Lamborghini, still with overhead valve gear, but much more ambitiously tuned, with fuel injection, fabricated exhaust manifolds, and every feasible performance trick. With a dry sump lubrication system, it produced a bellowing 400bhp – and not even Chevrolet's Corvette XZR-1 could match that. The performance – which included a top speed of nearly 160mph – was at a level very few would ever experience, but the potential, the traffic light kudos, and the general threatening character, all made it a matchless prospect.

Most original Viper owners always used their cars with the top open, though wimps could use a rather flimsy soft-top (which was almost a Surrey top, in view of the large and functional roll-over hoop behind the seats) if it rained. All of them loved the six-speed Borg Warner transmission which allowed them to produce engine booming noises at every opportunity. With no automatic transmission option, this was a uniqiue American car for the period.

Sales, as expected, were steady – thousands rather than millions, every year – but market appeal was improved by the arrival of the fastback GTS Coupé in 1993. Further even-higher-powered types were raced with success, and sold in small numbers, the Viper entering the new century as the continuing sporty icon of the Chrysler corporation's range.

Duesenberg Model A

Model A, built from 1921 to 1927
Built by: Duesenberg Motor Co., United States.
Engine: Eight cylinders, in line, in three-bearing cast-iron cylinder block. Bore and stroke 73.0mm by 127.0mm, 4,261cc (2.875in × 5.00in, 260cu.in). Detachable cast-iron cylinder head. Two overhead valves per cylinder, opposed to each other in part-spherical combustion chamber, and operated by rockers from single overhead camshaft. Single updraught Stromberg carburettor (later cars had Schebler unit). Maximum power 90bhp at 3,6000rpm. Maximum torque 170lb.ft at 1,500rpm.
Transmission: Single-dry-plate clutch and three-speed manual gearbox (without synchromesh), bot in unit with front-mounted engine. Direct-acting central gearchange. Propeller shaft enclosed in torque tube to spiral-bevel 'live' rear axle.
Chassis: Separate pressed-steel chassis frame, with channel-section side members, fabricated and tubular cross bracings. Tubular front axle beam. Front and rear suspension by half-elliptic leaf springs; rear axle located by radius arms. Watson Stabilator dampers at front and rear. Four wheel, hydraulically acting on drum brakes fixed to transmission shaft behind gearbox. Centre lock wire wheels, with 5in × 33in tyres.
Dimensions: Wheelbase 11ft 2in (340cm), front and rear tracks 4ft 8in (142cm).

Overall length depending on coachwork, from 15ft 11.5in (486cm).

History: The Duesenberg brothers first made their names as racing car designers, but decided to make road cars just a year after their 'straight eight' machine won its first big event. The road car was intended to have engines with horizontal valve gear, but 1920 race engines were so successful that their single-overhead-camshaft layout was adopted for road use, in a much bigger unit altogether. This was odd in that it only had three main bearings (which is theoretically undesirable), but was reliable in service.

The Duesenberg Eight (the 'A' followed years later, as a bastardisation of 'Eight' and was never an official title), pandered to the richest and most sporting North Americans, who wanted a lot of passenger space, and refused to use more than three gears. Therefore a splendidly detailed chassis was provided, and some extremely attractive American-vintage coachwork was conceived to suit. There were many racing-inspired details in chassis layout. Duesenbergs were used in all manner of long-distance and record attempts, and got involved very successfully in stock car racing. Supercharged versions were tried by the factory, but never sold. The company was taken over by E. L. Cord in 1926, who then prepared for a bigger, better and even more magnificent Duesenberg, the Model J.

Left: The Duesenberg brothers' first production car was the 'Eight' (which later became known as the 'A'), with a 4.3-litre straight-eight engine. Only the richest and most sporting of North Americans bought one, to enjoy the overhead camshaft engine's performance – this tourer body is by Springfield.

Duesenberg J and SJ

J and SJ models, built from 1928 and 1938 (data for Model J)
Built by: Duesenberg Motor Co., United States.
Engine: Eight cylinders, in line, in five-bearing cast-iron block/crankcase. Bore and stroke 95.25mm by 120.6mm, 6,882cc (3.75in × 4.75, 420cu.in). Detachable cast-iron cylinder head. Four overhead valves per cylinder (two inlet and two exhaust), opposed to each other at 70 degrees in part-spherical combustion chambers and operated by twin overhead camshafts. Single updraught twin-choke Schebler carburettor (from 1932, downdraught twin-choke Stromberg carburettor). Maximum power 265bhp (gross) at 4,250rpm.
Transmission: Double-dry-plate clutch and three-speed manual gearbox (without synchromesh), both in unit with front-mounted engine. Direct-acting central gearchange. Propeller shaft, enclosed in torque tube, to hypoid-bevel 'live' rear axle.
Chassis: Separate pressed-steel chassis frame, with channel-section side members, and tubular cross members. Forged front axle beam. Front suspension by half-elliptic leaf springs. Rear suspension by half-elliptic leaf springs and radius arms. Lever-type hydraulic dampers. Cam-and-lever steering. Four-wheel, hydraulically-operated drum brakes (with vacuum-servo assistance from 1930 models). Drum transmission handbrake. 19in centre-lock wire wheels, (17in optional from 1935).
Dimensions: Wheelbase 11ft 10.5in or 12ft 9.5in (362cm or 390cm), tracks

(front and rear) 4ft 8in (142cm). Overall length depending on coachwork 16ft 8in (508cm). Unladen weight from 5,000lb (2.268kg).

History: After his purchase of Duesenberg, E. L. Cord asked his engineers to produce an all-new car. This was revealed in December 1928, at the height of the American economic 'boom', and was advertised as 'The World's Finest Motor Car'. The Model J was magnificently engineered without an eye to cost, with a beautiful twin-cam engine, modern features, and some of the most sumptuous body styling America had yet seen.

The chassis price in 1929 was $8,500, which rose to $9,500 by 1932, and Cord intended it to be as good as a Rolls-Royce. To boost the performance even more (production cars could beat 110mph without much difficulty), the SJ arrived in 1932, where 'S' stood for 'supercharged', and the power output was boosted to an astonishing claimed 320bhp at 4,750rpm. Even if we take this as an exaggeration, the SJ was probably the world's most powerful production car. Two very special SSJ cars (Short Supercharged J models) were made – for Clark Gable and Gary Cooper.

Js and particularly SJs were sometimes stripped out for record attempts with great success, Ab Jenkins taking international class records at Utah at 152mph in 1935. The Cord Corporation collapsed in 1937, taking the J/SJ cars with it, which was rough justice after the car had survived the Great Depression. Rather fewer than 500 examples were built in all.

Left: Perhaps the most desirable of all American vintage cars was the Duesenberg Model J, with twin-cam 6.9-litre engines. SJs were supercharged.

Ferrari 250GT Berlinetta

250GT series, built from 1953 to 1964 (data for 1959 Berlinetta)
Built by: SEFAC Ferrari, Maranello, Italy.
Engine: 12 cylinders, in 60-degree vee-formation, in seven-bearing light-alloy block/crankcase. Bore and stroke 73mm by 58.8mm, 2,953cc (2.86in × 2.31in, 180.2cu.in). Two detachable light-alloy cylinder heads. Two overhead valves per cylinder, opposed to each other in part-spherical combustion chambers and operated by rockers from single overhead camshaft per cylinder head. Three down-draught twin-choke Weber carburettors. Maximum power 260bhp (net) at 7,000rpm.
Transmission: Twin-dry-plate clutch and four-speed, synchromesh manual gearbox, both in unit with front-mounted engine. Remote-control central gearchange. Open propeller shaft to hypoid-bevel 'live' rear axle.
Chassis: Separate multi-tubular chassis frame, with large-section side members and tubular cross bracing. Independent front suspension by coil springs, wishbones and anti-roll bar. Rear suspension by half-elliptic leaf springs and radius arms. Lever-arm hydraulic dampers. Worm-and-wheel steering. Four-wheel hydraulically operated disc brakes. Centre-lock wire wheels. 175 × 400 tyres.
Dimensions: Wheelbase 7ft 10.5in (240cm), track (front) 4ft 5.3in (135.4cm), track (rear) 4ft 5.1in (135cm). Overall length 13ft 7.5in (415cm). Unladen weight 2,400lb (1,088kg).
History: Ferrari's first attempt at building a Gran Turismo car was the 250 Europa of 1953, but unlike all its descendants this model was powered by the large Lampredi-designed V12. The 250GT, which followed in 1954, reverted to the original Colombo V12. The chassis was Ferrari-conventional, being built up of large-diameter tubing, and there was a front-mounted all synchromesh gearbox and a live rear axle located by leaf springs and radius arms. The Berlinetta cars (much lighter than production two-seater coupés) began to appear in the mid

Above: Inevitably the 250GT range was stretched – the original 250GT 2 + 2 was a Farina-styled 1960 model.

1950s and were intended for competition purposes. The name has been applied indiscriminately to *all* 250GTs, particularly those with short wheelbases, although the true Berlinettas, which became famous in GT racing, were built from 1959 to 1962, with that distinctive body by Scaglietti. Steel-bodied versions of these cars, rightly, became legendary and about 80 were made all in all. Out of the Berlinetta, of course, came the 250GTO, which was a pure competition car, and the 250GT Lusso, which was a pure road car. Successor to all of them, of course, was the smooth 275GTB, with its axle-mounted gearbox and 'rope-drive' propeller shaft. The 250GT cars, however, are those which truly signify Ferrari's change from being a racing car maker to being a production car maker.

Below: Simply styled but brutally attractive short-wheelbase Ferrari 250GT Berlinetta, bodied by Scaglietti – made 1959 to 1962.

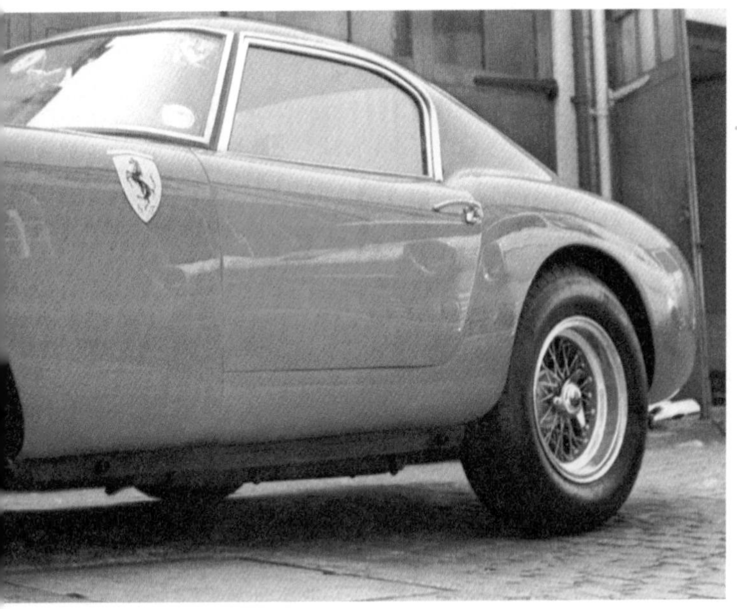

Ferrari Type 340/375 Sports Cars

340 and 375 models, built from 1951 to 1954 (data for 1954 Le Mans car)
Built by: Auto Costruzione Ferrari, Italy.
Engine: 12 cylinders, in 60-degree vee-formation, in seven-bearing cast-alloy block/crankcase. Bore and stroke 84mm by 74.5mm, 4,954cc (3.31in × 2.93in, 302.3cu.in). Two detachable light-alloy cylinder heads, complete (when assembled) with screwed-in cylinder liners. Two overhead valves per cylinder, opposed to each other at 60 degrees in part-spherical combustion chambers and operated by rockers from single overhead camshaft per cylinder head. Three down-draught twin-choke Weber carburettors. Maximum power 344bhp (net) at 6,500rpm.
Transmission: Multi-dry-plate clutch in unit with engine. Open propeller shaft to four-speed manual gearbox in unit with chassis-mounted spiral-beval final drive, with limited-slip differential. Remote-control central gearchange. Exposed, universally jointed drive shafts to rear wheels.
Chassis: Separate tubular-steel frame, with large elliptic-section side members and tubular cross-bracing. Independent front suspension by transverse leaf spring, wishbones and rubber blocks. Rear suspension De Dion, by transverse leaf spring and radius arms. Lever-arm hydraulic dampers. Worm-and-wheel steering. Four-wheel, hydraulically operated drum brakes. 16in centre-lock wire wheels. 6.50 × 16in (front) and 7.50 × 16in (rear) tyres.
Dimensions: Wheelbase 8ft 6.5in (260cm), track (front) 4ft 2in (127cm), track

Above: Mike Hawthorn driving a 340MM sports-racing Ferrari at Silverstone in 1953. It had a 4.1-litre vee-12 engine and the body is by Touring of Milan. He won the sports car race outright.

(rear) 4ft 2.5in (128cm). Overall length 13ft 7.5in (415.5cm) Unladen weight 2,204lb (1,000kg).

History: This very successful impressive and at times brutally fast series of sports-racing cars evolved directly from the fact that Ferrari had developed a powerful and very reliable new V12 engine for Grand Prix racing. Whereas the Colombo-designed Type 125 V12 started life at 1½ litres and grew eventually to well over 3 litres, the new unit by Lampredi was always laid out with a 4½-litre GP capacity in mind and proved capable of even further stretching. In sports-racing, or even in production-car form, it was produced in 3.3-litre, 4.1-litre, 4.5- ▶

Below: The sleek lines and the usual Ferrari badging do nothing to hide the brutal menace of Gonzales' 1954 Le Mans 375S model. Its 4.9-litre engine produced a dead-reliable 344bhp.

litre and in two 4.9-litre forms, usually with a combination of twin-choke Weber carburettors and always with the classic single- overhead-camshaft cylinder heads to which non-GP Ferraris were faithful for so long. The GP cars of 1950 and 1951, which used the basic 'building block' of this engine, were fitted with twin-cam cylinder heads. Apart from the fact that the engine was physically larger (and was therefore stronger with some built-in stretch), it was also distinguished by the fact that the wet cylinder liners were screwed into the cylinder heads, thereby ensuring a water-tight and gas-tight head/cylinder joint. Especially with his supercharged V12s. Colombo had experienced trouble with gasket failures, which this new design very effectively overcame.

The Type 275S car was not a success, because the transmission to deal with massive increases in torque and power was not ready, but the Type 340/342 cars which followed in 1951 were much improved. The chassis, used by racing cars and production America models alike, was based on elliptic-section tubing, with transverse-leaf-spring front suspension. The gearbox was front mounted at first, but for the 1954-6 375 Plus and 410 Plus models a four-speed unit, placed together with the differential of the De Dion rear axle was fitted, being a direct crib from the old Grand Prix car thinking. The Type 340MM (Mille Miglia) won its first event – appropriately enough the Mille Miglia of 1953, but the Type 340 Mexico had already won the Panamerica Road Race in Mexico in 1951. After that Italian success the cars' engines were enlarged to 4.5-litres and given extremely attractive closed Pininfarina bodies. They had no success at Le Mans, but won several other long-distance sports car races that year. For 1954 the ultimate 375 Plus car appeared, with a low-revving 4.0-litre engine and the back-axle-mounted gearbox. It was really the ultimate in brute-force machines, very powerful, very noisy and rather unwieldy, but it was geared for something like 180mph at Le Mans and other fast circuits and seemed to have a completely unburstable engine which, after all, was considerably derated from the Grand

Prix units. In the event the Gonzales/Trintignant car won the 1954 Le Mans outright from the first of the D-type Jaguars, but it was not the easy victory which had been prophesied, as the car suffered various electrical problems. The same model of car was good enough to win the Carrera Panamerica again and also to take the Buenos Aires 1,000km sports car race, before Ferrari were ready to supersede it with a new family of straight-six-engined cars. The last cars, however, were phenomenally powerful – their outright output of 380bhp was not to be beaten until the more-developed rear-engined 330P racing sports cars arrived at the beginning of the 1960s – but even shortened wheelbases and attention to suspension could not solve their brutish handling. The series had been developed specifically to attack so-called 'sports car' races, but were so obviously related to the 4½-litre Formula One cars that it brought this class of racing into disrepute. The only Ferrari production cars to benefit from their experiences were the small-production Americas and Superfasts.

Below: The nose was typical of early-1950s Ferraris, and on this car most of the tail was filled by the vast fuel tank. The gearbox was fixed to the differential, and the car could reach 180mph in a straight line.

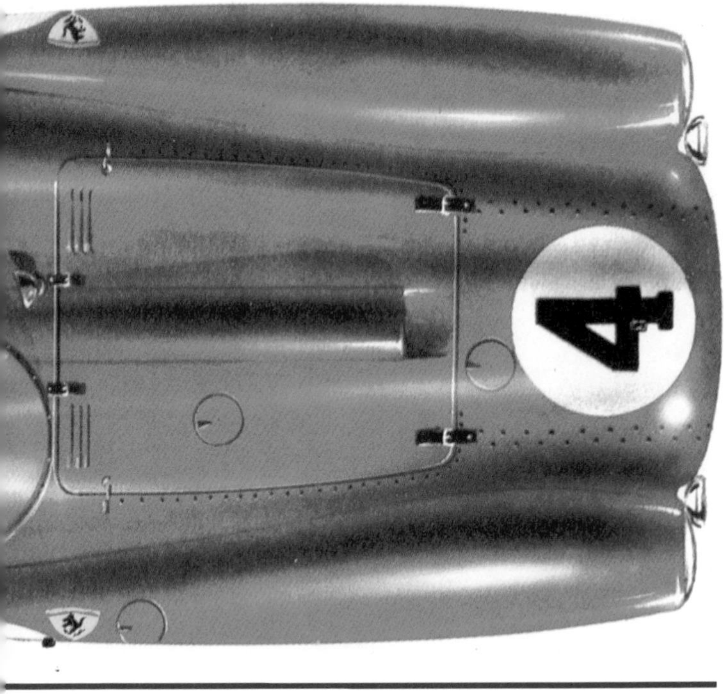

Ferrari 365GTB4 Daytona

Daytona model, built from 1968 to 1974
Built by: SEFAC Ferrari, Maranello, Italy.
Engine: Twelve cylinders, in 60-degree vee-formation, in seven-bearing cast-alloy block/crankcase. Bore and stroke 81mm by 71mm, 4,390cc (3.10in × 2.79in, 268cu.in). Two detachable light-alloy cylinder heads. Two overhead valves per cylinder, inclined to each other in part-spherical combustion chambers and operated by inverted-bucket tappets from twin overhead camshafts per cylinder head. Six down-draught twin-choke Weber carburettors. Maximum power 352bhp (DIN) at 7,500rpm. Maximum torque 318lb.ft at 5,500rpm.
Transmission: Single-dry-plate clutch in unit with front-mounted engine. Torque tube and enclosed propeller shaft to combined gearbox/differential transaxle. Five-speed, all-indirect, all-synchromesh manual gearbox, and hypoid-bevel differential with limited-slip device, all chassis mounted. Exposed, universally jointed drive shafts to rear wheels.
Chassis: Separate multi-tubular steel chassis frame, with light-alloy closed two-seater coupé coachwork by Scaglietti. All independent suspension coil springs, wishbones and anti-roll bars, with telescopic dampers. Worm-and-nut steering. Four-wheel, hydraulically operated ventilated disc brakes, with vacuum servo assistance. 15in centre-lock cast-alloy road wheels. 215/70VR15in tyres.
Dimensions: Wheelbase 7ft 10.5in (240cm), track (front) 4ft 8.5in (143.5cm), track (rear) 4ft 8in (142cm). Overall length 14ft 6in (442cm). Unladen weight 3,530lb (1,600kg).
History: To replace the long-running 250GT production cars, with their conventional mechanical layout and obligatory V12 engines, Ferrari launched the 275GTB in 1964. This was improved to become the 275GTB4 in 1966. Although it remained true to the traditions, with front-mounted V12 engine and two-door

two-seater coupé body, it had a multi-tubular chassis frame, all-independent coil-spring suspension and the five-speed gearbox in unit with the chassis-mounted differential.

There was little doubt that the four-cam 275GTB4 (with the final stretch of the original Colombo-type engine) was one of the fastest cars in the world, but Ferrari was not satisfied. In the autumn of 1968, his engineers had produced the delectable 365GTB4 Daytona car, which did everything that the now obsolete 275GTB4 could have done, but also had the massively powerful four-cam 4.4-litre engine and dramatically styled body (by Pininfarina) constructed as usual by Scaglietti. The 275GTB4's basic chassis and mechanical layout were retained, including the rear-positioned gearbox. However, the front and rear wheel tracks were wider and the shovel-nosed shape, with its hidden headlamps, was more shapely even than before. With all that power, the Daytona was tremendously fast. Its maximum speed was between 175 and 180mph, it could break almost any limit in the world in its 86mph second gear, and beat 140mph in fourth! Without any doubt it was the world's fastest production car, faster even than the Lamborghini Miura, in the six years it was on sale. Yet the whole business of going fast was carried out in exemplary Ferrari manner, with refinement to suit the high price, and the most amazingly flexible engine, as one had come to expect from the Maranello-built products.

The only way for the car to be significantly improved would have been to make it faster, or even more docile, but Ferrari was not interested in half-measures. He had decided that the Daytona should be the last of his front-engined super-car two-seaters and from 1974 it was deposed by the wickedly attractive mid-engined Berlinetta Boxer, with a new flat-12 power unit, also of 4.4-litres. To drive a Daytona was a truly memorable and exciting experience.

Left: When launched in 1968, the Daytona set new standards in several areas, notably in performance, and in its startling looks. Speeds of 170mph+ were always possible, and were achieved with huge panache.

Ferrari Type 375 America

America models, built from 1951 to 1959 (data for 375 model of 1953)
Built by: SEFAC Ferrari, Maranello, Italy.
Engine: 12 cylinders, in 60-degree vee-formation, in seven-bearing light-alloy block/crankcase. Bore and stroke 84mm by 68mm, 4,522cc (3.31in × 2.68in, 276cu.in). Two detachable light-alloy cylinder heads, complete (when assembled) with screwed-in cylinder liners. Two overhead valves per cylinder, opposed to each other at 60 degrees in part-spherical combustion chambers and operated by rockers from single overhead camshaft per cylinder head. Camshaft drive by chain from nose of crankshaft. Hairpin valve springs. Three down-draught twin-choke Weber carburettors. Maximum power 300bhp (net) at 6.300rpm.
Transmission: Multi-dry-plate clutch and four-speed, synchromesh manual gearbox, both in unit with front-mounted engine. Remote-control central gearchange. Open propeller shaft to hypoid-level 'live' rear axle.
Chassis: Separate multi-tubular chassis frame, with elliptic-section-tubing side members and tubular cross bracing. Independent front suspension by transverse leaf spring, wishbone and integral rubber block. Rear suspension by semi-elliptic leaf springs and twin radius arms. Lever-arm hydraulic dampers. Worm-and-wheel steering. Four-wheel, hydraulically operated drum brakes.

15in centre-lock wheels. 7.10 × 15in tyres.
Dimensions: Wheelbase 9ft 2.7in (280cm), track (front) 4ft 2in (132.5cm), track (rear) 4ft 3in (132cm). Unladen weight 2,205lb (1,000kg).
History: To add to the limited appeal of the 166s, 195s and 212 Inters. Ferrari introduced a much bigger car specifically for the North American market, the first being the Type 342 America of 1952. Much of the chassis engineering was based on Ferrari's racing sports cars and the engine was a detuned Lampredi-type V12, as used in the 4½-litre Grand Prix cars. The 375 America followed, with 4,522cc in place of 4,101cc and 300bhp instead of 220bhp, which made it more attractive to the customers. Once the big 4.9-litre engine had proved itself at Le Mans and in other road races, it was adopted (in detuned form) for the Type 410 Superamerica, which carried on in small-scale and exclusive production until 1959. The cars' charm was in their exquisite engines and in their parentage. Both styles varied, according to customer taste, but those magnificent and sensuous-sounding V12 engines persisted. Enormously fast two-seater cars could not possibly be very practical, but they were *the* most glamorous form of transport. Out of the Americas came the Type 410 Superfast, the even more rare Type 500 Superfast and – eventually – the more modern Type 365GT 2 + 2 cars. All these were the largest, the fastest and the most desired of Ferrari's road cars.

Below: The 342 America donated much of its chassis and drive line to this Type 375MM racing sports car, a two-seater where roadholding and sophistication were always subservient to brute power.

Ferrari Boxer

Boxer 365GT4/BB and 512GT4/BB – 1971 to 1984 (data for 365GT4/BB)
Built by: SEFAC Ferrari, Maranello, Italy.
Engine: Twelve cylinders, in horizontally opposed formation, based on seven-bearing light-alloy crankcase and cylinder blocks. Bore and stroke 81mm by 71mm, 4,390cc (3,19in × 2.79in, 267cu.in). Two light-alloy cylinder heads. Two valves per cylinder, inclined in part-spherical combustion chambers and operated by inverted bucket tappets from twin overhead camshafts per bank. Four triple-choke Weber carburettors. Maximum power 380bhp (DIN) at 7,700rpm. Maximum torque 318lb.ft at 3,900rpm.
Transmission: Mid-engine layout, with engine above and ahead of line or rear wheels. Single-dry-plate clutch behind transaxle and five-speed, all-synchromesh manual gearbox in unit with, and under, engine. Spiral-bevel final drive unit with limited-slip differential at rear of gearbox. Exposed, universally jointed drive shafts to rear wheels.
Chassis: Separate multi-tube steel chassis frame, mainly square-section tubes, with box and sheet cross bracing. Independent front suspension by coil springs, wishbones and anti-roll bar. Telescopic dampers. Rack-and-pinion steering. Four-wheel, hydraulically operated disc brakes with vacuum servo assistance. 15in cast-alloy, centre-lock road wheels. 215VR15in tyres.
Dimensions: Wheelbase 8ft 2.5in (250cm), track (front) 4ft 11in (150cm), track (rear) 5ft (152cm). Overall length 14ft 3.7in (436cm). Unladen weight 2,480lb (1,123kg).

Below: The original Boxer was the first 12-cylinder mid-engined Ferrari road car, though there was much racing expertise to draw on. Shaped by Pininfarina, it looked much like the 3208GTB which followed.

Above: Unmistakeable in looks, character, performance and sheer presence, the 365GT4/BB was a stunning mid-engined Supercar. In various forms, the Boxer would be built for 13 years.

History: Having developed, and made a success of, the mid-engined Dino, Ferrari next turned their attention to a really fast and brutal supercar. The result, first shown as a prototype in 1971, was the Berlinetta Boxer, which probably had more performance than any other car in the world. Only Lamborghini, with the Countach, would argue with that claim. Later, with a five-litre engine in the Boxer (since the autumn of 1976) Lamborghini's claim goes by default.

The engine itself was derived from that of the Grand Prix 3-litre unit, but had – sensibly – the same bore and stroke as the front-engined Ferraris. Unlike the smaller Dino, however, the engine/transmission layout was entirely different. Although the flat-12 sat in front of and above the final drive, its clutch was behind the centre line, and drop gears transferred the drive to a shaft into the gearbox which was below the engine and also ahead of the final drive. By comparison, the rest of the car was conventional Ferrari, with a multi-square-tube chassis frame, all-independent coil-spring suspension

and a sleekly-styled (by Pininafarina) body made in light alloy at the Scaglietti works near Maranello.

The secret of the car is not in the specification, nor in the looks, but in the manner of its performance. With a maximum speed of more than 170mph, Ferrari-like acceleration, and the noise that no other car in the world can match, the Boxer has to be the sexiest of all expensive GT cars. As a Ferrari, it has roadholding, aerodynamics and stability to match the colossal performance, and (if any car with this performance can be safe) it is immensely safe. Yet, for all that, it suffers from the mid-engined car's habitual disadvantage of having just two seats and very little stowage space. But the queuing customers for this superfast beauty seem not to care about this for a second.

Below: The Boxer was an elegant car, whose flat-12 engine was mounted behind the cabin. It was the ultimate playboy's Supercar, with enormous charisma.

Ferrari Dino

Dino 206GT and 246GT, built from 1967 to 1973 (data for 246GT)
Built by: SEFAC Ferrari, Maranello, Italy.
Engine: Six cylinders, in 65-degree vee-formation, in four-bearing cast-iron block, transversely mounted behind driving compartment. Bore and stroke 92.5mm by 60mm, 2,418cc (3.64in × 2.36in, 147.5cu.in). Light-alloy cylinder heads. Two valves per cylinder inclined to each other, in part-spherical combustion chambers and operated by inverted-bucket tappets from twin overhead camshafts per bank. Three down-draught twin-choke Weber carburettors. Maximum power 195bhp (DIN) at 7,600rpm. Maximum torque 166lb.ft at 5,500rpm.
Transmission: Single-dry-plate clutch and train of transfer gears to five-speed, all-synchromesh manual gearbox, mounted in unit with, but behind and below, the cylinder block. Remote control central gearchange. Hypoid-bevel final drive unit, with limited-slip differential at rear of gearbox. Exposed, universally jointed drive shafts to rear wheels.
Chassis: Fabricated tubular and sheet steel load-bearing chassis frame, with steel and light-alloy welded to it on assembly. Light-alloy skin panels, in two-seat coupé or spider construction. Engine/transmission unit behind driving compartment. All-independent suspension, by coil springs, wishbones, anti-roll bars and telescopic dampers. Rack-and-pinion steering. Four-wheel, hydraulically operated disc brakes, with vacuum servo assistance. 14in bolt-on cast-alloy road wheels. 205VR14in tyres.
Dimensions: Wheelbase 7ft 8.2in (234cm), track (front) 4ft 8.1in (142cm), track (rear) 4ft 7.1in (140cm). Overall length 13dt 9in (420cm). Unladen weight 2,400lb (1,088kg).
History: Ferrari's first mid-engined road car came about because of a desire to go racing in the 1967 Formula Two (which meant that engines had to be 'production' based), and because they were already committed to supplying such engines to Fiat for the same validation purpose. Mid-engined Dinos,

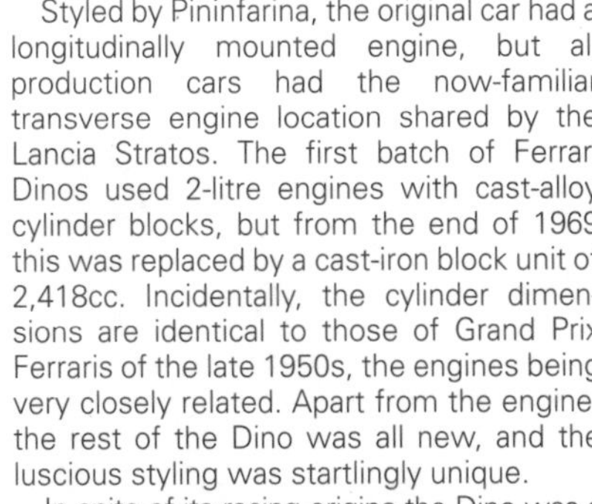

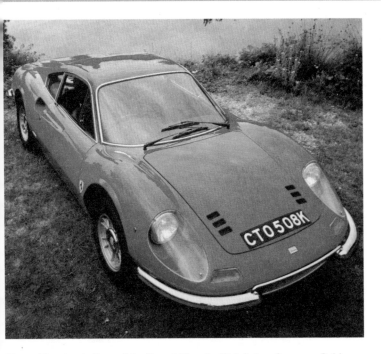

Above: The classic lines of the Ferrari Dino, by Pininfarina. Coupe or Spider versions were built. First cars had mid-mounted 2-litres, later 2.4-litres.

entirely different from the road cars, were raced in 1965 to 1967, but the first true prototype was shown in 1967.

Styled by Pininfarina, the original car had a longitudinally mounted engine, but all production cars had the now-familiar transverse engine location shared by the Lancia Stratos. The first batch of Ferrari Dinos used 2-litre engines with cast-alloy cylinder blocks, but from the end of 1969 this was replaced by a cast-iron block unit of 2,418cc. Incidentally, the cylinder dimensions are identical to those of Grand Prix Ferraris of the late 1950s, the engines being very closely related. Apart from the engine, the rest of the Dino was all new, and the luscious styling was startlingly unique.

In spite of its racing origins the Dino was a thoroughly practical road car, fast enough (about 140mph maximum speed) for almost everybody, and had remarkable roadholding powers. It was replaced in 1974 by the new and larger 308GTB car, with a new V8 engine.

Left: The lines effectively hide the mid-mounted engine position. The car was small, with impeccable road manners.

Ferrari F40

Ferrari F40 sports coupé, built from 1987 to 1992
Built by: Ferrari S.p.A., Italy.
Engine: Eight cylinders, in 90-deg formation, in cast-alloy cylinder block, crankcase. Bore and stroke 82 x 69.5mm, 2,936cc (3.23 x 2.74in, 179cu.in). Two light-alloy cylinder heads. Four valves per cylinder, in narrow vee-angle, operation by twin overhead camshafts and inverted bucket-type tappets. Weber-Marelli fuel injection and twin IHi turbochargers. Maximum power 478bhp (DIN) at 7,000rpm. Maximum torque 425lb.ft at 4,000rpm.
Transmission: Rear-wheel-drive, diaphragm spring clutch and five-speed all-synchromesh manual gearbox, all in unit with mid-mounted engine. Remote-control, central gearchange.
Chassis: Separate tubular/fabricated steel chassis frame, topped by Kevlar/carbon fibreglass-fibre body shell. Independent front suspension by coil springs, wishbones, telescopic dampers, anti-roll bar. Independent rear suspension by coil springs, wishbones, telescopoc dampers, and anti-roll bar. Rack-and-pinion steering. Four-wheel disc brakes, no servo assistance. Cast-alloy 17in road wheels, 245/40-17in (front) and 335/35-17in (rear) tyres.
Dimensions: Wheelbase 8ft 0.5in (245cm), front track 5ft 2.8in (159.4cm), rear track 5ft 3.2in (160.6cm). Overall length 14ft 3.6in (435.8cm). Unladen weight 2,425lb (1,100kg).
History: As every Ferrari enthusiast knows, the F40 model was designed as a fortieth anniversary model, to commemorate the birth of Ferrari road cars in 1947, and to offer the very best, the very latest, and the most astonishing combination of Ferrari engineering that was possible at the time. Within five years of its launch, the F40 was superseded by other, more exuberant, Ferraris,

Right: Once seen, never forgotten, the F40 had a low, ground-hugging, front end, complete with NACA-type air intakes. The vast rear spoiler was visible from all angles.

Below: Although the F40 was a road car, it was equipped as if motor racing was planned - hence the figure-hugging Sparco seats and full-harness safety belts.

but somehow it has never lost its reputation as the most exciting Ferrari road car of all time.

By comparison with some of its so-called rivals, in 1987 the F40 might have been considered unadventurous – no four-wheel-drive, no ABS brakes and no sophisticated suspension systems, for instance – yet it offered an abundance of sheer excitement. Preposterously fast (nobody seriously contested Ferrari's claim that it would exceed 200mph), achingly beautiful, and blessed with the sort of in-built charisma that stopped traffic at two hundred paces, the F40 didn't need any more equipment or a higher specification to make its point.

Without taking five years to design and develop the new car, and without using end-to-end whizz-bang high technology, Ferrari intended only to provide the fastest Ferrari so far, in its rawest form. They succeeded, totally. Having made 1,200 F40s in five years, they would close the production line and ignore a still bulging order book. Customers, they decided, would have to wait for another 'limited-edition' Ferrari in the mid-1990s – if the company could be bothered to make one.

The F40 was a direct descendant of the limited-production 288GTO, with a lot more power, and more obviously unique styling. Whereas the 288GTO had been derived from the 328GTB of the period (it looked very similar, even though the engine/transmission layout had been re-aligned), the F40 went its own, glorious, ▶

way. It was, above all, a light machine, for whereas the Porsche 959 which some might consider to be a rival tipped the scales at no less than 2,977lb/1,350kg, the more starkly presented F40 weighed no more than 2,425lb/1,100kg, which was a massive saving. Less weight equated to higher performance and, if anyone cared, potentially better fuel economy.

The chassis was essentially a tubular steel structure, which also incorporated bonded composite panels to endow greater rigidity and torsional stiffness. Ferrari reckoned that this was three times as rigid as a conventional steel frame would have been, but weighed perhaps 20 per cent less. There was tubular steel all around the passenger compartment, to provide a safety cage.

This Supercar was so characteristically Ferrari (and, in some ways, with typically rough-and-ready finishing to some joints and assemblies), in which the twin-turbocharged four-camshaft 90-degree V8 engine was mounted amidships, behind the two-seater cabin, driving the rear wheels through a five-speed transmission. To get the sort of power they required – 478bhp in this case – and to keep the weight down, Ferrari engineers developed the 288GTO's V8 a stage further (and, let us remember, this V8 had its original roots in the 308GTB of the mid-1970s). Keeping to the twin turbocharger layout – the F40, in fact, using one Japanese IHi turbo for each bank of four cylinders – the engine was enlarged to 2,936cc, further developed in detail, and eventually rated at 478bhp at a rousing 7,000rpm. Although the 288GTO had produced 400bhp, up to that time no other Ferrari road car unit had pushed out anything like the same power. Although the engine, the transmission, the rock-solid artisan-engineering tubular chassis and the all-independent suspension were all a logical development of what had gone before, it was the body style, its construction and the materials used which were so very advanced.

With the exception of the Testarossa of 1984, almost all previous Ferraris had been rounded, sinuous, creatures (not machines, you understand, but creatures), with sweeping lines over their wheels and their passenger cabins. Not the F40. Here was a two-seater coupé whose lines had been suggested by Pininfarina, but whose detail had then been finalised after many hours of wind-tunnel testing.

The shell itself was made up of 12 pieces of Kevlar/carbon fibre/glassfibre composite material – strong and light, so that the F40 could perform at its best.

Below: In spite of having a 478bhp/2.9-litre engine, the F40 was quite a compact car, its two-seater cabin being ahead of the turbocharged V8 engine. That spoiler was functional, not for decoration.

Above: The F40 was tightly but expertly packaged, with the turbocharged V8 engine behind the seats. Up front there was space only for the spare wheel - and a toothbrush. Note the huge width of rear tyres.

At the front it had a squared-up, almost flat, shovel-like nose, with a deep spoiler to channel air in the required direction. Headlamps were behind lift-up flaps, while there were two discreet NACA ducts in the 'bonnet' panel to channel fresh air to the interior. Air intakes for the engine bay were at the sides, 328GTB/288GTO-like, though detailed differently, and at the rear there was a large, full-width, fixed-incidence transverse aerofoil, the better to trim the high-speed handling. The cabin itself was pure two-seater, the roof blending sweetly into a tinted Perspex cover over the exposed engine, and liberally slatted to provide cooling.

It went as well, even better, than everyone expected. In a straight line, where excellence was expected, it always delivered – raucously, in a full-blooded way, time and time again. At speed it was as stable as hoped for – no high-speed journey, even on a limit-free German autobahn, ever caught out an F40 – and on twisty going it was sure-footed up to enormously high limits. The big disparity in tyre sections – 235/40 section at the front, and road-roller width 335-/35 section at the rear – saw to that. All this, allied to race-proved independent suspension, steering that was remarkably light even though there was no power assistance, and the sort of response that only professional racing drivers could treat as familiar, made it irresistible.

Even as the new century opened, the F40 was probably still the most desirable, the most spine-tingling, Ferrari of all, and one only has to look at the proven performance to see why. Maybe to experience the 200+ top speed was an academic wish, but the thrill of sprinting from rest to 100mph in a mere 8.8 seconds could make up for all that (current hot hatchbacks such as the Peugeot 205GTI and the Golf GTI were just hitting 60mph as the F40 sprinted past 'the ton').

So, what if the interior trim was stark, and the ground clearance flinched at every road hump in the world? What if it was almost impossibly expensive to insure, and costly to service? This was an F40, and this was the best.

Ferrari F355

Ferrari F355 sports coupé and cabriolet, built from 1994 to 1998
Built by: Ferrari S.p.A., Italy.
Engine: Eight cylinders in 90-deg V8 formation, in five-main-bearing light-alloy cylinder block/crankcase. Bore and stroke 85 x 77mm, 3,496cc (3.35 x 3.03in, 213.4cu.in). Two light alloy cylinder heads. Five valves per cylinder (three inlet, two exhaust), operation by twin overhead camshafts per head, with inverted bucket-type tappets. Bosch/Ferrari fuel injection. Maximum power 380bhp (DIN) at 8,250rpm. Maximum torque 268lb.ft at 6,000rpm.
Transmission: Rear-wheel-drive, diaphragm spring clutch and six-speed all-synchromesh manual gearbox, all in unit with mid/rear-mounted engine. Remote-control, central gearchange.
Chassis: Separate multi-tubular steel, with reinforcements, chassis frame, clad in steel-and-light alloy two-seater body shell. Independent front suspension by coil springs, wishbones, electronically adaptive telescopic dampers, anti-roll bar. Independent rear suspension by coil springs, wishbones, electronically adaptive telescopic dampers, anti-roll bar. Rack and pinion steering, with speed-sensitive power assistance. Four-wheel disc brakes, with power asistance, and ABS. Cast-alloy 18in road wheels, 225/40-18in (front) and 265/40-18in (rear) tyres.
Dimensions: Wheelbase 8ft 0.5in (245cm), front track 4ft 11.6in (151.4cm), rear track 5ft 3.6in (161.5cm). Overall length 13ft 11.3in (425cm). Unladen weight 3,135lb (1,422kg).
History: If the F40 was Ferrari's best-ever road car, so called, the F355 which arrived in 1994 was a contender for the best civilised, all-purpose, two-seater from the same stable. The two cars could not have been more different. The F40 was all about performance, and brushed aside many creature comforts, whereas the F355 was the all-can-do two-seater which could be fast or slow, could be driven in cities or on the highways, and would appeal to thousands.

Ferrari's 'small' V8 family had been founded in 1973 with the 308GTB, and progressed to the 328GT, which had then been supplanted by the 348tb of 1989. The F355 replaced the 348tb, and built on the previous reputation. The displaced 348tb had been good, but by Ferrari standards not quite good enough, particularly in its performance and its on-the-limit roadholding. For the F355 (note the new type of model naming policy) Ferrari aimed to improved on that.

Although the chassis, complete with its 96.5in/245cm wheelbase, was much as before, there had been development changes everywhere. The engine, too,

while still the same basic 90-degree V8 (and thus related to that of the F40), was 3,496cc instead of 3,405cc, had brand new cylinder heads with the fashionable five valves per cylinder which Ferrari F1 V12s were already using – and produced no less than 380bhp at 8,250rpm.

Because the F355, with its new, rounded, but somehow understated styling, was smaller than the 512TR (the reworked Testarossa, which was still being made) it was a faster, and better car in all respects – and this with 'only' 3.5-litres, only and with eight cylinders. It was no wonder that road testers raved the moment they were let loose in it, and why the customers' queues soon built up.

This time, it seemed, Ferrari had thought of everything. Not only was this the fastest V8-engined 'everyday' Ferrari so far, but it also seemed to be the most complete. The style, by Pininfarina, was smooth and understated (no side strakes this time, unlike the 2348tb), but this time it incorporated a smooth undertray to improve aerodynamic performance still further. Traditionalists saluted the return of circular tail lamps, while others wanted to know why there were no extravagant spoilers.

To match the 380bhp there was a new in-line close-ratio six-speed transmission (not even the F40 had had one of those), where the claimed top speed was 184mph, but where you could also beat 150mph in fifth. Acceleration was just as ferocious as expected, though the 265/40-section rear tyres did their very best to keep wheelspin in check.

The F355's most impressive feature was its completeness, for this was a car with roadholding as good as its performance, with looks matched to its equipment, with superlative power-assisted steering, sensitive brakes, ABS to take away all the pain and the worry, and a cabin in which (not always possible in earlier Ferraris, by the way) one could also relax.

Perhaps it was as well that the flat-12 Testarossa-based cars were already in their last manifestation, for the F355 surely out-gunned them in every respect. It was only when the 360 Modena came along in 1999 that we all realised that improvements were possible, after all.

Below: The F355 had its 380bhp engine behind the seats, and could reach 184mph. Until ousted by the new F360 Modena, it was the best all-round Ferrari ever built.

Ferrari Testarossa

Ferrari Testarossa sports coupé, built from 1984 to 1992

Built by: Ferrari S.p.A., Italy.

Engine: Twelve cylinders, horizontally opposed (sometimes called '180-deg vee'), in seven-bearing light-alloy cylinder block/crankcase. Bore and stroke 82 × 78mm, 4,942cc (3.228 × 3.071in, 301.7cu.in). Two light-alloy cylinder heads. Four valves per cylinder, arranged in narrow vee, operation by twin overhead camshafts per head, and inverted bucket-type tappets. Bosch KE-Jetronic fuel injection. Maximum power 390bhp (DIN) at 6,300rpm. Maximum torque 362lb.ft at 4,500rpm.

Transmission: Rear-wheel-drive, single-dry-plate diaphragm spring clutch and five-speed all-synchromesh manual gearbox, all in unit with mid-mounted engine. Remote-control, central gearchange.

Chassis: Separate multi-tubular steel chassis frame with reinforcements. Independent front suspension by coil springs, wishbones, telescopic dampers and anti-roll bar. Independent rear suspension by coil springs, wishbones, telescopic dampers, and anti-roll bar. Rack-and-pinion steering. Four-wheel disc brakes with hydraulic servo assistance. Cast-alloy 16in wheels, 225/50-16in (front) and 255/50-16in (rear) tyres.

Dimensions: Wheelbase 8ft 4.4in (255cm), front track 4ft 11.8in (151.8cm), rear track 5ft 5.4in (166cm). Overall length 14ft 8.6in (448.5cm). Unladen weight 3,675lb (1,670kg).

History: In the 1980s Ferrari would need a remarkable new model to improve on the charismatic Boxer, and they succeeded, flamboyantly, with the Testarossa. Bigger, better, faster and more recognisable than the Boxer had ever been, the Testarossa was Ferrari's most desirable road car in the late 1980s. The name itself – Testarossa, meaning 'red head' in Italian – was a nostalgic throwback to Ferrari's racing sports cars of the 1950s, though there was no mechanical connection of any type. The name, simply, referred to the colour in which the cylinder head castings were painted – just as they had been with the Le Mans race cars of the 1950s.

The looks – styling by Pininfarina, of course – told their own story, but there was much novelty under that lovely skin. Whereas the Boxer had always been a rounded two-seater, closely related to the 308/328 models with which it was

Below: Mechanically, the Testarossa was an evolution of the Boxer, but the wide body style made it all look brand new.

Above: Wider, lower and somehow squatter than the Boxer, the Testarossa fed its cooling radiators by air intakes behind the doors.

contemporary, the Testarossa was one on its own. Much flatter, squatter and somehow closer to the ground that the Boxer had ever been, the Testarossa was a wide two-seater coupe (Ferrari never sold drop-top versions, though handbuilt examples were eventually produced by privateers), with flamboyantly detailed air intakes for the radiators moulded along the sides, creasing the doors and piercing the rear wings.

Ferrari made no secret of the fact that the chassis was a logical and linear development of that of the final Boxer (the 512BBi), though with improvements at every turn, not only by relocating radiators and widening the tyres, but by radically upgrading the engine. The flat-12 engine, still of 4,942cc, still sat atop/ahead of the five-speed transmission/transaxle, and was placed behind the seats, but it now featured four-valves per cylinder, and produced 390bhp. The noise from this complex power unit was so intense that Ferrari owners ignored cabin sound levels, merely enjoying the music they could perceive.

Helped along by the need to cover the massive 255/50-16in rear tyres (which ran on 10in wide cast alloy rims), the Testarossa was the widest-yet Ferrari at 6ft 5.8in/197.6cm, looking and sounding as purposeful as any Supercar, anywhere in the world.

It performed the way that the looks suggested that it might – with colossal acceleration, and an exuberant combination of exhaust noise, camshaft thrash and general commotion. Yet, because of the rear-biased weight distribution, one needed to be an accomplished driver to get the best out of the car. The sprint to 100mph, or even to 150mph, was one thing, but the ability to push hard, along a winding road, was something to be learned, not assumed. It was a sports car, in other words, which delivered amazing speed, uncomplainingly, but could bite back, suddenly and viciously, if driven in the wrong way.

Eight years after its introduction, the Testarossa was displaced by the new 512TR, a much-modified and upgraded version with a 428bhp engine, that car in its turn being replaced by the 440bhp F512M in 1994. Although none of these cars could ever reach the 200mph which so many claimants would have liked, they all shared the same magnificent power plant, running gear, and basic layout, which persisted from 1973 (the arrival of the Boxer) until 1996, when the 512M was finally discontinued.

Fiat 8V

8V model, built from 1952 to 1954
Built by: Fiat SpA., Italy.
Engine: Eight cylinders, in 70-degree vee-formation, in three-bearing light-alloy block/crankcase with cast iron cylinder liners. Bore and stroke 72mm by 61.3mm, 1,996cc (2.83in × 2.41in, 121.8cu.in). Detachable light-alloy cylinder heads. Two overhead valves per cylinder, operated by pushrods and rockers from single camshaft mounted in centre of cylinder block 'vee'. Two downdraught twin-choke Weber carburettors. Maximum power 105bhp or 114bhp (net) at 6,000rpm. Maximum torque with 115bhp engine, 107lb.ft at 4,600rpm.
Transmission: Single-dry-plate clutch and four-speed, all-synchromesh manual gearbox, both in unit with front-mounted engine. Direct-acting central gearchange. Open propeller shaft to chassis-mounted hypoid-bevel final drive. Exposed, universally jointed drive shafts to rear wheels.
Chassis: Tubular-steel chassis frame, with sheet-steel floor and reinforcements, and steel bodywork all welded up into a unitary-construction structure. Independent front suspension by coil springs, wishbones and anti-roll bar. Independent rear suspension by coil springs, wishbones and anti-roll bar. Two-piece track rod steering. Four-wheel, hydraulically operated drum brakes. Centre-lock wire wheels. 165 × 400mm tyres. Two-seat closed coupé coachwork by Fiat, with passenger's seat set back to give driver more elbow room.
Dimensions: Wheelbase 7ft 10.5in (240cm), tracks (front and rear) 4ft 2.7in (129cm). Overall length 13ft 2.6in (403cm). Unladen weight 2,34olb (1,061kg).
History: Fiat were such a vast company by the 1950s that they could indulge themselves in a sporting whim when it took their fancy. The 8V coupé, of which not more than 114 examples were ever made, was such a fancy. It pandered to

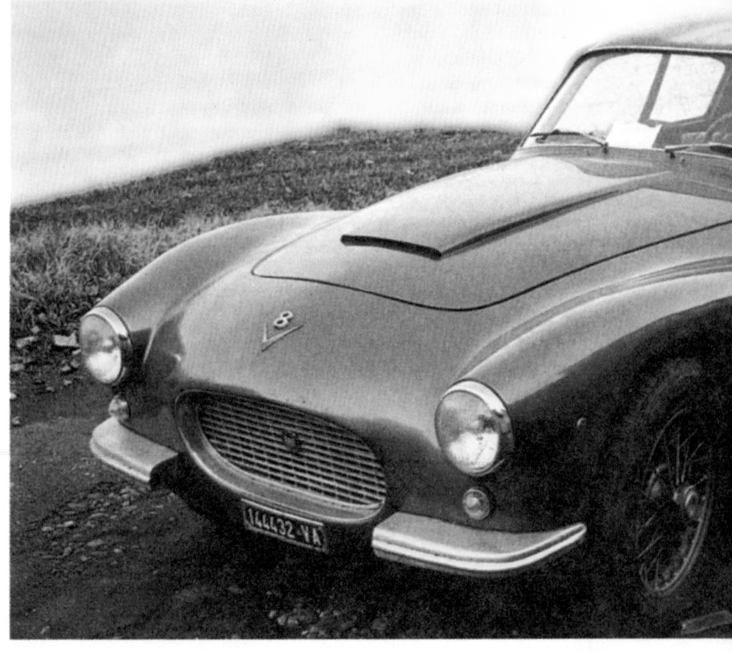

the rich Italian sportsmen who wanted a competition car, but would not pay out for a very exclusive Alfa Romeo or wildly impractical Ferrari or Maserati. The 8V's engine itself was entirely special and was never shared with another model. Its 70-degree vee engine was specifically designed to fit under narrow bonnets, which explains the unique included angle. The body made no compromises to comfort and convenience: the passenger/co-driver seating position was set back by at least a foot to give the driver's elbows room to operate and there were only two seats.

The combined multi-tube/sheet-steel shell could only ever be made in small quantities. Under the skin, however, the front and rear suspension components were lifted from Fiat's popular 1100 saloon, while the axle and drive shafts were *front* components from the Campagnola cross-country car. The gearbox was all-synchromesh, at a time when such things were rare and the body had actually been wind-tunnel tested at a time when many competition cars were shaped by eye and by personal preference. It was a car once described as 'Fiat engineers thinking aloud' – in other words the sort of engineering they would like to see adopted on a large scale if only their masters would agree. As a potential competition car, the 8V was well-designed, although the overhead-valve engine could not be tuned much above 130bhp. The cars won the Italian 2-litre GT championship in 1954, and Ghia and Zagato both produced unique-looking and very purposeful machines, Ghias with a five-speed gearbox. The last series of production cars were given a 'Chinese' slant-eye four-headlamp system, which predated Triumph by several years.

Fiat's only gas-turbine-powered car, which ran in 1954, used an 8V's chassis and suspensions as its base. The last of the 8Vs were built in 1954 and there were no other sporting Fiats until the beginning of the 1960s.

Left: Fiat's 8V model is unique in several respects. It is the only vee-8 Fiat car sold to the public, and was the only model in which the engineers' whims triumphed over sales requirements. 8Vs were sold in tiny numbers – only 114 were built in three years – and it was intended mainly for competition use. There were only two seats, that of the passenger being set back to give more elbow room to the hard-working driver! Bodies were usually by Ghia or Zagato, and made few concessions to comfort or silence. The 8V was a very successful sports car of its day.

Fiat 500 'Topolino'

Type 500, models built from 1936 to 1955 (data for 1936 model)
Built by: Fiat SpA., Italy.
Engine: Four cylinders, in line, in two-bearing cast-iron block. Bore and stroke 52mm by 67mm, 569cc (2.05in, 34.7cu.in). Detachable cast-iron cylinder head. Two sidevalves per cylinder, operated directly from single camshaft in cylinder block. Single side-draught Solex carburettor. Maximum power 13bhp (net) at 4,000rpm.
Transmission: Single-dry-plate clutch and four-speed manual gearbox (with synchromesh on top and third gears), all in unit with front-mounted engine. Direct-acting central gear-change. Open propeller shaft to spiral-bevel 'live' rear axle.
Chassis: Separate press-steel chassis frame, with channel-section side members, liberally pierced with holes for lightness, tubular and pressed cross-bracing. Independent front suspension by transverse-leaf spring and wishbones. Rear suspension by quarter-elliptic cantilever leaf springs and radius arms. Hydraulic piston-type dampers. Four-wheel, hydraulically operated drum brakes. 15in bolt-on pressed-steel wheels. 4.00 × 15in tyres.
Two-door saloon coachwork by Fiat themselves, with two seats and large luggage/occasional seating space behind seats, in pressed steel.
Dimensions: Wheelbase 6ft 6in (200cm), track (front) 3ft 7.5in (110.5cm), track (rear) 3ft 6.5in (108cm). Overall length 10ft 8.5in (326cm). Unladen weight 1,185lb (537kg).
History: Fiat's tiny little 'Topolino' ('little mouse') 500 model was the first of that company's really small cars, for which they are now justly famous. They had toyed with a small 'peoples' car' in 1919, and even published catalogues, but

never sold any cars. The 500 was designed in 1934 to slot into a Fiat range of which the 1-litre Balilla was then the smallest. It was new from end to end and caused as much of a sensation in Italy as the Austin Seven had done in Britain, more than a decade earlier. It was, in every way, an 'ordinary' car in miniature, with no compromises or crudities due to the small size. Fiat never attempted to give it four seats, which was wise, as it had a small 78.5in (200cm) wheelbase and a conventionally mounted front engine. The independent front suspension was advanced by its rivals' standards and it had a very cheerful and cheeky character. It was a huge success, if slow but sure, right from the start, but inevitably, like the Austin Seven, it began to grow up.

In 1939 the frame was lengthened so that conventional half elliptic springs could be added and a rear seat provided. The car therefore put on weight and, after the war, the original side-valve engine was displaced by a 16bhp overhead-valve conversion, which raised the maximum speed to something approaching a creditable 60mph. An aluminium cylinder head arrived in 1949, at the same time as the half-timbered Giardiniera estate car. Minor restyling gave it a recessed-headlamp nose, but the car carried on basically unchanged until 1955, when it was discontinued in favour of the brand-new rear-engined 600 model. More than 120,000 500s were built between 1936 and 1948 and these were followed by 376,000 of the overhead-valve 500Cs. Apart from being reliable and incredibly versatile, the 'Topolino' really scored because it looked like, sounded like and behaved like a much bigger car. More than any other Italian car of the period, it was an ideal machine for the new motorist, or for the ex-motor cycle customers. Like later mini-Fiats, it was meant to take the place of the horse-and-cart in areas which were not used to cars, and it succeeded admirably.

Left: In its way Fiat's Topolino was as popular and versatile as the Austin Seven or the Model T Ford. The first was sold in 1936, and half a million were built up to 1955, with a break during the war years. Though tiny, its engineering was conventional, with a four cylinder engine in the nose, and rear wheel drive. It was always sold as a two-seater, with open or closed bodywork. It was really indestructible.

Fiat 508 Balilla

Type 508 and 508s, side-valve and overhead-valve, built from 1932 to 1937 (data for 508S overhead-valve)
Built by: Fiat SpA., Italy.
Engine: Four cylinders, in line, in three-bearing cast-iron block. Bore and stroke 65mm by 75mm, 995cc (2.56in × 2.95in, 60.7cu.in). Cast-iron cylinder head. Two overhead valves per cylinder, operated by pushrods and rockers from single side-mounted camshaft. Zenith down-draught carburettor. Maximum power 36bhp at 4,400rpm.
Transmission: Single-dry-plate clutch and four-speed manual gearbox (synchromesh on top and third gears), both in unit with engine. Central direct-acting gearchange. Open propeller shaft to spiral-bevel 'live' rear axle.
Chassis: Separate steel chassis frame, with channel-section side members, and cruciform bracing. Forged front axle beam. Half-elliptic leaf springs at front and rear and friction type dampers (hydraulic on earlier 508 models). Worm-and-wheel steering. Four-wheel, hydraulically operated drum brakes. Separate drum handbrake on transmission, behind gearbox. 17in bolt-on wire wheels 4.00 × 17in tyres. Coachwork to choice, on 508, but 508S built as two-seat sports car.
Dimensions: Wheelbase 7ft 6.5in (230cm), tracks (front and rear) 3ft 10in (117cm). Overall length (depending on coachwork) about 12ft 10.8in (368cm). Unladen weight 1,300lb (590kg).
History: Fiat's all-new Balilla model was launched in 1932, at the very depth of the depression years. Fiat were well-protected against economic disaster (with 90 per cent of the Italian market), but could not afford to make another bad car

Right and below: Because it had a separate chassis, the Balilla was sold with several different body styles. On the right is one of the original 1932 Roadsters (a 'Spider Lusso') with twin exposed spare wheels and rather upright lines. By 1935 the car was a 508S, with overhead valves, and the fast back coupé competed with honour in the Mille Miglia. The large illustration shows the typical two-seater open sports car style which went well with the final engine. The pronounced tail fin was a 1930s fashion. Although only 2,000 508S models were made, a few being licence-built in France and Germany, they were loved.

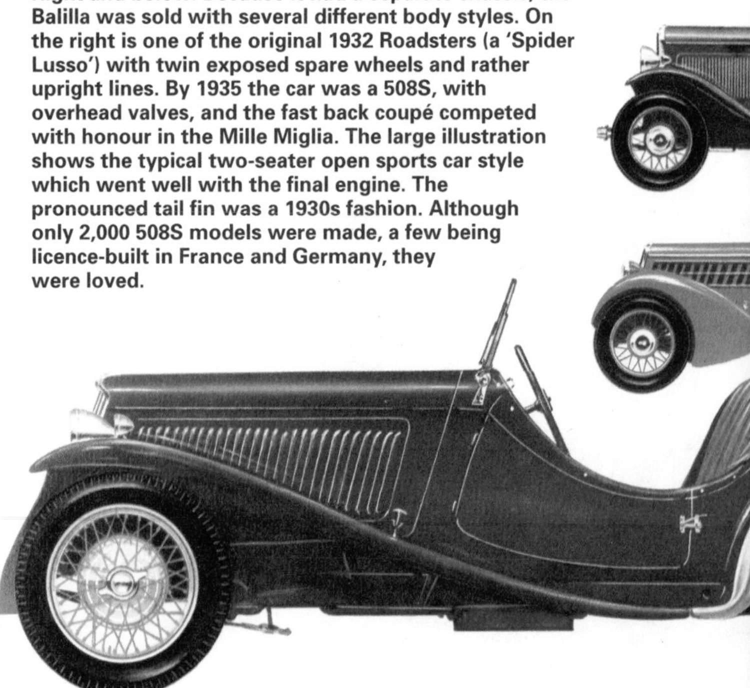

after the Type 514, which had failed. The 508 was typical in most ways of the small family machine developed to expand the European market in the 1930s, with a one-litre engine, strictly conventional mechanical layout and lightweight construction. Fiat, better than most, engineered their car well, made it reliable and somehow ensured that it was interesting to drive. The original 508 had a marginally shorter wheelbase than the later 508S and a side-valve engine, but otherwise the specification remained mainly settled for five years. 'Balilla', incidentally, means 'plucky little one' and had rather sinister connotations with a Mussolini/fascist youth movement.

The 508S, built first as a side-valve car, but from 1934 with an overhead-valve conversion of the same basic 995cc engine, arrived in 1933 and eventually made its name in trials, rallies, and even in endurance racing. Class for class it was very competitive, although it was overshadowed by such exotic machinery as the supercharged MG Magnettes. Cars sold in Britain were usually given British two-seater bodywork, of which a recognition point was usually the pronounced tail-fin behind the cockpit. One very desirable version of the car was the *berlinetta aerodinamica,* a fastback coupé with attractive flowing lines; maximum speed was raised, but the car was not much faster overall than open versions. A bald look at the specification tells us little about a Balilla's charm, except that it had an unusually 'short stroke' and small-capacity engine for the period. Somehow it was much more of a small car than a scaled down battle cruiser, and handled accordingly. All in all, about 2,000 508S were built, and a few were licence-made by Simca in France and by NSU in Germany.

Below: Fiat's Balilla sports car was a real advance over the heavy type of 'vintage' car – small, light, and with up-to-date engineering. In five years the styling was improved and the engine converted from side to overhead valves. This car had British-built bodywork.

Ford Escort RS1600

Escorts – Twin-Cam, RS1600 and RS1800 (data for RS1600) – 1968 to 1977
Built by: Ford Motor Co. Ltd., Britain.
Engine: Four cylinders, in line, in five-bearing light-alloy block (1970/72 models with cast-iron cylinder block). Bore and stroke 80.97mm by 77.62mm, 1,601cc (3.19 × 3.06in, 97.7cu.in). Light-alloy cylinder head. Four overhead valves per cylinder head. Four overhead valves per cylinder, operated by inverted-bucket tappets from twin overhead camshafts. Twin side-draught dual-choke Weber carburettors, Maximum power 120bhp (DIN) at 6,500rpm. Maximum torque 112lb.ft at 4,000rpm.
Transmission: Single-dry-plate clutch and four-speed, all synchromesh manual gearbox, both in unit with front-mounted engine. Remote-control central gearchange. Open propeller shaft to hypoid-bevel 'live' rear axle.
Chassis: Unitary-construction pressed-steel two-door saloon body/chassis unit. Front suspension independent by MacPherson struts and anti-roll bar. Rear suspension by half-elliptic leaf springs with radius arms and telescopic dampers. Rack-and-pinion steering. Hydraulically operated and servo-assisted front wheel disc brakes, and rear wheel drums. Cable-operated handbrake to rear wheels. 13in pressed-steel disc wheels. 165 × 13in tyres.
Dimensions: Wheelbase 7ft 10.5in (240cm), track (front) 4ft 3.7in (131cm), track (rear) 4ft 4in (132cm). Overall length 13ft 0.6in (398cm). Unladen weight 1,920lb (870kg).

History: The Ford Escort, announced in 1968, was the latest in a long line of conventional small family saloons from Ford. One version of it – the Escort Twin-Cam – was a very special, limited-production car intended for use in touring car racing and rallying. This car used Lotus-Cortina mechanicals, including the twin-overhead-cam engine. It was extremely successful, but the two-valves-per-cylinder engine was obsolescent.

In 1970, it was replaced by the RS1600, almost identical to the Twin-Cam except for its magnificently conceived four-valves-per-cylinder Ford-Cosworth BDA engine. This was a twin-overhead-cam conversion of the pushrod 1,600cc Cortina unit, with belt-driven overhead camshafts. It was also, in effect, a productionised variant of the wildly successful Cosworth FVA Formula 2 racing engine. Thus equipped, and with all manner of tuning gear added, an Escort could have up to 280bhp in enlarged (2-litre) racing guise, and could win rough rallies all over the world. The first RSs had cast-iron cylinder blocks, which could only safely be bored out to 1,800cc; the aluminium block, adopted in 1972, allowed boring to give the full 'capacity limit' of 2-litres.

In 1975, when the Escort's styling was changed, the RS1600 became the RS1800, with a larger but more simply carburated engine. All previous competition extras could be fitted. The RS1800 was dropped in 1977. Other popular Escorts for sporting purposes have been the 1,600cc Mexico and the 2,000cc RS2000.

Left: Without any doubt, Ford Escorts were the world's most successful rally car of all time. The factory used them for 12 years in Twin-Cam, RS1600 (the model shown), and RS1800 form. More recent cars had 16-valve Cosworth BDA engine producing 245bhp.

Ford GT40

GT40 I, to III (data Mk I)
Built by: Ford Advanced Vehicles Ltd., Britain.
Engine: Eight cylinders in 90-degree vee-formation, in cast-iron block. Bore and stroke 101.6mm by 72.9mm, 4,727cc (4.00 × 2.87in, 289cu.in). Cast-iron cylinder heads. Two overhead valves per cylinder, operated by pushrods and rockers from a single camshaft positioned in the vee of the cylinder block. Four down-draught, 48mm, dual-choke Weber carburettors. Fabricated tubular exhaust manifolds, with silencers positioned above the transmission. Wet-sump lubrication system. Maximum power 390bhp at 7,000rpm in 'production' form. Maximum torque 325lb.ft at 5,000rpm. Engine derived from quantity-production Mustang/Cobra design, and built by Ford in Detroit.
Transmission: Transaxle and five-speed ZF gearbox mounted integrally behind mid-positioned engine. No propeller shaft. Gear ratios and final drive gearing depended on racing application; many alternatives available. Limited-slip differential standard. Engine mounted ahead of axle and drive shafts, gearbox behind it. Exposed drive shafts with two universal joints. Maximum speed, depending on overall gearing, could be between 140mph and 200mph.
Chassis: Sheet-steel monocoque, with integral roll hoop and cockpit supports. Glassfibre skin panels. Doors cut high into the roof, also made of glassfibre. All-independent suspension by coil springs and wishbones; rear suspension pivoted direct from the transaxle. Four-wheel ventilated disc brakes, outboard all round. Cast-alloy 15in road wheels with centre-lock 'knock-off' nuts, originally with 6in front rims, 9in rears. Tyre size according to racing requirements; racing tyres obligatory.
Dimensions: Wheelbase 7ft 11in (241cm), track (front) 4ft 6in (137cm), track (rear) 4ft 6in (137cm). Overall length 13ft 8.6in (418cm). Unladen weight 1,835lb (832kg).

Below: A GT40 Mk II won the Le Mans 24 Hour race in 1966, but not this car. Ford also won in 67/68/69.

Above: Among the 107 GT40s built were seven de-tuned road cars like this 1966 model.

History: In 1963, Ford of Detroit turned to high performance and motor sport in a big way. Apart from their Indianapolis engine projects, their main effort went into an assault on the Le Mans 24-hour race. Their original Ford GTs were partly based on Eric Broadley's Lola GT and they raced without success in 1964 with light-alloy 4.2-litre engines and Colotti transmissions. For 1965, the race cars, further developed by Carroll Shelby's team in California, won the World Championship event at Daytona.

Production cars, called GT40 because 40in was the height of the machine, were built to the1965 design, in the FAV Ltd. factory in Slough, Bucks. Fifty had to be sold for the car to qualify as a 'Production Sports Car' in racing circles, but demand was such that a total of 107 were constructed before 1968, when the FAV Ltd. business was closed down. Almost every GT40 built was sold specifically for competition use, but 31 were converted for road use and seven detuned, silenced and better-trimmed Mark IIIs were specially built for the road. The price of a Mk III, in 1967, was £7,254 in Britain.

Ford of Detroit rapidly developed the original car into a Mk II version, which first ran at Le Mans in 1965, with the larger and heavier 7-litre V8 engine and a Kar-Kraft transmission utilising Ford Galaxie internals. Also in this special GT40-based (but factory-only) Mk II was a dry-sump lubrication system and minor aerodynamic changes to the glassfibre bodywork. Mk IIs in this form could easily top 200mph with Le Mans gearing and they dominated most events in 1966. Ford's first Le Mans win came in that year, with the winning car driven by Bruce McLaren and Chris Amon.

For 1967, Ford built a few very special Mk IV Ford FTs, which used Mk II mechanicals in entirely new monocoque chassis with light-alloy honeycomb structural members. The company took their second Le Mans victory at a record 135.48mph (218kph) average speed. Immediately after this race they retired from racing.

GT40s, further refined and developed by JW Automotive (whose chief, John Wyer, had been Managing Director of FAV Ltd.) went on to win many more races in 1968 and 1969, including the Le Mans 24-hour event each year. Latterly their engines were enlarged from 4.7 litres to the full 5-litre limit, and fitted with Gurney-Weslake cylinder heads. JWA also raced the Ford Mirage, which was really a GT40 fitted with a non-standard engine and more streamlined bodywork.

Ford Model T

Model T, built from 1908 to 1927
Built by: Ford Motor Co., United States.
Engine: Four cylinders, in line, in three-bearing cast-iron block/crankcase. Bore and stroke 95.2mm by 101.6mm, 2,896cc (3.75in × 4.0in, 176.7cu.in). Cast-iron cylinder head. Two side valves per cylinder, directly operated by camshaft in cylinder block. Single Holley or Kingston carburettor. Splash lubrication. Maximum power 20bhp.
Transmission: Epicyclic transmission, two forward speeds and reverse, incorporating take-up clutches, in unit with engine, and running in engine oil. Contracting bands applied to epicyclic drums for low gear and reverse, as appropriate; direct drive top gear with multi-disc clutch fixed to engine. Propeller shaft in torque tube to straight-bevel 'live' axle (overhead worm gear on light commercials).
Chassis: Very simple separate steel chassis frame, with channel-section side members, and minimal cross bracing. Forged front axle beam. Front and rear suspension by transverse leaf springs. No dampers. Epicyclic reduction gear steering in steering wheel boss; direct connection from column to drag link by

Below: Motoring for Everyman, USA-style, was what Ford's Model T offered for two decades. More than 16 million were built.

drop arm. Foot brake by contracting band on to direct-drive transmission clutch. Handbrake mechanically connected to drums on rear wheel hubs. 30in artillery-type wheels. 30 × 3in or 30 3.5in tyres. Coachwork: many Ford-sourced choices, from two-seat tourers to five-seat four-door saloons. All on same basic chassis and mechanicals.

Dimensions: Wheelbase 8ft 4in (254cm), tracks (front and rear) 4ft 8in, or (late models) 5ft (142cm or 152cm). Overall length slightly dependent on coachwork from 11ft 4in (345cm). Unladen weight from 1,450lb (658kg).

History: Before the VW Beetle came along, the Model T Ford could be described in one sentence – it was the world's highest selling car. Between 1908, when production began at Highland Park in Detroit, and 1927 when the last Model T was built, 15,007,033 examples were sold. The car, which started modestly enough at 10,000 units in 1909, came to dominate the American market with just over two *million* sales in 1923. It was also assembled at several overseas Ford plants, not least at Trafford Park, Manchester, in Great Britain. Even so the Model T had two basic faults – in almost every way it was unimproved between 1908 and 1927, and Henry Ford hung on to it for far too ▶

long, before replacing it by the new Model A. The hiatus this caused – the Mode A having to be developed in a rush and the factory having to be closed down fo re-equipment – set back Ford very seriously, and it was not until World War I that stability was really achieved.

Although the Model T was not the first ever Fort to be put into production (tha was the original Modal A, of course), it was the first ever mass-production Ford Indeed, it was really the world's first mass-produced car and, in spite of its mechanical crudities, the facilities and production techniques developed to assemble it very easily and quickly were advanced and modern. Ford, for instance, undoubtedly 'invented' the moving production line, where cars were moved on from one specific assembly station to the next.

Henry Ford's theory was that the great mass of the American people wanted reliable and basic transportation, not necessarily modern styling and complex mechanical equipment, and with the Model T he set out to give this to them. By developing the Ford service network all over the world, and by making the Mode T very simple to strip down and repair, he kept the whole concept as cheap as possible. The fact that the Model T was by no means as reliable nor as simple as other cars made no difference. The time it spent off the road was minimal.

The chassis was not at all rigid; it was very simple and had the most rudimentary of transverse-leaf suspensions. Bodies, more and more variations of which became available over the years, were light and also simple. It was a long time before weather protection and enclosed cabins became the norm for Ford customers. The engine, too, was as basic as Ford could make it. Of nearly 2.9-litres, it nevertheless had very undeveloped manifolding, and produced about 20bhp. The only real mechanical complication was in the transmission, which had two forward gears and one reverse, relying heavily on epicyclic gearing. Not only that, but the 'clutch' pedal was really a gearchange pedal. In its mid position, held by applying the handbrake, the transmission was in neutral; when pressed right down, the epicyclic low gear was engaged and when released completely the direct-drive top gear was in use. There was no foot accelerator pedal, and engine speed changes were effected by hand levers under the steering wheel which controlled throttle opening and spark advance.

In addition to the T's reputation for low running costs Henry Ford had an affinity for regularly cutting selling prices. The five-seat tourer cost $850 in 1909, and $950 in 1910, but thereafter the price-cutting began. By mechanising more and more of the production process, Ford was able to cut that same car's price to $360 by 1916. In Britain, for instance, where the Model T had a larger engine than many cars (and an RAC horsepower rating absurdly high for its performance) it was by far the cheapest car on the market. The only thing which could

Right: All Model Ts had the same chassis, but Ford offered a multitude of body styles, open and closed, private and for commercial use.

Above: This was the nearest Ford got to offering a Model T sports car, for it was low cost, rather than performance, which mattered most.

kill the T in its home country was complete and absolute obsolescence. Sales began to fall after the record year of 1923 and by the time it was discontinued in 1927 the T was on its last legs. Not only had the opposition advanced too much technically, but their cars were reliable, cheap *and* smart. The new Model A would have to match them, in a way that the T could not.

Ford Mustang

Mustang, built from 1964 to 1968, six-cyl and V8 models (data for 289cu.in)
Built by: Ford Motor Co., United States.
Engine: Eight cylinders, in 90-degree vee-formation, in cast-iron cylinder block. Bore and stroke 101.6mm by 72.9mm, 4,727cc (4.0in × 2.87in, 289cu.in). Two cast-iron cylinder heads. Two overhead valves per cylinder, operated by pushrods and rockers from single camshaft mounted in cylinder block 'vee'. Downdraught four-choke Ford carburettor. Maximum power 271bhp (gross) at 6,000rpm. Maximum torque 312lb.ft at 3,400rpm.
Transmission: Single-dry-plate clutch and four-speed all-synchromesh manual gearbox, both in unit with engine. Central remote-control gearchange. Open propeller shaft to hypoid-bevel 'live' axle. Optional limited-slip differential. Optional three-speed Ford automatic transmission with torque converter.

Below: These views of the Mustang show that the original cars had striking styling, but still found space for four full-size passengers. The car was a 'tourer' in every way, and was raced and rallied in the standard saloon car categories. Mustangs won the Tour de France in 1964, hundreds of races all over the world, and were a virility symbol to American youth of the 1960s. Through the years it grew up gradually but recent cars are smaller and slower, with European power trains. This convertible has the optional 289cu.in high-performance vee-8 engine, special wheels and tyres. Softer versions had six-cylinder engines and rather less performance. More than a million Mustangs sold in the first three years.

Chassis: Unitary-construction, pressed-steel body-chassis unit, sold as open tourer four-seater, closed two-door coupé, or with fastback closed coupé style. Independent front suspension by coil springs, wishbones and anti-roll bar. Rea suspension by half-elliptic leaf springs. Recirculating-ball steering with powe assistance optional. Four-wheel, hydraulically operated and servo-assisted drum brakes, with optional front discs. 14in pressed-steel disc wheels.
Dimensions: Wheelbase 9ft (274cm), track (front) 4ft 8in (142cm), track (rear 4ft 8in (142cm). Overall length 15ft 1.6in (461cm). Unladen weight from 2,925lb (1,327kg) depending on equipment and bodyshell.
History: Ford's Mustang can probably thank the first very sporting Thunderbirds for its birth. The T-Bird, a two-seater at first, soon grew up and became a much larger car. By the early 1960s, with compact cars popular and sporting motoring again important to Ford, a place for a 'small' sporting machine developed. By European standards, of course, the Mustang has never been small – in origina production form it was more than 15ft long, which is Aston Martin size, and bulkier than any sporting Jaguar. By Detroit standards, however, it was a very neat little package.

The production car was launched in April 1964, but had already been trailered by other prototype 'Mustangs' for the company to gauge reaction. The mid-engined car (the engine being a German V4) made public in 1962 was far too sophisticated for Ford to build in quantity and was made purely as a 'taster' Mustang II, revealed at the US Grand Prix in the autumn of 1963, was still a non-production car, but since it was closely based on a prototype Mustang and redecorated lightly, its impact on the public was important. The public liked it and Ford went ahead to build the cars.

Chief of the Mustang project was Lee Iacocca, who was no innovative designer, but was sporting minded and already had the successful development of the compact Ford Falcon to his credit. It was therefore no surprise that the Mustang was such an enjoyable car to drive. It was more of a surprise that it could be persuaded to become a winner on the race tracks, but this was mostly because of the very imaginative list of high-performance options made available. The car used many Falcon components, including the basic engines and

Below: For 1968 the Mustang received its first major re-style, becoming longer, smoother and more expensive. This was the fastback 2+2 GT.

Above: The original Mustang of 1964 was craggily styled, but struck a chord with America's affluent young, offering high performance at low first cost.

transmissions, and in true Detroit style there was a vast range of choice right from the start. One option much discussed, and even pictured in 1964, was an independent rear suspension for racing, but this was never proceeded with, and all Mustangs had to rely on the very basic half-elliptic leaf spring layout for location.

Engines ranged from the cheapest and least powerful straight six of 2,781cc to the highest-performance V8 of 4,727cc. The difference in power was from 101bhp to 271bhp, and shows the spread of owners' preferences for which Ford was aiming. By 1966, indeed, two tunes of sixes and five tunes of eights had already been listed, and as the years went by this choice widened. Cars could have manual or automatic transmission, drum or disc brakes, manual or power-assisted steering, soft or hard-tops, 13in or 14in wheels, extra instruments, special colour schemes and many other options.

Mustangs were successful in factory-sponsored teams almost at once, and their biggest early win was in the 1964 Tour de France where two cars prepared in Britain finished first and second overall, the winning car being driven by Peter Procter. As a racing 'saloon' car (for the Mustang was ideally dimensioned to satisfy international regulations), it was only ever beaten by other and even more special Fords, usually the lightweight Falcons. No young man, or young-at-heart man in North America could live until he had owned a Mustang, with the result that 400,000 were sold within twelve months, and the first million sales were notched up in 1966. Engine tuners like Carroll Shelby hurried to market their own special Mustangs (Shelby's was the GT350 and was very fierce indeed), while the 'add-on' accessory suppliers made a good living with special customising kits. The Mustang was an aggressively marketed runaway success in North America and (because of its reasonable size) was well-received in other countries. So much so, in fact, that Ford did not need to go for an important restyling operation until 1968. With that move, the Mustang, like the Thunderbird before it, began to move 'up-market' and to put on weight and bulk. Apart from the 5-litre 'Boss' of the late 1960s, it became less of a sporting car and more of a virility symbol. It was completely redesigned in the early 1970s and Mustang II was a much smaller, simpler and slower car.

Ford RS200

Ford RS200 sports coupé, built in 1985 and 1986
Built by: Ford Motor Co. Ltd., Britain.
Engine: Four cylinders, in line, in five-main-bearing light-alloy cylinder block. Bore and stroke 86 x 77.62mm, 1,803cc (3.39 x 3.06in, 110cu.in). Light alloy cylinder head. Four valves per cylinder, in narrow vee, operation by twin overhead camshafts and inverted bucket tappets. Ford/Bosch fuel injection and AiResearch turbocharger. Maximum power 250bhp (DIN) at 6,500rpm. Maximum torque 215lb.ft at 4,000rpm. Tune-up kits in 300bhp, 350bhp and 450bhp were all optionally available.
Transmission: Four-wheel-drive, AP Racing type of diaphragm spring clutch and five-speed all-synchromesh manual gearbox, all in unit with mid-mounted engine. Remote-control, central gearchange.
Chassis: Unitary-construction body-chassis unit, based around aluminium honeycomb/carbon fibre composite/steel tub, with integral steel roll cage, and glassfibre body skin panels. Independent front suspension by double coil springs, wishbones, telescopic dampers, anti-roll bar. Independent rear suspension by double coil springs, wishbones, telescopic dampers, and anti-roll bar. Rack-and-pinion steering, with optional power assistance. Four-wheel disc brakes, with hydraulic power assistance, but no ABS. Cast-alloy 16in road wheels, 225/50-16in tyres.
Dimensions: Wheelbase 8ft 3.6in (253cm), front track 4ft 11.1in (150.1cm), rear track 4ft 11in (150cm). Overall length 13ft 1.5in (400cm). Unladen weight 2,607lb (1,183kg).
History: Although rallying's Group B formula lasted only a few years, it inspired the birth of some remarkable four-wheel-drive monsters. The prettiest by far, though not the most successful in the sport, was Ford's RS200. Because only 200 such cars had to be built (to meet the Group B requirements), and Ford's mainstream factories could not cope, the company leased a redundant Reliant building at Shenstone to do the assembly job. Starting late, but with the intention of producing a car which could

Below: The RS200's turbocharged engine was mid-mounted, and drove all four wheels. Twin coil spring/damper units for each wheel were standard.

Above: The RS200's style was by Ghia, a beautiful two-seater with roof-mounted scoop for the turbo intercooler, and with rear spoiler to add downforce.

not only win at world level, but also carry a familiar family style, Ford designed the RS200 as a mid-engined four-wheel-drive two-seater coupé, complete with Cosworth-type turbocharged BDT engine and transmission developed by FF Developments but incorporating Hewland gears.

The chassis was a combined steel/carbon fibre composite tub, with a steel tubular safety cage around the cabin, and with steel tubular front and rear sub-frame extensions. The engine itself, driving forward rather than back, was behind the two-seater cabin, but the bulky four-wheel-drive transmission was between the driver's and passenger's footwells. On rally cars it was possible to lock up the transmission (thus negating the centre differential).

Suspension was by coil springs wrapped around shock absorber units, two of them at each corner, and because this was a light car there was no power assistance for the steering, and no ABS assistance to the all-disc-brake installation. Remarkably, the road cars had a soft ride and near-neutral handling characteristics.

In standard form the 1.8-litre engine produced 250bhp, with the turbocharger affect being felt over 3,500rpm, but when fully prepared for rallying the same engine could produce between 450 and 500bhp. Engine Tune-up kits in 300 and 350 bhp were offered from new, a fair proportion of the cars produced actually having these. Even in standard form, the cabin was noisy, there being a good deal of turbocharger wastegate chatter and transmission whine to assail the driver's ears.

The style, by Ford's subsidiary Ghia, was extremely graceful, for it was difficult to realise that the same screen, and cut-down versions of the doors, had been lifted from the Sierra family car. Luggage space was restricted to a box, up front, where a second spare wheel might be placed, while ventilation was best described as basic. Major skin panels were all in glass-fibre. Even so, road cars had wind-down glass windows in the doors, carpets on the floor, and the option of comfortable recaro seats, but competition cars were more starkly equipped. A few road cars even had radio/cassette and mobile phone installations.

Production began in mid-1985, the 200th (and last) being cobbled together in January 1986. Refurbishing and preparation for delivery was finally ceded to Tickford of Coventry, who were still delivering 'new' RS200s as late as 1989.

Although Group B was cancelled in 1986, the RS200 was successful in international rallies in that year. Versions with 2.1-litre/700bhp BDT-E engines then became dominant in rallycross in the following years – until, that is, the regulations were re-written to outlaw such an effective car.

Ford later admitted to losing several millions of pounds on this project, which was nonetheless a great image raiser for the company.

Ford Sierra RS Cosworth

Ford Sierra RS and RS500 Cosworth sporting hatchback, built 1986 and 1987 (data for Sierra RS Cosworth)
Built by: Ford Motor Co. Ltd., Britain.
Engine: Four cylinders, in line, in five-main-bearing cast iron cylinder block. Bore and stroke 90.8 × 76.95mm, 1,993cc (3.60 × 3.03in, 121.7cu.in). Aluminium-alloy cylinder head. Four valves per cylinder, in narrow vee, operation by twin overhead camshafts and inverted bucket tappets. Weber-Marelli fuel injection and Garrett AiResearch turbocharger. Maximum power 204bhp (DIN) at 6,000rpm. Maximum torque 205lb.ft at 4,500rpm.
Transmission: Rear-wheel-drive, single-dry-plate diaphragm spring clutch and five-speed all-synchromesh manual gearbox, all in unit with engine. Remote-control, central gearchange.
Chassis: Unitary-construction pressed-steel body-chassis unit, in three-door hatchback style with large rear spoiler. Independent front suspension by MacPherson struts, coil springs, lower wishbones, telescopic dampers and anti-roll bar. Independent rear suspension by coil springs, semi-trailing arms, telescopic dampers and anti-roll bar. Rack-and-pinion steering with hydraulic power assistance. Four-wheel disc brakes. Cast light alloy 15in wheels, 205/50-15in tyres.
Dimensions: Wheelbase 8ft 6.6in (260.6cm), front track 4ft 9.1in (145cm), rear track 4ft 9.7in (146.6cm). Overall length 14ft 7.5in (446cm). Unladen weight 2,688lb (1,216kg).
History: Ford had been so used to winning saloon car races in Europe that when the sequence faltered in the early 1980s, a special model was designed to rectify all that. Developed as an out-and-out 'homologation special', the Sierra RS Cosworth (and the RS500 Cosworth which followed) was exactly right for the job. To win in Group A racing Ford decided that they needed a 350bhp 2-litre car with an appropriate aerodynamic package to provide high-speed downforce. With no such model in production, or on the stocks, they therefore enlisted Cosworth, and their own motorsport engineers, to create such a car.

Starting with a Sierra three-door body shell (which up to then had been inflicted with a series of quite uninspiring engines), adding a front chin spoiler, and a vast 'whale-tail' aerofoil at the rear, the shape became suitable. Cosworth

Below: The first 'whale-tail' Sierra RS Cosworth had a 204bhp turbocharged engine up front, and a vast rear spoiler to balance the handling at high speeds.

Above: Didier Auriol won the World Championship Tour de Corse Rally in 1988, with this 300bhp-plus version of the Sierra RS Cosworth.

then took an ageing 'Pinto' cylinder block, designed a 16-valve twin-cam cylinder head for it, turbocharged it with a Garrett Airesearch component – and the output was assured. A Borg Warner five-speed gearbox, as already used in Ford-USA Mustangs, and a big Scorpio-size rear axle did the rest. Detuning for road use (only 204bhp instead of the 340bhp available for racing) took time, but the car was previewed in 1985, went on sale in 1986, and was ready to start winning races and rallies in 1987. By that time, more than 5,000 cars had been manufactured, so sporting approval was certain.

Ford's rivals were horrified enough by this – it was, after all, the world's first road car to offer more than 100bhp/litre in standard form – but became positively suicidal later in 1987 when the RS500 Cosworth was revealed. Five hundred such cars, built up by converting already-part-built RS Cosworths, featured engines with even larger turbos, eight fuel injectors instead of four, and slightly improved aerodynamics (including a 'Gurney flap' at the tail). Although the RS500 was no faster on the road, in racing tune the engine could develop up to 550bhp, with long-term reliability. This was enough to give Ford the World Touring Car Championship in 1987, the European series in 1988, and innumerable national championships until the early 1990s, when regulations were speedily re-written to eliminate such dominant machinery.

In spite of this race-car character, road cars were remarkably civilised, flexible and practical machines, for they were 150mph full four-seaters with only minimal turbo-lag (the turbos made all the right whistling noises too). They could be serviced by any Ford RS dealership, and had a soft ride with nice features such as ABS braking and comfortable seating and interiors. Regrettably, they were also attractive to thieves all over the world, so insurance premiums soon went through the roof.

Ford followed up by launching the 'Sapphire' Cosworth in 1988, which had the same running gear but a four-door saloon shell, topping it off in 1990 by the Cosworth 4x4, which combined four-door comfort with Cosworth power and four-wheel-drive transmission. Even then the pedigree was not dead, for the same running gear was then to be used in the Escort RS Cosworth, a specialised 'homologation special' introduced in 1992.

Ford Thunderbird

Thunderbird two-seater cars built from 1955 to 1957 (data for 1956 model)
Built by: Ford Motor Co., United States.
Engine: Eight cylinders, in 90-degree vee-formation, in five-bearing cast-iron block. Bore and stroke 96.5mm by 87.4mm, 5,113cc (3.80in × 3.44in, 312cu.in). Two detachable cast iron cylinder heads. Two overhead valves per cylinder, operated by pushrods and rockers from single camshaft mounted in centre of cylinder block 'vee'. Single down-draught four-choke Ford carburettor. Maximum power 225bhp (gross) at 4,600rpm. Maximum torque 324lb.ft at 2,600rpm.
Transmission: Single-dry-plate clutch and three-speed, all-synchromesh manual gearbox, both in unit with front-mounted engine. Direct-acting central gearchange. Optional three-speed automatic transmission, with torque converter. Open propeller shaft to hypoid-bevel 'live' rear axle.
Chassis: Separate pressed-steel chassis frame, with box-section side members, and pressed cross bracing. Independent front suspension by coil springs, wishbones and anti-roll bar. Rear suspension by half-elliptic leaf springs. Telescopic dampers all round. Four wheel, hydraulically operated drum brakes, with vacuum-servo assistance. 15in pressed-steel road wheels. 6,70 × 15in tyres. Two-seat sporting bodywork by Ford, supplied with folding hood or detachable hardtop.
Dimensions: Wheelbase 8ft 6in (259cm), tracks (front and rear) 4ft 8in (142cm). Overall length 15ft 5.2in (470.5cm). Unladen weight 3,450lb (1,565kg).
History: The Thunderbird took shape in 1953, and was publicly launched in

Above, below and over: Only in the first three years of its long life was the Ford Thunderbird a true sporting two-seater. It persisted in growing up, and from 1958 became a close-coupled four-seater 'personal car' in advertising parlance. Conceived in 1953 the Thunderbird was Ford's first sporty two-seater for many years, and aimed to beat Chevrolet's new Corvette. The T-Bird used mainly standard Ford touring parts under a sleek pressed-steel skin, had optional automatic transmission, and a big selling point was that every car had a V8 engine. More than 53,000 were built in three seasons.

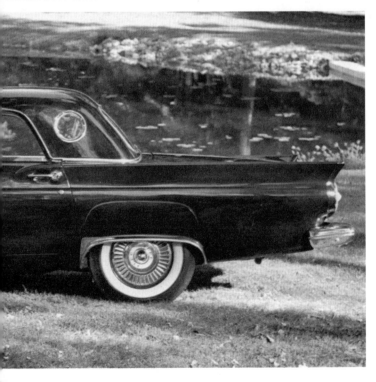

1954, as the first true 'sporting' two-seater Ford for many years. Although a multitude of normal saloon car parts were used under the skin, the styling was fresh, youthful in its appeal and unique to this model. The importance of the early T-Birds was that their appeal was not compromised by other commercial considerations. Although Ford were already looking ahead to a more sporting future in the early 1950s, the arrival of the deadly rival from Chevrolet, the first of the Corvettes, was a great spur to their ambitions. Even though the T-Bird was – by North American standards – a sports car, it was by no means small. The first cars had 4.8 litre V8 engines and weighed in at around 3,500lb (1,587kg), which put them a full size class ahead of the Jaguars even though they were no more expensive in their native North America. Styling of the first two-seaters was crisp and clean, certainly by Detroit's saloon car styling standards, and the first cars in particular had virtually no extraneous decoration to spoil the overall

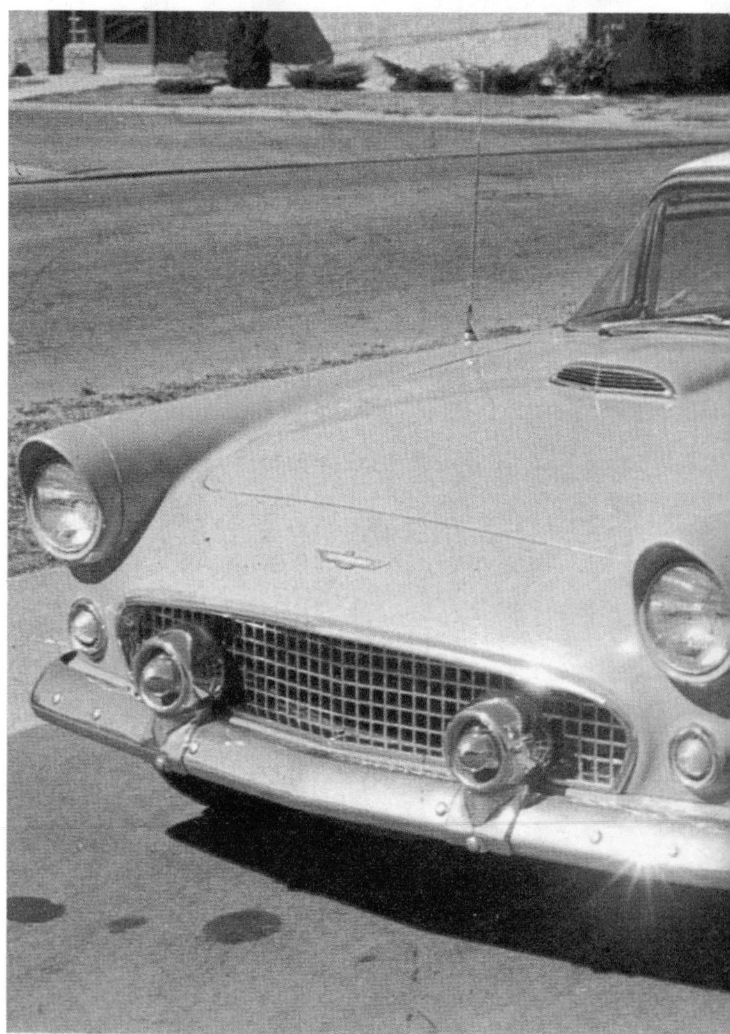

effect. The windscreen was well swept, as were all such cars from Detroit, and the lines were very low, with a height of only 4ft 5in (135cm). Either manual transmission or Ford-o-Matic automatic transmission was available. Unlike the rival Corvette, and this was thought to be a great selling point, every T-Bird was equipped with a V8 engine; there was no 'cheap' six-cylinder option. A feature of 1956 and later models was the optional external mounting of the spare wheel, atop the back bumper, to give a 'continental' look. There was an extensive retouching of the style for 1957, which included portholes in the optional hardtop, but the car's whole character was lost in 1958 when it was rebodied into a much less sporting four-seater. After that the T-Bird became just another Ford, and it was not until 1964 and the arrival of the Mustang that sporting motoring really came back to Ford's ranks.

Ford V8 1930s

V8 cars, built from 1932 to 1941 (data for 1932 model 18)
Built by: Ford Motor Co., United States
Engine: Eight cylinders, in 90-degree vee-formation, in three-bearing cast-iron block/crankcase. Bore and stroke 77.8mm by 95.25mm, 3,622cc (3.06in × 3.75in, 221cu.in). Two detachable cast-iron cylinder heads. Two side valves per cylinder, operated directly from single camshaft positioned in centre of cylinder block 'vee'. One single-choke down-draught Detroit Lubricator carburettor. Maximum power 65nhp (gross) at 3,400rpm.
Transmission: Single-dry-plate clutch and three-speed manual gearbox (without synchromesh on first gear), both in unit with front-mounted engine. Direct-acting central gear-change. Propeller shaft, enclosed in torque tube, driving spiral bevel 'live' rear axle.
Chassis: Separate pressed-steel chassis frame, with channel section side members and tubular cross bracing. Forged front axle beam. Front suspension by transverse leaf spring and radius arms. Rear suspension by transverse leaf spring and radius arms. Lever-arm hydraulic dampers. Four-wheel, rod operated drum brakes. 18in bolt-on wire spoke wheels. 5.25 × 18in tyres.
Dimensions: Wheelbase 8ft 10in (269cm), track (front) 4ft 7.2in (140cm), track (rear) 4ft 8.7in (144cm). Overall length 13ft 9.5in (420cm). Unladen weight 2,580lb (1,170kg).
History: To replace the obsolete Model T, Ford developed the new Model A at the end of the 1920s and from the beginning of 1932 they further improved their range by slotting the first of the now-legendary side-valve V8 engines into the Model A's chassis and body styles. There was nothing remarkably new about the V8 engine in the United States, but at the time the straight-8 configuration was fashionable and it was the first real sign Ford had given of being interested in making powerful cars. The V8s were always quick, for they combined lusty torque with light weight. In Europe, where modified versions were built in several countries (in Britain, for instance, from 1935 onwards) the V8 soon became a recognised rally car and one won the Monte Carlo Rally in 1936. The V8 was always hampered by its crude suspension (transverse leaf springs at front and rear) and its eventual development was always to be hindered by the side-valve layout with exhaust gases being let out across the cylinder block casting, but it formed the backbone of Ford's world-wide power-plant engineering until the beginning of the 1950s. There were several

Above: President of the United States Franklin D. Roosevelt in a 1936 Ford V8 model 68, one of the very popular cabriolet versions of this car.

changes in body style which transformed the V8 from an upright saloon to a much smoother machines by the outbreak of World War II. After an initial period the engines soon got their reputation for being dead reliable and the cars always offered extremely good value. The engine was the symbol of Ford's modernisation at the end of the 1920s.

Below: Ford V8 styling was instantly recognisably in the late 1930s, complete with this 'fencers' mask' type of grille. This was a UK version of the North American car.

Franklin Air-cooled Model IIB Six

Six-cylinder Franklins, built from 1905 to 1934 (data for 1927 model)
Built by: Franklin Automobile Co., United States.
Engine: Six cylinders, in line, in individual finned (air-cooled), cast-iron blocks, with seven-bearing light-alloy crankcase. Bore and stroke 82.55mm by 101.6mm, 3,263cc (3.25in × 4.0in, 199cu.in). Detachable cast-iron cylinder heads. Two overhead valves per cylinder, operated by pushrods and rockers from single camshaft mounted in side of crankcase. Exposed valve gear. Air impeller at front of engine, blowing air across cylinder head and down radially finned cylinders. Single up-draught carburettor.
Transmission: Single-dry-plate clutch and three-speed manual gearbox (without synchromesh), both in unit with front-mounted engine. Direct-acting central gearchange. Open propeller shaft to spiral-bevel 'live' rear axle.
Chassis: Separate chassis frame, with laminated ash wood side members, reinforced by steel plates and tubular and pressed cross bracing. Forged front axle beam. Front and rear suspension by full-elliptic leaf springs. Worm-and-gear steering. Mechanically operated foot brake on transmission drum and hand brake on rear-wheel drums. Artillery-style wheels, fixed to hubs. 32 × 4in tyres.
Dimensions: Wheelbase 9ft 11in (302cm), tracks (front and rear) 4ft 8in (142cm). Overall length 14ft 8in (447cm). Unladen weight 3,255lb (1,476kg).

History: Franklin's claim to fame in the history books is that they were America's most successful makes of air-cooled cars. In more than 30 years of manufacture they never made a water-cooled machine and sold more than 150,000 cars in all. At their peak, with the final development of the six-cylinder engines, they sold 14,000 in 1929. Not only this, but until 1927, even with the big cars of the vintage years, they stayed loyal to a chassis frame with wooden side members and used full-elliptic springs to give the best possible ride (not losing out all that much on precision of steering or handling).
Externally, a vintage Franklin looked conventional, with a dummy 'radiator' grille hiding the big engine-driven fan; this is impelled air along the top of the engine, where ducts channelled this down the finned sides of the individually cast cylinders. The rest of the chassis and layout was entirely conventional and none the worse for that. Before the end of the decade Franklin had espoused four-wheel hydraulic brakes and he finally adopted a pressed-steel chassis. By 1932, indeed, synchromesh had been fitted. Also Franklin announced their splendid 'white elephant' in 1932 – a 6.8-litre supercharged V12, still with air-cooling.

The United States Depression caught out Franklin, as it did most of the other independents. The technology carried on, however, in aero-engines.

Left: The most successful maker of air-cooled cars was Franklin. This late vintage six-cylinder machine had a 3.3 litre engine and a wooden chassis frame but in 1932 Franklin even tried a V12! Franklin sold 14,000 cars in 1929.

Frazer Nash 'Chain Gang'

'Chain gang' models, built from 1924 to 1939 (data for TT Replica model)
Built by: A.F.N Ltd., Britain.
Engine: Meadows manufactured. Four cylinders, in three-bearing cast-iron block/crankcase. Bore and stroke 69mm by 100mm, 1,496cc (2.72in × 3.94in, 91.3cu.in). Cast-iron detachable cylinder head, modified by Frazer Nash. Two overhead valves per cylinder, operated by pushrods and rockers from single block-mounted camshaft. Twin horizontal constant-vacuum SU state of tune, but normally 62bhp at 4,500rpm.
Transmission: Single-dry-plate clutch in unit with engine. Open propeller shaft to bevel box. Four-speed-and-reverse transmission by chain drive, from cross shaft, with dog engagement. Chains exposed, and no differential. Remote-control right-hand gearchange.

Chassis: Separate pressed-steel chassis frame, with channel-section side members, tubular and fabricated cross bracing. Tubular front axle beam. Front suspension by cantilever semi-elliptic springs and radius arms. Rear suspension

Below: Full and glorious detail of the TT Replica 'chain gang', so called as cars had run successfully in the Tourist Trophy of the early 1930s. Not more than 350 'chain gang' cars, all of the same general design, were built in fifteen years. There were several different engines, but all used the unique transmission, with a separate and exposed chain and sprockets for each gear. This needed regular greasing, but put up with a lot of abuse. The cars' ride was very hard, the steering direct, and creature comforts very few. Owners loved them!

by cantilever quarter-elliptic springs and radius arms. Hartford-type adjustabl friction damps. Rack-and-pinion steering with fore-and-aft drag link. Four-whee cable operated drum brakes. 19in centre-lock wire wheels. 4.50 × 19in tyres Two-seater open sports coachwork of light-alloy on ash frame.

Dimensions: Wheelbase 8ft 6in (259cm), track (front) 4ft (122cm), track (rea 3ft 6in (106.7cm). Overall length 12ft 6.3in (351cm). Unladen weight 1,800l (816kg).

History: After Archie Frazer-Nash left the defunct GN concern, he set up i business on his own to make two-seat sports cars carrying his own name. It i not surprising, therefore, to see several design points from the GN in the earlies Frazer Nash cars, including the extremely simple but effective chain-driv transmission. Even the first cars, however, were much more 'grown-up' tha the GN had ever been, as they had a proper channel-section chassis frame an always used water-cooled four-cylinder or six-cylinder engines. In spite of hi engineering prowess, however, Frazer-Nash himself was not always a pruden business man and his company was taken over by H. J. Aldington in 1929. Th Aldington family controlled the destinies of Frazer Nash, through AFN Ltd., unt the cars were finally taken out of production in the 1950s. Production, albeit o a very limited scale, was moved from Kingston-on-Thames to Islesworth i 1926, where it settled permanently. Even so, cars were hand-built at a very lov rate. Between 1924 and 1939, no more than 350 'chain gang' cars were bui and production of these cars, now legendary, had been reduced to the meres trickle after about 1936, when the Aldingtons were more interested in buildin up their British concession to sell the Fiedler-designed BMW cars.

The GN ancestry showed up in the Frazer Nash (as it did in the HRG car whic was master-minded by GM's other partner, Godfrey). The chassis was ver simple and easy to repair, with cantilever springs fore and aft to keep the fram short and the wheels well under control. The suspension was very hard, whic was exactly what the sporting-minded Frazer Nash customers wanted, an weather protection minimal. The chain-drive transmission was so simple tha critics often used to disbelieve its efficiency. If, however, the chains wer cleaned and oiled regularly – about every 500 miles was best – they operate

well, and the consequences of a snapped chain were not so serious as those of smashed gear wheels. There was no torque-splitting differential, because of the (literally) solid rear axle, which explains the fact that all 'chain gangs' had very narrow wheel tracks and extremely sensitive handling characteristics. Traction in all conditions, of course, was superb.

The main changes over the years centred around engines. The original cars were built with Plus Power four-cylinder engines, but after that firm closed down (with only 16 engines delivered) British Anzani engines were used for the next six years. In the early 1930s, a whole series of units were tried, including the Meadows overhead-valve engine sold in the first batch of TT Replica cars. These progressively became more of Frazer Nash and less of Meadows as their designer (Gough) developed special components. As a more refined alternative to the sporting Gough-Meadows. Aldington then began to fit the six-cylinder, 1½-litre Blackburne units, redesigned to have twin overhead camshafts. However, even at the same time, the company were developing their own single-overhead cam 'Gough' engine, which was entirely special but rather under-developed.

Many of the car's variants were named after the races or circuits where competition success had been gained, which explains the naming of the 'Shelsey' and 'Boulogne' cars. TT Replicas, first built in 1931, as prototypes, were named after the cars ran in the British Tourist Trophy races of 1931, 1932 and 1934, and the first 'production' car was sold in the spring of 1932. Because of its no-nonsense specification, it became the most popular of all 'chain gangs', a total of 85 being manufactured between 1932 and 1938; 54 of the cars were equipped with the Meadows engine (complete with 'Gough' improvements. Only a few had the splendid twin-cam Blackburne engine, which in racing form (and supercharged) could be persuaded to give more than 150bhp.

It might be fair to say that the Aldingtons had new ideas for improved models, but that they did not need to introduce them because the basically vintage 'chain gang' was popular as long as they needed to make it. Their ideas for post-war Frazer Nash cars, in the 1940s, were as interesting and advanced as the 'chain gangs' had been twenty years earlier.

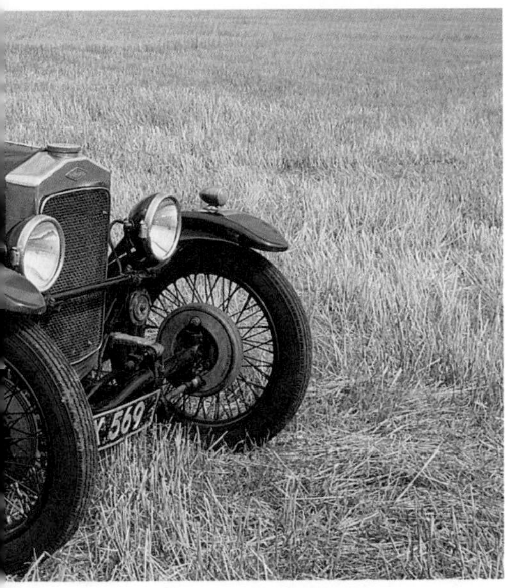

Left: The 'Chain Gang' model was expensive and exclusive, but steered and handled well, and was remarkably fast in its class. Addicts loved them then - and today.

GN

GN models, built from 1911 to 1925 (data for 1913 vee-twin models)
Built by: G.N. Ltd., Britain.
Engine: JAP manufactured. Two air-cooled cylinders, in 90-degree vee-formation in cast-iron cylinder barrels on light-alloy crankcase. Bore and stroke 84mm by 98mm, 1,086cc (3.31in × 3.86in, 66.3cu.in). Detachable cylinder heads. Two valves per cylinder; overhead inlets operated by pushrods and rockers, side exhausts operated direct from crankcase-mounted camshaft. Single B&B carburettor. Maximum power about 12bhp at 2,400rpm.
Transmission: Clutch on rear of engine crankcase, mounted in nose of car. Open propeller shaft drive to bevel box driving countershaft. Two-speed dog-and-chain transmission to counter shaft and final drive to solid rear axle by side-mounted belts. Remote-control right-hand gearchange.
Chassis: Separate ash chassis frame with tubular cross bracing. Tubular front axle. Front suspension by quarter-elliptic leaf springs, cantilevered forward, and lower radius arms. Rear suspension by quarter-elliptic leaf springs. No dampers. Wire-and-bobbin steering. Belt-rim brakes on rear wheels only, footbrake working on inside of rims and handbrake on outside of rims. Centre-lock wire wheels 650 × 65 tyres. Rudimentary two-seat open coachwork by GN.
Dimensions: Wheelbase 8ft (244cm), tracks (front and rear) 3ft 6in (106.7cm). Overall length 11ft (335cm). Unladen weight 670lb (304kg).
History: Viewed from the new millennium the GN is a joke, but in its day it was a popular and effective little cycle car. This type of machine was an ultra-cheap half-way house between motor cycles and light cars and most owners graduated to them from motor cycles, when they found sidecar progress too tedious. GN was founded by H. R. Godfrey and Archie Frazer-Nash in 1910 and the first cars sold a year later. To keep the price down to around 100 guineas (the cheapest of all, in 1915, sold for 88 guineas) the cars had to be as light and simple as possible. This no doubt explains the use of a wooden (ash) chassis frame, steering by wires which passed round strategically placed bobbins, and a two-speed chain-and-belt transmission, which was open to attack by the elements.

All the early models used proprietary vee-twin JAP motor cycle engines, which kept the passengers' feet warm as they were set right up against the toe board. Bodywork was minimal, in line with the rest of the specification, so an early GN built in 1911 or 1912 (before the inevitable refinement process set in) weighed no more than about 400lb (181kg). In many ways a GN was crude, but

Below and below right: The GN's charm lay in its light weight, its simplicity and in its sporting potential. This two-seater was built in 1922. The radiator was a dummy as the JAP vee-twin engine was air-cooled. Final drive was by chain and there were only two forward gears. From 1923 the Austin Seven killed GN.

Above: This boat-tailed sporting GN was built in 1921, by which time it cost around £315 – and was expensive for the type of motoring offered. The weight was low, but equipment was very sparse. The chassis frame was made of wood, and body panels from aluminium alloy. Total weight was about 700lb.

it was also practical and very easy to repair when it went wrong. Almost everything in the design was simple, accessible, and with an obvious function, and the steering and (within reason) the performance were most satisfactory.

GN made very few machines before World War I (perhaps fewer than 200 in all), but in a post-war factory, production rose to the dizzy heights of 50 cars a week in the cycle-car boom, even though the price of the vee-twin-engined machines had risen to £275 or even £315. Engines were modified persistently at the start of the 1920s and right at the end an attempt was made to upgrade the car with an imported Chapuis-Dornier engine with four-cylinders and water-cooling.

In fact it was a vain hope; the GN was not only being beaten by its own price, but by the fact that the customers were demanding more weather protection and by the fact that the mass-produced Austin Seven became available in 1923 for not more than £165. Both Godfrey (with HRG) and Frazer-Nash (with cars bearing his own name) went on to build more modern and even better 'classic' cars.

Hispano-Suiza Alphonso

Alphonso model – short and long chassis, built from 1911 to 1914
Built by: S.A. Hispano-Suiza, Spain.
Engine: Four cylinders, in line, running in four-bearing light-alloy crankcase and detachable cast-iron block. Bore and stroke 80mm by 180mm, 3,620cc (3.15in × 7.09in, 220.9cu.in). Non-detachable cast-iron cylinder head. T-head valve arrangement, side inlet valves directly operated by offside camshaft, side exhaust valves by nearside camshaft. Single Hispano-Suiza carburettor, directly bolted to block/head. Maximum power 64bhp (net) at 2,300rpm.
Transmission: Multi-dry plate clutch on short-chassis cars, cone clutch on long-chassis cars, and three-speed gearbox, without synchromesh (early versions), or four-speed gearbox (later versions), both in unit with engine. Right-hand gearchange. Open propeller shaft to bevel 'live' rear axle.
Chassis: Separate steel chassis frame, with channel-section side members. Forged front axle beam. Half-elliptic leaf springs at front and rear; later cars had three-quarter-elliptic leaf springs at the rear. Transmission drum footbrake, aided by rear wheel drum handbrake. Worm-and-sector steering. Centre-lock wire wheels. 815 × 105mm or 820 × 120mm tyres. Variety of sports two-seat or four-seat coachwork.
Dimensions: Wheelbase 8ft 8in or 9ft 10in (264cm or 300cm), tracks (front and rear, short chassis cars) 4ft (122cm), tracks (front and rear, long chassis cars) 4ft 3in (130cm). Overall length (short chassis) 12ft 9in (389cm). Unladen weight, chassis only (short) 1,450lb (658kg), chassis only (long) 1,680lb (762kg).
History: Every Hispano-Suiza car designed between 1904 and 1934 was the work of Marc Birkigt, who also designed the first Spanish car of all, the La Cuadra. This company, along with Birkigt, was taken over by Hispano. Like many other Edwardian companies, Hispano used motor sport for publicity and were encouraged by the Spanish monarch King Alfonso XIII when he put up a cup for a voiturette race at Sitges in 1909. A team of Hispano-Suiza cars looked to be possible winners, and led at one stage, but all succumbed to troubles. The team fared better at the *Coupe de l'Auto* races at Boulogne, the best car finishing fifth overall. A year later the revised cars took third place at Sitges, but won outright at Boulogne. It was but a short step for Birkigt to decide that his customers should be able to buy near replicas. He enlarged the engine from 2.6-litres to 3.6-litres, but the basic chassis and mechanical layout was the same.

Right: In many ways the Alphonso laid down guide lines for many vintage sports cars which would follow it in the 1920s. Simple lines, an efficient engine and no excess weight were all keynotes.

Above: Looking rather frail and spidery, the Hispano-Suiza Alphonso was a very rugged little sports car. Like all other Hispanos, it was the work of Marc Birkigt, and this model had a light-alloy 3.6-litre engine. The Alphonso raced with distinction – the name was from King Alphonso XIII.

He named his car in honour of the Spanish monarch. The Alphonso XIII, probably, was one of *the* first 'production sports cars', as opposed to pensioned-off Grand Prix cars, or vast open-bodied tourers. By our modern standards the Alphonso was not a small nor delicate car, but it was thought very advanced for 1911. By Edwardian standards it was adequately fast, with a maximum speed probably of about 80mph – this at a time when anything approaching 100mph was almost Grand Prix car pace. It was renowned for its ease of control and the very long-stroke engine made it a very easy car to drive in give-and-take country. Among its features were the engine/clutch/gearbox in unit – most cars still placed their gearboxes in isolation in the centre of the chassis – and the centre-lock wire wheels when the artillery type was more usual.

In spite of its engine size the Alphonso was not a very large car. Most Hispanos succeeding it were mechanically more complex, larger and much more expensive.

Hispano-Suiza H6B

H6B models, built from 1919 to 1938 (data for 1919 model)
Built by: S.A. Hispano-Suiza, Spain
Engine: Six cylinders, in line, in light-alloy block, with seven-bearing light-alloy crankcase. Bore and stroke 100mm by 140mm, 6,597cc (3.94in × 5.52in, 402.5cu.in). Non-detachable cylinder head. Two overhead valves per cylinder operated by disc-type tappets from single over-head camshaft. Single up-draught Hispano-Suiza carburettor. Maximum power approx 135bhp at 3,000rpm.
Transmission: Multi-dry-plate clutch and three-speed manual gearbox (without synchromesh), both in unit with front-mounted engine. Remote-control right hand gearchange. Two-piece propeller shaft, front half open, and rear half enclosed in torque tube, connected to spiral-bevel 'live' rear axle.
Chassis: Separate pressed-steel chassis frame, with channel-section side members and pressed and tubular cross bracings. Forged front axle beam. Front and rear suspension by semi-elliptic leaf springs. No dampers (friction-type dampers added to later models). Four-wheel mechanically operated drum brakes, with Hispano-type mechanical servo assistance, driven from side of gearbox. Centre-lock wire wheels. 935 × 135 tyres.
Dimensions: Wheelbase 12ft 1in (368cm), tracks (front and rear) 4ft 8in (142cm). Overall length 15ft 10in (482.6cm). Unladen weight 3,360lb (1,524kg)
History: After the great success of Hispano-Suiza aero-engines during World War I, motoring enthusiasts looked forward with great anticipation to seeing Marc Birkigt's post-war private car design. They were not disappointed. The H6B, revealed at the 1919 Paris show, was technically in advance of any other car in the world. Its six cylinder engine was conventional enough if one had

studied the famous aeroplane engines (indeed, it was at once simpler and more effective), but there was also the question of servo-assisted four-wheel brakes, with a mechanically driven servo invented by Birkigt, the sheer quality of the chassis, the magnificent stability and performance and the matchless coachwork styles which the specialists felt inspired to produce for this car. It was without any doubt the last word in advanced motor engineering for the very rich, and if you had to ask the price you could not afford it! Not surprisingly, Hispano pursued what was effectively a 'one-model' policy for some years – with all H6Bs and H6Cs made in the Paris factory. From the H6B, itself at a pinnacle of achievement. Birkigt then developed the H6C cars – Sport or Boulogne models – in 1924. These used the same basic chassis, but had an engine enlarged to nearly eight litres. The 'Boulogne' title was earned because modified H6Bs had won the Coupe Boillot at the Boulogne racing circuit in 1921, 1922 and 1923. One exceptionally beautiful Boulogne was built for the 1924 Targa and Coppa Florio races, with a wooden body shell, and in this guise probably produced about 200bhp, with maximum speed getting on for 120mph. It was the detail in the building of an H6B which made is so remarkable, like the machining of the massive crankshaft from a steel billet originally weighing 770lb and the way the steel (later cast-iron) cylinder sleeves were individually screwed into the light-alloy cylinder block from below. The mechanical servo-assistance to the brakes (where friction clutches driven from the transmission helped increase braking effort) was so good that it was eventually adopted by Rolls-Royce for their own cars. This was the final compliment which Birkigt richly deserved. Even the best were willing to copy the best. An H6B deserved that title.

Left: In the 1920s there is little doubt that the H6B Hispano-Suiza was the best car in the world, though Rolls-Royce disagreed. The model was built for nearly twenty years, to 1938.

Hispano-Suiza V12

V12 models, built from 1931 to 1938 (data for 1931 Model 68)
Built by: Société Francaise Hispano-Suiza, France.
Engine: Twelve cylinders, in 60-degree vee-formation, in combined light-alloy blocks and heads, with seven-bearing crankcase. Bore and stroke 100mm by 100mm, 9,424cc (3.94in × 3.94in, 575cu.in). Two overhead valves per cylinder, operated by pushrods and rockers from single camshaft mounted in centre of engine 'vee'. Two down-draught twin-choke Hispano-Suiza carburettors. Maximum power (on 5.0:1 compression ratio) 190bhp at 3,000rpm; (on 6.0:1 compression ratio) 220bhp at 3,000rpm.
Transmission: Multi-plate clutch and three-speed, synchromesh manual gearbox (without synchromesh on first gear), both in unit with front-mounted engine. Direct-acting central gearchange. Propeller shaft, enclosed in torque tube, to spiral-bevel 'live' rear axle.
Chassis: Separate pressed-steel chassis frame, with channel-section side members and pressed and tubular cross-bracing. Forged front axle beam. Semi-elliptic leaf springs at front and rear. Hydraulic dampers. Four-wheel, mechanically operated drum brakes, with Hispano-type mechanical-servo assistance. Centre-lock wire wheels. 17 × 50 tyres. Coachwork in many styles by European specialist builders.
Dimensions: Wheelbase 11ft 3in, 12ft 2in, 12 6in or 13ft 2in (343cm, 371cm, 381cm or 401cm). Tracks (front and rear) 4ft 11in (150cm). Overall length, depending on wheelbase and coachbuilder, from 16ft (488cm). Weight, depending on wheelbase and coachwork, from 4,900lb (2,222kg).
History: Having built some of the world's finest cars between 1904 and 1930, Hispano-Suiza were not prepared to face the depression with mundane machinery. Instead, Marc Birkigt decided to replace the company's splendid six-cylinder machines with an even finer V12 Hispano, drawing on all his company's aero-engine experience in the designing of it. The company's V8 aero-engine had been built in several Allied countries during World War I and details of its valve gear and general layout were to filter down to many other makes.

The new Type 68 engine, displacing an impressive 9.4-litres, was really a comprehensive up-date of a V12 aero-engine Birkigt had designed in the war, but to achieve quieter running the famous single-camshaft design was abandoned in favour of a conventional pushrod system. The car, announced in the autumn of 1931, was magnificently built and magnificently priced (it was certainly the most expensive French car if one discounts the 'white elephant'

Above and below: Marc Birkigt's masterpiece, the best of all his splendid creations, was the V12 Hispano-Suiza. Much of his experience with successful World War I aeroplane engines went into the V12 which was a 9.4-litre with conventional pushrod overhead valves. At least 220bhp was produced on the high compression, and a V12 could reach 100mph with great ease, and in complete serenity. Any V12 was enormously expensive, especially the later 11.3-litre examples like this with a Saoutchick two-seater touring body. The elegant stork radiator mascot would be dismissed as dangerous these days, but was a symbol of wealth and mechanical good taste in the 1930s.

Bugatti Royale). It was probably the fastest saloon/limousine in the world and, in terms of mechanical excellence, could only be matched by such marvels as the 16-cylinder Cadillacs. Although the chassis was truly 'vintage' in concept, there were advanced features like the gearbox-driven brake servo and, of course, the engine was very powerful (190bhp or 220bhp to choice).

The Type 68 sold in small numbers, as one would expect, but the makers then added an even more impressive option the 68-Bis, with nothing less than an 11.3-litre V12 engine. This produced more than 250bhp and left all the opposition gasping. Hispano had, in the meantime, taken over Ballot, and for a short time made a 'small' six-cylinder car of only 4.9 or 4.6 litres. It is worth noting that the massive and over-bodied Hispanos could reach 100mph without trouble, and there were very few out-and-out sports cars in the world which could approach these magic figures. The last of the cars were made in 1938.

Honda NSX

Honda NSX sports coupé, introduced in 1990 (original specification)
Built by: Honda Motor Co. Ltd., Japan.
Engine: Six cylinders, in 90-degree formation, in four-main-bearing light-alloy cylinder block. Bore and stroke 90 × 78mm, 2,977cc (3.54 × 3.07in, 181.7cu.in). Two light-alloy cylinder heads. Four valves per cylinder, in narrow vee, operation by twin overhead camshafts and intermediate rockers. PGM-F1/Honda electronic fuel injection. Maximum power 274bhp (DIN) at 7,000rpm. Maximum torque 210lb.ft at 5,300rpm.
Transmission: Rear-wheel-drive, single-dry-plate diaphragm spring clutch and five-speed all-synchromesh manual gearbox, all in unit with transverse-mid-mounted engine. Remote-control, central gearchange. Optional four-speed automatic transmission.
Chassis: Unitary-construction pressed and fabricated aluminium alloy body-chassis unit. Independent front suspension by coil springs, wishbones, telescopic dampers, anti-roll bar. Independent rear suspension by coil springs, wishbones, telescopic dampers, and anti-roll bar. Rack-and-pinion steering, electric power asistance on automatic-transmission models. Four-wheel disc brakes, with Honda ALB anti-lock installation. Cast alloy road wheels, 15in front, 16in rear, 205/50-15in (front) and 225/50-16in (rear) tyres.
Dimensions: Wheelbase 8ft 3.6in (253cm), front track 4ft 11.4in (151cm), rear track 5ft 0.2in (153cm). Overall length 14ft 5.4in (440.5cm). Unladen weight 3,020lb (1,370kg).
History: At the height of the 1980s economic boom, when all things looked possible to Japanese car makers, Honda decided to take on Ferrari at their own game. Having studied the latest in 328GTBs, Honda decided that it could do better – and developed the new mid-engined NSX. Along with most other supercars of the period, the NSX's general layout was conventional – it was a two-seater, the engine was behind the seats driving the rear wheels, there was all-independent suspension, and the main air intakes for the engine bay were on the flanks.

Honda, being Honda, then went their own way. Instead of a separate chassis with steel tubes, there was a carefully detailed aluminium – yes, aluminium – monocoque, which ensured that the NSX was much lighter – some estimates quoted 300lb/136kg – than if it had been crafted in pressed steel. The engine, which both looked and sounded sensational, was the already-known aluminium four-cam V6 whose smaller-capacity ancestors had already been seen in cars such as the Honda Legend and Rover 827 executive saloons. Mounted transversely (Ferrari 308/328-style) it drove the rear wheels through a five-speed transmission.

Compared with a Ferrari, the NSX was different in so many ways. Purists (for which read 'Ferrari fanatics') suggested that Honda had developed all the soul and all the passion out of the car. Even if this had been true, the compensation was that they had also engineered in reliability, comfort, a driver-friendly cabin with good ventilation, and the sort of fail-safe handling which made every driver feel like Ayrton Senna. Senna? Indeed, for the great Brazilian Grand Prix driver, who was contracted to McLaren-Honda at the time, had driven the car at every stage of its development.

The style was smooth rather than agressive, and had seen many hours in Honda's own wind-tunnel. The result was a subtly rounded shape which needed no flashy spoilers to provide stability, though a transverse wing section was provided to make the rear aspect look more suitable for the job in hand.

Structurally and functionally, the NSX road car hardly ever put a foot wrong, but it struggled constantly to make its mark. Although there was

Above and below: When Honda developed the NSX, they set out to beat Ferrari at its own game. Did they succeed? The looks, the performance, the engine sounds and the general character were all absolutely in line with this: the rust-proof aluminium construction was a bonus.

nothing, absolutely nothing, wrong with its engineering, its behaviour or its performance (Honda claimed a top speed of 167mph though this was rarely delivered on production cars) it did have one failing which Honda could not solve – it was not a Ferrari. Not even in the USA, where cynicism about Ferrari reliability was well established, and where the NSX sold behind an 'Acura' instead of a Honda badge, could sales stand up against those of the Italians. Sales in the UK were abysmally small – once again, entirely without justification.

Honda persevered – a loss of face would have been unthinkable – adding a 'Targa roof' type in the 1990s, and a 290bhp/3.2-litre version with a six-speed transmission from 1997, though there were no changes to the long, low, sleek style. Secondhand values were low, and in view of the rust-resistant aluminium structure this made an older NSX a real performance bargain.

Horch Type 850

Type 850 straight-eight, built from 1935 to 1939 (data for 1936 model)
Built by: A. Horch & Co., Motorwagenwerke A.G., Germany.
Engine: Eight cylinders, in line, in ten-bearing cast-iron combined block/crankcase. Bore and stroke 87mm by 104mm, 4,946cc (3.43in × 4.09in, 301.8cu.in). Detachable cast-iron cylinder head. Two overhead valves per cylinder, operated by single overhead camshaft. One twin-choke down-draught Solex carburettor. Maximum power 100bhp at 3,200rpm.
Transmission: Single-dry-plate clutch and four-speed, synchromesh manual gearbox (without synchromesh on first gear), both in unit with front-mounted engine. Direct-acting, central gearchange. Open propeller shaft to worm-drive 'live' rear axle.
Chassis: Separate pressed-steel chassis frame, with box-section side members and pressed and cruiciform cross bracing. Independent front suspension by two transverse leaf springs and radius arms. De Dion rear suspension by semi-elliptic leaf springs. Lever-arm hydraulic dampers. Worm-and-wheel steering. Four-wheel, hydraulically operated drum brakes, with servo assistance. Centralised chassis lubrication. 17in bolt-on wire wheels, or bolt-on-steel-disc wheels. 7.00 × 17in tyres. Open touring and sporting roadster coachwork.
Dimensions: Wheelbase 11ft 6in (350cm), tracks (front) 4ft 11in (150cm), track (rear) 5ft 0in (152cm). Overall length 17ft 6in (533cm). Unladen weight 5,070lb (2,300kg).
History: August Horch was one of the motor industry pioneers in Germany, selling his own cars from 1900, after working for Benz for three years. The company's reputation for making prestige models was founded in the 1920s,

beginning with the 33/80PS 8.4-litre car. In the meantime, however, Horch himself had quarrelled with his fellow directors and had gone off to found the Audi marque. Paul Daimler (son of Gottlieb) joined Horch in 1923 and began to develop even more splendid machines. Overhead-cam fours and sixes were already under development, but his first designs were the straight-eights of 1926 and onwards, with twin-camshaft engines. This range grew and grew and before Daimler himself left the company, in 1930, he had also supervised the design of the Type 450 single-cam straight-eights and that of the splendid 6-litre V12 engine, which followed in 1931. That car, splendid and dignified as it was, was just too much for the impoverished times and in 1933 the basic chassis was relaunched with a 3.5 litre V8.

By this time Horch had joined with Wanderer and Audi to form the 'Auto Union', and it was here at Zwickau that the legendary 16-cylinder Grand Prix cars were built. After the end of 1933, small-engined versions of the eight were dropped and the 5-litre became the company's prestige model. It was sold in a confusing number of versions, really as a second-division Mercédès (especially to the Nazi heirarchy), some with rigid axles, some with independent front suspension and some (like the Type 950 and the 951 models) with a De Dion type of rear suspension.

The V8 and the straight-eight models continued right up to the outbreak of war – the single-cam eight, therefore, had had a life of nearly ten years – and many were put to good use by high-ranking German staff officers during the war. Production could not be resumed in 1945 as the factory had been over-run by the Russian forces and found itself in East Germany.

Left: Horch was one of the four German marques which combined to make up the Auto Union. The Type 850 model, with 5-litre straight-eight engine, was splendid, and individually made.

Hotchkiss Six-Cylinder Cars

Six-cylinder cars, built from 1929 to 1954 (data for Type 686 – Grand Sport)
Built by: Hotchkiss et Cie (Automobiles Hotchkiss from 1935), France.
Engine: Six cylinders, in line, in seven-bearing cast-iron block/crankcase. Bore and stroke 86mm by 100mm, 3,485cc (3.39in × 3.94in, 212.6cu.in). Detachable cast-iron cylinder head. Two overhead valves per cylinder, operated by pushrods and rockers from single camshaft mounted in side of cylinder block. Twin down-draught Stromberg carburettors; alternatively one downdraught twin-choke Stromberg. Maximum power 125bhp at 4,000rpm.
Transmission: Single-dry-plate clutch and four-speed, synchromesh manual gearbox (with out synchromesh on first gear), bot in unit with front-mounted engine. Direct-acting central gearchange. Open propeller shaft to spiral-bevel 'live' rear axle.
Chassis: Separate pressed-steel chassis frame, with channel section side members, and pressed and tubular cross bracings, with cruciform. Forged front axle beam. Front and rear suspension by semi-elliptic leaf springs. Lever-type hydraulic dampers. Worm-and-nut steering. 16in pressed-steel bolt-on disc wheels. 6.00 × 16in tyres. Variety of coachwork, open or closed.
Dimensions: Wheelbase 9ft 2in (279cm), tracks (front and rear) 4ft 8in (142cm). Overall length depending on coachwork, from 14ft 7in (444cm). Unladen weight 3,050lb (1,383kg).
History: Harry Ainsworth led the French Hotchkiss fortunes through most of the inter-war years and in many ways the well-known six-cylinder cars ignored current Gallic trends. The first, the AM80, was revealed at the 1928 Paris salon, and was seen to have a conventional but efficient 3-litre pushrod engine, but used several features well proven in the pushrod AM2 four-cylinder car. Over the years the design improved logically, with lowered and stiffened chassis frames, hydraulic instead of cable brakes and synchromesh gears in place of 'crash' gearing.

Rallying was always a Hotchkiss strong point, with outright Monte wins in 1932, 1933 and 1934. After a gap, and some near misses, Trevoux's Grand Sport model tied for first place in 1939 and a pre-war model won again in 1950.

Smaller-engined versions were tried in countries where taxation demanded

Above: Smart and sober saloon version of the original Model AM80 Hotchkiss, built in 1930 with a 3-litre engine. Harry Ainsworth inspired the design.

them, but the classic 3,485cc unit arrived in 1933. The Grand Sport in particular, with its short wheel-base, was very fast (up to 100mph was claimed) and cost about £825 in France.

The French luxury cars lost their market after World War II, but even a Detroit-style full-width facelift could not save the big Hotchkiss. No important mechanical redesign was attempted and the last were made in 1954.

Below: An exciting Type 686 Hotchkiss Grand Prix 3½-litre, with a Le Mans Sports body. The chassis was a rally-winner; this body was well-equipped.

continued on next page

FGY 400
FGY 400

Below: The epitome of the fast and very glamorous French Grand Touring car of the 1930s – the Hotchkiss Model 686 Grand Sport with its drop head body by Henri Chapron. Along with Delahaye and Delage, Hotchkiss provided a clear statement of French fashion of the period. There were four full-size seats and a snug convertible hood. The chassis was conventional, but the push-rod 3½-litre engine pushed out 125bhp. and 100mph was possible.

Invicta

Invicta 1½-litre, 2½-litre, 3-litre and 4½-litre, built from 1925 to 1933 (data for 4½-litre S)

Built by: Invicta Cars, Britain.

Engine: Meadows-manufactured. Six-cylinder, in line, in cast-iron block or detachable five-bearing light-alloy crankcase. Bore and stroke 88.5mm by 120.6mm, 4,467cc (3.46in × 4.75in, 272.5cu.in). Cast-iron cylinder head. Two over-head valves per cylinder, operated by pushrods and rockers from single side-mounted camshaft. Two SU constant-vacuum carburettors. Maximum power in excess of 115bhp.

Transmission: Single-dry-plate clutch and Meadows four-speed manual gearbox (without synchromesh), both in unit with engine. Right-hand gearchange. Open propeller shaft to hypoid-bevel 'live' rear axle.

Chassis: Separate steel chassis frame, with channel-section side members, tubular and channel-section cross-bracing members. Forged front axle beam. Front and rear suspension by half-elliptic leaf springs. Hydraulic piston-type dampers, with Hartford friction dampers in over-riding control. Rod-operated

drum brakes. Coachwork to choice from nominated coachbuilders, including Invictas' own two-seat light-alloy sports body on ash framing.

Dimensions: Wheelbase 9ft 10in (300cm), tracks (front and rear) 4ft 8in (142cm). Overall length 13ft 6in (411cm). Unladen weight 2,800lb (1,270kg).

History: Noel Mackin got together with Oliver Lyle (of sugar-making family) in 1924 to produce cars of a type new to the British market – cars that would combine British standards of quality and roadholding with American standards of performance and engine flexibility. To do this, as their company was to be very small, they had to be skilful assemblers of proprietary parts and 'bought-out' components. The first Invicta 'factory', indeed, was the three-car garage of Macklin's own home at Cobham, Surrey, south-west of London.

The first three cars, with 2½-litre six-cylinder Coventry-Climax engines did not match Macklin's high standards, so for future production he turned to Henry Meadows of Wolverhampton, who were already producing engines for various uses. From 1925, all Invictas with the exception of the 1½-litre model announced in 1932, used Meadows 'sixes'. Macklin's designer was W. G. ▶

Left and below: Perhaps the most famous of all Invictas, the 'flat iron' 4½-litre of 1931. Donald Healey won the Monte Carlo Rally in one, and up to 100mph was possible. Only 77 of these cars were built, and they were as fierce as any Bentley or Bugatti, though without the glamour. The rivetted bonnet was a trademark, carried on to the Railton.

Watson, later renowned for his post-war twin-camshaft Invicta Black Prince, and in the eight years of what are now thought of as 'vintage' Invictas he was loyal to one basic chassis layout. The 2½-litre Meadows model was succeeded a year later by the enlarged-bore 3-litre, but by 1928 the big six-cylinder unit had been further stretched to give a powerful and reliable 4½-litres. Mechanically the Invictas' performance was way ahead of their brakes, and indeed of their styling. Before the end of the decade there was nothing very striking about the cars' lines, even though the radiator was simple and noble, and the bonnet rivets aped those of Rolls-Royce to a very obvious degree.

The 4½-litre NLC Invicta, often with a body as expensive and individually produced as those for Rolls-Royce, was the company's most expensive car of all; its chassis price of £1,050 was only £50 under that of the contemporary 20/25 Rolls. Unlike the Rolls, however, the Invicta had an engine not noted for smoothness or silence, even if it *was* powerful. An 85mph maximum speed was normal for this car – far better than the average.

By 1930, the 4½-litre chassis was being supplied in two forms – the 'high' A-Type, and an entirely different lowered S-Type. The latter, usually supplied with lightweight sporting coachwork, formed the basis of really sensationally effective competition cars. Though colloquially known as the '100mph' Invicta, the production car was really capable of a 90-plus maximum. Nevertheless, Invicta, who sold only 77 of these scarce sports cars, did nothing to discourage the unofficial title, as it could only be good for sales. The chassis was reputedly inspired by that of the successful Delage Grand Prix cars, was very rigid, and was passed underneath the back axle. This rather limited wheel movement, and may have contributed to the rather knife-edge road-holding for which the 'flat iron' Invicta was later renowned. One lurid accident involving 'Sammy' Davis of *The Autocar*, which happened in front of thousands of spectators at Brooklands, did nothing to help.

During the production run, really a misnomer as all cars were hand-built at Cobham, engine power was increased and the last cars probably boasted

140bhp at 3,600rpm. The maximum speed of this bluff-fronted machine would undoubtedly have been over 100mph by then. It is worth recalling that Meadows also sold this engine to Lagonda for their 4½-litre machines, and that W. O. Bentley joined Lagonda in 1935, refined the installation and ensured the engine's life right up to 1939.

No attempt was ever made by Invicta to prove their products on the race track, but they were keen on competition in long-distance trails of various types. In 1930 several top events in Europe were tackled with great success, and in 1931 Donald Healey astonished the motoring world by winning the Monte Carlo Rally outright. A year later the same car and driver took second overall, but as before were fastest of all on the tests where performance was at a premium. The world depression had the same effect on Invicta as on other luxury-car makers, and an entirely different 1½-litre Blackburne-engined car was briefly sold. The company stopped making cars in 1933 and Macklin turned to Railtons in their place.

Below: A Cadogan-bodied 4½-litre Invicta of 1929, with normal 'high' frame and four-seater layout. The chassis cost £1,050, body another £300.

Isotta Fraschini Tipo 8 Series

Tipo 8 models, built from 1919 to 1935 (data for 1919 model)
Built by: Fabbrica Automobil Isotta Frashchini, Italy.
Engine: Eight cylinders, in line, in light-alloy block with nine-bearing light-alloy crankcase attached. Bore and stroke 85mm by 130mm, 5,902cc (3.35in × 5.12in, 360cu.in). Fixed cylinder head. Two overhead by pushrods and rockers from single side-mounted camshaft. Two side-draught Zenith carburettors Maximum power 80bhp at 2,200rpm.
Transmission: Multi-dry-plate clutch and three-speed manual gearbox (without synchromesh), both in unit with front-mounted engine. Direct-acting central gearchange. Enclosed propeller shaft, to spiral-bevel 'live' rear axle.
Chassis: Separate pressed-steel chassis frame, with channel-section side members and fabricated and tubular cross bracing. Forged front axle beam Front and rear suspension by semi-elliptic leaf springs, and friction-type dampers. Four-wheel drum brakes, foot pedal or hand operated. 895 × 135mm tyres. Open or closed four/five seater coachwork.
Dimensions: Wheelbase 12ft 1in (368cm), front and rear tracks 4ft 8in (142cm) Overall length depending on coachwork, from 16ft 3in (495cm). Unladen weight (chassis only) 3,100lb (1,406kg).
History: Before the end of World War I, Isotta Fraschini already had a fine

eputation, not only for making cars, but also for making military machines, narine engines and aero engines. During the war, prototypes of a new eight-ylinder car, designed by Giustino Cattaneo, were on the road and these went n sale in 1919. The Tipo 8, as it became known, was the world's first quantity-roduction 'eight', and was intended to provide the ultimate in luxurious notoring for the rich – particularly in the United States, where Isotta's sales fforts were very strong.

The Tipo 8 was very American in some ways particularly in the flexibility of ts 6-litre engine, and was renowned for impeccable roadholding and a great leal of solid engineering. It was by no means as refined as either Rolls-Royce r Hispano-Suiza cars, but this did not harm its image at first. Cars were sold o Rudolph Valentino, Clara Bow, Jack Dempsey and William Randolph Hearst, vhich did wonders for its image. The Tipo 8A arrived in 1924, with 7.4-litre ngine and more performance, and the 8ASS (Super Spinto) cars were offered o counter Hispano's claims. After the luxury car market collapsed at the end f the 1920s, Isotta turned more to aero engines, and sold only a handful of Bs (further improved Tipo 8S) before closing down car production in 1935. he car had been truly 'vintage' but did not advance with the rest of the ndustry.

eft: The straight-eight Isotta-Fraschini range – the Tipo 8 – was meant to e one of the world's best cars, and had a splendid reputation for more han ten years. It was the first quantity-production straight-eight in the vorld, and sold very well in North America. Like Rolls-Royce or Hispano-Suiza cars, it was built without regard to cost, and was almost the ltimate in prestige machines, with customers among the tycoons and ilm stars of the day. The concept was 'vintage' in every way, and as the ipo 8 was not improved in the 1930s it was eventually eclipsed by its restigious opposition.

Jaguar D-Type

D-types, 3.4-litre and 3.8-litre (data for 3.4-litre)
Built by: Jaguar Cars Ltd., Britain.
Engine: Six cylinder, in line, in seven-bearing cast-iron block. Bore and strok 83mm by 106mm, 3,442cc (3.27in × 4.17in, 210cu.in). Aluminium cylinder head Two overhead valves per cylinder, in part-spherical combustion chambers directly operated by inverted-bucket tappets from twin overhead camshafts Dry-sump lubrication system, with oil tank alongside engine in engine bay. Thre Weber twin-choke carburettors. Maximum power 250bhp (net) at 6,000rpm Maximum torque 248lb.ft at 4,500rpm.
Transmission: Triple-dry-plate clutch and four-speed, all-synchromesh manua gearbox, both in unit with engine. Short open propeller shaft to hypoid-beve 'live' rear axle. Several alternative final-drive ratios.
Chassis: Front section a multi-tube 'space frame', bolted to centre-section stee monocoque tub. Front suspension by wishbones, longitudinal torsion bars an anti-roll bar. Rear suspension by trailing arms and 'A' bracket, with transvers torsion bars. Telescopic dampers. Rack-and-pinion steering. Four-wheel multi pot disc brakes, without servo. 16in centre-lock light-alloy disc wheels. 6.50 16in racing tyres. Almost-two-seat open sports-racing coachwork, with minima screen and no hood.
Dimensions: Wheelbase 7ft 6.6in (230cm), track (front) 4ft 2in (127cm), trac (rear) 4ft (122cm). Overall length (short nose) 12ft 10in (391cm). Unladen weigh 1,900lb (862kg).
History: Jaguar's distinguished racing history began with an XK120' appearance at Le Mans in 1950. The first 'specialised' racing Jaguars were th streamlined 150mph C-types, used between 1951 and 1953, which won the L Mans 24-hour race outright twice. To replace them, both for factory and privat owners' use, Jaguar designed the D-type. The new car appeared in 1954 narrowly failed to win at Le Mans on its maiden appearance and won th Rheims 12-hour race only weeks later. Shaped, as was the C-type, b aerodynamicist Malcolm Sayer, the car was a very efficient wind-cheater an could reach 180mph in wrap-round windscreen trim.

Many components – including the basic engine, front suspension and axle – were production based, making the D-type *the* least exotic of all 1950s racing two-seaters. Not content with winning races themselves, the factory laid down a short production line. Between 1955 and 1957 a total of 45 production cars were sold. 'Works' specials totalled 17 cars. Although the car was designed specifically to win at Le Mans (which it did in 1955, 1956 and 1957) it won races all over the world, including the Sebring 12-hour event in Florida. D-types could be, and were, used on the open road, being docile and surprisingly economical. For 1957, inspired by a private conversion, the factory made a few road-equipped cars with proper screen and hood, called the XK-SS. Only 16 were sold before a disastrous fire destroyed assembly fixtures and caused policy changes. The E-type, none the less, was directly descended from the philosophy of XK-SS.

Right: The fastest D-Types had wrap-round single-seat screens. Le Mans rules in 1956 enforced this version.

Above: The Jaguar D-Type, used by the factory from 1954 to 1956. The final 1956 cars like this had fuel injection.

Jaguar E-Type

E-type 3.8-litre, 4.2-litre, and Series III V12 (data for V12 car)
Built by: Jaguar Cars Ltd. (later British Leyland Motor Corporation Ltd.) Britain.
Engine: Twelve cylinders, in 60-degree vee-formation, in seven-bearing cast aluminium block. Bore and stroke 90mm by 70mm, 5,343cc (3.54 × 2.76in 326cu.in). Aluminium-alloy cylinder heads. Two overhead valves per cylinde opening into 'bowl in piston' combustion chambers and operated by inverted bucket tappets from single overhead cam per bank. Four constant-vacuum SU carburettors, positioned at the outside of the engine, feeding through vertica inlet ports. Maximum power 272bhp (DIN) at 5,850rpm. Maximum torqu 304lb.ft at 3,600rpm. Exhaust emission restrictions caused both figures to drop slightly during the model's production run.
Transmission: Single-dry-plate clutch and four-speed, all-synchromesh gearbox both in unit with engine. Remote-control central gear-change. Open propelle shaft to subframe-mounted hypoid-bevel final drive. Limited-slip differentia standard. Exposed, universally jointed drive shafts to rear wheels. Optional Borg Warner automatic transmission.
Chassis: Front section a multi-tube 'space frame', bolted to centre/tail section steel monocoque tub, with rear subframe for suspension and final drive Independent front suspension by wishbones, longitudinal torsion bars and anti roll bar. Independent rear suspension by lower wishbones, fixed-length drive shafts, radius arms and double coil springs to each wheel. Telescopic dampers Four-wheel hydraulically operated disc brakes, with vacuum-servo assistance inboard at the rear. Rack-and-pinion steering, power assisted 15in steel-disc wheels. ER70VR15in tyres. Open two-seater or closed coupé 2 + 2 seater bodies to choice, plus optional hard-top.
Dimensions: Wheelbase 8ft 9in (267cm), track (front) 4ft 6.3in (138cm), track (rear) 4ft 5.3in (135cm). Overall length 15ft 4.4in (468cm). Unladen weight 3,230lb (1,453kg).
History: The E-type Jaguars, even more successful than the XK series they replaced, were – like the XKs – popular by chance. The first E-type, designed in 1956, was a racing sports car to replace the D-type. Only after Jaguar retired from racing was the order given to 'productionise' the car. It was, in all major design respects, a direct descendent of the D-type/XK-SS family, but with one major difference. It was a completely refined, docile, and roadworthy machine. It was also unbelievably cheap and used very few sophisticated special parts.

Like the D-type, the basis of the E-type (or XKE as the North Americans called it) was a combined monocoque/multi-tube chassis, covered by a sleek, aerodynamically tested bodyshell in which the headlamps were faired into the long nose, and in which the air-intake was as small as possible. All-independent suspension was new from Jaguar. The rear suspension, hung with its differential and inboard brakes from a separate steel subframe, set a pattern followed by every other Jaguar for many years. The fixed-length drive shaft effectively formed an upper wishbone and to keep stresses in check there were *two* combined coil-spring/damper units controlling each rear wheel – one at each side of the drive shaft. The famous six-cylinder XK engine was used, in 3.8-litre 'S' tune, and specially prepared road test cars, running on Dunlop racing tyres, beat 150mph in otherwise standard form, when tested in 1961. ▶

Above: One of the final batches of E-types, with the vee-12 5.3-litre engine. Early 'sixes' had short wheelbases and less passenger space. Headlamps were exposed after 1968, partly to improve lighting at night, but this marginally spoiled the sleek lines. The vast majority of all E-types were exported, many to the USA.

Below: From any angle, the E-Type Jaguar was slinky and beautiful. The original lines were settled in a wind tunnel, as in the beginning the car was to have raced at Le Mans.

The racing E-type project had been for an open car, but for production a slee fast-back coupé with what we would now call a 'third door', was offered. Thi the afterthought, was by far more the more popular version. The first *publ* appearance of a prototype was at Le Mans in 1960, when the Cunninghar racing team were asked to run a works-built light-alloy version. This, althoug fast, did not finish the race.

The early cars were none-too-large inside, and had poor ventilation. Th United States market also found that they overheated too rapidly in heavy traffi and summer conditions. These, and other minor problems, were all rectified. I 1964, the engine was enlarged to 4,235cc and the first of the all-synchromes gearboxes was fitted. Over the years the engine power dropped a little (due t having to meet US exhaust emission limits), the headlamp cowls wer discarded and the interior was revised. Disc wheels supplanted wire-spok 'knock-ons', and power steering was made optional.

The big change, however, was in 1971, when the six-cylinder E-type wa dropped and replaced by a brutal and very rapid V12 car! This, like the X engine, was a quantity-production 'first' in the whole world, at least of any V1 that could be called modern and technically advanced. Jaguar intended th V12, also, for their saloon cars, and for their long-term future. The rest of th E-type, basically unchanged, was extensively redeveloped to cope with th V12's power. Fatter wheels and tyres from the XJ6 were fitted, which mean that the bodywork had to be altered to suit. Early cars had had a 96in (244cm wheelbase, supplemented by a 105in wheelbase (267cm) for the 2 + 2 coup announced in 1966. For the Series III cars, the longer wheelbase wa standardised, which made the open version that much more spacious. A six cylinder version of the Series III was announced, but none was ever produced The last of the V12s were produced in the winter of 1974/75 (the last fift were painted black, and specially plaqued) and the E-type had been replace by the XJ-S. A total of 72,507 were made in all, more than 15,000 of then being V12s.

Below: All the early-model E-Types had faired-in headlamps and small front intakes. Every owner had the registration number painted onto the bonnet.

Above: The late 1960s SII cars had exposed headlamps, 4.2-litre engines, and an all-synchromesh gearbox: much better than the originals.

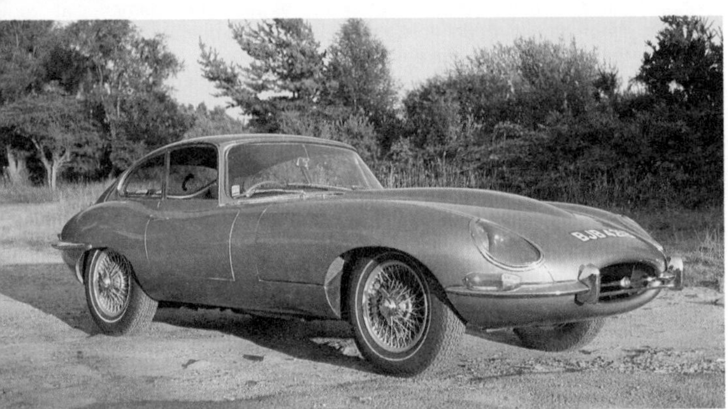

Above: Fixed-head coupé cars with the 3.8-litre engine were near-150mph machines and quite stunning lines. Very desirable, then and now.

Below: Final E-Types were SIIIs, with 5.3-litre V12 engines, wider grilles and wheelarches and a choice of 2+2 coupé or Roadster styles.

Jaguar SS100

Originally known as SS100, SS90, SS100 2½-litre and 3½-litre (data fo 3½-litre)

Built by: SS Cars Ltd., Britain.

Engine: Six cylinders, in line, in seven-bearing cast-iron block. Bore and stroke 82mm by 110mm, 3,485cc (3.23in × 4.33in, 213cu.in). Cast-iron cylinder head. Two overhead valves per cylinder, operated by pushrods and rockers from camshaft mounted in side of cylinder block. Compression ratio 7:1. Twin constant-vacuum SU carburettors. Maximum power 125bhp (gross) at 4,250rpm.

Transmission: Single-dry-plate clutch and four-speed, synchromesh manual gearbox (without synchromesh on first gear), both in unit with engine. Central remote-control gearchange. Open propeller shaft spiral-bevel 'live' rear axle.

Chassis: Separate steel chassis, with channel-section side members, and pressed-steel cross-bracing members. Forged front axle beam. Half-elliptic leaf springs front and rear. Hydraulic piston and extra friction dampers at front, hydraulic piston-type dampers at rear. Four-wheel, rod-operated drum brakes to all four wheels. Fly-off handbrake. Worm-and-nut steering. 18in knock-off wire-spoke wheels 5.50 × 18in tyres. Two-seaters open sports coachwork fitted, of alloy panels on ash framing. No alternatives.

Dimensions: Wheelbase 8ft 8in (264cm), track (front) 4ft 4.5in (133cm), track (rear) 4ft 6in (137cm). Overall length 12ft 9in (398cm). Unladen weight 2,680lb (1,215kg).

History: William Lyons entered the motor industry in the 1920s as a designer and builder of special coachwork for ordinary cars like the Austin Seven and the Standard Nine as well as for sidecars. His 'Swallow' car designs, like his

Above and below: Styled by William Lyons, the SS100 sports car was sensationally fast and attractive. There were 2½-litre and 3½-litre versions.

sidecars, were soon launched in 1931 and built in Coventry. The first SS sports car, the SS90, was an attractive short-wheelbase mechanical version of the 20hp SS1 with a side-valve 2½-litre engine. The SS100, which was born in 1935, used the same SS1 type of chassis, but with suspensions and other details from the also-new SS-Jaguar saloon cars. The engine was a Heynes-designed overhead-valve conversion of the original side-valve 2,663cc Standard six-cylinder unit.

The first SS100 was sensational enough, but the 3½-litre version, announced in 1937, was even more so. The 3,485cc engine, although keeping some Standard parentage, was largely new, and very powerful. The car, priced at a mere £445 in Britain, could achieve just over 100mph and had the looks usually associated with Italian-designed thoroughbreds. The SS100s, in 2½-litre and 3½-litre form, did much for the SS company's prestige up to the outbreak of World War II.

The car made few concessions to comfort. Style and function was considered all-important, with performance a great selling point. One has to remember that in those days a 100mph maximum speed was rare. The new engine was found to be very tuneable and a Jaguar development car eventually lapped the Brooklands oval at 125mph in tests. Only 23 of the SS90 side-valve cars were made, but SS sold 190 2½-litre SS100s and 118 3½-litres. Only one car was built up (from a partly-complete war-time state) in post-war years. In Ian Appleyard's hands it was a remarkably competitive rally car. One fixed-head coupé SS100 was built and exhibited at the 1938 Earls Court Motor Show: this car still exists.

Jaguar XJ220

Jaguar XJ220 sports coupé, previewed in 1989, on sale 1992 to 1994
Built by: Jaguarsport Ltd., Britain.
Engine: Six cylinders in 90-degree vee formation in four-main bearing cast allo cylinder block/crankcase. Bore and stroke 94 × 84mm, 3,498cc (3.70 × 3.307in 213.5cu.in). Two light-alloy cylinder heads. Four valves per cylinder, and operation b inverted bucket tappets from twin overhead camshafts. Zytek electronic fuel injectio with twin Garrett AiResearch turbochargers. Maximum power 542bhp (DIN) a 7,000rpm. Maximum torque 475lb.ft at 4,500rpm.
Transmission: Rear-wheel-drive, AP Racing diaphragm spring clutch and five-spee all-synchromesh manual gearbox, all in unit with mid-mounted engine. Remote control, central gearchange.
Chassis: Separate aluminium honeycomb chassis tub, clad in light-alloy body shel Independent front suspension by coil springs, wishbones, telescopic dampers an anti-roll bar. Independent rear suspension by coil springs, telescopic dampers and anti-roll bar. Rack-and-pinion steering. Four-wheel disc brakes, but no anti-loc provision. Alloy road wheels, 17in at front, 18in at rear, with 255/45-17in (front) an 345/35-18in (rear) tyres.
Dimensions: Wheelbase 8ft 7.9in (264cm), front track 5ft 7.3in (171cm), rear track 5f 2.5in (158.8cm). Overall length 16ft 2.1in (493cm). Unladen weight 3,241lb (1,470kg)
History: The mid-engined 208mph XJ220 which went on sale in 1992 was ver different from the hastily completed non-running prototype which had bee previewed at the Birmingham Motor Show of 1988. A car that had started out as a cost-no-object one-off by Jaguar's 'Saturday club' of engineers, was turned into a limited-production machine by Tom Walkinshaw's Jaguarsport operation. Only the styling – in truncated, and slightly simplified, form – remained. The first car, complete with a detuned version of TWR's 48-valve racing Jaguar V12, had four-wheel-drive and was enormous. At the time intended as no more than a fascinating project car, i attracted so much attention (and waving cheque books) that Jaguar then put it away to think about its future. Within months it had been farmed out for study to Tom Walkinshaw's Jaguarsport business, which was 50 per cent owned by Jaguar Concluding that a lookalike, but mechanically different, machine *could* sell in limitec numbers, Walkinshaw head-hunted Mike Moreton from Ford as his project manage to make it happen.

During 1989 the entire project was recast. Pressured by Walkinshaw, and taking the pragmatic view of costs, development headaches, and the time involved, Jaguarsport decided to ditch the V12 engine and four-wheel-drive system in favour of

a turbocharged four-camshaft V6 was smaller, the XJ220's wheelbase could be shorter, the whole car considerably lighter.

It would take more than two years to move the car from a 'For Sale' brochure to a ready-for-delivery machine.

Although the definite style looked similiar to the original, it was considerably shorter (the wheelbase was reduced by eight inches), and a lot lighter. Ex-racing car designer Richard Owen led a small design team at Bloxham – there was no input from mainstream Jaguar (or from Ford) engineers – the result being a relatively simple package which could be hand-assembled at the rate of three or four cars a week.

The aluminium honeycomb chassis tub surrounded a compact two-seater cabin, the MG Metro 6R4-derived V6 engine (complete with twin turbochargers, just as the XJR race cars had had) was behind the cabin, and transmission was through a specially-developed FF Developments five-speed transmission. Bloxham would only be an assembly plant, since the tubs and the sinuously shaped aluminium body panels would be supplied by Midlands-based specialists. Although the cabin was carefully and comfortably fitted out, and there were aerodynamic 'ground effect' tunnels under the floor of the structure, there was no place in this project for anti-lock brakes, one reason beging that a proper ABS system always takes ages to refine, and the XJ220 was always running to a very tight schedule.

By 1991 prototypes had completed their tests, and some startling top speed runs had been carried out at the superfast Nardo circuit in southern Italy, but in the meantime the world's economy had turned down into recession, many so-called rich people found their funds disappearing and, suddenly, the XJ220's order book was under pressure.

This all detracted from the worth of the £400,000 cars, which started reaching customers in mid-1992. Those who honoured their 1989 instincts found that they had a magnificent-looking, capable and amazingly fast road car, which would be outpaced by only one other machine – the McLaren F1 – later in the 1990s.

Yet everything about the XJ220 was extreme. It was large – very wide and substantially proportioned for a two-seater – far too fast to be unleashed on public roads, with the sort of gearing which made top (and sometimes fourth) gears quite redundant. Expensive to repair whenever anything went wrong – one only had to look at the 18in rear tyres, and the alloy road wheels, to realise how costly a simple kerbing incident would be – it was definitely a car for high days and holidays. Faced with reneging customners, Jaguar struggled long and hard to 'move the metal', eventually winding up the project in 1994 when just 271 cars had been built.

Left: The XJ220 was a massive car with huge performance. The mid-mounted engine produced 542bhp, and the top speed was nearly 210mph.

Jaguar XK Series

XK120, XK140, XK150 and XK150S models (data for XK120)
Built by: Jaguar Cars Ltd., Britain.
Engine: Six-cylinders, in line, in seven-bearing cast-iron block. Bore and stroke 83mm by 106mm, 3,442cc (3,27in × 4,.17in, 210cu.in). Aluminium cylinder head. Two overhead valves per cylinder, in part-spherical combustion chambers, directly operated by inverted-bucket tappets from twin overhead camshafts. Twin SU constant-vacuum carburettors. Maximum power 160bhp (gross) at 5,000rpm. Maximum torque 195lb.ft at 2,500rpm.
Transmission: Single-dry-plate clutch and four-speed, synchromesh manual gearbox (without synchromesh on first gear), both in unit with engine. Open propeller shaft to hypoid-bevel 'live' rear axle.
Chassis: Separate steel frame, with box-section side members, braced by pressed cruciform members and pressed and tubular cross members. Independent front suspension by wishbones and longitudinal torsion bars, with anti-roll bar. Rear suspension by semi-elliptic leaf springs. Telescopic dampers at front, piston-type at rear. Recirculating-ball-steering. Four-wheel, hydraulically operated drum brakes and fly-off handbrake. 16in centre-lock wire wheels 6.00 × 16in tyres. Coachwork (first 200 cars), in light alloy on ash frame base; (all other cars) pressed-steel bodywork in two-seat drop-head, and two-seat fixed-head versions.
Dimensions: Wheelbase 8ft 6in (259cm), track (front) 4ft 3in (129cm), track (rear) 4ft 2in (127cm). Overall length 14ft 5in (439cm). Unladen weight (drop-head version) 2,920lb (1,324kg).

History: The XK Jaguars are rightly, legendary. Announced in 1948, they combined smooth and ultra-modern styling with fine engineering and were powered by an advanced twin-overhead-camshaft engine. This last, incidentally, was the first quantity-production 'twin cam' in the world.

The XK's success was all rather accidental. The engine and longer-wheelbase version of the chassis were intended for Jaguar's new Mark VII saloon car and William Lyons planned his XK sports car as a small-production publicity project. The customers thought otherwise. In six years, more than 12,000 XK120s were sold. The XK140 (9,000 sold) and the XK150 (9,400 sold) all added to the reputation. XK140s had better steering and more power. XK150s had revised styling, even more power and four-wheel disc brakes. The last versions also had 3.8-litre engines. Apart from looking beautiful, the XKs were always very good value for money and very fast. The twin-cam engine, although quite an oil-slinger, lasted for ever.

XKs were great rally cars and successful race cars, although they were really too heavy to take on the specialised French and Italian machines. Production eventually ceased in 1961, 13 years after launch. The XKs, successor – the E-type – made as much of a stir as its ancestor.

Below: The legendary XK120 sports car, powered by the twin-cam 3,442cc engine. It could reach 120mph at a time when most cars struggled at 80.

Jaguar XK8 and XKR

Jaguar XK8 sports coupé and convertible, introduced in 1996, with supercharged XKR type added in 1998

Built by: Jaguar Cars Ltd (a subsidiary of Ford Motor Co. Ltd.), Britain.

Engine: Eight cylinders, in 90-deg vee, in five-main-bearing cast alloy cylinder block. Bore and stroke 86 x 86mm, 3,995cc (3.385 x 3.385in, 243.9cu.in). Two light-alloy cylinder heads. Four valves per cylinder, in vee, operation by twin overhead camshafts and hydraulic tappets. Electronic fuel injection. Maximum power 290bhp (DIN) at 6,100rpm. Maximum torque 290lb.ft at 4,250rpm. (The XKR derivative, introduced in 1998, had a supercharged engine, with 370bhp (DIN) at 6,150rpm, and 387lb.ft. at 3,600rpm.)

Transmission: Rear-wheel-drive, torque converter and five-speed automatic transmission, all in unit with front-mounted engine. Remote-control, central gearchange.

Chassis: Unitary-construction pressed-steel body-chassis unit, made as 2+2 seater fastback coupe or cabriolet. Independent front suspension by coil springs, wishbones, telescopic dampers, anti-roll bar. Independent rear suspension by coil springs, wishbones, telescopics, and anti-roll bar. Rack-and-pinion steering, with hydraulic power assistance. Four-wheel disc brakes, with ABS as standard. Cast alloy 17in road wheels, 245/50-17in tyres.

Dimensions: Wheelbase 8ft 5.9in (258.8cm), front track 4ft 11.2in (150.4cm), rear track 4ft 11in (149.8cm). Overall length 15ft 7.4in (476cm). Unladen weight 3,645lb (1,653kg).

Below: The XK8 replaced the long-serving XJS in 1996, and was a much smoother and more elegant car, powered by Jaguar's new V8 engine.

Above: The XK8 was available in fixed-head coupé or convertible form, both sharing the same sleek lines, 290bhp engine, and soft ride.

History: Although the Jaguar XK8 of 1996 was broadly based on the platform and chassis engineering of the long-running XJS, the earlier car's controversial looks always precluded it from being seen as an out-and-out classic. Of the engineering heritage, though, there were never any doubts. The original XJS Coup'é of 1975 had evolved from the shortened platform of the XJ6 saloon, and in a 21-year career it had evolved through different engine families, a restyle, and two different convertible versions, but by the early 1990s it was time for a change. In the 1980s there had already been one false start (Project XJ41), and four-wheel-drive had been mooted, but after a lot of work had been carried out, this was abandoned.

Fortunately for Jaguar, Ford had taken control in 1989, the funds were finally available for a new start – styling and mechanically engineering – and, in particular, a brand-new V8 engine was designed. A new car to be called XK8 was previewed in March 1996, and was widely praised for its sleek good looks, and its quality.

Compared with the old XJS, the XK8 used the same basic (though much-refined) 102in/259.1cm wheelbase platform and suspension systems (though much of the front-end componentry was new), but not only had the new four-cam 4-litre V8 engine (which was also to be used in the XJ8 saloons) been perfected, but there was a choice of coupé or full convertible body styles.

Where the XJS had been craggy, the XK8 was sleek and rounded, for there was a low nose with a wide-mouth oval grille, specially sculptured headlamps and lines which rose gently, but persistently, towards a rounded tail. There was space in the cabin for 2+2 seating – or, to be honest, for generous two-seater accomodation with very occasional rear seats for legless adults or willing children . . .

The equipment was as carefully detailed as expected, with airbags ahead of both front-seats, and a full display of instruments and controls in the traditional walnut dashboard, though every car was to be built with ZF five-speed automatic transmission. ABS brakes were standard, there was electronic traction control, the soft top was power-operated, and the new 290bhp V8 guaranteed instant and seamless acceleration, and a top speed of at least 155mph. This was all done in silence, with a soft yet well-controlled ride, and in a quality atmosphere that loyal Jaguar buyers from the 1960s might never recognise.

Above: Fifty years of Jaguar sports car development separate the styling of these two models - the late 1990s XK8 and the late 1940s XK120.

As if this was not enough for an impressed market-place (particularly in the USA, where most Jaguars were being sold), Jaguar then set out to develop an even more colossally performing version, the XKR, which made its debut in 1998. The already lusty V8 was treated to an Eaton-type supercharger (not, please note, a turbocharger), which pushed the power up to 370bhp. Although this car's top speed was electronically limited to 155mph, the acceleration and general behaviour was even more outstanding before. By the end of the 1990s, the XK8 was selling faster than its predecessor had ever done, and more innovation was expected in the early years of the next century.

Left: The secret hidden away under the bonnet of the XKR of 1998 was a 370bhp supercharged version of Jaguar's modern 4-litre V8 engine. The top speed was electronically limited to 155mph.

Jensen FF

Jensen FF I, II and III (data for FF Mk 1)
Built by: Jensen Motors Ltd., Britain.
Engine: Chrysler manufactured. Eight cylinders, in 90-degree vee-formation, in five-bearing cast-iron block. Bore and stroke 108mm by 86mm, 6,276cc (4.25in × 3.3in), 383cu.in). Detachable cast-iron cylinder heads. Two overhead valves per cylinder, operated by pushrods and rockers from single camshaft mounted in centre of cylinder block 'vee'. One down-draught four-choke Carter carburettor. Maximum power 325bhp (gross) at 4,600rpm. Maximum torque 425lb.ft at 2,800rpm.
Transmission: Four-wheel-drive layout, comprising Chrysler Torqueflite torque convertor and automatic three-speed gearbox, and central torque-splitting gearbox (Ferguson Formula), all in unit with front-mounted gear shift. Open propeller shaft to hypoid-bevel 'live' rear axle. Transverse chain drive from central gearbox, then exposed propeller shaft to front chassis-mounted hypoid-bevel final drive. Exposed, universally jointed drive shafts to front wheels.
Chassis: Fabricated chassis frame, with tubular-steel side members and pressed-steel floor, scuttle and cross-bracing members. Steel/light-alloy three-door coupé bodyshell welded to chassis after assembly. Independent front suspension by double coil-spring/telescopic damper units, wishbones and anti-roll bar. Rear suspension by semi-elliptic leaf springs. Panhard rod and telescopic dampers. Power-assisted rack-and-pinion steering. Four-wheel, hydraulically operated disc brakes, with vacuum-servo assistance and with 'Maxaret' anti-skid sensor connected to central gearbox. 15in disc road wheels. 6.70 × 15in tyres.
Dimensions: Wheelbase 9ft 1in (277cm), tracks (front and rear) 4ft 8.9in (145cm). Overall length 15ft 11in (485cm). Unladen weight 4,000lb (1,814kg).
History: In the 1960s, Jensen of West Bromwich got together with Harry Ferguson Research of Coventry to develop a practical four-wheel-drive private car. Ferguson had tried, and failed, to get their own car project adopted by the

Above: The four-wheel-drive Jensen FF – a unique private car, with Ferguson transmission and a 6.3-litre Chrysler vee-8 engine.

British motor industry. Now they were happy to sell their expertise and components to a customer in the normal way. Jensen first built a prototype in 1964/65 on the basis of the CV8, which was a 6.3-litre V8-engined GT car with glassfibre coachwork. To accommodate the chassis-mounted front final drive of the Ferguson Formula, the chassis had to be lengthened. The mechanically similar FF went into production at the end of 1966, but this carried the striking Vignale light-alloy coachwork shared with the new Interceptor.

The four-wheel-drive system was much more sophisticated than that of a Land-Rover or Jeep 4 × 4, and incorporated Ferguson's patented central torque-splitting gearbox, which dramatically cut down any tendency for lightly loaded wheels to spin. In addition, the Dunlop 'Maxaret' anti-skid device was added to the braking system; this was connected to the transmission and sensed a sudden deceleration of a drive shaft (ie, if a wheel locked up), whereupon brake line pressure to those wheels would be released. Thus equipped, the FF was probably the safest car in the world to drive on slippery surfaces. Handling and roadholding were excellent, and the FF system's reliability adequate for a pilot scheme. On the other hand every car had to be adjusted individually before delivery and this helped to make the first cost very high indeed – £6,000 in 1968. The last FF was built at the end of 1971 – 318 were built in all. The Interceptor on which the FF was based carried on until Jensen closed down in 1976.

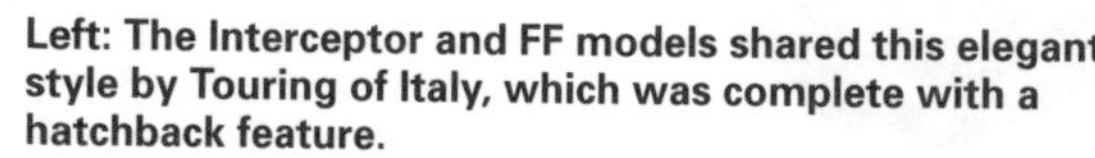

Left: The Interceptor and FF models shared this elegant style by Touring of Italy, which was complete with a hatchback feature.

Lagonda V12

V12 model, built from 1937 to 1939
Built by: Lagonda Ltd., Britain.
Mechanical specification as for Lagonda LG45 six-cylinder model, except for the following.
Engine: Twelve cylinders, in 60-degree vee-formation, in four-bearing cast-iron block/crankcase. Bore and stroke 75mm by 84.5mm, 4,480cc (2.95in × 3.33in, 273cu.in). Detachable light-alloy cylinder heads. Two overhead valves per cylinder, operated by adjustable tappets from single overhead camshaft per cylinder head. Two vertical single-choke Solex carburettors. Maximum power 180bhp (gross) at 5,500rpm.
Transmission and chassis: The transmission and the chassis, with independent front suspension, were shared with the LG6 and the same type of coachwork could be fitted to either motor car.
History: W. O. Bentley's first job after joining Lagonda was to refine the existing six-cylinder 4½-litre car, but once this was achieved he designed a magnificent new V12 engine – apart from Rolls-Royce's Phantom III unit, the only such 1930s British design – and an independently sprung chassis to suit it. The engine was actually shown at the 1936 motor show, fitted to an existing LG45 frame, but the car did not go into production until the end of 1937. The engine itself was everything one could have expected from the designer of great Bentleys, and though it was never developed properly (the war saw to that) it was good enough for special Lagondas to finish third and fourth overall at Le Mans in 1939.

The design was at once advanced and behind the times. Each cylinder bank had single-over-head camshaft valve gear, which was ahead of the times, but there was only a four-bearing crankshaft and rather rudimentary breathing arrangements. The maximum speed of a V12 was at least 100mph, but some cars were fitted with elephantine coachwork, which rather hampered acceleration.

The engine found naval use in the war, but the jigs and tools were destroyed later and the magnificent V12 car and engine were never built again. They were arguably W. O. Bentley's finest products.

Above: Langonda's vee-12 car was designed by W. O. Bentley, no less. No car needs any other recommendation. It was fast, expensive, and exclusive. This standard saloon model was registered in 1938, and its owner is Mr David Wall.

Below: The LG6 of 1938 shared frame and body with the rarer vee-12, and had a 4½-litre six-cylinder Meadows engine.

Lamborghini Diablo

Lamborghini Diablo sports coupé, introduced in 1990 (original specification)
Built by: Automobile Ferruccio Lamborghini, Italy.
Engine: Twelve cylinders, in 60-degree formation, in seven-bearing cast-alloy cylinder block/crankcase. Bore and stroke 87 x 80mm, 5,729cc (3.42 × 3.15in, 350cu.in). Two light-alloy cylinder heads. Four valves per cylinder, in narrow angle vee, operation by twin overhead camshafts and inverted bucket-type tappets. Maximum power 492bhp (DIN) at 7,000rpm. Maximum torque 428lb.ft at 5,200rpm.
Transmission: Rear-drive (four-wheel-drive version also available), diaphragm spring clutch and five-speed all-synchromesh manual gearbox, all in unit with mid-mounted engine. Remote-control, central gearchange.
Chassis: Separate multi-tubular and reinforced steel chassis frame, topped by light-alloy two-seater body shell. Independent front suspension by coil springs, wishbones, telescopic dampers, anti-roll bar. Independent rear suspension by coil springs, wishbones, telescopic dampers, anti-roll bar. Rack-and-pinion steering, no power assistance. Four-wheel disc brakes, with vacuum-servo assistance. Cast-alloy 17in road wheels, 245/40-17in (front) and 335/35-17in (rear) tyres.
Dimensions: Wheelbase 8ft 8.3in (265cm), front track 5ft 0.6in (154cm), rear track 5ft 4.6in (164cm). Overall length 14ft 7.6in (446cm). Unladen weight 3,474lb (1,576kg).
History: Lamborghini had upset the Supercar establishment (Ferrari and Maserati) way back in the mid-1960s with the launch of the mid-engined Miura, had followed it up in the early 1970s with the extreme Countach, and then moved such machinery into an entirely new dimension in 1990 with the introduction of the Diablo. It was not merely that the Diablo was so powerful, so wickedly styled, and so demonstrably special – it was that it laid down a 'beat this for power' challenge to Ferrari, and that it was also to be made available with

Below: Wickedly purposeful from any angle, the Diablo was the fastest Lamborghini. There were rear wheel and (this 'VT' version) four-wheel-drive types.

Above: Lamborghini hired Marcello Gandini to shape the Diablo for them, and he produced this unique wedge-nose/high-tail layout.

a choice of rear-wheel-drive or four-wheel-drive. What must have depressed Ferrari even more was that Lamborghini was now controlled by Chrysler of the USA, so the technical and financial muscle behind the new venture was assured.

Like its predecessors, the Diablo (Devil, in Italian, of course) was a mid-engined beast, its styling being in the capable hands of Marcello Gandini, who had already shaped the Miura and Countach models. Like the Countach, it was based on a multi-tube chassis layout (this time, though, in square-tube instead of round-tube form), with the hugely powerful V12 engine mounted longitudinally behind the two-seater cabin. Like the Countach too, the five-speed gearbox was ahead of the engine (between the seats), and the transaxle behind it, the two being neatly linked by a final drive shaft located neatly alongside the engine sump. About the engine, one needed to say no more than – V12, four overhead camshafts and four valves per cylinder, 5.7-litres and a colossal 492bhp.

The looks, complete with doors which swung forwards and upwards, coleopter-insect-fashion, when opened, rather than outwards, with a low snout, extrovert air intakes in the flanks, and with garden-roller-width rear tyres, all told a story, which was backed up by the amazing V12 sounds – and a top speed of more than 200mph. Exciting enough in rear-drive form, the Diablo was even more impressive in four-wheel-drive VT guise, with a package that not even Ferrari's Testarossa developments could offer. Lamborghini, though, always had to work hard to maintaiun their image, especially as Chrysler's resolve weakened in the early 1990s, and before VW-Audi came in to offer financial stability again in the late 1990s.

The need to impress perhaps explains why later Diablos had 6.0-litre engines with up to 550bhp, why an open-top version (think of the wind chill factor at very high speeds!) was eventually offered, and why extreme competition GT2 types were offered with no less than 630bhp, which was more than any other car in the world.

Throughout this process, the style remained basically unchanged, and it is a tribute to Gandini's experience that a Diablo seemed to be stable even as speeds approached 200mph. The fact that it was still in production in 2000, at the rate of more than 200 cars a year, proved that the concept had always been right, and that VW-Audi was going to have great difficulty in providing a better successor.

Lamborghini Miura and Countach

Miura models, built from 1966 to 1972 (data for P400S)
Built by: Automobili Ferruccio Lamborghini S.p.A., Italy.
Engine: Twelve cylinders, in 60-degree vee-formation, in seven-bearing light-alloy block. Bore and stroke 82mm by 62mm, 3,929cc (3.23in × 2.44in, 240cu.in). Two detachable light-alloy cylinder heads. Two overhead valves per cylinder, opposed to each other at 70 degrees and operated camshafts per bank. Six down-draught twin-choke Weber carburettors. Maximum power 370bhp (DIN) at 7,700rpm. Maximum torque 286lb.ft at 5,500rpm.
Transmission: Transverse, mid-mounted engine ahead of line of rear wheels. Single-dry-plate clutch and gear-driven connection to five-speed, transversely mounted, all-synchromesh gearbox, also ahead of rear wheel line. Spur-gear final-drive unit, with limited-slip differential. Exposed universally joint drive shafts to rear wheels.
Chassis: Pressed and fabricated punt-type steel floor pan/chassis, clothed by light-alloy two-seat coupé body from Bertone. Independent suspension on all four wheels, by coil springs, wishbones and anti-roll bars. Telescopic dampers. Rack-and-pinion steering. Four-wheel, hydraulically operated disc brakes, with vacuum-servo assistance. 7 × 15in centre-lock cast-alloy wheels. GR70VR15 tyres.
Dimensions: Wheelbase 8ft 2.6in (250cm), tracks (front and rear) 4ft 7.8in (141.7cm). Overall length 14ft 3.5in (435.6cm) Unladen weight 2,860lb (1,300kg).
History: Italian industrialist Ferruccio Lamborghini, a fast-car enthusiast, was unhappy about the reliability of his Ferraris, and decided to do the job better himself. His timing, in 1963, was ideal, as the Supercar market was booming. The first Lamborghini coupés – the 350GT and 400GT models – were bulbous front-engined cars, with shattering performance provided by a brand new twin-cam engine. This masterpiece, by Giotti Bizzarrini, was a beautiful and enormously powerful 60-degree vee-12, machined at a new factory at Sant'Agata Bolognese, not far from the Ferrari and Maserati factories.

At the end of 1965 Lamborghini caused a sensation by showing a rolling chassis with the vee-12 engine mid-mounted across the car, behind the seats. The design was by Gianpaolo Dallara, and was topped by an unforgettable Bertone coupé body style in 1966. Too many cynics thought that the new car (called Miura, which was a type of Spanish fighting bull) was a one-off indulgence, but deliveries

Right: The Countach took over from the Miura in 1974, still with vee-12 power, this time mounted in an 'in-line' position. Like the Miura, the Countach was styled by Bertone, and had doors which hinged forwards rather than sideways. Top speed was well over 180mph.

Above: The Miura was the most sensational Italian Supercar of the 1960s, not only for its looks, but for its specification, which featured a mid-mounted four-cam, 4-litre vee-12 engine. Its top speed was more than 170mph.

began later that year. The Miura was strictly a two-seater, but it was extremely fast (British machines achieved more than 170mph), had extremely good handling, and it was practical into the bargain. Not only that, but it was unique, for no other Italian maker of Supercars had a mid-engined car to sell for a couple of years.

Bertone's body style made the Miura memorable, for the entire nose and tail sections could be lifted up for access to the mechanical equipment, and in the daytime the pop-up headlamps laid back, flush with the bonnet lines, looking up into the sky. It was a car which appealed particularly to the "Beautiful People", for no car came more beautiful than this, and merely to look at it evoked visions ▶

of fast, high-speed dashes down the hot autoroutes or autostradas of Europe.

Lamborghini never found it necessary to enlarge the engine from its origina size of 3,929cc, but the original Miura P400, with 350bhp was later boosted t 370bhp for the P400S, and to an amazing 385bhp for the P400SV of 1971, b which time the top speed was under threat once the new Countach prototyp had been shown in 1971, but a total of 775 Miuras of all types had been bui when production ceased in 1973.

COUNTACH

Announced in 1971, in production from 1974. Many components as for Miura except engine mounted in fore-and-aft position behind driver. 375bhp (DIN) a 8,000rpm. Maximum torque 266lb ft at 5,500rpm. Five-speed box in unit wit engine and hypoid-bevel final drive trans-axle. Multi-tube chassis frame, an coupe body style by Bertone, 7.5 × 15in (front) and 9 × 15in (rear) wheels, wit 205 (F) or 215 (R /70VR14 tyres.

Dimensions: Wheelbase 8ft 5.0in (245cm), track (front) 4ft 1.9in (125cm), trac (rear) 4ft 1.8in (126cm). Overall length 13ft 7in (414cm). Unladen weight 3,000l (1,360kg).

History: To improve on the Miura, Lamborghini needed something trul remarkable, and this duly arrived in 1971 as the Countach. Compared with th Miura, the Countach production car had a multi-tube chassis, and the vee-1 engine was now placed fore-and-aft, with the gearbox ahead of it, and almos between the two seats. The styling, by Bertone as it had been for the Muira was not so much 'sexy' as brutally powerful, with a marked wedge front style and with NACA-style air intakes in the flanks to channel cooling air into th engine bay. The official explanation of the title 'Countach', incidentally, is tha this is a Piemontese slang expression suggesting astonishment and admiratio – and had been used by a craftsman putting finishing touches to the firs prototype.

The prototype, incidentally, had a 5-litre Lamborghini vee-12 engine, but th production cars (which started to emerge in 1974, after a long delay fo development of the concept) reverted to 4 litres when the true top speed (wh knows...?) was between 170mph and 190mph. The most controversial featur of the body construction, apart from the looks themselves, was that the door were arranged to open forward from a front bottom hinge, rather than sideway or upwards, which apparently made safety-conscious authorities think twic

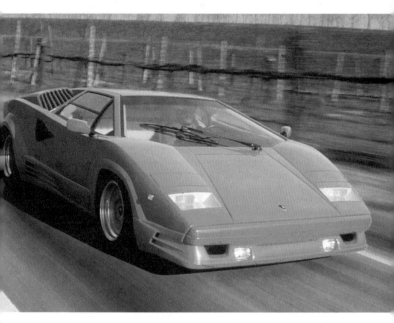

Above: The Countach's wedge-nose style by Bertone, and a peerless 375bhp V12 engine all helped to guarantee top speeds of more than 170mph.

about the after-effects of a serious accident.

Countach was badly affected by the social and financial changes occurring after the 1973-1974 Suez energy crisis, and by Lamborghini's own financial traumas of the 1970s. Signor Lamborghini himself sold out during the decade, and there were other changes of ownership, at least one of which resulted in production being stopped. A total of 1111 Countachs had been built by the end of 1990 when production ended.

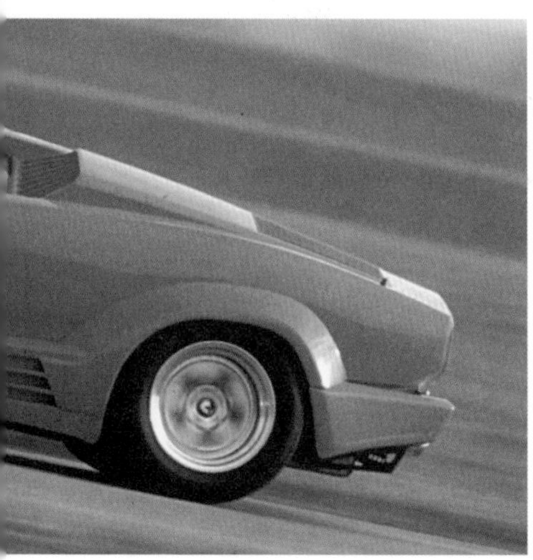

Left: The two-seater Countach, styled for Lamborghini by Bertone, looked startlingly attractive from any angle. The massive V12 engine was mounted 'in-line', ahead of the rear wheels.

Lanchester 40

Lanchester 40, built from 1919 to 1929
Built by: Lanchester Motor Co. Ltd., Britain.
Engine: Six cylinders, in line, in two three-cylinder cast-iron blocks fixed to aluminium crankcase. Bore and stroke 101.6mm by 127mm, 6,178cc (4.0in × 5.0in, 377cu.in). Non-detachable cylinder head. Two overhead valves per cylinder, operated by rockers from single overhead camshaft. Single Smith carburettor. Maximum power approximately 100bhp.
Transmission: Single-dry-plate clutch and Lanchester three-speed epicyclic gearbox, both in unit with engine. Propeller shaft in torque tube, attached to 'live' rear axle incorporating Lanchester worm-gear and differential.
Chassis: Separate chassis frame, with two principal cross members. Front axle beam suspended on semi-elliptic leaf springs. Rear suspension by trailing cantilever quarter-elliptic plate springs. Choice of wheelbase lengths depending on coachwork desired. Single transmission foot-operated drum transmission brake and handbrake lever connected to rear wheel drums (pre 1924); four-wheel, hydraulically operated drum brakes, with vacuum-servo assistance (post 1924), no transmission handbrake. 895 x135 tyres (early models), or 33 × 6½in (later models). Normally Lanchester-constructed coachwork – steel and light-alloy panels on cast-aluminium and ash framing. Special coachwork to choice.
Dimensions: Wheelbase 11ft 9in or 12ft 6in (358 or 381cm), tracks (front and rear) 4ft 10in (147cm). Length from 15ft 8in (478cm), depending on coachwork and wheelbase. Unladen weight, chassis only, 4,480lb (2,031kg).
History: The Lanchester 40 was a magnificent engineering masterpiece, built to the highest possible standards of workmanship and quality and therefore priced

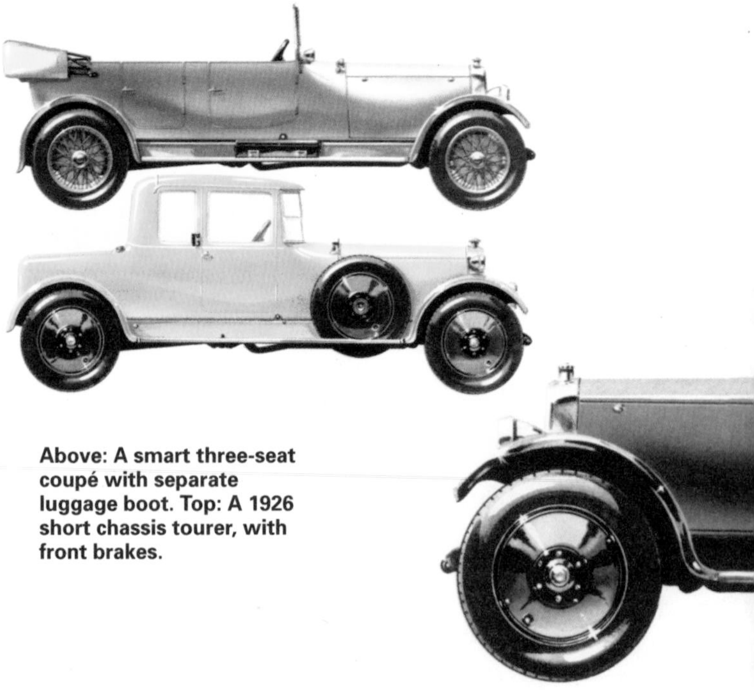

Above: A smart three-seat coupé with separate luggage boot. Top: A 1926 short chassis tourer, with front brakes.

accordingly. It rivalled Rolls-Royce and later Daimler as the finest car in the world for its period. It sold in restricted numbers to the gentry, to royalty and to many foreign potentates. Lanchester had made their name in Edwardian times and the 40, designed by George Lanchester (assisted by his brother Frederick), was spiritually descended from both the pre-war 38hp model and the Sporting Forty. It was big and heavy – up to 5,500lb (2,494kg), with long-wheelbase limousine coachwork – and therefore ponderous and stately. A maximum of 65mph was all that a limousine would normally achieve, but it did this with great dignity and refinement. This was exactly what its customers wanted. On sale from 1919 to 1929 (and, in theory, still available until 1931, although replaced by the new 'Straight Eight'), the car made no concessions to cost-saving. The original price of £2,200 was reduced to £1,800 in 1921, but the model was still among the world's most costly cars. The Duke of York, later King George VI, preferred his '40' to all other machines.

The Lanchester brothers never trusted others to do their own engineering, which explains why not only the engine, but the complex and effective epycyclic gearbox and the worm-drive axle were also Lanchester-made. The four-wheel brakes, adopted in 1924 (because Rolls-Royce were also rumoured to be doing so), were not truly hydraulic, but had servo-assisted mechanical linkages connected to a hydraulic accumulator pressed from the gearbox, which assisted the driver's own efforts.

One 40 was extensively modified, tuned, lightened and rebodied, and in 1921 achieved great things as a racing car at Brooklands. The car was easily capable of beating 100mph and later took a clutch of long-distance endurance records.

Below: By the start of the Vintage years, Lanchester were building very conventional, but grand and impressive carriages. This three-quarter landaulet, built in 1923, was rated at 40hp, and carried its 12ft 6in wheelbase with great elegance.

Lancia Aurelia

Aurelia model, built from 1950 to 1958 (data for Aurelia GT 2500)
Built by: Fabbrica Automobil Lancia e Cia., Italy.
Engine: Six cylinders, in 60-degree vee-formation, in four-bearing cast-alloy block. Bore and stroke 78mm by 85.5mm, 2,451cc (3.07in × 3.37in, 149.1cu.in). Two detachable light-alloy cylinder heads. Two overhead valves per cylinder opposed to each other at 52 degrees, longitudinally, in part-spherical combustion chambers and operated by pushrods and rockers from single camshaft mounted in centre of cylinder block 'vee'. Single down-draught twin-choke Weber carburettor. Maximum power 118bhp at 5,000rpm. Maximum torque 134lb.ft at 3,500rpm.
Transmission: Front-mounted engine and two-piece open propeller shaft, single-dry-plate clutch and four-speed, synchromesh manual gearbox (no synchromesh on first gear), both in unit with chassis-mounted spiral-bevel final-drive unit. Remote-control steering column gear-change. Exposed, universally jointed drive shafts to rear wheels.
Chassis: Box-section and pressed-steel platform chassis frame, with steel and light alloy two-door coupé 2 + 2 body shell by Pininfarina. Independent front suspension by sliding-pillar Lancia-type coil springs and telescopic hydraulic dampers. De Dion rear suspension, with semi-elliptic leaf springs and Panhard rod. Worm-and-sector steering. Four-wheel, hydraulically operated drum brakes, inboard at rear. Bolt-on pressed-steel-disc wheels. 165 × 400mm tyres.
Dimensions: Wheelbase 8ft 8.7in (266cm), front track 4ft 2.4in (128cm), rear track 4ft 3.2in (130cm). Overall length 14ft 4in (437cm). Unladen weight 2,630lb (1,193kg).

Right: The Aurelia GT's classic lines – in 1950 it was a sensational shape.

listory: Lancia's first post-war model, the Aurelia, was delayed until 1950,)ut was an outstandingly up-to-date layout. As with most Lancias, a V-engine ayout was chosen, this time with a conventional 60-degree cylinder bank ngle. New and very advanced was the transmission, with clutch, gearbox nd final drive all grouped together at the rear. The saloon came first, with ,754cc, but this was enlarged in stages to nearly 2½ litres. The star of the ange, the Aurelia Grand Tourismo coupé, arrived in 1951, at first in 2-litre orm. Bracco drove the car into second place overall in the Mille Miglia and he car won its class at Le Mans. The 2½-litre Aureli GT was announced in he autumn of 1953 and Louis Chiron won a protested victory in the 1954 Aonte Carlo Rally. Production of GTs ceased at the end of 1955 although the :ar was listed for another couple of years, and the last saloons had gone by 958. In place of the Aurelia was the dramatically-styled Flaminia, which ievertheless used some of the well-proven Aurelia engineering. The GT is jenerally accepted as being the first of that elusive breed, the 'grand ouring' car.

Lancia Delta Integrale

Lancia Delta Integrale sports hatchback, built from 1987 to 1994 (data for original version, of 1987–1989)

Built by: Lancia & Co. (a subsidiary of Fiat Auto), Italy.

Engine: Four cylinders, in line, in five-main-bearing cast iron cylinder block. Bore and stroke 84 × 90mm, 1,995cc (3.31 × 3.54in, 121.8cu.in). Aluminium alloy cylinder head. Two valves per cylinder, in vee, operation by twin overhead camshafts and inverted bucket tappets. IAW-Weber fuel injection and Garrett AiResearch turbocharger. Maximum power 185bhp (DIN) at 5,300rpm. Maximum torque 224lb.ft at 3,500rpm.

Transmission: Four-wheel-drive, single-dry-plate diaphragm spring clutch and five-speed all-synchromesh manual gearbox, all in unit with transverse front-mounted engine. Remote-control, central gearchange.

Chassis: Unitary-construction pressed-steel body-chassis unit. in three-door four-seater sports hatchback style. Independent front suspension by MacPherson struts, coil springs, wishbones, telescopic dampers, and anti-roll bar. Independent rear suspension by MacPherson struts, coil springs, wishbones, telescopic dampers and anti-roll bar. Rack-and-pinion steering with hydraulic power-assistance. Four-wheel disc brakes. Cast alloy 15in wheels, 195/55-15in tyres.

Dimensions: Wheelbase 8ft 1.4in (247.5cm), front track 4ft 8.1in (142.5cm), rear track 4ft 7.3in (140.5cm). Overall length 12ft 9.3in (389.5cm). Unladen weight 2,679lb (1,215kg).

History: By the mid-1980s, Lancia was not only committed to a massive rally programme, but was willing to develop special cars to make success inevitable. The limited-production Delta S4 of 1985/1986 was one such car, but was outlawed by a change in regulations. Fortunately a less specialised, but still four-wheel-drive, version of the humble five-door Delta hatchback had already been introduced.

Evolution progressed in this way. First there was the front-wheel-drive Delta, complete with a transversely mounted two-valves-per-cylinder 2-litre twin-cam engine, and from 1986 a four-wheel-drive version with turbocharged 2-litre engine, the Delta HF 4x4, also became available. This was Lancia's original 'Group A' rally car, hampered by having only about 240bhp in tuned-up form, but it was still good enough to win the World Rally Championship of 1987. Through its Abarth associates, Lancia then began to evolve this car, and from the end of that year the first Delta Integrale was launched. Based on the HF 4x4, it had

Below: The four-wheel-drive turbocharged Delta Integrale was the ideal base for a rally car, as this 'works' Martini-liveried example shows.

Above: Over the years the Delta Integrale became more and more powerful, first with 8-valve, then with 16-valve turbocharged engines.

more power in road trim (185bhp), wider track and wider rim wheels, with flared wheelarches to cover the fat tyres, and a beefed up four-wheel-drive layout.

Lancia needed to sell 5,000 cars of this type to gain sporting homologation, but this was never a problem, for far more than this number would be produced every year until the early 1990s. Even in this original eight-valve turbo form, it was good enough to dominate World Championship rallying until 1990.

Road cars, which were only ever built in left-hand-drive form, were extremely successful. Not only were these fast and nimble, but they were smaller, lighter and cheaper than any of their opposition, and seemed to have more character – more sheer Italian brio – than could possible have been expected from the specification. The looks, square-rig and distinctly unaerodynamic, cannot have been responsible. On the other hand fine handling, inch-accurate steering and response were all spine-tinglingly satisfying, as was a top speed of almost 140mph. Not even traditionally doubtful Lancia build quality could detract from all this.

But there was more. For 1990 and beyond Lancia introduced the Integrale 16V, where the new 16-valve cylinder head helped deliver 200bhp (a bulged bonnet was needed to cover this new head), while even this was exceeded from mid-1993, in the Integrale's final manifestation, where 215bhp was delivered through an exhaust-cleaning catalyst, and where there was an extra transverse aerofoil on the rear of the roof to trim the high-speed performance.

Buyers of Integrales worrying about the strength of the running gear could always take comfort in the marque's rally successes, for a record-breaking sequence saw the 'works' cars take the World Rally Championship for Makes from 1987 to 1992 inclusive, and saw the 'works' cars regularly producing 340–360bhp from the same basic engine which was used in the road cars. Years after production and sales ended in 1994, the Integrale's reputation was still high, and residual values remained. Lancia never attempted to produce a better and more balanced car than this.

Lancia Lambda

Lambda Series 1 to 9, built from 1923 to 1931 (data for Series 1 Lambda)
Built by: Fabbrica Automobili Lancia e Cia., Italy.
Engine: Four cylinders, in 13-degree vee-formation, in three-bearing light-alloy block/crankcase. Bore and stroke 75mm by 120mm, 2,120cc (2.95in × 4.72in, 129.4cu.in). Single detachable cast-iron cylinder head. Two overhead valves per cylinder, operated by rockers and cam followers from single overhead camshaft. Single Zenith carburettor at rear of head, feeding to middle of engine. Maximum power 50bhp at 3,000rpm. Maximum torque 38lb.ft at 2,125rpm.
Transmission: Multiple-dry-plate clutch and three-speed manual gearbox (without synchromesh) both in unit with engine, direct-acting central gearchange. Two-piece open propeller shaft to spiral-bevel 'live' rear axle unit.
Chassis: Separate sheet-steel chassis, really a unitary structure forming frame and basic body structure in one. Independent front suspension by Lancia-type coil springs and sliding pillar linkage, with vertical telescopic dampers. Rear suspension by semi-elliptic leaf springs, with Hartford friction-type dampers. Worm-and-wheel steering. Centre-lock wire wheels. 765 × 105 tyres. Four-wheel drum brakes. Coachwork to choice – tourer, sports, or saloon. Structural boot compartment supplied as part of Lancia unitary-construction chassis structure.
Dimensions: Wheelbase 10ft 2in (310cm), tracks (front and rear) 4ft 4in (132cm), overall length 14ft 4in (437cm). Unladen weight (depending on coachwork) about 2,400lb (1,088kg).

History: Narrow-angle vee-formation engines had been an obsession in Vincenzo Lancia's plans for many years before his Lambda was announced in 1921, but the Lambda will also be remembered for its remarkable, unique, and rigid chassis. The engine, with only 13 degrees between banks (the block casting was actually almost cubic) was very short and stubby, with no attempt to deal with the out of balance dynamic forces. It is interesting to note that later Lambdas used 14-degree engines and final versions a 13-degree 40-minute layout.

The chassis was even more remarkable. It was a skeleton framework of flanged pressed-steel members, riveted together in ship fashion, with cut-outs for doors and for lightening. Cross bracing for these deep side members was provided by scuttle and bulkhead panels, and a rigid backbone, which included the propeller shaft tunnel. Suspension and steering were hung from strategically placed tubular cross members. Front suspension was independent, by coil springs bearing above and below on to the sliding pillar stub axles – an arrangement used by Lancia for another thirty years. The firm was even forced to invent its own type of hydraulic dampers, integral with the 'king pin' housing.

The Lambda, made in nine series between 1923 and 1931, was at once light, low, and with exceptional roadholding, by any standards. More than 12,000 were made and Lancia's reputation for making 'way out' engineering work was established.

Left: Lancia's famous Lambda model was introduced in 1923 and ran through to 1931. The example shown was a 1928 version, mechanically very similar to the originals, and with that unique type of narrow-angle vee-4 light-alloy engine. The chassis frame was the other Lambda advance – of sheet steel and very deep – really an early example of unit-construction, now universal.

Lancia Stratos

Stratos model, built from 1974 to 1975
Built by: Fabbrica Automobili Lancia e Cia. (now part of Fiat), Italy.
Engine: Ferrari manufactured. Six cylinders, in 65-degree vee-formation, in four-bearing light-alloy block, transversely mounted behind seats. Bore and stroke 92.5mm by 60mm, 2,418cc (3.64in × 2.36in, 147.5cu.in). Light-alloy cylinder heads. Two overhead valves per cylinder, inclined to each other in part-spherical combustion chambers and operated by twin overhead camshafts. Three down-draught twin-choke Weber carburettors. Maximum power 190bhp (DIN) at 7,000rpm. Maximum torque 159lb.ft at 4,500rpm. Four-valve cylinder heads also available for competition purposes, along with fuel injection in some applications.
Transmission: Single-dry-plate clutch and five-speed, all-synchromesh manual gearbox, behind and below the main engine block. Remote-control central gearchange. Direct gearbox shaft to hypoid-bevel final-drive unit. Exposed, universally jointed drive shafts to rear wheels.
Chassis: Fabricated sheet-steel chassis structure, with tubular and other fabricated cross-bracing members. Glassfibre body skin panels, non-load-bearing. Engine/transmission behind driving compartment. Two seats in closed coupé layout. All independent suspension, by coil springs, wishbones, and anti-roll bars. Telescopic dampers. Rack-and-pinion steering. Four-wheel, hydraulically operated disc brakes. 14in bolt-on cast-alloy wheels. 205/70VR14 tyres. Wider wheels optional.
Dimensions: Wheelbase 7ft 1.8in (218cm), track (front) 4ft 8.2in (143cm), track (rear) 4ft 9.5in (146cm). Overall length 12ft 2in (371cm). Unladen weight about 2,160lb (980kg).
History: The Stratos was born out of Lancia's desire to dominate international production car motor sport, and particularly rallying. Cesare Fiorio, at once sales director and competition chief at Lancia, knew that the front-drive Fulvia coupés were no longer competitive and co-operated with Bertone in evolving a very special machine. It was nothing less than a full-blown mid-engined competition car, of which the minimum number (400 in a 12-month period) would be made to ensure approval for Group 4 competition. The first 'show car' by Bertone was a non-runner and was fitted with a Lancia Fulvia V4 engine, but as Lancia and

Below: The Lancia Stratos was a purpose built competition car, of which only a few hundred were made between 1974 and 1975. It could win races or survive the roughest and toughest rallies, with a combination of over powerful 2.4-litre vee-4 Ferrari engine, and a light but rigid structure.

Above: The Stratos's style was by Bertone, the rear-drive engine was behind the seats, and rally-tuned 24-valve engines produced up to 280bhp.

Ferrari were now both controlled by Fiat it seemed reasonable to go the whole way to domination. The 'production' Stratos, therefore, was given a straight transplant, without any need for modification, of the 2.4-litre, four-cam, V6 Ferrari Dino engine and transmission, which was already engineered for mid-mounting. The Stratos, although stubby, low, and wickedly purposeful-looking, was also very strong. It had to be – it was meant to win not only the fastest tarmac rallies, and road races to be found in Europe, but also to tackle the rough events like the East African Safari, the Moroccan rally and the RAC rally. After some development problems, speedily solved because the solution could be applied to the small batch of production machines, the Stratos soon began to win, more or less as it pleased. It has to be said that the 'works' machines were usually stronger and more reliable than those supplied to private owners, but this is only to be expected.

The production Stratos disposed of 190bhp, but competition versions usually had 240bhp, and – once the four-valve cylinder heads were homologated – up to 280bhp was available. This along with the splendid traction and road-holding of the cars, allied with the bravery of factory-hired drivers, made the cars almost unbeatable. Only the Safari (where dust in the engines is a major hazard) has really defeated the arrow-shaped projectile from Turin. The Stratos was never a serious road car, although some wealthy enthusiasts use the cars in this way. The factory continued to campaign the machines years after production ceased.

Leyland Eight

Leyland Eight, built from 1920 to 1922 (data for one-off 1927 sports car)
Built by: Leyland Motors Ltd., Britain.
Engine: Eight cylinders, in line, in six-bearing light-alloy block. Bore and stroke 89mm by 140mm, 6,987cc (3.50in × 5.5in, 425cu.in). Cast-iron cylinder head. Two overhead valves per cylinder, inclined in part-spherical combustion chambers and operated by short rockers from single overhead camshaft. Leaf valve-return springs. Single Zenith carburettor. Maximum power 200bhp (net) at 2,800rpm.
Transmission: Single-dry-plate clutch and separate four-speed, sliding gear manual gearbox. Right-hand gearchange. Propeller shaft, enclosed in torque tube, to spiral-bevel 'live' rear axle. Splayed drive shafts, giving positive wheel chamber.
Chassis: Separate steel chassis frame, with channel-section side members and tubular and pressed cross braces. Forged front axle beam. Front suspension by semi-elliptic leaf springs. Rear suspension by cantilever quarter-elliptic leaf springs, connected by anti-roll torsion bar. Marles steering. Rear-wheel drum brakes, vacuum-servo assisted; no front brakes. Steel-disc road wheels. 895 × 135 tyres.
Dimensions: Wheelbase 10ft 6in (320cm), tracks (front and rear) 4ft 8.5in (143.5cm). Overall length 16ft 1in (490cm). Unladen weight 3,140ln (1,424kg).

History: Before the 1960s there was, quite literally, only one design of Leyland private car. This was the magnificent Leyland Eight, designed by J. G. Parry Thomas during World War I. Shown for the first time at London's Olympia motor show, it was dropped in little more than two years. Reputedly only 18 cars were built and sold, although when Thomas when off to indulge his passion for motor racing, at Brooklands, he took several spare chassis and other components with him. The Eight was meant to be the best car in the world, regardless of cost, and was aimed squarely at the Rolls-Royce market. The design was good enough for its purpose, but Leyland themselves never backed Thomas's skills with their facilities. Trucks were more important to them and when post-war financial problems intruded the project was unceremoniously dropped.

The only surviving Leyland Eight is the short-chassis sports car now owned by B.M.I.H.T., built up in 1927 from parts held at the Thomson and Taylor workshops in Brooklands. The engine was remarkable for its detail – including leaf spring control of the valves, and eccentric camshaft drive. The live axle was arranged to give positive road wheel camber to match the steeply cambered roads of the day. The starter motor, incidentally, was fixed to the gearbox. A few engines were enlarged from 7 litres to 7,266cc by means of a 6mm (0.24in) stroke increase. Opinion is that, mechanically at least, the Leyland Eight was the best car in the world during its short life.

Left: Not until Leyland took control of Jaguar in 1968 did they build a finer car than the Leyland Eight. It was grand and exclusive – only 18 cars were built in three years – with an advanced 'straight eight' engine.

Lincoln Continental

Continental, built from 1940 to 1948 (data for 1940 model)
Built by: Lincoln Motor Co. (a division of Ford Motor Co.), United States.
Engine: 12-cylinders, in 75-degree vee-formation, in cast-iron block. Bore and stroke 73.0mm by 95.25mm, 4,784cc (2.87in × 3.75in, 292cu.in). Aluminium cylinder heads. Two side valves per cylinder, operated by hydraulic tappets from single camshaft mounted in centre of cylinder block 'vee'. Single downdraught Holley carburettor. Maximum power 120bhp (gross) at 3,500rpm.
Transmission: Single-dry-plate clutch and three-speed manual gearbox (synchromesh on top and second gears), both in unit with engine. Remote-control steering column gearchange. Propeller shaft in torque tube to spiral-bevel 'live' rear axle. Optional two-speed Columbia 'over-drive' axle, giving 23 per cent higher gearing when in use.
Chassis: Separate steel chassis frame, with channel-section side members and pressed and tubular cross braces. Forged front axle beam. Transverse-leaf suspension with radius arms, at front and rear. Hydraulic lever-arm dampers. Four-wheel hydraulically operated drum brakes. Mechanical hand brake operating on rear wheels. 16in pressed-steel wheels. 7.00 × 16in tyres.
Dimensions: Wheelbase 10ft 5in (317cm), track (front) 4ft 7.5in (141cm), track (rear) 5ft 0.7in (154cm). Overall length 17ft 6in (533cm). Unladen weight (coupé) 3,890lb (1,764kg).
History: Unlike the KV2 and the Lincoln-Zephyr models, the Continental was a very exclusive, high-priced machine for the status conscious. It was the brainchild of none other than Edsel Ford, who was president of his father's Ford Motor Company from 1919 to 1943. Edsel was much more interested in engineering and up-to-the-minute styling than his father (who was much more attracted to the idea of selling millions of cars at the lowest possible price) and it was his decision which led to the formation of a styling department in the

Above and below: In the beginning the Lincoln 'Continental' name meant much more than it does today. The vee-12 engine was shared with other models but the two-door bodies (coupé or drop head) were sleek and special.

corporation at a time when such things were still unusual in Detroit. Edsel Ford always regretted that Lincoln's fine name had progressively been downgraded since the 1920s, when Ford had bought it, and by the mid 1930s he was determined to do something about this. The styling studio was set up in 1932 and within a year their first Edsel-inspired efforts were on the road. Commercial pressures meant that Lincoln had to concentrate on the bread-and-butter Zephyrs in the mid and late 1930s, but by 1938 the fashion-conscious Edsel Ford decided to have a very special looking model developed. He was much influenced by the cars being made (at high prices) in Europe, and it was natural that the new car should immediately be known as a 'Continental' – a name which stuck to Lincoln even when the first famous model was discontinued, and which appears on modern products to this day.

Sales, Ford had no doubt, would be restricted, especially as he was prepared to see a $4,000 showroom price, so all his team's efforts were put in the body and fitting. Under the skin, disappointing to those more interested in engineering than in styling, was the 1939-model Lincoln-Zephyr convertible coupé chassis. The engine, a 75-degree V12 side-valve unit already sold in the Lincoln-Zephyr, owed much to Ford's famous V8 engine and was none the worse for that, even though it was a very simple and cheap engine to make. Aluminium cylinder heads, three-speed gearbox with steering column gearchange and the Columbia two-speed axle were also familiar components. Unfortunately, so was the transverse-leaf suspension insisted on by Henry Ford himself for many years. In spite of the fact that General Motors had adopted independent front suspension years earlier, the elderly Ford was adamant and the Continental was way behind in this respect. The styling, on the other hand, was not. Although enthusiasts now look on the car as very special, it shared some panels with the Lincoln-Zephyr cars. Prototypes were built in 1939 and the first batch of production cars was delivered early in 1940. All were two-door machines, in coupé or cabriolet form, and at first an exposed rear-mounted

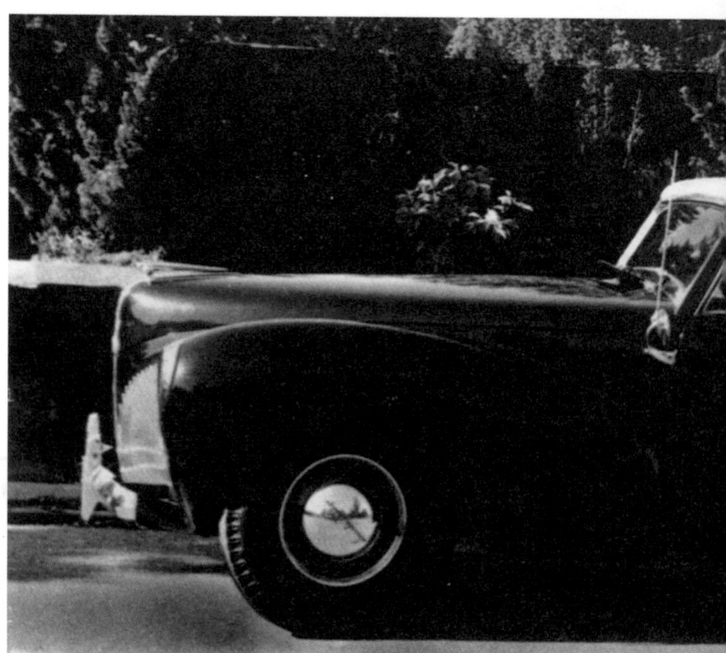

spare wheel was a recognition point. Mechanically the car was changed very little over the years, but for 1942 (a short-lived season because of the war) the Lincoln-Zephyr type of nose was superseded by a modern trend with box-style wings and coffin-type nose. The engine was bored out to a full five litres at the same time, but unreliability caused this change to be reversed in 1946. Very important too was the option of 'Liquimatic' automatic transmission but it was not a success. Overdrive, to replace the two-speed axle, was much more popular. Post-war production of Continentals was resumed in 1946, but the model's sponsor Edsel Ford had died in 1943, so there was little impetus to develop a successor. The price shot up with post-war inflation, but there was no shortage of buyers. This is proved by looking at sales figures – 5,324 cars were sold in all, but nearly 1,300 of these were sold in January to March 1948, after which the model was discontinued. One reason for the high price was that fittings and furnishings were always individually specified and much of the bodywork was hand-formed by craftsmen – a most unlikely thing for any Detroit-based concern to attempt. Only 404 were made in the 1940 model year, and 1,250 in the 1941 series.

The Continental was to reappear, with similar success and distinction, as the Mark II in the mid 1950s and as the Mark III in the late 1960s. In neither case, however, was it so exclusive, or so sought-after by the well off. Continentals live on, but are no more than super de luxe Fords.

Below: Collectors now look on the drop-head cabriolet Lincoln Continental as the most desirable of the range. Edsel Ford inspired the styling, after much study of European trends. From 1940 to 1948, only 5,324 Continentals were built. The chassis was standard vee-12 Lincoln – but the bodies had special fixtures and fittings. The quality rivalled Cadillac – something Ford always wanted. Few other Detroit cars have such an aura.

Lincoln K-Series V12s

K-Series cars, built from 1932 to 1939 (data for 1932 V12)
Built by: Lincoln Motor Co., United States.
Engine: 12 cylinders, in 65-degree vee-formation, in two cast-iron blocks, with seven-bearing light-alloy crankcase. Bore and stroke 82.55mm by 114.3mm, 7,340cc (3.25in × 4.5in, 448cu.in). Two detachable cast-iron cylinder heads. Two side valves per cylinder, operated by tappets from single camshaft mounted in top of crankcase. One twin-choke down-draught carburettor.
Transmission: Twin-dry-plate clutch and three-speed, synchromesh manual gearbox (without synchromesh in first gear), both in unit with front-mounted engine. Freewheel mounted in tail of gearbox. Propeller shaft, enclosed in torque tube, driving spiral-bevel 'live' rear axle.
Chassis: Separate pressed-steel chassis frame, with channel-section side members and pressed and tubular cross-bracing. Forged front axle beam. Front and rear suspension by semi-elliptic leaf springs, rear location by torque tube. Lever-arm hydraulic dampers. Worm-and-roller steering. Four-wheel, rod-operated drum brakes, with vacuum-servo assistance. 18in bolt-on wire wheels. 7.50 × 18in tyres. Choice of coachwork, saloon, convertible or limousine.
Dimensions: Wheelbase 12ft 1in (368cm), track (front and rear) 5ft (152cm). Overall length 17ft 10in (543.5cm). Unladen weight, depending on coachwork, from 5,800lb (2,630kg).
History: Henry Leland resigned from Cadillac in 1917 and evolved a new car for 1921 which he called the Lincoln. However, the new concern was not financially successful and it was acquired by Henry Ford in 1922. Ford himself was happy to let Lincoln carry on making small numbers of exclusive machines for well over ten years before the first 'Ford -Lincoln' (the Zephyr) was designed. The new management carried on building V8 Lincolns for ten years, but in 1932 they announced the splendid and rather exclusive K-Series cars, one of which (the KB) was given a new V12 engine of 7.3 litres. The cars were beautifully made and were impressive rather than attractive to look at. Their quantity-production precision engineering was obvious, but they were just one of seven 12s on the market in 1932, so sales were low: only just over 2,000 were sold in 1933. Even though the KA, which had been V8 powered, acquired a smaller-edition 6.2-litre V12 in 1933, it had to retail for $2,700, which put it in the luxury category and

out of reach of most impoverished rich Americans. Even so, there was much of interest in the technical details. The chassis and suspension were entirely conventional, but the engine was a mixture of old and new – among its features being a 65-degree angle between banks (60 degrees would have been normal and would have given perfect balance), side valves and detachable cylinder blocks on a light-alloy crankcase. There was synchromesh in the gearbox (all America was fast following GM's 1928 example) and a freewheel feature into the bargain. Surprisingly the brakes were mechanically operated, but they had a vacuum servo to assist the driver.

A new Model K was announced for 1934 to replace both the original KAs and KBs; this had a slightly smaller engine, of 6.8 litres (414cu.in), aluminium cylinder heads and a top speed of about 100mph. There was important restyling a year or two later, but sales gradually died away and the last of this type of V12 was built in 1939. In the meantime the Ford-designed Lincoln Zephyr, much cheaper yet still fast, had begun to sell like hot cakes. As one Lincoln tradition had been destroyed, another was beginning to burgeon.

Above and left: One of Lincoln's finest cars was the K-Series vee-12, built throughout the Depression years. Quality and engineering always came ahead of price, though in later years the styling was recognisably related to cheaper Fords.
Left: A 1932 KB sedan with the 7.3-litre side-valve engine.
Above: A 1934 Model K with Dietrich convertible body, 6.8-litres, and a top speed of 100mph.

Lincoln Zephyr

Zephyr, built from 1935 to 1948 (data for 1936 model)
Built by: Lincoln Motor Co. (Division of Ford Motor Co.), United States.
Engine: 12 cylinders, in 75-degree vee-formation, in four-bearing cast-iron block/crankcase. Bore and stroke 69.8mm by 95.2mm, 4,375cc (2.75in × 3.75in 267cu.in). Two detachable aluminium cylinder heads. Two side valves per cylinder, operated directly by single camshaft positioned in centre of cylinder block 'vee'. One single-choke down-draught Stromberg carburettor. Maximum power 110bhp (gross) at 3,900rpm.
Transmission: Single-dry-plate clutch and three-speed, synchromesh manual gearbox (without synchromesh on first gear), both in unit with front-mounted engine. Propeller shaft, enclosed in torque tube, driving spiral-bevel 'live' rear axle.
Chassis: Unitary-construction pressed-steel body/chassis unit. Forged front axle beam. Front and rear suspension by transverse leaf spring and radius arms. Lever-arm hydraulic dampers. Four-wheel, cable-operated drum brakes. 16in bolt-on pressed-steel-disc wheels. 7.00 × 16in tyres.
Dimensions: Wheelbase 10ft 2in (310cm), track (front) 4ft 7.2in (140cm), track (rear) 4ft 8.7in (144cm). Overall length 16ft 10.5in (514cm). Unladen weight 3,350lb (1,519kg).
History: By 1935, Ford were in the full flow of their success, having capitalised perfectly on the reliability, performance, and low cost of the V8 car. They now turned their attention to the prestigious Lincoln marque, which had been making no more than about 40 cars every week in the V12 K-Series for some time. In a clever and entirely successful marketing move, a 'new' Lincoln was created

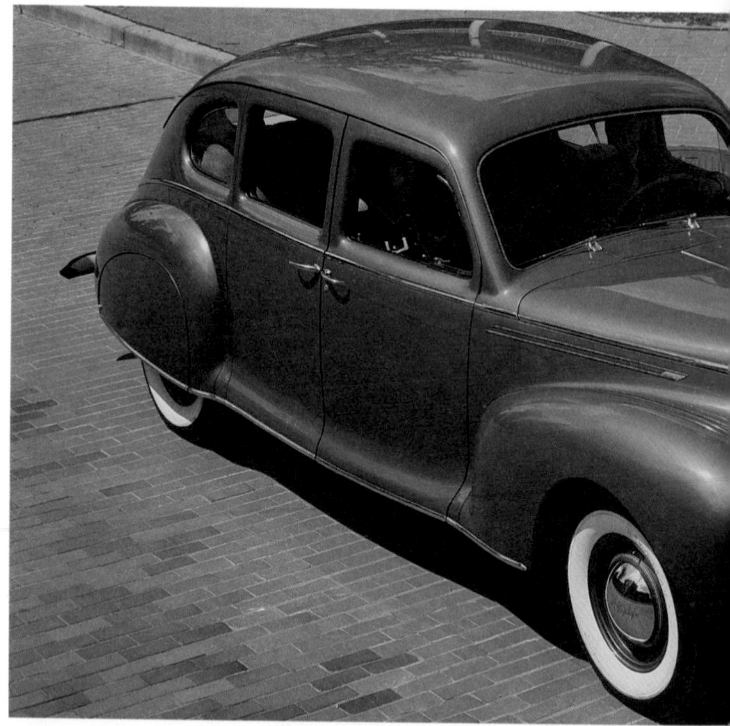

with much family resemblance to Ford's current models, and with a new side-valve V12 engine which drew on the Ford V8 for many of its parts and all of its design philosophy. It was a big 4.4-litre design, but it produced only 110bhp. The main innovation was that the car had unitary construction (the first time in a car from the Ford empire); it was also by far the cheapest 12-cylinder car in the world. That outweighed other carryover points like the transverse-leaf suspension and the wide-ratio three-speed gearbox. The styling, with headlamps recessed in the wings, a six-window shape and a fastback tail with spatted rear wheels, was no more 'modern' than Chrysler's Airflow, but was much more commercially successful. A year later Ford's own styling was brought into line and the two marques shared identical noses and many sheet metal panels.

The V12, at first, was not entirely successful, for the exhaust passages were brought out across the cylinder block from the line of valves in the centre of the 'vee' and there were overheating problems. These were soon overcome, and the Lincoln Zephyr went on to become a very important model in Ford's line-up. The engine, too, became popular with other manufacturers (like Allard and Jensen in Britain), as it was a sure-fire way to develop enough power and torque to power any self-respecting trials or rally car. A facia-mounted gearchange was adopted in 1938, but it was replaced by a column change in 1940 and there were hydraulic brakes from 1939. Over-drive, a fluid coupling and power windows all became optional before production closed down in 1941. The same model was built between 1945 and 1948.

Left: Designed specifically to fill a gap between Ford V8s and the expensive K-Models, the Lincoln Zephyr had an advanced unit-construction shell, and a simple, new, vee-12 engine based on the Ford V8. This is a saloon version built in 1937. There was also a coupé version.

Lotus Elan SE

Lotus Elan, with front-wheel-drive, produced 1989 to 1994 (data for original S model)

Built by: Lotus Cars Ltd., Britain.

Engine: Isuzu, four cylinders, in line, in five-main-bearing cast-iron cylinder block Bore and stroke 80 × 79mm, 1,588cc (3.15 × 3.11in, 96.9cu.in). Light-alloy cylinde head. Four valves per cylinder, in narrow vee, operation by twin overhead camshaft and inverted hydraulic tappets. Rochester fuel injection and IHi turbocharge Maximum power 165bhp (DIN) at 6,600rpm. Maximum torque 148lb.ft at 4,200rpm (Non-turbocharged version, with 130bhp and 105lb.ft, available on entry level Elan not badged as 'SE'.)

Transmission: Front-wheel-drive, single-dry-plate diaphragm spring clutch and five speed all-synchromesh manual gearbox, all in unit with transverse front-mounte engine. Remote-control, central gearchange.

Chassis: Separate chassis frame, backbone shape, in presswed and fabricate steel, clad in glassfibre/advanced composite two-seater style, open roadster or wit hardtop. Independent front suspension by coil springs, wishbones, telescopi dampers and anti-roll bar. Independent rear suspension by coil springs, wishbone and transverse links, telescopic dampers, and anti-roll bar. Rack-and-pinion steerin with hydraulic power assistance. Four-wheel disc brakes, no ABS. Cast alloy 15in wheels, 205/50-15in. tyres.

Dimensions: Wheelbase 7ft 4.6in (225cm), front track 4ft 10.5in (148.6cm), rea track 4ft 10.5in (148.6cm). Overall length 12ft 5.7in (380.2cm). Unladen weigh 2,253lb (1,022kg).

History: During the 1980s, Lotus went through agonies in trying to develop a nev 'small' sports car to slot into a product range under the existing Esprit models. It wa not until General Motors took control, and provided finance to underpin developmen and investment, that a new car, the Elan, was finalised. Although this was traditional Lotus in many ways – including the use of the stubby steel backbone typ chassis, and the VARI-patented way of manufacturing a glass-fibre body shell – ther was sensation in other aspects. Not only was this the first (and only) Lotus to use

Below: From this view the Elan's style had similarities with earlier Lotus sports cars. The turbocharged SE delivered a 136mph top speed.

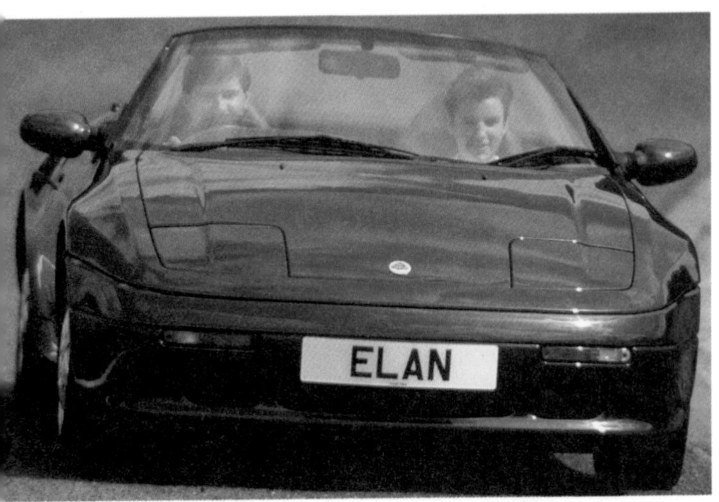

Above: Wide, squat but above all purposeful, the 1989 Elan was the first-ever front-wheel-drive Lotus, with remarkable steering and handling.

apanese Isuzu engine, but it also had front-wheel-drive.

The choice of front-wheel-drive, with a transverse engine and five-speed gearbox, went hand in hand with the use of the Isuzu power pack, this being provided ourtesy of General Motors, who also had a controlling interest in the Japanese oncern. The engine itself was a sturdy 16-valve 1.6-litre twin-cam unit being eveloped for use in front-drive Isuzus of the 1990s, and was ideal for this purpose. Although Isuzu had never previously been known for producing fine engines, this was a typical, smooth, high-revving, Japanese 16-valver, which worked well in the Lotus. Two engine tunes were to be offered – a normally aspired unit with 130bhp, nd an IHi-turbocharged version with no less than 165bhp – but sales experience howed that few people took up the low-powered option. With 165bhp the new Elan SE (without a turbo, it was not an SE either . . .) could reach 136mph.

Naturally there was independent front and rear suspension, but a front-end novelty was that the suspension was mounted on a separate 'raft' or sub-frame, which allowed the Lotus engineers to provide peerless refinement to go with the steering and suspension accuracy all such Hethel-built cars always had. Here was a short-wheelbase car with wide tracks, which could so easily have looked stubby, but Peter Stevens (who would later go on to shape the McLaren F1 road car) did a marvellous design job to prevent this possibility. Neat, rounded, with a front-to-rear wing line rising steadily towards the tail, and with a vast multi-curvature windscreen, this was an unmistakeable Lotus which could never be taken for anything else.

UK sales began in 1989, with USA sales starting in 1991, but orders were always disappointingly low. Although this was a fast car which handled superbly, it was always expensive. This, and the fact that Lotus's once-unreliable build quality reputation took ages to be killed off, did not help.

At the development stage Lotus had made sure that the engineering, and the behaviour, was right, at the (to them) laudable expense of neglecting product cost. This Elan, too, was difficult to build and (in view of the finicky nature of the front suspension system) time-consuming to set up. Faced with an on-going loss-maker, General Motors pulled the plug in 1992, closed down the assembly lines, and shortly after decided to sell off the entire company. Kia, of South Korea, bought the design and manufacturing rights to the Elan, installed its own normally aspirated engine, and called it a Roadster from 1995, but it was no Lotus, and sales ended in 2000.

Lotus Elise

Lotus Elise two-seater sports car, introduced in 1995
Built by: Lotus Cars Ltd., Britain.
Engine: Rover K-Series four cylinders, in line, in five-main-bearing light-allo cylinder block/crankcase. Bore and stroke 80 × 89.3mm, 1,796cc (3.15 × 3.51in 109.6cu.in). Light-alloy cylinder head. Four valves per cylinder, in narrow vee operation by twin overhead camshafts and inverted bucket tappets. MEM electronic fuel injection. Maximum power 118bhp (DIN) at 5,500rpm. Maximum torque 122lb.ft at 3,000rpm.
Transmission: Rear-wheel-drive, single-dry-plate diaphragm spring clutch an five-speed all-synchromesh manual gearbox, all in unit with transverse-mounte mid engine. Remote-control, central gearchange.
Chassis: Separate extruded aluminum tub, bonded together from sections clothed in a glassfibre advanced composite two-seater body style. Independent front suspension by coil springs, wishbones, telescopic dampers, anti-roll bar Independent rear suspension by coil springs, wishbones and telescopi dampers. Rack-and-pinion steering. Four-wheel disc brakes without ABS. Light alloy 15in and 16in road wheels, 185/55-15in (front) and 205/50-16in (rear) tyres
Dimensions: Wheelbase 7ft 6.5in (230cm), front track 4ft 8.7in (144cm), rea track 4ft 9.2in (145.3cm). Overall length 12ft 2.7in (372.6cm). Unladen weight 1,594lb (723kg).
History: The miracle is not that the lightweight and appealing Lotus Elise eve became a success, but that it ever went into production at all, for it wa conceived when Lotus's entire business was in turmoil, and when complete closure was forecast on more than one occasion. Lotus, at one time a Genera Motors subsidiary, had been sold off to Romeo Artioli's business empire (he was also trying to revive Bugatti) in 1993, and although he always talked big, neithe the financial backing nor the deeds ever backed this up. After a great deal o strife, which included the aborted sale to other interests, Lotus was finally sold to Proton of Malaysia in 1996.

In the meantime, the Elise project had stuttered into life, a light, back-to

Below: Not a line out of place, and not a kilo of surplus weight – that was the philosophy behind the mid-engined Elise.

Above: The basis of the Elise was a bonded-together extruded aluminium tub, with a Rover K-Series engine mounted behind the seats – ultra-light, and very effective.

basics two-seater being built around a bonded-together aluminium chassis/tub whose technology and original execution hailed from Denmark. The engine/transmission unit, mounted behind the starkly trimmed two-seater cabin, was the modern Rover K-series installation, where the aluminium engine had a 16-valve twin-cam cylinder head, and where 118bhp was developed from 1.8-litres.

Linked to a neat five-speed transmission, this all looked very familiar, and so it should, for the same combination was also to be found in the also-new MG MGF. The body itself was in glass-fibre, as was every modern Lotus of the 20th Century, but trim was almost non-existent, there were no carpets on the floor, and the 'all-weather' equipment could best be described as skimpy. Yet this was precisely the type of car, it seemed, that sporty young customers were seeking, exspecially as the initial price – originally set at £18,950 in the UK – looked to be so reasonable. Previewed in September 1995, the Elise was ready for sale by mid-1996, but deliveries were originally hampered because many suppliers (especially Rover) demanded cash-on-delivery before they would release components, and it was not until Proton took charge towards the end of 1996 that continuity was assured.

Once the first independent road tests were published, the Elise's charm became common knowledge. Fast (124mph) but not astonishing, it was light and possessed of simply incredible mid-engine-type road holding. Its natural rival, the new mid-engined Renault Spider, had no answer to its capabilities which, in one tester's opinion, 'Rewrites the book on driver appeal.'

With more unpainted aluminium on show in the cabin that trim materials, one would not expect it to sell to the staid, and the pernickety, but Lotus never expected that. Within two years, in any case, 3,000 Elise types were being delivered every year, which was more than Lotus had ever sold, of any one model, at any time. By 2000 the range had been further expanded, not only with a 145bhp Elise 111S derivative, but there was also talk of an Exige model with a permanent hardtop and a bigger, more powerful engine. For the first time in decades, it seemed, Lotus had a sure-fire winner on its hands, the back-to-basics decision of 1994 having been responsible for this.

Lotus Elite (1950s Type)

Lotus Elite, built from 1957 to 1963 (data for 1959 car)
Built by: Lotus Cars Ltd., Britain.
Engine: Coventry Climax manufactured. Four cylinders, in line, in three-bearing light-alloy block. Bore and stroke 76.2mm by 66.6mm, 1,216cc (3.0in × 2.62in, 74.2cu.in). Light-alloy cylinder head. Two overhead valves per cylinder, in line in wedge-shaped combustion chamber, operated by inverted-bucket tappets from single overhead camshaft. Single or twin side-draught constant-vacuum SU carburettors to choice. Maximum power with single carburettor 71bhp (net) at 6,100rpm. Maximum torque with single carburettor 77lb.ft at 3,500rpm. Maximum power with twin carburettors 83bhp at 6,300rpm.
Transmission: Single-dry-plate clutch and four-speed, synchromesh manual gearbox (no synchromesh on first gear), both in unit with engine. Remote-control central gearchange. Exposed propeller shaft to chassis-mounted hypoid-bevel differential. Exposed, universally jointed drive shafts to rear wheels.
Chassis: Three main piece glassfibre monocoque, with steel-tube reinforcements. No separate chassis frame. Independent front suspension by coil springs, wishbones and anti-roll bar. Independent rear suspension by Chapman strut and coil springs. Telescopic dampers. Rack-and-pinion steering. Four-wheel, hydraulically operated disc brakes, inboard at rear. 15in centre-lock wire wheels, with 4.90 × 15in tyres.
Dimensions: Wheelbase 7ft 4in (224cm), tracks (front and rear) 3ft 11in (119cm). Overall length 12ft (366cm). Unladen weight 1,200lb (544kg).
History: Colin Chapman had established Lotus's reputation on the race track by 1956, but the Elite coupé, conceived in 1956 and revealed in 1957, was his first true road car. Nearly 1,000 were made between 1959, when full production began, and 1963 when it ceased, but although it was attractive and very functional the Elite was never a profit-maker for the company. In particular the cost of making the bodies became prohibitive, which is one reason why the Elan sports car had a steel chassis.

The Elite's concept was of a glassfibre monocoque – made in three major

Above: The Elite, revealed in 1957, was beautiful and technically clever. A unit-construction shell in glassfibre was unique, the car was very light, and used a Climax engine.

sections, floor, structural centre section and one-piece outer skin – on to which all mechanical and suspension parts would be mounted. This worked remarkably well, even if there were refinement problems in bolting the axle and engine units to the shell, and it certainly made the whole car very light. The shape was sleek, and the fuel company therefore very good. Series II cars, produced in the 1960s, incorporated revised rear suspension and other improvements, and late in life Coventry-Climax engines of up to 100bhp were offered.

Perhaps the Elite's biggest disadvantage was that the roof was stressed and a convertible version was therefore impossible. Ventilation was also poor, because door shape did not allow for opening side windows. It is already a collector's piece in many countries.

Left: Inspired by Peter Kirwin-Taylor, the two-seater monocoque Elite was sinuous and sleek from every angle.

Lotus Elite

Lotus Elite and Eclat built from 1974 to 1982 (data for first Elite)
Built by: Lotus Cars Ltd., Britain.
Engine: Four-cylinders, in line, in five-bearing light-alloy block. Bore and stroke 95.2mm by 69.3mm, 1,973cc (3.75in × 2.73in, 120.5cu.in). Engine inclined at 45 degrees. Light-alloy cylinder head. Four overhead valves per cylinder, operated by twin overhead camshafts. Twin side-draught twin-choke Dell'Orto carburettors. Maximum power 160bhp (DIN) at 6,500rpm. Maximum torque 140lb.ft at 5,000rpm.
Transmission: Single-dry-plate clutch and five-speed, all-synchromesh manual gearbox, both in unit with engine. Remote-control gearchange. Open propeller shaft to chassis-mounted hypoid-bevel differential. Optional Borg Warner automatic transmission on some versions. Exposed, universally jointed drive shafts to rear wheels, doubling as suspension location links.
Chassis: Pressed-steel separate chassis frame forming a 'backbone construction. Independent front suspension by coil springs and anti-roll bar Independent rear suspension by coil springs and combined link/radius arm arrangement. Telescopic dampers. Rack-and-pinion steering (optionally power assisted). Four-wheel, hydraulically operated brakes, front discs and rear drums Glassfibre three-door bodywork.
Dimensions: Wheelbase 8ft 1.7in (248cm), track (front) 4ft 10.5in (149cm) track (rear) 4ft 11in (150cm). Overall length 14ft 7.5in (446cm). Unladen weight 2,550lb (1,156kg).
History: As Lotus entered the 1970s, their founder Colin Chapman decided to move the product further up the social and price scale and gradually to phase out kit-built cars. When the Elan Plus Two became obsolete, he decided to replace it with something altogether more grand. The new Elite, confusingly given the same name as the coupé of the 1950s, was this car. Coded the M50 at Lotus, it was just the first of a whole new family of Lotus cars. Alongside it were the Eclat (mechanically like the Elite, but with fastback instead of square-back styling) and

Above: From the rear the Elite looks like a fast estate car, but there is nothing commercial about the engine, which produces 160bhp from only two litres. Lotus built most of the car themselves – a far cry from the 'kit-car' Lotus machines of the 1960s.

the mid-engined Esprit, which effectively replaced the Europa at greatly increased cost. All shared the completely Lotus-manufactured Type 907 2-litre 16-valve twin-cam engine (which was also sold to Jensen for use in their Jensen-Healeys until Jenson closed down in 1976). The Elite was designed to meet all existing and projected safety regulations, and in spite of being made with a glassfibre body was very strong and rigid. Lotus, in their Norfolk factory, made most of the motor car, instead of merely assembling proprietary parts. The Elite's backbone steel chassis frame carried on the Lotus tradition established with the 1962 Elan sports car and the all-independent suspension followed racing car lines of wheel location and control. The five-speed gearbox actually used British Leyland internals. Performance was high – maximum speed being over 120mph – because of the light weight and efficient aerodynamic shape, and the fuel consumption was low because of the car's light weight. It is well known that a larger V8 engine could easily be fitted into the Elite's engine bay; performance then would be quite phenomenal. Styling is mainly the work of Lotus staff, with suggestions from the Ital Design offices. The cheaper and more simple Eclat used an Elite chassis, together with nose and centre sections from that car. Only the tail styling was unique.

Left: The Elite of the 1970s had nothing in common with the 1950s car. The modern version has a pressed steel chassis and Lotus's own slant-four twin-cam engine. The glassfibre body is built from two large pieces. The Eclat is mechanically similar, with fast-back styling.

Lotus Esprit Family

Esprits built from 1976 to 1987 (data for 1981 Turbo Esprit)
Built by: Lotus Cars Ltd., Britain.
Engine: Four cylinders, in line, in five-bearing light-alloy cylinder block, crankcase, installed in car at 45 degree angle. Bore and stroke 95.2mm by 76.2mm, 2,174cc (3.75 × 3.50in, 132.7cu.in). Light-alloy cylinder head. Four overhead valves per cylinder, operated directly by inverted bucket-type tappets from two overhead camshafts. Twin side-draught twin-choke Dell'Orto carburettors and Garrett AiResearch turbocharge. Maximum power 210bhp (DIN) at 6,000rpm. Maximum torque 200lb.ft at 4,000rpm.
Transmission: Mid-engine, rear drive. Single dry plate clutch, and five-speed all-synchromesh manual gearbox, all in unit with engine and hypoid bevel final drive. Remote control, central gearchange. Exposed, universally jointed drive shafts to rear wheels.
Chassis: Separate pressed-steel chassis frame forming 'backbone' construction. Independent front suspension by coil springs, wishbones and anti-roll bar. Independent rear suspension by coil springs, transverse links, fixed length drive shafts, and radius arms. Telescopic dampers. Rack-and-pinion steering. Four-wheel hydraulically operated disc brakes, with vacuum servo assistance. 15in cast-alloy road wheels, with 195/60VR15in tyres (front) and 235/60VR15in tyres (rear). Two-seat fastback mid-engined coupe body style in glass-fibre.
Dimensions: Wheelbase 8ft 0in (244cm), track (front) 5ft 0.5in (154cm), track (rear) 5ft 1.2in (155,5cm). Overall length 13ft 9in (419cm). Unladen weight 2,650lb (1,202kg).
History: In line with Lotus's determination to make more of their own cars than hitherto, and to make full use of facilities planned for the 1974 Elite, it was decided to replace the mid-engined Europa with a new mid-engined car utilising the same new 16-valve 2-litre engine, installed at 45 degrees in the chassis. However, although the new car, to be called Esprit, retained the backbone pressed-steel frame layout of the old Europa, it was entirely new in detail.

Also new was the wedge-style glassfibre body shape, carried out for Lotus by

the famous Italian stylist, Giugiaro, and the use of a modified Citroën SM gearbox and final drive assembly – the difference being that the SM's transaxle had originally been front-mounted, for a front-wheel-drive installation, through it had also been adapted for use in the mid-engined Maserati Merak as well.

The all-independent suspension was engineered for series-production use, but used geometry akin to that found on racing sports cars, and the entire vehicle showed signs of Lotus's racing car roots. Like other contemporary Lotuses, too, it had flip-up headlamps, and a more luxurious interior and facia layout than any previous road car from this factory. One of the clever tricks used by Lotus to keep their investment to a minimum was that they picked up components from other cars if they could not afford to develop their own – which explains why the first Esprits had Opel Ascona front suspension components, and modified Lancia Beta disc brakes.

Production did not begin until 1976, when the first Esprits were found to be rather disappointingly slower than had been claimed for them on announcement. Lotus then took time to rectify this – which was due to the variable performance of the Lotus-built engines – before the cars' full 135/140mph performance could be guaranteed.

In the next few years, however, more intensive development work was carried out without disturbing the general style or concept of the car. Series 2 models, from mid-1978, had new styling details, while by 1980 not only had the engine been enlarged to 2,174cc, but a very powerful (210bhp instead of the original 156bhp) turbocharged version had also been developed. Great publicity had also been gained by the use of a specially modified Esprit in one of the popular James Bond films, when the car was supposed to be able to manoeuvre under water!

In the face of difficult economic conditions, particularly for personal 'indulgences' like the Esprit, demand for the car turned down about this time. Like many other mid-engined cars, its engineering and general handling had been found to be more attractive than its practicality.

Left: Styling of the mid-engined Lotus Esprit is by Giugiaro, but the twin-cam engine is Lotus's own, and the roadholding is peerless. There is a 'turbo' too.

Lotus Esprit (from 1987)

Re-styled Lotus Esprit, introduced in 1987 (data for original Turbo model c 1988)
Built by: Lotus Cars Ltd., Britain.
Engine: Four cylinders, in line, in five-main-bearing light alloy cylinder block. Bor and stroke 95.28 × 76.2mm, 2,174cc (3.75 × 3.00in, 132.7cu.in). Light alloy cylinde head. Four valves per cylinder, in narrow vee, operation by twin overhead camshaft and bucket type tappets. Twin-choke Dellorto carburettors with Garrett AiResearc turbocharger. Maximum power 215bhp (DIN) at 6,500rpm. Maximum torqu 220lb.ft at 4,250rpm.
Transmission: Rear-wheel-drive, single-dry-plate diaphragm spring clutch and five speed all-synchromesh manual gearbox, all in unit with mid-mounted engine Remote-control, central gearchange.
Chassis: Separate chassis, backbone style, in folded or fabricated sheet stee topped by glassfibre/advanced composite two-seater sports coupé body shel Independent front suspension by coil springs, wishbones, telescopic dampers, an anti-roll bar. Independent rear suspension by coil springs, lower wishbones, trailin and transverse links, and telescopic dampers. Rack-and-pinion steering wit hydraulic power assistance. Four-wheel disc brakes, with vacuum-servo assistance Cast alloy 15in. wheels, 195/60-15in (front) and 235/60-15in (rear) tyres.
Dimensions: Wheelbase 8ft 0.76in (245.7cm), front track 5ft 0in (152.4cm), rea track 5ft 1.2in (155.4cm). Overall length 14ft 2.5in (433cm). Unladen weight 2,800l (1,270kg).
History: By the mid-1980s Lotus's mid-engined Esprit had been in production for full decade, and was overdue for improvement. Lotus, however, did not have th resources to develop a completely new model, so a makeover (what a multi-nationa company would probably call a 'mid-term facelift') was appropriate. It was not tha Lotus, then owned by General Motors, was currently short of backing, but that ther was only a limited development capability at Hethel – most of which was alread committed to the all-new front-wheel-drive Elan. In any case, Lotus judged that th existing slant-four twin-cam 16-valve 2.2-litre still had life in it.

Accordingly a new project, coded X180 at Hethel, was started. Led by Coli Spooner, with body styling in the hands of Peter Stevens, the object was to make a many changes as possible without spending much capital! The result, in the end was that Stephens produced a new body style around the original basic wedge-nos proportions. Instead of a sharp-edged, typically Giugiaro, shape, Stevens shaped th

Below: After its re-style in 1987, the mid-engined Esprit went through further improvements, reaching S4, and 305bhp, by 1994.

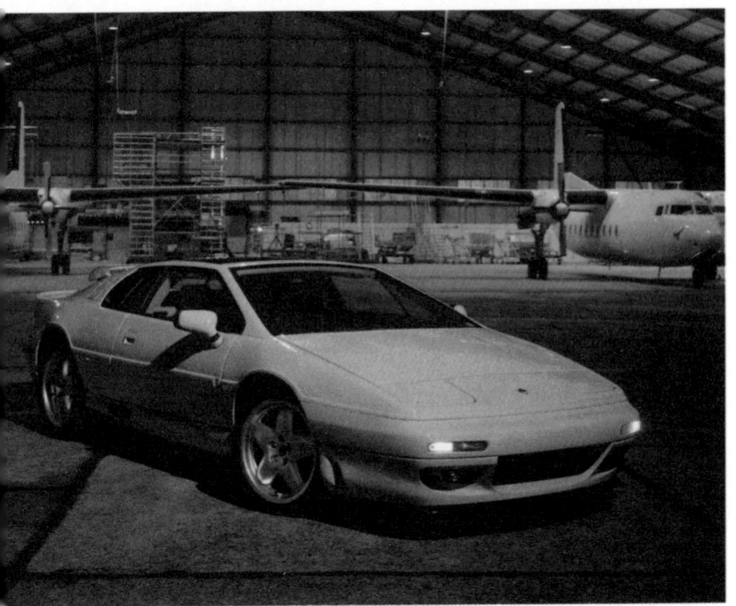

Above: Compared with the first Giugiaro-styled Esprit of the 1970s, the re-shaped late-1980s Esprit was smoother from any angle.

revised Lotus with rounded lines, though Lotus claimed that no part of any new profile was more than one inch/2.54cm away from that of the old at any point. This meant that the old-type VARI fibre-glass production moulds could be reworked without completely new frames and structures being required.

Although it was not impossible to pick the normally aspirated from the turbocharged versions of this new car (the Turbo had extra driving lamps at the front and each type had its own specially styled road wheels), badges also helped give the game away, while on the turbocharged car there was initially a large pane of clear glass between the 'flying buttress' panels which linked the sides of the roof to the tail lamps. Inside the cabin there was more space than before (on the original Giugiaro-styled car it had always felt a touch cramped). Instruments and the facia panel were new and (praise be!) the ventilation too was better than before.

As launched at the end of 1987, Lotus marketed the two distinct types with 172bhp (normally aspirated) and 215bhp (turbocharged), respectively. Behind them (USA markets only, at first) there was a new-type of five-speed transaxle, this time the Renault GTA type.

Lotus, being Lotus, did not leave this 1988-model specification alone for long. Being small, flexible, ambitious and (let us be honest) always enthusiastic about ways of improving their cars, they were always ready to improve the latest Esprits, especially if this meant tinkering with the engine and suspension.

Normally aspirated Esprits did not sell well (and not at all in the USA), so that version of the car was dropped in 1990, after which it was only turbocharged 2.2-litre types which held sway until the big 3.5-litre/354bhp V8-engined version of the car arrived in 1996. By this time the design had progressed through Esprit S4 to GT3, and the power output of the 2.2-litre engine had risen to 243bhp. With a top speed of more than 150mph (the V8 car reached 172mph), the four-cylinder Esprit was still selling slowly, but steadily, as the 21st Century opened.

Lotus Europa

Lotus Europa, Europa Twin-Cam and Europa Special, built from 1966 – 1975 (data for Europa of 1967)
Built by: Lotus Cars Ltd., Britain.
Engine: Four cylinders, in line, in five-bearing light-alloy block. Bore and stroke 76mm by 81mm, 1,470cc (2.99in × 3.19in, 90.5cu.in). Light-alloy cylinder, operated by pushrods and rockers from high-mounted camshaft in cylinder block. Single down-draught dual-choke Solex carburettor. Maximum power 78bhp (net) at 6,000 rpm. Maximum torque 76lb.ft at 4,000rpm.
Transmission: Combined clutch/gearbox/axle unit in transaxle, mounted behind mid-positioned engine. Single-dry-plate clutch ahead of axle unit and four-speed, all-synchromesh, all-indirect manual gearbox behind axle unit. Remote linkage to central gearchange. Hypoid-level final-drives. Exposed, universally jointed drive shafts to rear wheels.
Chassis: Separate pressed-steel chassis frame, in backbone 'tuning fork' shape. Engine mounted behind seats, but ahead of rear wheels, longitudinally. Independent front suspension by coil springs and wishbones. Independent rear suspension by coil springs, transverse links and radius arms. Telescopic dampers. Rack-and-pinion steering. Front disc and rear drum brakes. 13in pressed-steel wheels. 155 × 13in tyres. Two-seater glassfibre bodywork, coupé construction, bounded to chassis frame (later made detachable).
Dimensions: Wheelbase 7ft 7in (231cm), tracks (front and rear) 4ft 5in (135cm). Overall length 13ft 0.5in (397cm). Unladen weight 1,350lb (613kg).
History: The Elite, expensive to make, was followed by the simpler but very successful front-engined Elan sports car. In 1966, as a complete contrast, Lotus then announced their mid-engined Lotus Europa, which in Europe was the cheapest production Lotus yet sold. Its concept was a marketing arrangement between Renault and Lotus. Renault would supply Renault 16 engines and transmissions (suitably modified for driving the rear wheels of the Lotus – in the 16 they drove front wheels), Lotus would build the rest of the car, and the first sanction of cars would be sold only through Renault outlets in Europe – hence the car's appropriate name. Within a couple of years Lotus had gained

agreement to sell the Europa all over the world. The car carried on the Elan's backbone chassis philosophy, but the mid-engined layout was new. Lotus, with their vast knowledge of mid-engined racing cars, had plenty of experience to call upon, and the Europa's handling was exemplary. It was, incidentally, one of the world's first quantity-production mid-engine cars, and certainly has always had the most renowned road manners.

Originally, the glassfibre body was bonded to the chassis frame on assembly, but for ease of maintenance and repair the mating became a bolt-on affair when the Europa was upgraded to Series II in July 1969. The biggest problem with the car was that it always seemed to be under-engined, but this complaint was stilled in October 1971 when the Europa Twin-Cam was announced, having the Elan's 1,558cc engine with 105bhp. This engine was a Lotus-converted twin-overhead-cam unit, based on the Cortina 1,500cc pushrod engine, and was also in use by Ford at the time in their Escort competition cars. A year later the Twin-Cam became the Special, with 126bhp and a five-speed gearbox. Production ran out in 1975, and the car was replaced by the mid-engined Esprit.

Above and left: The first mid-engined Lotus was the Renault-engined Europa of 1966, which became the Europa Twin-Cam in 1971 with Lotus-Ford power. Roadholding was splendid, but passenger space was tight.

Lozier Type I 50hp

Type I 50hp, built from 1907 to 1911 (data for 1910 model)
Built by: Lozier Motor Co., United States.
Engine: Six cylinders, in line, in three cast-iron blocks, with four-bearing light-alloy crankcase. Bore and stroke 117.5mm by 139.7mm, 9,089cc (4.62in × 5.5in, 554.6cu.in). Three non-detachable cast-iron cylinder heads. Two side valves per cylinder, in T-head layout with exposed valve stems and springs, operated via tappets from two camshafts mounted in sides of crankcase. Single up-draught carburettor.
Transmission: Multiple-dry-plate clutch, in unit with front-mounted engine, and shaft drive to separate four-speed manual gearbox (without synchromesh) – third gear direct and fourth gear an overdrive. Remote-control right-hand gear-change. Propeller shaft, enclosed in torque tube, driving straight-bevel 'live' rear axle.
Chassis: Separate pressed-steel chassis frame, with channel-section side members and pressed and tubular cross bracing. Forged front axle beam. Front suspension by semi-elliptic leaf springs. Rear suspension by semi-elliptic leaf springs, with transverse 'platform' leaf spring picking up rear of these springs, plus torque tube and radius arm location. Friction-type dampers. Worm-and-sector steering. Foot-operated transmission drum brake. Hand brake on rear wheel drums. Artillery-style road wheels. 36 × 4½in tyres. Choice of coachwork.
Dimensions: Wheelbase 10ft 11in (333cm), tracks (front and rear) 4ft 8in (142cm).

Right: Lozier's Type I was one of North America's finest cars. Only a few were built, and raced successfully.

History: Lozier cars, like Pierce-Arrows and Packards, were among the finest American cars of the highest quality in the halcyon days before the outbreak of World War I. Unhappily, like many other firms around them, the social and financial changes which followed this conflict served to kill off many of the bespoke car makers. Lozier was one of the unlucky ones. The original Loziers had 'conventional American' T-head engines and chain drive, but only two years later they adopted shaft drive, and the 'platform' type of leaf spring suspension so beloved of the American designers. The engines had alloy crankcases and paired cast-iron blocks, which made it easy and straightforward to build fours or sixes. The 1907 range was precisely that – a high-quality mixture of components and a 40hp four alongside a 50hp six. Aids to luxury motoring were the chassis-long cast-alloy undertray (which protected the mechanicals from the dust of the era's unmade roads), and, in the case of the Type I, the geared-up fourth speed, which gave an 'overdrive' effect. It was no wonder that the Lozier marque was active in motor sport – in 1910 they won the National Stock car championship, and in 1911 the Vanderbilt Cup, with a second place overall in the Indianapolis 500.

Maserati 3500GT, 3500GTi, Sebring and Mistral Family

3500GT family built 1957 to 1969 (data for 3500GTi Sebring)
Built by: Officine Alfieri Maserati SpA, Italy.
Engine: Six cylinders, in line, in seven-bearing light-alloy cylinder block, with steel dry liners. Bore and stroke 86mm by 100mm, 3,485cc (3.39in × 3.94in, 212-7cu.in). Detachable light-alloy cylinder head. Two overhead valves per cylinder, inclined to each other in part-spherical combustion chambers, operated in inverted-bucket tappets from twin overhead camshafts. Lucas fuel injection, indirect into inlet ports. Maximum power 235bhp (net) at 5,550rpm. Maximum torque 232lb.ft at 4,000rpm.
Transmission: Front engine, rear drive. Single-dry-plate clutch, and five-speed all-synchromesh manual gearbox, all in unit with engine. Remote control centre gearchange. Open propeller shaft to hypoid-bevel 'live' rear axle.
Chassis: Separate multi-tubular chassis frame, with large oval section side-members, tubular cross-bracing and sheet steel reinforcements. Independent front suspension by coil springs, wishbones, and anti-roll bar. Rear suspension by semi-elliptic leaf springs, and longitudinal torque arm. Telescopic dampers. Recirculating ball steering. Four-wheel hydraulically operated disc brakes, with vacuum-servo assistance. 6.5 × 16in centre-lock wire-spoke wheels. 185-16in tyres. Two-seater closed coupé body style, in steel, by Vignale.
Dimensions: Wheelbase 8ft 2.5in (250cm), track (front) 4ft 6.7in (139cm), track (rear) 4ft 5.3in (135cm). Overall length 14ft 8in (447cm). Unladen weight 3,330lb (1,510kg).
History: Maserati were a noted Italian company, building racing cars, for some years before they built their first true road car. There were Grand Prix cars in the 1930s, and nice but not very fast 1,500cc and 2,000cc limited-production sports cars in the 1940s and early 1950s. It was not until 1957, however, that the Orsi family, which had owned Maserati for some time, decided to 'productionise' the famous six-cylinder twin-cam racing engine, and put it into limited, but series, production.

The result was the 3500, which was built up around a typical Italian Supercar

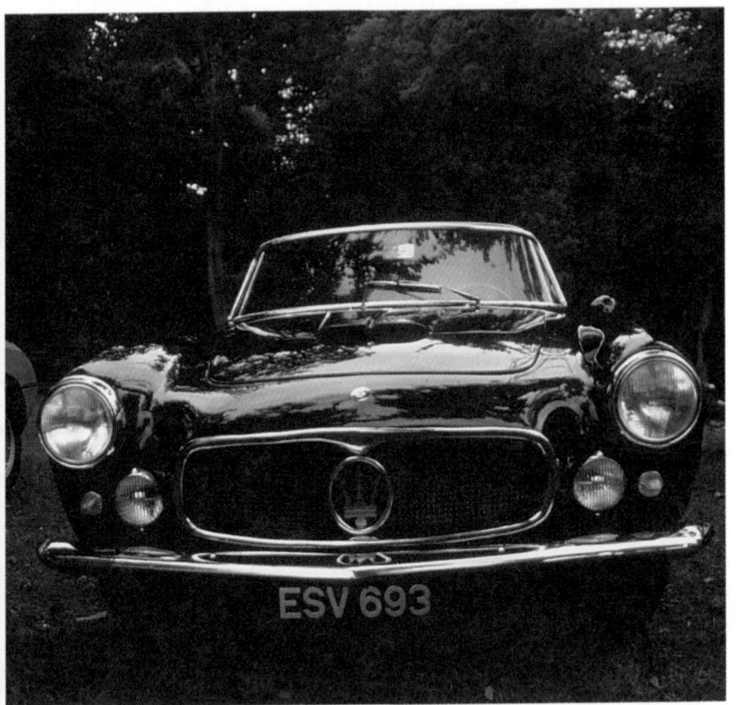

Above: Maserati's 3500GT of 1957 was that company's first six-cylinder-engined road car, originally with 220bhp and a 130mph top speed.

Below left: The 3500GT was a neat 3.5-litre coupé, with which Maserati set out to challenge Ferrari in the exotic road car market.

chassis layout, having a large-diameter tubular members, and a variety of sheet steel reinforcements, with coil spring independent front suspension, and very basic leaf-spring rear suspension of the large and bulky beam axle. As with Ferrari, at the time, the magic of owning a Maserati 3500 lay in the engine itself, and in the body styles.

Even in its original guise, a 3500 and 230bhp, and this was before the use of Lucas fuel injection (the 'i' in the title), was standardised at the beginning of the 1960s. Other and more exciting Maseratis took more limelight as the 1960s progressed, but the basic design of the 3500GT led to the 3500GTi, into the Sebring (with Vignale coupé body) by 1962, and finally into the Mistral.

The fact that these cars were what had once been called 'assembled models', with German ZF gearboxes. British Salisbury axles, and bought-in body styles, never took away their attraction to the customers, many of whom wanted simplicity of the six-cylinder engine instead of the open-cheque-book horrors of a Ferrari or Lamborghini vee-12. By the Supercar standards of the day, the 3500 family was always popular, for more than 120 cars were built in the first full year (1958).

Most 3500GTs and GTis had coupé bodies by Touring and spider bodies by Vignale. All the Sebrings were coupés, by Vignale, but the last series of cars based on this chassis, the Mistral, had coupé and spider styles by Frua. All in all, a total of 3,617 cars were built in 12 years.

Maserati Bora and Merak

Bora V8 model and Merak V6 model, built from 1971 to 1983 (data for Bora of 1972-3)

Built by: Officine Alfieri Maserati SpA, Italy.

Engine: Eight cylinders, in 90-degree V8 formation, five-bearing light-alloy block. Bore and stroke 93.9mm by 85mm, 4,719cc (3.70in × 3.34in, 290cu.in). Light-alloy cylinder heads. Two overhead valves per cylinder, inclined to each other in part-spherical combustion chambers and operated by inverted-bucket tappets from twin-choke Weber carburettors. Maximum power 310bhp (DIN) at 6,000rpm. Maximum torque 340lb.ft at 4,200rpm.

Transmission: Mid-mounted engine ahead of final drive and five-speed, all-synchromesh manual gearbox behind final drive. Single-dry-plate clutch, all indirect gearbox and straight-bevel final drive, all in unit with the engine. Remote-control central gearchange. Exposed, universally jointed drive shafts to rear wheels.

Chassis: Unitary-construction fabricated steel (sheet and tubular) structure, with tubular extensions to support engine and transmission. Engine mid mounted, between two-seat closed passenger cabin and transaxle. All-independent suspension by coil springs, wishbones, anti-roll bars and telescopic dampers. Rack-and-pinion steering. Four-wheel, hydraulically operated disc brakes, with vacuum-servo assistance. 15in bolt-on cast-alloy wheels. 215/70VR15 tyres.

Dimensions: Wheelbase 8ft 6.2in (260cm), track (front) 4ft 9.9in (147cm), track (rear) 4ft 9.1in (145cm). Overall length 14ft 2.4in (433cm). Unladen weight 3,090lb (1,400kg).

History: It was Citroën, which had taken a controlling interest in Maserati in 1968, who provided the inspiration, and the impetus, for the mid-engined Maseratis built in the 1970s. The Bora evolved around a 4.7-litre V8 engine, which Maserati had steadily been refining since the days when it had powered the lusty 4½-litre two-seat racing sports cars. Mid-engined cars were not new to

Below: The V8-engined Bora and the V6-engined Merak were based on the same chunky but rounded mid-engined body style by Giugiaro.

Above: Recognition points on the vee-6 Merak are the road wheels and the more sloping rear quarters. There is also a very occasional rear seat.

them (their first rear-engined 'birdcage' racing two-seaters had been used in 1961), although they knew little about the unitary-construction techniques which went with them. The Bora, revealed at Geneva in March 1971, was at once a gamble and a technical triumph. Like other supercars to come from the Modena region (such as the soon to follow Ferrari Boxer and Lamborghini Countach), it followed a predictable trend, with mid-mounted in-line engine, five-speed gearbox and transaxle bolted to it, and a wedge-shaped two-seater body.

The performance – 160mph was a perfectly usable maximum speed – was sensational, and the roadholding and response for experienced and skilful drivers was also superb. Not that the Bora was by any means an excuse for a road-going racing car, not by any means. Air-conditioning and electric windows were standard, along with adjustable pedals and many other creature comforts. Styling was by Giugiaro (Ital Design). Citroën influence, incidentally, was obvious ▶

in the fully powered braking circuits, with the zero-travel brake pedal.

To supplement the Bora, Maserati next revealed the Merak, which once again owed its existence to Citroën. The kernel of the Merak was the V6 engine, a Maserati development which the Italian firm could never have afforded to put into production without a contract also to supply it to Citroën for their SM coupé. In effect the V6 engine (3 litres in the Merak but 2.7 litres in the Citroën SM) was developed from the ageing Maserati V8, but was very different in detail. The overhead-camshaft drives, for instance, were taken up the centre of the engine, between one end pair and the centre pair of cylinders. The angle between banks, at 90 degrees, was unusual for a V6, but allowed the V8's production tooling, such as it was, to be used in another application. The Merak itself looked virtually identical to the Bora, except in detail, but because the engine was substantially shorter than the V8, Maserati managed to insert a pair of almost useless 'jump seats' behind the existing front seats. Even with only a 3-litre engine installed, the Merak had a maximum speed of around 140mph, together with much improved operating economy. Maserati struck financial difficulties soon after their agreement with Citroën had been dissolved in 1973 and stopped trading for a time in 1975. With government finance, Alejandro de Tomaso made a take-over bid and restored the factory to activity during the year. Boras and Meraks were still being made at the end of the 1970s, in developed form, the Bora boasting a full 5-litre engine and the Merak more power than ever before. Some Citroën influence was still present – both cars having the Citroën brakes, the Merak having the SM's gearbox and the Bora having hydraulic adjustment to seats and pedals. The Merak incidentally, had inboard rear brakes (Citroën SM style) while the Bora's were outboard. These two cars were joined by a new front-engined Quattroporte four-door saloon.

Above and below: Both Merak (vee-6 engine) and Bora (vee-8 engine and 4.7-litres) share the same basic chassis. In each case the unit is mid-mounted, behind the seats, with all-independent suspension. The Bora (below) is a strict two-seater; the Merak has a shorter engine, set back, and room for a bit more space in the shape of an upholstered shelf. The Merak (above) has craggy wheels and sloping rear, the Bora a squared-off tail.

McLaren F1

McLaren F1 sports coupé, built 1993 to 1997
Built by: McLaren Cars Ltd., Britain.
Engine: Twelve cylinders, in 60-degree vee-formation, in seven-bearing light-alloy cylinder block. Bore and stroke 86 × 87mm, 6,064cc (3.38 × 3.42in, 370cu.in). Two light-alloy cylinder heads. Four valves per cylinder, operation by twin overhead camshafts. Bosch/BMW fuel injection. Maximum power 627bhp (DIN) at 7,400rpm. Maximum torque 479lb.ft at 4,000rpm.
Transmission: Rear-wheel-drive, triple-plate carbon clutch and six-speed all-synchromesh manual gearbox, all in unit with mid-mounted engine. Remote-control, central gearchange.
Chassis: Unitary-construction carbon fibre advanced composite monocoque structure and combined bodyshell with three-seater accommodation. Front and rear suspension mounted on subframes. Independent front suspension by coil springs, wishbones, telescopic dampers and anti-roll bar. Independent rear suspension by coil springs, wishbones, telescopic dampers and anti-roll bar. Rack-and-pinion steering. Four-wheel disc brakes with vacuum servo assistance, but no ABS. 17in cast-alloy wheels, 235/45-17in (front) and 315/45-17in (rear) tyres.
Dimensions: Wheelbase 8ft 11in (271.8cm), front track 5ft 1.7in (157cm), rear track 4ft 10in (147cm). Overall length 14ft 0.8in (429cm). Unladen weight 2,509lb (1,138kg).
History: Vaunting ambition is often thwarted, as it was with McLaren and their incredibly fast F1 road car. Conceived in 1990 when it was thought that they could easily sell cars priced at £540,000, it did not go on sale until 1993. By this time the world's economy had turned down, potential customers fled for cover, and sales were extremely sluggish. In the end the project had to be wound down in 1997, after only 100 machines (a proportion of them GTR competition cars, and LM types) had been built.

Technically, however, the F1 was superb. Because of the way that world attitudes to motoring changed so much in the last years of the 20th Century (when enjoying high performance became politically incorrect), its top speed of 231mph will probably never be bettered by a rival.

Gordon Murray, poached from the Brabham F1 team to head McLaren's design team, was allowed to indulge himself with the F1 road car. There were, effectively, no limits to what he might specify, for this car had to be the best, the fastest and the most desirable: it was always understood that it could also be the most exclusive, and the most expensive. Like the Jaguar XJ220, which it followed, and surpassed, it was to have amazingly high performance, but lack several partly expected amenities. There was, for instance, no provision for four-wheel-drive, none for traction control, and none for ABS anti-lock brakes. Nor was there any power assistance for the rack-and-pinion steering, or even a spare wheel.

Murray was, above all, a deep thinker, so the layout of the Supercar which he conceived was unique. Although, like many other such machines, it had a mid-mounted engine driving the rear wheels, it had a wide cabin with not two, but three, seats, the driver occupying the central seat, which was set ahead of the others. Although the F1 was neither light enough or small enough to be considered as a single-seater with a roof, the (wealthy) driver might fantasise that he was in just such a car.

Structurally, the F1 was built up around a full F1-race-style carbon fibre monocoque, and was powered by a brand-new engine. McLaren went to BMW of Germany, explained its need for a normally aspirated engine with more than 550bhp, and placed a contract. BMW therefore designed a brand-new V12 (which, in detail, had much in common with their latest M3 straight-six), and within 18 months had it thrumming away on their test beds in Munich. It was

Above: The McLaren F1 road car, immensely fast and very expensive, was the world's fastest car in the 1990s.

altogether typical of BMW that it not only surpassed every contract requirement, but produced a stunningly civilised, refined and reliable engine too. Having settled on a capacity of 6,064cc, it then delivered no less than 627bhp at 7,400rpm – this from a normally aspirated layout which had to pass every one of the world's exhaust emission tests.

The rest of the car lived up to these standards. With carbon fibre body panels, doors which (when opened) swung upwards and forwards, Lamborghini Diablo-fashion, and without the need for a single aerodynamic spoiler to keep it stable at 200mph-plus speeds (except a discreet, flush-mounted, spoiler on the tail which popped up when the brakes were applied from high speed), the style was stunning. But this had always been expected, for the F1 had been shaped by Peter Stevens, whose reputation (for designing cars like the front-wheel-drive Lotus Elan) had already been made.

The sheer, mind-boggling, record-breaking performance of this car caused every jaw to drop, especially as it was linked to impeccable stability, roadholding and general behaviour. Only a handful of the owners were ever likely to see the speedometer indicate more than 200mph (with a lot more to come, please note . . .), but most of them would revel in the acceleration.

Tyre wear, for sure, from those massive 315/45-17in 'rollers' at the rear might be expensive, but rich men would not mind, preferring to bury the throttle from a standing start, see 60mph come up in 3.2 seconds, 100mph in a mere 6.3 seconds, and 150mph in 12.8 seconds. The quarter-mile post would be passed in 11.1 seconds.

All such figures completely annihilated the opposition from any other car in the '200-Club', and not even recognised iconic Supercars like the Ferrari F40 and the Jaguar XJ220 could match them. And there was more. Every one of the world's open road speed limits could be passed in the second (of six gears), where 95mph was possible; fourth gear was good for 150mph; and, before changing up out of fifth gear, the F1 could be passing most Ferraris (which would be flat out) at 180mph.

Put another way, if an owner was content to trundle through towns and cities with a 30mph speed limit, he would be obliged to change down to fifth or even fourth gear so that the magnificent BMW V12 was not turning over too slowly. At sensible speeds, all this, mind you, was delivered in near silence – to witness an unmodified F1 at speed on a test track was almost to watch a silent movie – and, if it mattered to the sort of driver this car would attract, the fuel consumption was a totally acceptable 15mpg.

Part of the F1's attraction, however, was not in its style, or its performance, but in its detailing. Gordon Murray and Peter Stevens, having been given their head, did not skimp on a single detail. To keep the flanks smooth (or, at least, to ensure that the style was not compromised), the

engine air intake was in the roof, immediately behind the top of the screen, with a long, carbon fibre, channel leading back from there and dividing the rear window glass.

The six-speed gearbox, especially designed for McLaren by Traction Products of America, had a magnesium casing, while the final drive was packaged alongside the clutch. Like the XJ220, the carbon body shell included under-floor venturi sections to add downforce at high road speeds. The engine silencer had a volume of no less than 65 litres. Discs, by Brembo, were Formula 1 type, massive, light and incredibly effective.

The GTR, developed as a racing car for Le Mans, was even more extreme, and the incredibly rare Lm type, with all the GTR chassis, but in road-legal form, was a £799,000 indulgence. The F1 was that sort of car, unsurpassed, and unsurpassable. At the end of the day, it must have been a big loss-making project, but for McLaren the prestige bonus was immeasurable. We may never see another car like it.

Below: The F1's 6.1-litre V12 BMW engine was behind the cabin, which had three seats, with the driver sitting in the centre.

Mercédès 60 Model

60 models, built from 1903 to 1904 (data for 1903 model)
Built by: Daimler Motoren Gesellschaft, Germany.
Engine: Four cylinders, in line, in two cast-iron blocks, with three-bearing light alloy crankcase. Bore and stroke 140mm by 151mm, 9,293cc (5.52in × 5.94in 567cu.in). Non-detachable cylinder heads. Two valves per cylinder: over-head inlet valves, with special Mercédès annular construction, operated by pushrods and rockers, and side exhaust valves; both valves operated from single camshaft in side of crankcase. Single up-draught Mercédès-Simplex carburettor. Maximum power about 65bhp at 1,100rpm.
Transmission: Scroll clutch in unit with front-mounted engine and separate four speed manual gearbox (without synchromesh) and straight-bevel differential in rear of gear case. Final drive by countershaft from transmission to sprockets. Drive to rear wheels by chains.
Chassis: Separate pressed-steel chassis frame, with channel-section side members and tubular cross bracing. Forged front axle beam. Front and rear suspension by semi-elliptic leaf springs. No dampers. Worm-and-nut steering. Externally contracting drum brake, foot-pedal and mechanically operated, on gearbox counter shaft. Hand lever operating drums on rear wheel hubs. Wooden artillery style wheels. 910 × 90mm tyres (front) and 920 × 120mm tyres (rear). Open two-seat or four-seat bodywork.
Dimensions: Wheelbase 9ft 0.2in (275cm), tracks (front and rear) 4ft 7.5in (141cm). Overall length 12ft 3.5in (375cm). Unladen weight 2,204lb (1,000kg).
History: Emil Jellinek was a wealthy admirer of the German Daimlers and ordered a series of cars to his own requirements at the end of the 19th century. For 1901, he persuaded Daimler's Wilhelm Maybach to design him a completely new type of car, one which is now recognised as the forerunner of modern designs. The chassis, much lower than before, was of pressed steel and the layout and detail represented a complete change from 19th century practice. These Mercédès-Simplex cars were progressively developed in racing after

1901, until Mercédès 60 cars were announced for 1903. The name Mercédès, incidentally, is that of Jellinek's own daughter.

For the infamous 1903 Paris-Madrid race a 90bhp car was produced, but it was beaten by the 60s and a fire at Cannstatt destroyed all five special racing cars. For the Gordon Bennett races in Ireland the factory appealed for owners to return their cars on loan. The American Clarence Gray Dinsmore lent his car, and Camille Jenatzy duly won the race in it, achieving 49.2mph in average speed, and notching up a 66mph maximum speed.

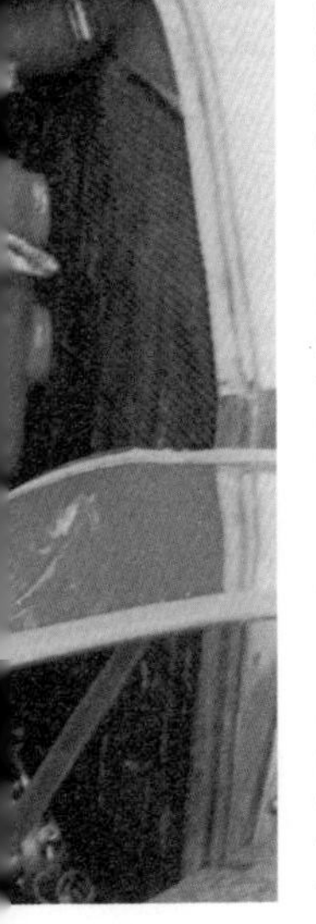

The transmission, with countershaft and chain drive to the rear wheels, was typical of the period, as was the braking system, with foot brake operating on the transmission drum. The engine, with its cast-alloy crankcase and paired cast-iron cylinders, had an integral cylinder head and overhead inlet valves which, admitted mixture through annular slots. The basic design of these cars was so good that the 12.7-litre 90 and the 14-litre models used virtually the same chassis and details, and all used the same robust family of four-cylinder engines. The success of the predecessors of the famous 60 cars caused the name Mercédès to be applied to all private cars built at Cannstatt from 1902. Jellinek himself had been on the board of the company since 1900. By 1908, however, when Mercédès won the Grand Prix, their cars had become even more advanced and with repeat wins in 1914 (with overhead-camshaft engines) they were established as leading makers of really fast cars.

Left and above: Sheer exciting modern engineering in the Mercédès 60. It is hard to believe that this splendid car was built as early as 1903. Most truly modern cars seem to have evolved from this brilliant design. A Mercédès 60 won the Gordon Bennett race in 1903.

Mercedes-Benz 38/250

36/220 and 38/250 models, built from 1927 to 1933 (data for 1929/30 SS model)
Built by: Daimler-Benz A.G., Germany.
Engine: Six cylinders, in line, in four-bearing light-alloy combined block/crankcase. Bore and stroke 100mm by 150mm, 7,069cc (3.94in x 5.91in, 431.4cu.in). Detachable cast-iron cylinder head. Two overhead valves per cylinder, vertically mounted, but staggered, and operated by fingers from single overhead camshaft. Two up-draught single-choke Mercédés-Benz carburettors, with or without assistance from Roots-type supercharger driven from nose of crankshaft. Maximum power (supercharged) 200bhp at 3,000rpm (140bhp if not supercharged).
Transmission: Multi-dry-plate clutch and four-speed manual gearbox (without synchromesh), both in unit with front-mounted engine. Direct-acting central gearchange. Propeller shaft enclosed in torque tube, driving spiral-bevel 'live' rear axle.
Chassis: Separate pressed-steel chassis frame, with channel-section side members and pressed and tubular cross bracing. Forged front axle beam. Front suspension by semi-elliptic leaf springs. Rear suspension by semi-elliptic leaf springs and torque tube. Lever-arm hydraulic dampers or friction-type dampers (depending on customer). Four-wheel, shaft and rod-operated drum brakes (some cars with vacuum-servo assistance). Centre-lock wire wheels. 6.50 x 20 tyres. Two-seat or four-seat open coachwork.
Dimensions: Wheelbase 11ft 4in (345.4cm), tracks (front and rear) 4ft 10in (147.3cm). Overall length 15ft 5in (470cm). Unladen weight 2,800lb (1,270kg).
History: Following the completion of the merger between Mercédès and Benz, in 1926 (the accents on the name were dropped thereafter), the new combine continued to develop a fabulously fast, brutally impressive, starkly attractive and very successful series of supercharged sports cars. These cars are, in the beginning, to the credit of Dr. Ferdinand Porsche, who worked for the company after leaving Austro-Daimler earlier in the 1920s and before leaving to set up his own engineering consultancy business. The origins of a remarkable series of cars lie in the Mercédès (pre-merger, that is) 24/100/14PS of 1924. This car was designed around a vast new six-cylinder unit and the three figures, respectively, referred to the tax horsepower, the unsupercharged peak power output and the supercharged peak power. The blower itself was mounted at the nose of the engine, in an upright position, and could be clutched in or out of engagement (by friction clutches at the front end of the crankshaft) by the driver. Mercedes were at pains to point out to owners that the supercharger should be used only when needed, as it vastly increased the stresses on the engine and on the transmission. The engagement linkage was connected to the throttle pedal. Newer and faster models followed with great industry. First came the 36/220S, with its engine enlarged to 6/8-litres and that 220 referring to supercharged peak horsepower; this then paved the way for the 7-litre 38/250. This last car, in more and yet more developed form, was the basis of all the Mercedes sports racing two-seaters of the late 1920s and early 1930s, which culminated in the very rare SSKL cars with their 300bhp and a top speed of more than 145mph in

Below: The 38/250 (or SSK) was typical of late-1920s Mercedes-Benz design, complete with an outside exhaust system.

Above: Dr. Ferdinand Porsche's masterpiece of design for Mercedes was the six-cylinder supercharged car, built up to 1933.

streamlined form. After the Mercédès and Benz merger, the 'basic' 140bhp supercharged car was given a shorter chassis and became the K (K = Kurz). This car was fast, but was not yet nimble enough, so it was reengineered for an S version to be built alongside it. The S had a new chassis frame dropped considerably by comparison with the K, and with the engine moved back by about 12in along with a lowered radiator. This car, in German numbering, was the 26/120/180PS, which indicated how the power was being increased. The 1928 cars which, among other things, won the German Grand Prix, were SSs (27/140/200PS), and had 7.1 litres compared with 6.8 litres for the original S. The cars were now becoming very specialised and a series of SSK cars (K = Kruz again, for shortened chassis) were raced with great success. These, in German terms, were 27/170/225PS cars. There was now only one more development to come – the SSKL – which was incredibly expensive to build, very specialised, much lightened, even more highly tuned, and intended for factory use only. The SSKLs were 27/170/300PS cars – which gives an idea of the engine boost they were asked to withstand from the latest enlarged elephant blowers. No doubt Mercedes-Benz could have improved the cars still further, but by then they were committed to a large-scale single-seater racing programme, with cars being built for the new 750kg Grand Prix formula, and the sports car programme was dropped. Perhaps even more than the much-vaunted Bentleys and Hispano-Suizas, and certainly more so than the bigger Bugattis, the Mercedes supercharged sports cars said everything about the magnificence of the vintage era. The cars were, frankly, expensive, fast and exhilarating toys for their rich buyers; with usually more than 200bhp on tap and often only a token four-seater body shell without much weather protection provided, they were hardly practical every-day machines. Their 'optional' supercharging was a unique way of providing, at one and the same time, a potential race-winning car which could also be cruised around when the pressure was off and which could also be used on the road in its less forceful state. Even if the supercharger could not be used with impunity, the howl emitted when it was in use must have made quite an impact on its opposition. Strangely enough, a weak point with these cars was the brakes, which is hardly surprising when one considers that they were, relatively speaking, faster in their day than a Ferrari or Lamborghini road car is today *and* cable-operated drum brakes were all that could be provided. Such performance, too, was achieved without any pretence to streamlining. Cycle type wings, which did not turn with the front wheels, were the order of the day, and between them was the bluff and legendary vee-shape of the Mercedes radiator, with the equally famous three-pointed star fixed to its apex. Yet this immense performance, much feared by any rival met on road or track, was mostly to the credit of Dr. Porsche's splendid engine, the rest of the chassis engineering, although carried out with great care and in high-quality materials, was entirely conventional, and was on a par with cars like the W.O. Bentleys and the Hispanos.

Mercedes-Benz 300SL

300SL models, built from 1954 to 1963 (data for 1954 model)
Built by: Daimler-Benz AG. West Germany.
Engine: Six cylinders, in line, in seven-bearing cast-iron block, installed in car at angle of 45 degrees. Bore and stroke 85mm by 88mm, 2,996cc (3.35in × 3.46in, 182.8cu.in.) Detachable light-alloy cylinder head with joint not perpendicular to cylinder bores. Combustion chamber formed in top of piston and top of cylinder block. Two overhead valves per cylinder, staggered (with inlet valves in one line and exhaust valves in other line) and operated by rockers from single overhead camshaft. Dry-sump lubrication. Bosch direct fuel injection. Maximum power 215bhp (net) at 5,800rpm. Maximum torque 228lb.ft at 5,000rpm.
Transmission: Single-dry-plate clutch and four-speed, all-synchromesh manual gearbox, both in unit with engine. Direct-acting central gearchange. Open propeller shaft to chassis-mounted hypoid bevel final drive.
Chassis: Separate multi-tubular spaceframe, with many small-diameter steel tubes linking points of stress. Lightweight aluminium two-seater body shell – coupé with gull-wing doors or open 'roadster' with conventional doors. Independent front suspension by coil springs, wishbones and anti-roll bar. Independent rear suspension by coil springs and swing axles. Telescopic dampers. Steering wheel hinged for access to driving seat and steering by recirculating-ball unit. Four wheel, hydraulically operated drum brakes, vacuum-servo assistance. 15in pressed-steel road wheels. 6.70 × 15in tyres.
Dimensions: Wheelbase 7ft 10.5in (240cm), track (front) 4ft 9in (145cm). Overall length 15ft (457cm). Unladen weight 3,000lb (1,364kg).

History: Mercedes-Benz began to introduce a new series of passenger cars in 1950 and 1951, among which was a big and impressive six-cylinder 3-litre car, but they made a sensation when re-entering motor sport in 1952 with the futuristic 300SL sports-racing car. The fact that this car won its very first Le Mans race was startling enough, but that Mercedes were proposing to put it into some sort of quantity production was even more astonishing. Apart from the obvious facts that it was at the same time very fast and very attractive, it was also exceedingly complex, mechanically, and was not really designed for quantity production. The heart of the car's performance lay in its engine, which had direct fuel injection on production cars (although the Le Mans winner had used an engine with conventional carburettors), but the main interest was in the structure. Mercedes had gone all the way towards a theoretically perfect multi-tube 'spaceframe' structure, where all tubes were slim and absolutely straight and none had to withstand bending or torsional stresses of any nature. Taken to extremes, this would deny access to the car altogether, so there were inevitable compromises in the region of the passenger compartment. To ease this problem as much as possible, the frame was very deep along the sills and the doors were ▶

Below: Striking comparison between the world-famous gull-wing Mercedes 300SL (on the right), and the mid-engined four-rotor Wankel engined Mercedes C111 Coupé. Both are from the same stable, but the progress made in less than 20 years is obvious. The 300SL engine is front-mounted, on its side; the Wankel is mid-mounted.

arranged to hinge along their top edge and open upwards in 'gull-wing' fashion. The car's only failing, more noticeable at very high speeds than at touring speeds, was that Mercedes were then wedded to swing-axle independent rear suspension. This allowed large (driven) rear wheel camber changes and produced serious and possibly dangerous oversteer at times. To handle a 300SL at really high speeds required good 'racing-driver' reflexes. Far more of the 300SLs were ordered than Mercedes had bargained for and in 1957 they introduced the open-topped 300SL Roadster, which was a little easier to make, and handled better by virtue of its low-pivot swing-axle rear suspension. This model continued to be made at Stuttgart until the early 1960s and a total of 3,250 of both types were eventually sold.

There was no doubt that a suitably-geared 300SL, particularly in the more-streamlined coupé condition, had a very high maximum speed. The original publicity claims were that the car could accelerate from 15mph to no less than 165mph in top gear (which said a lot for the flexibility of the fuel-injected engine),

Below: The gull-wing Mercedes-Benz 300SL, of which more than 1,000 examples were built, is one of two different types of 300SL, the other being the open Roadster, with conventional doors. Both had multi-tube 'space-frame' chassis, fuel injection for their 3-litre six-cylinder engines, and swing-axle rear suspension, but retained drum brakes.

but the higher figure was not attainable by a normally equipped road car. In British tune the cars could certainly beat 130mph, which made them supreme; however, with very high gearing it was possible for something like 150mph to be passed. The 300SL was forecast to start a new trend in sports car design, but even Mercedes themselves did not really want to have to build a spaceframe chassis in quantity and they were not copied by any other serious production-car concern. The multi-tube layout was very expensive and very difficult to build properly, as Mercedes soon found out. Neither did the gull-wing doors find favour elsewhere and when the Roadster 300SL was announced it was seen to have a modified frame with conventionally hinged doors.

The 300SL's descendants, truly, were the W196 Grand Prix car, which had many family resemblances, and the 300SLR sports-racing-car (which in unique closed-coupé guise looked astonishingly similar to the 300SL). A car does not have to be a commercial success to be an all-time 'classic'. In looks, in performance and in the sheer exuberance of its complex engineering, the 300SL stood quite apart from any really fast supercar of the 1950s. Not even Ferrari, with exotic V12 engines in more mundane chassis, could match their ambience. The 300SL's engine, in less highly tuned form, was a mainstay of the Mercedes production car range until the end of the 1960s, when it was at last replaced by a new 3½-litre/4½-litre V8 unit. The direct-injection system in the 300SL was unique for many years.

Mercedes-Benz 'Grosser' 770

'Grosser' models, built 1930 to 1940 (data for 1938 model)
Built by: Daimler-Benz A.G., Germany.
Engine: Eight cylinders, inline, in cast-iron block, with nine-bearing light-alloy crankcase. Bore and stroke 95mm by 135mm, 7,655cc (3.74in × 5.31in, 467cu.in). Detachable cast-iron cylinder head. Two overhead valves per cylinder, operated by pushrods and rockers from single camshaft mounted in side of crankcase. Single up-draught Mercedes-Benz twin-choke carburettor, with optionally engaged Roots-type supercharger, driven through friction clutch and gearing at nose of crankshaft and engaged by flooring throttle pedal. Maximum power 155bhp (unsupercharged) or 230bhp (supercharged) at 3,500rpm.
Transmission: Single-dry-plate clutch and five-speed, synchromesh manual gearbox (without synchromesh on first gear), both in unit with front-mounted engine. Direct-acting central gearchange. Open propeller shaft to chassis-mounted spiral-bevel final-drive unit. Universally jointed drive shaft enclosed in swinging half-axles.
Chassis: Separate steel chassis frame, made up of oval-section tubes, with tubular side members and tubular and pressed cross-bracing. Independent front suspension by coil springs and wishbones. De Dion rear suspension by coil springs and radius arms. Lever-arm hydraulic dampers. Worm-type steering. Four-wheel, hydraulically operated drum brakes, with servo assistance. 17in bolt-on steel disc wheels. 8-25 × 17in tyres. Open or closed coachwork, four doors in each case.

Above: By 1937 the 'Grosser' Mercedes was looking more and more American. The final flowering was a technically clever machine with GP-type chassis.

Dimensions: Wheelbase 12ft 11.1in (394cm), track (front) 5ft 4in (162.6cm), track (rear) 5ft 6in (167.6cm). Overall length 20ft 6in (625cm). Unladen weight (depending on coachwork and amount of armour-plating) 7,600lb to 8,100lb (3,673kg).

History: There had been Grosser Mercedes models since 1930, when the first model with its exclusive 7.7-litre engine was announced. These cars were intended for state ceremonial use, and for selected and prestigious private owners. At first the cars had classic chassis with beam axles and leaf springs, but in 1938, the massive Type 770 model was announced. Production was even more restricted – to Adolf Hitler and his party colleagues – and the car's design leaned heavily on the company's newly gained Grand Prix racing expertise. The oval-tube frame, the advanced suspensions, and the general layout, were all inspired by the W125 racing cars, although there were no common parts. The usual Mercedes 'optional' supercharger feature was present, together with a firm injunction *not* to use it for more than a minute at any one time. The five-speed gearbox, like the massive but conventional engine, was unique to the Grosser model and no other passenger car used the oval-tube type of chassis. There was never any economic reason for building these cars, which were purely prestige models, yet they were magnificently engineered in every way. As most of them carried armour plate and bullet-proof glass they were heavy and ruinously un-economical. Something less than 5mpg was normal in most conditions!

Left: There was always one 'Grosser' Mercedes in the range in the 1930s. This model was a Type 770 of 1930 with a vast coachbuilt four-door drophead body.

Mercedes-Benz SLK

Mercedes-Banz SLK, two-seater convertible/hardtop, introduced in 1996 (data for original Kompressor model)
Built by: Daimler-Benz AG, Germany.
Engine: Four cylinders, in line, in five-bearing cast iron cylinder block. Bore and stroke 90.9 × 88.4mm, 2,295cc (3.58 × 3.48in, 140.1cu.in). Light-alloy cylinder head. Four valves per cylinder, in vee, operation by twin overhead camshafts, and hydraulic inverted bucket tappets. Electronic fuel injection and supercharger. Maximum power 190bhp (DIN) at 5,300rpm. Maximum torque 206lb.ft at 2,500rpm.
Transmission: Rear-wheel-drive, torque converter and five-speed manual or automatic transmissions, all in unit with front-mounted engine. Remote-control, central gearchange.
Chassis: Unitary-construction pressed-steel body-chassis unit, in combined two-seater roadster or hardtop style. Independent front suspension by coil springs, wishbones, telescopic dampers, and anti-roll bar. Independent rear suspension by coil springs, multi-link location, and telescopic dampers. Recirculating ball steering with hydraulic power assistance. Four-wheel disc brakes, servo assisted, with ABS as standard. Cast alloy 16in road wheels, 205/55-16in (front) and 225/50-16in (rear) tyres.
Dimensions: Wheelbase 7ft 10.4in (240cm), front track 4ft 10.6in (148.8cm), rear track 4ft 10.3in (148cm). Overall length 13ft 1.3in (399.5cm). Unladen weight 2,950lb (1,338kg).
History: In the 1990s, as in many previous decades, Mercedes-Benz was adept at squeezing every possible derivative from a particular model range. Although the two-seater SLK roadster of 1996 looked completely new, therefore, it hid a great deal of existing technology under the skin. It may have appeared to be related to the existing, longer, heavier and much more upmarket SL series, but it was actually based on the pressed-steel platform of the latest C-Class saloons, which had been launched in 1993. The use of 'K' (for Kurz, or 'short' in the German language) showed that it had a shorter wheelbase, but the basic suspension, steering and running gear were all lifted from that car.

Because it was a Mercedes-Benz model, of course, there was no sign of

Below: The SLK, introduced in 1996, was a compact and carefully detailed two-seater, with an electric fold-up hardtop feature.

Above: The SLK, naturally, had a strong family resemblance to the longer and larger SL, but at first was available only with 4-cylinder engines. A V6-engined derivative was added in 2000.

compromise in this design, for it had all been carefully developed, integrated, and tested. The new R170 style (to use Mercedes-Benz's own internal description of this model) not only had a family resemblance to other current cars from Stuttgart, but it was as rigid and as wind-cheating as possible.

More than that, this was a car which could be used as an open roadster or as a snug two-seater coupé, for it incorporated a clever fold-away steel roof feature, which might have made the boot space rather restricted, but was an extremely neat and versatile way of providing two cars in one. One interesting feature, which caused a great deal of worry among customers, was that there was no spare wheel (no space in the tail, apparently), but instead the car was supplied with tyre sealant and an electric pump.

Although it was small by other Mercedes-Benz standards (it was only 157.3in/399.5cm long), it was also sturdily built, so powerful engines were needed to push it along. In the beginning there were to be two types of the ubiquitous four-cylinder C-Class unit – a normally aspirated 135bhp two-litre and an Eaton-supercharged 193bhp 2.3-litre, badged 'Kompressor' for obvious reasons. Although this car was offered with a choice of five-speed manual or automatic transmissions in continental Europe, only the automatic was available in the UK. The lower powered car, frankly, was not fast enough for what its customers required, most of whom chose the blown example.

The car's initial reception was friendly, but not ecstatic, reflecting the balance of Mercdes-Benz build quality against a certain lack of refinement (the four-cylinder engine did not help) and sporting character. Early in 2000, therefore, without changing the car's style, or its clever packaging, there was a major reshuffle of engines and transmissions. The 'entry level' machine became a supercharged 2.0-litre/163bhp unit, the 2.3-litre 'Kompressor' was slightly uprated to 197bhp, while a range-topping 218bhp 3.2-litre V6 engine was also added. Newly developed six-speed manual transmissions were introduced, the five-speed automatic box was continued, and all of a sudden the SLK began to look like a more integrated package. In the meantime, none of the hewn-from-solid build quality feel was destroyed, nor was the full range of safety equipment, and the SLK became one of Mercedes-Benz's best-selling roadsters ever.

Mini

Austin and Morris Minis, built from 1959 to 1969 and Minis, built from 1969 to 2000 (data for 850 version)

Built by: (Originally) British Motor Corporation Ltd., Britain. (From 1968 to 1975) British Leyland Motor Corporation Ltd., Britain. (From 1975 to date) British Leyland Ltd., Britain.

Engine: Four cylinders, in line, three-bearing in cast-iron block. Bore and stroke 62.9mm by 68.3mm, 846cc (2.48 × 2.69in, 51.7cu.in). Cast-iron cylinder head. Two overhead valves per cylinder, operated by pushrods and rockers from single camshaft side-mounted in the block. Engine itself transversely mounted in nose of car, on top of and in unit with transmission. Single semi-down-draught SU carburettor. Maximum power 33bhp (DIN) at 5,300rpm. Maximum torque 40lb.ft at 2,500rpm. Other versions (including Cooper and Cooper S models) have had 970cc, 997cc, 998cc, 1,071cc, 1,098cc and 1,275cc displacement and Coopers and Cooper Ss had twin SU carburettors.

Transmission: Single-dry-plate clutch and four-speed, synchromesh manual gearbox (all-synchro since 1968, before that with unsynchronised first gear) mounted in case immediately underneath engine. Direct or extension gear-change on floor between seats. Drive on right of engine through overhung clutch

Top right: In the late 1960s the fastest Minis were the 1275S Mini-Coopers, which could reach 95mph, and were race and rally winners.

Right: This 1976 model Mini had a 998cc engine, and was capable of nearly 80mph, but had evolved very little since launch in 1959.

Bottom right: The most finely-tuned Minis of all were the 'works' cars from Abingdon. This was a 1275S rally car, with more than 100bhp, a special gearbox, and masses of extra fittings, in the 1968 Swedish Rally. Minis won the Monte Carlo Rally three times, and dozens of other events round the globe.

Below: Most famous, if not most numerous, of all the Minis, was the Mini Cooper S, built from 1963 to 1971. Three versions – 970S, 1071S and 1275S – all won races and rallies. A powerful engine, disc front brakes, and remarkable handling all helped.

ROU 11G

MOC 205R

U8448

and drop gears. Spur-gear final drive with differential mounted behind transmission. Exposed drive shafts to front wheels, with Rzeppa-type outboard, constant-velocity joints. Transmission shares lubricating oil with engine. AP four-speed automatic transmission (with manual override) optional from 1965, mounted in same way under engine. Only available on some versions of the car.
Chassis: Unitary-construction pressed-steel body structure. Several coachwork variations. Most are two-door saloons but longer-wheelbase estates, vans and pick-ups also sold. Riley and Wolseley 'Minis' had extended tails with bigger boots. Mini Clubman series has longer nose and different style. All-independent suspension, mounted on pressed-steel subframes, by wishbones (front) and trailing arms (rear). Suspension by rubber cone springs, except 1964 to 1969 when by interconnected Hydrolastic suspension. Hydraulic drum brakes on most versions – Cooper, Cooper S and 1275GT versions have front discs with servo assistance. 145 × 12in Dunlop 'run-flat Denovo wheels/tyres on 1275GT. 10in pressed-steel-disc wheels and 5.20 × 10in or 145 × 19in tyres on other versions.
Dimensions: Wheelbase 6ft 8in (204cm), track (front) 3ft 11.4in (120cm), track (rear) 3ft 9.8in (116cm). Overall length 10ft 0.25in (305cm). Unladen weight 1,398lb (635kg).
History: In the aftermath of the first Suez war of 1956, the BMC Mini was Alec Issigonis's brilliant concept of what a new generation of tiny economy cars should be like. Transverse engines with front drive were not entirely new, but the Issigonis layout with a conventional four-cylinder water-cooled engine was unique. His principle has since been copied by car makers all round the world.

As remarkable as the power plant installation were the car's very small size, its space utilisation and the suspension system chosen. Developed in collaboration with Alex Moulton, it brought rubber compression units back into the limelight. Geometry, apart from the reversed rubber cone actuation at the rear (to save space), was conventional. Between 1964 and 1969 BMC's later Hydrolastic

Right: This is a specially developed private-venture Mini, the Mini-Sprint, which had a lowered body, but retained the same running gear.

Below: The original Minis - this is a 1959 model - were sold as Austin or Morris types, had 848cc engines, and could reach only 72mph.

system, where road shocks and suspension displacements were signalled from front to rear wheels through interconnecting high-pressure water/alcohol pipes, was more expensive but did not achieve a great advance in ride.

Front-drive, splendid balance, and sensitive steering combined to give startling handling and roadholding. Apart from being everybody's idea of a cheap and practical runabout the Mini soon became an important competition car. Minis began winning races at once and Cooper versions were followed by the very formidable Cooper S competition cars. Apart from winning the Monte Carlo rally on three occasions (and being spectacularly disqualified from a fourth), the Cooper S won British and European touring car race championships, international rallies, ice races – in fact any kind of motoring event.

The first million minis were built by spring 1965 and the four millionth arrived in the winter of 1976/7. Since 1969, rationalisation has eliminated many specialised versions like the long-tail Riley/Wolseley Minis and – alas – all the Coopers after nearly 150,000 had been delivered. One ultra-special variant – the stark and almost non-bodied Mini Moke – was withdrawn after hoped-for military contracts did not materialise.

Certainly Mini features, like the ingenious installation of the Automotive Products automatic transmission, have never been matched by the competition. Neither (except by the Fiat 126) has its small size. Apart from being a true 'Classic Car', the Mini is also Britain's best selling car of all time, for production continued slowly until October 2000, by which time nearly 5.4 million of all types had been made.

MG M-Type Midget

M-Type Midget, built from 1929 to 1932
Built by: M.G. Car Co. Ltd., Britain.
Enginer: Four cylinders, in line, in two-bearing cast-iron block. Bore and stroke 57mm by 83mm, 847cc (2.24 × 3.27in, 51.8cu.in). Cast-iron cylinder head. Two overhead valves per cylinder, operated by single overhead camshaft. Single SU side-draught carburettor. 5.4:1 compression ratio. Maximum power 20bhp at 4,000rpm (raised to about 27bhp at 4,500rpm after 2,000 cars had been built). Engine (like chassis) derived from that of Morris Minor saloon.
Transmission: Single-dry-plate clutch and three-speed manual gearbox (without synchromesh), both in unit with engine. Optional four-speed gearbox (also without synchromesh) from autumn 1930. Open propeller shaft to spiral-bevel 'live' rear axle.
Chassis: Simple channel-section frame with five pressed cross members, Semi-elliptic leaf springs at front and rear, with Hartford friction-type dampers. Four-wheel, cable-operated drum brakes. 19in wire wheels. 4 × 19in tyres. Original coachwork was light and simple two-seat sports car layout with pointed tail, framed in ash and fabric covered. First cars had rear-hinged doors (changed in 1930, but later versions had metal panels with a folding hood. A closed two-door

Above: The standard production Midget M-Type, built from 1929 to 1932. This car is a 1930 example, with appropriate 'MG' registration plate found on many such London-sold Midgets in the 1930s. The chassis and engine were developed form the Morris Minor. Note fabric body.

Left and below: M-Type Midgets prepared for competition had tiny and lightweight bodies. This 1930 Double-12 car averaged 60.23mph for 24 hours at Brooklands, and was the highest-placed of the Team Prize winning cars, driven by C.J. Randall and F.M. Montgomery.

'Sportsman's coupé was also offered as an extremely attractive alternative.
Dimensions: Wheelbase 6ft 6in (198cm), track (front) 3ft 6in (106.7cm), track (rear) 3ft 6in (106.7cm). Overall length 10ft 3in (312cm). Unladen weight 1,120lb (508kg).
History: The very first MGs were built in 1924 and were no more than lightly modified and rebodied 'Bullnose' Morris Cowleys. They were inspired by Cecil Kimber at Morris Garages Ltd. In Oxford, which was owned by William Morris himself. The M.G. Car Co. Ltd. was formally established in 1928, by which time Kimber was already planning to build a tiny new two-seater sports car. Morris, having bought Wolseley Motors of Birmingham, were proposing to announce their new Morris Minor in the autumn and Kimber decided that this car's little chassis and Hispano-inspired overhead-camshaft engine would be an ideal starting point.

Mechanically, therefore, the M-Type MG Midget, announced in 1928, first sold in April 1929 and withdrawn in June 1932 after 3,235 examples had been delivered, was almost pure Morris Minor. To make it a proper MG, the suspension was lowered, the steering column was re-angled and that distinctive MG radiator was added. The initial bodies were simplicity themselves, having a very light plywood and ash frame mainly covered by fabric. The ensemble was completed by cycle-type wings, a neat little vee-shaped windscreen and a very elementary hood.

Apart from its cheekily attractive lines, the car's main attraction was the price – £175 in Britain – much lower than for almost any other sportscar in the world. Performance was good for its size, with maximum speed of more than 60mph and an average fuel consumption of around 40mpg. The brakes were not very efficient, but the handling and roadholding made up for this.

The press and the first customers loved the car and it was not long before it started to appear in competition, being used equally in sporting trials and on the

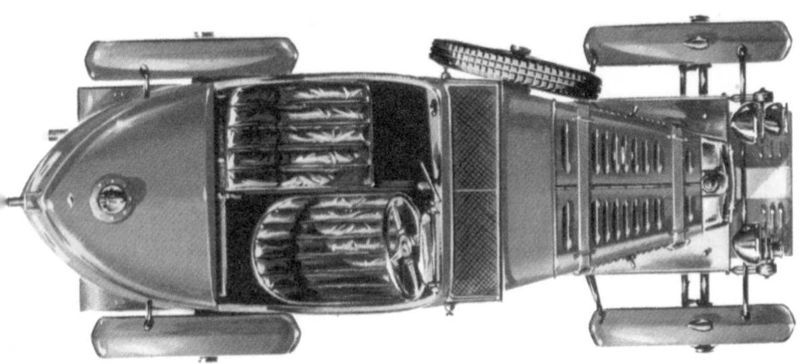

Above: Not much space for the riding mechanic in the Double-12, whose seat was set back. Note bonnet straps and wire mesh screen.

Brooklands race track. Camshaft changes intended to make the car competitive boosted the power from 20bhp to 27bhp and several factory-backed cars raced with distinction in 1930. The C-Type Montlhéry Midgets, out-and-out competition cars, were derived directly from the M-Type and its racing experiences.

Even with the optional four-speed gearbox and a tuned engine, the M-Type was not quite competitive enough in international racing, although it established the pedigree of all other MGs built before 1950. Production moved from Oxford to Abingdon in September 1929.

Below: 1930 Le Mans M-Type Midget.

MG Midgets–'Overhead Cam' Types

D-Type, J-Type four-cylinder models, built from 1931 to 1936 (data for 1934 PA two-seater)
Built by: MG Car Co. Ltd., Britain.
Engine: Four-cylinder, in line, with three-bearing cast-iron cylinder block. Bore and stroke 57mm by 83mm, 847cc (2.24 × 3.27in, 51.8cu in). Cast-iron cylinder head. Two overhead valves per cylinder, operated by single overhead camshaft. Twin semi-downdraught SU constant-vacuum carburettors. Maximum power 35bhp at 5,600rpm.
Transmission: Single-dry-plate clutch, with four-speed non-synchromesh manual gearbox, both in unit with engine. Open propeller shaft to spiral-bevel 'live' rear axle.
Chassis: Simple channel section pressed steel frame with pressed and tubular cross-members. Semi-elliptic leaf springs at front and rear, with Hartford friction-type dampers at front, and lever-arm hydraulic dampers at rear. Bishop cam steering. Four-wheel, 12in diameter, cable-operated drum brakes. 19in centre-lock wire-spoke wheels, with 4 × 19in tyres. Choice of coachbuilt bodywork, of steel panels on ash framing – two-seat open sports, four-seat open tourer, and two-seater closed 'Airline' coupé.
Dimensions: Wheelbase 7ft 3.3in (221.7cm), track (front and rear) 3ft 6in (106.7cm). Overall length (two-seat sports) 11ft 3in (343cm). Unladen weight (two-seat) 1,568lb (711kg).
History: After the original small MG sports car, the M-Type, had made its mark, there was never much doubt that it would have successors. Even so, nobody could have forecast that there would be a continuous and recognisable strain of MG Midgets in production until 1955, when the last of the TFs was finally replaced by the first of the Midgets built between 1931 and 1936 were all designed around the same basic mechanical layout (only the very rare R-Type single-seater racing Midget had all-independent suspension), with progressive

Below: The PA Midget of 1934 was one of the last Midgets to be sold with an overhead-cam engine. Separate simple steel frames meant that other styles were offered – including four-seaters. The engine size was 847cc and four-cyl.

Above: Perhaps not the copybook way to corner a racing Midget, but at least we get a good view of the front end and the good steering lock! This particular car is a TC, built in large numbers immediately after the Second World War. By then all of MG's design traditions were thoroughly established and the car sold well in export markets.

development of the four-cylinder overhead camshaft engine originally designed for the humble little Morris Minor of 1928. All had narrow, flexible, channel-section chassis frames with the rear slung under the spiral bevel back axle, and with rock-hard half-elliptic front and rear suspension, three- or four-speed manual gearboxes without synchro-mesh, cable brakes, centre-lock wire wheels, and a fly-off handbrake. Most of them had narrow, starkly trimmed, British-traditional styling, with separate front wings and free-standing head-lamps, most were open sports two-seaters, and all were enormous fun to drive. Bodies were cheap and simple, with ash frames supporting pressed or hand-formed steel panels; creature comforts were few, and not demanded by customers.

The M-Type's successor was the short-lived D-Type of 1931 and 1932, with 27bhp and a three-speed box, of which only 250 were built, but it was followed by the J1/J2 models of 1932-1934 (2,463 built in two years), and finally by the PA and PB cars of 1934-1936 (which sold to the tune of 2,526 cars. Compared with the D-Type, the J-model had 36bhp, a four-speed gearbox and rather more rakish styling, which included the use of cutaway doors to allow driver and passenger more elbow room. Like the D-Type, J1 and J2 models, the original P-series cars of 1934 and 1935 (retrospectively known as PAs) still retained an 847cc overhead camshaft engine, but now allied to a three-bearing block and crankshaft. There was no more power than before, but this was rectified for the PB of 1935-1936, which had 939cc, 43bhp, and a top speed of nearly 80mph.

Other MG models were built during the same incredibly prolific period, under the direction of Cecil Kimber, but other Midgets like the C-Type Montlhery, J3, ▶

J4, Q-Type and R-Type models were all strictly for competition, and the complex series of Magnas and Magnettes all had six-cylinder engines of the same basic design, related to the original Midget 'fours'.

MG's problem, at Abingdon, was that although success upon success was being gained by the competition cars, the road cars were becoming more and more expensive and (by Morris Motors standards) more and more specialised. Lord Nuffield, who personally owned MG throughout this period, saw that sales were dropping steadily, as losses began to mount. In 1935 he sold MG to his corporate Nuffield Group, where they came under the direct control of Morris Motors. Immediately the competitions programme was cancelled, and a new and cheaper-to-build Midget was put in hand. The last PB was built in 1936, when it was replaced by the entirely different TA model.

It is worth noting that although the MG Midget was *the* most popular British sports car, in fact and in legend, of the early 1930s, a total of only 8,474 overhead-camshaft engined road cars were sold in eight years.

Right: A TC fully modified for circuit racing in Britain, with a roll cage and fat non-standard tyres on 16 inch wheels (a popular modification).

Below: The well-known overhead-cam 847cc or 939cc PA/PB engine, with twin SU carburettors, and three main bearings.

Below: The PA Midget of 1934, with a full range of instruments, and much evidence of Cecile Kimber's well-loved style feature on MGs, the octagonal emblem.

MG MGA Twin-Cam

Twin-Cams built 1958 to 1960
Built by: MG Car Co. Ltd., Britain.
Engine: Four cylinders, in line, in three-bearing cast-iron cylinder block. Bore and stroke 75.39mm by 88.9mm, 1,588cc (2.97in × 3.50in, 96.9cu in). Detachable light alloy cylinder head. Two overhead valves per cylinder, inclined to each other in part spherical combustion chambers, directly operated by inverted bucket-type tappets from twin overhead camshafts in cylinder head. Twin semi-downdraught SU constant-vacuum carburettors. Maximum power 108bhp (net) at 6,700rpm Maximum torque 104lb ft at 4,500rpm.
Transimission: Front engine, rear drive. Single-dry-plate clutch, and four-speed manual gearbox (no synchromesh on first gear), all in unit with engine. Remote control central gearchange. Open propeller shaft to hypoid-bevel 'live' rear axle.
Chassis: Separate steel chassis frame, with box section side members, box and tubular cross bracing, and box section scuttle supports. Independent front suspension by coil springs and wishbones; later models also had anti-roll bars. Rear suspension by semi-elliptic leaf springs. Lever-arm hydraulic dampers. Rack and pinion steering. Four-wheel hydraulically operated disc brakes, no vacuum servo 15in centre-lock steel disc wheels, with 5.90-15in tyres. Choice of two-seater pressed steel body styles – open Roadster or closed coupé.
Dimensions: Wheelbase 7ft 10in (239cm), track (front) 3ft 11.9in (122cm), track (rear) 4ft 0.9in (124cm). Unladen weight (Roadster/Coupé) 2,185/2,245lb (991/1,018kg).
History: By the mid-1950s, MG's sports cars were looking thoroughly old-fashioned but the introduction of the MGA in 1955 changed all that. Only a few front suspension parts were carried over from the obsolete TF1500, while there was an all-new box-section chassis frame, a sleek and aerodynamic two-seater body style, and the engine was a tuned version of BMC's new B-Series standard design, matched to the corporate gearbox and back axle. It was something of a miracle, therefore, that the MGA had so much character – it could nearly reach 100mph, was amazingly refined and comfortable, and had beautifully satisfying handling and roadholding.

Right from the start, MG's John Thornley wanted to get the new car into

competition, and he encouraged the development of a new high-performance twin overhead camshaft engine to make this possible. Two different new engines appeared at the Tourist Trophy race of 1955, and one of them (designed by Morris Engines in Coventry) was eventually developed into a production unit. Among its other competition uses was that, in highly supercharged form, it powered MG's mid-engined record car, EX181, which achieved more than 250mph at the Utah Salt Flats in 1959.

The MGA Twin-Cam model was announced in the summer of 1958 and was available in open Roadster or bubble-top Coupé form – the coupé having glass wind-up windows and the attributes of a small, but perfectly habitable, saloon car. Not only did the new car have the twin-overhead-camshaft engine, which was effectively an extensively modified version of the MGA's normal pushrod overhead valve engine (though, at the time, the basic engine was only of 1,489cc), with 108bhp, but it also had four-wheel disc brakes, and was also fitted with unique centre-lock steel disc wheels of a type fitted to D-Type Jaguars and BRM Grand Prix cars.

Twin-Cams were always expensive, and known to be finicky to service and maintain, but this ought to have been matched by a top speed capability of 115mph and acceleration to match, if only the cars had been reliable. The problem was that in the early days the engines gained a reputation for oil-burning holes in pistons if they ran on inferior brands of petrol. By the time remedial action was taken (and it *was* taken, for later Twin-Cams were extremely nice cars to own) the car's reputation had been shot to ribbons. Production, which began in earnest in the autumn of 1958 was running down rapidly by the end of 1959, and the last of all was built months later.

Between 1960 and 1962, when the separate-chassis MGA family was dropped in favour of the monocoque MGB, a series of rather mysterious MGA 1600 De Luxe models were also built – which were effectively Twin-Cam chassis, with the disc brakes and the special wheels, but without the expensive twin-cam engine. A total of 2,111 Twin-Cams and 395 De Luxes were built, and the surviving cars are now looked upon as real collectors' pieces. The special engine was the only twin-overhead-camshaft unit ever fitted to an MG motor car, and the experiment has never been repeated.

Left: The MGA Twin-Cam had a special engine, but otherwise looked like a normal MG sports car. Behind the centre-lock disc wheels there were Dunlop disc brakes, and the roadholding was superb. Only engine reliability let the car down.

MG MGB

MGB sports car and GT coupé, built from 1962 to 1980
Built by: BMC (later British Leyland), Britain.
Engine: Four cylinders, in line, in three-main-bearing (later five-main-bearing) cast iron cylinder block. Bore and stroke 80.26 × 88.9mm, 1,798cc (3.16 × 3.50in, 109.8cu.in). cast iron cylinder head. Two overhead valves per cylinder, in line, operation by pushrods and rockers from a camshaft in the cylinder block. Two semi-downdraught SU carburettors. Maximum power 95bhp (DIN) at 5,400rpm. Maximum torque 110lb.ft at 3,000rpm.
Transmission: Rear-wheel-drive, single-dry-plate diaphragm spring clutch and four-speed manual gearbox, no synchromesh on first gear originally, all-synchromesh from 1967, all in unit with engine. Remote-control, central gearchange.
Chassis: Unitary-construction pressed-steel body-chassis unit in two-seater style, open Roadster or fastback/hatchback GT. Independent front suspension by coil springs, wishbones, lever arm dampers, and optional anti-roll bar. Beam axle rear suspension by half-elliptic leaf springs and lever-arm dampers. Rack-and-pinion steering. Front disc, rear drum brakes, no servo assistance. 14in wheels, steel disc or centre-lock wires, 5.60-14in tyres.
Dimensions: Wheelbase 7ft 7.0in (231cm), front track 4ft 1.0in (124.5cm), rear track 4ft 1.25in (125cm). Overall length 12ft 9.3in (389.4cm). Unladen weight (Roadster) 2,030lb (921kg), (GT) 2,190lb (993kg).
History: Is there anyone in the world who has not seen, admired, driven or owned an MGB? Until Japanese cars like the Datsun Z-class, and the Mazda MX-5/Miata finally racked up higher figures in the 1990s, the MGB was the world's best-selling sports car. Announced in 1962, made steadily until 1980, yet recognisably the same at the end, as in its beginning, the four-cylinder MGB notched up sales of 513,272. Along the way, another nine thousand six-cylinder MGCs, and 2,591 MGB GT V8s were also built. Nor was that all, for in the early 1990s the Rover group briefly revived a restyled, V8-engined version of the car, calling in the MG RV8, and selling most of them to Japan.

Below: The elegant MGB was, and is, Britain's best-selling sports car, with more than half a million built in eighteen years.

Above: The smart MGB GT style, complete with hatchback, was introduced in 1965. Most were 1.8-litre, but from 1973-1976 there was also a V8-engined car.

Conceived as BMC's mass-production sports car for the 1960s, and to replace the successful MGA, the MGB had a sturdy new monocoque shell, and a style devised by Abingdon (Italian influence was not needed), the running gear being a developed version of that used in the old MGA. With 95bhp from 1.8-litres, and a more slippery shape, the original roadster was capable of more than 100mph. Overdrive was optional (it would not be standardised until the 1970s), automatic transmission eventually became a short-lived option, and from 1965 there was even a smart and extremely successfull fastback coupé/hatchback version called the MGB GT.

Like many a previous MG, the sporty, stylish two-seater shape hid positively mundane running gear. Properly maintained by any competent mechanic or BMC dealer (which was one charm of this car, especially when being run thousands of miles from Britain), an MGB could go on forever, with saloon-type running costs. Engine and transmission were both shared with other mass-production BMC (later, British Leyland) cars, while the chassis, with its coil spring front suspension and beam axle/leaf-spring rear was extremely conventional, but here was a sports car which was more than the sum of its parts. The fabled 'Abingdon Touch' was certainly applied to this model.

Not only did it look good, but it handled well, and tuners soon found that race-prepared cars could be made to go very fast too. Although not outstanding on the track, the MGB still figured in endurance racing – the 'works' motorsport department, for instance, preparing a succession of long-nosed cars to contend, and complete, the legendary Le Mans 24 Hour race.

Although a new all-synchromesh gearbox was fitted from late 1967, and there were regular cosmetic retouchings in the 1970s, the MGB was really allowed to go on too long without a major update. For 1975 it was necessary to fit vast, controversially styled, rubber bumpers for the car to go on selling in North America, at which point the ride height went up and the roadholding suffered. By the late 1970s British Leyland had lost faith in it (they also favoured the in-house rival, Triumph, at this time), American emission rules had strangled the engine too far, and an overhead-camshaft engine transplant was ruled out. The consequence was that the MGB finally died of senile decay. The good news, though, is that body shells were later remanufactured in numbers, all parts were available through the 1990s, and the MGB was as much of an icon in the 2000s as it was all those years ago.

MG MGF

MG MGF sports car, introduced in 1995
Built by: Rover Group (originally BMW-owned), Britain.
Engine: Four cylinders, in line, in five-main-bearing light-alloy cylinder block. Bore and stroke 80 × 89mm, 1,796cc (3.15 × 3.50in, 109.6cu.in). Aluminium cylinder head. Four valves per cylinder, operation by twin overhead camshafts and inverted bucket tappets. MEMS electronic fuel injection. Maximum power 118bhp (DIN) at 5,500rpm. Maximum torque 122lb.ft at 3,000rpm, or 143bhp (DIN) at 7.000rpm. Maximum torque 128lb.ft. at 4,500rpm.
Transmission: Rear-wheel-drive, single-plate diaphragm spring clutch and five-speed all-synchromesh manual gearbox, all in unit with transverse mid-mounted engine. Remote-control, central gearchange. Optional Steptronic automatic on 118bhp versions.
Chassis: Unitary-construction pressed-steel body-chassis unit, in two-seater roadster style, with optional hardtop. Independent front suspension by Hydragas springs, wishbones, and anti-roll bar, with self-levelling connection to independent rear suspension by Hydragas springs, wishbones and anti-roll bar. Rack-and-pinion steering, with optional electric power assistance. Four-wheel disc brakes. Cast alloy 15in road wheels, 185/55-15in (front), 205/50-15in (rear) tyres.
Dimensions: Wheelbase 7ft 9.5in (237.5cm), front track 4ft 7.1in (140cm), rear track 4ft 7.5in (141cm). Overall length 12ft 10in (391.4cm). Unladen weight 2,366lb (1,073kg).
History: After the MGB died away in1980, British Leyland and its successors kept the MG badge alive on a series of lack-lustre, hotted-up Austin hatchbacks. Yet for many years in the 1980s and 1990s it looked as if no new sports car would ever be developed. Then came the period when the Rover Group was owned by BMW, who invested heavily in their new acquisition, saw the merits of MG, and commissioned a neat new two-seater, the MGF. It was, of course, too late to make this new car at Abingdon (which had been flattened after the MGB was killed off), so it was manufactured at Longbridge, alongside the Minis and Metros.

Below: The mid-engined MGF, first seen in 1995, had smart and timeless styling. This was the first-ever MG sports car to be built at Longbridge.

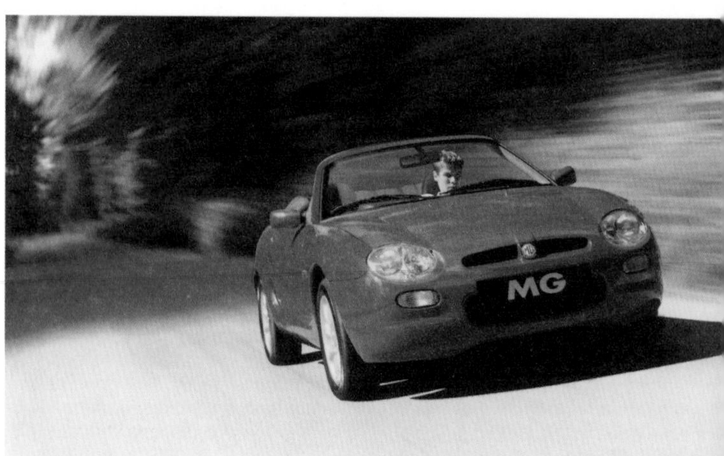

Above: The MGF was a curvaceous and roomy two-seater, with the transverse engine mounted behind the seats. A hardtop was also available.

In basic layout – it was a steel monocoque-shelled two-seater, with a transversely mounted four-cylinder engine positioned immediately behind the seats – the MGF followed other such successful cars as the Fiat X1/9 and the Toyota MR2, but there were many unique touches. Almost as expected, the chassis borrowed heavily from Rover 100 (as the Austin Metro had been renamed) and Rover 200 models.

In an interesting commercial deal, Mayflower of Coventry agreed to manufacture the body shells, take the commercial risk in producing tools, but also take an enhanced proportion of the profits. Rover engineers then slotted in an enlarged version of the modern K-series 16-valve – which boasted 1,796cc and a choice of 118bhp or 143bhp, all mated to the latest 5-speed transmission from the 200. (The same engine/transmission package, incidentally, would also be adapted by the Lotus Elise.)

Independent suspension at front and rear was by wishbones, with springing by interconnected Hydragas units, as previously used on cars like the Metro/100 and, before that, on the Austin Allegro and Princess 18/22 ranges. Rack-and-pinion steering was standard, shortly to be augmented by the option of electric power assistance, and there were disc brakes at all corners.

The style, stubby but rounded, was of a pure two-seater, with space for stowage ahead of the toeboard (not much) and also behind the transverse engine. Wind-up door glasses were standard, there was a vast, steeply sloping windscreen, and the cabin was well furnished with inviting-looking seats. A removable hardtop soon became optional.

The new car, in other words, was no more pure-bred than the previous MGB, or the Midget, had ever been, but the engineers somehow melded the whole into an appealing package, and the use of the traditional MG octagon badge was all-important. Even though it had a rear-based weight distribution, the new car proved to handle well (if a little biased towards safe-but-not-exciting understeer), and even in lower-power (118bhp) guise it was a brisk performer.

The 143bhp version, complete with its high-revving variable valve timing feature, was capable of 130mph, which was one extreme, while the 118bhp type, with the optional Steptronic transmission which was later added, was the other. Five years after its launch, with up to 15,000 MGFs being produced every year, the company's gamble in re-introducing an MG sports car had clearly paid off. More, and more specialised, MGs are expected in the 21st Century.

MG Midgets – T-Series Models

TA, TB, TC, TD and TF models, built 1936 to 1955 (data for 1946 model TC)
Built by: MG Car Co. Ltd., Britain.
Engine: Four-cylinder, in-line, based on three-bearing cast-iron block. Bore and stroke 66.5mm by 90mm, 1,250cc (2.62 × 3.54in, 76.3cu in). Cast-iron cylinder head. Two overhead valves per cylinder, operated by pushrods and rockers from single side-mounted camshaft. Twin semi-downdraught SU constant-vacuum carburettors. Maximum power 54bhp (net) at 5,200rpm.
Transmission: Single-dry-plate clutch and four-speed, synchromesh manual gearbox (un-synchronised first gear), both in unit with engine. Remote-control central gearchange. Open propeller shaft to spiral-bevel 'live' rear axle.
Chassis: Separate channel-section steel chassis, with two main longitudinal members, braced by pressed and tubular cross members. Semi-elliptic front and rear springs. Luvax-Girling piston type dampers. Bishop cam-and-lever steering. Four-wheel, hydraulically operated drum brakes. Fly-off handbrake. 19in centre-lock wire wheels. 4.50 × 19in tyres. Two seat open sports bodywork, of steel panels on an ash frame. No alternative coachwork.
Dimensions: Wheelbase 7ft 10in (239cm), tacks (front and rear) 3ft 9in (114cm). Overall length 11ft 7.5in (354cm). Unladen weight 1,736lb (787kg).
History: The T-Series MG Midget was conceived as a direct result of the sale of MG by Lord Nuffield to his own Nuffield Group, which was effectively passing control of the finances from one hand to another. The obsolete, and displaced PB had an overhead-camshaft engine, and a special 'crash' gearbox, whereas the original TA of 1936 had a more mundane overhead- valve engine, and a

Top right and below: The last of the T-Series Midgets was the TF of 1953-1955, which had a slightly updated styling, and 85mph performance.

synchromesh gearbox.

Although, in its general layout and design philosophy, the TA was like the PB, which is to say that it had a channel-section frame, a two-seater open sports body style panelling on a simple ash frame, sweeping front wings and free-standing headlamps, it was a larger, simpler, and altogether more pragmatic machine. Whereas the PB had been the final, and far-removed derivative of the 1928-1932 Morris Minor, the TA leaned heavily on the Wolseley 10/40 power train and transmission, a car that was itself a more advanced update of the Morris 10hp model.

The instant reaction of enthusiasts was that the TA was not a *true* Midget, but experience showed that it was a better, faster, and more roomy car in all respects, and that it offered remarkable value for money with a 1,292cc engine and 54bhp it sold for £222. The TA became the TB in 1939, with a new design of short-stroke 1,250cc engine, and in 1945 it became TC, with a rather wider cockpit but little modernisation. The TC was MG's first successful export-market car, and a total of exactly 10,000 were sold before the end of 1949.

In the meantime, Nuffield had produced the MG Y-Type, which was an amalgam of Morris 8hp Series E body, a new independent front suspension chassis, and the 1,250cc engine. This sold well, and in 1950 it led to the launch of the TD Midget, which was a much modified version of that chassis, the TC's running gear, and a wider, cobbier, but still essentially 1930s body style. It also had steel disc wheels (the firs Midget so to be equipped), but it was also available in left-hand drive, and the USA customer loved it. Nearly 30,000 TDs were built up to the summer of 1953.

By this time, MG were ready to replace the TD with a new modern car, but this (which later became the MGA of 1955) was frozen out by the new company management, called BMC (British Motor Corporation). In place of the new design, MG were only allowed to face-lift the TD into the TF of 1953-1955, which retained the same centre body and doors, but incorporated a slightly smoothed out nose and a more sloping tail, still on the same 7ft 10in wheelbase of all T-Series MGs.

The TF was not a car which was liked, even when the enlarged 1,466cc engine was made available in the autumn of 1954. The public had been offered old-style MGs in a modernising world for too long, and had eventually rebelled against this. Poor aerodynamics meant that even a TF1500 could only reach 85mph, which was so much slower than Triumph were offering with the TR2 that it was embarrassing. Like all other T-Series cars, however, the TF had excellent road manners.

Morgan Plus-Four and Plus-Eight

Morgan Plus-Four and Plus-Eight, built from 1950 (data for 1954 Plus-Four)
Built by: Morgan Motor Co. Ltd., Britain.
Engine: Triumph manufactured. Four cylinders, in line, in three-bearing cast-iron block. Bore and stroke 83mm by 92mm, 1,991cc (3.27in × 3.62in, 121.5cu.in). Cast-iron cylinder head. Two overhead valves per cylinder operated by pushrods and rockers from single camshaft mounted in side of cylinder block. Twin semi-downdraught constant-vacuum SU carburettors. Maximum power 90bhp (net) at 4,800rpm. Maximum torque 130lb.ft at 2,600rpm.
Transmission: Single-dry-plate clutch in unit with engine. Moss four-speed. Synchromesh manual gearbox (no synchromesh on first gear) mounted separately. Direct-acting central gear-change. Open propeller shaft to hypoid-bevel 'live' rear axle.
Chassis: Separate steel chassis frame, with A-section boxed side members and tubular and pressed cross-bracing members. Independent front suspension by sliding pillars and coil springs, with telescopic dampers. Rear suspension by semi-elliptic leaf springs, with lever-type hydraulic dampers. Worm-and-nut steering. Four-wheel hydraulically operated drum brakes (later models had front discs). Fly-off handbrake. 16in pressed steel-disc road wheels (optional centre-lock wire wheels). 5.25 × 16in tyres. Morgan-built two-seat sports, two-seat DH coupé or four-seat tourer coachwork to choice.
Dimensions: Wheelbase 8ft (244cvm), tracks (front and rear) 3ft 11in. (119cm). Overall length 11ft 8in (356cm). Unladen weight 1,900lb (862kg).
History: The present-day Morgan has, fairly accurately, been described as the only vintage car still in production. Like all *bon mots* this tends to be an exaggeration, but there is no doubt that the philosophy of Morgan design is

Above: Today's Morgan is the very fast vee-eight engined Plus Eight. The engine and gearbox are from Rover, but the rest is pure Morgan, built now to the standards and tastes of yester-year. Along with the 4/4, only about ten cars a week are built and sold.

Below: This Plus-Four coupé was built in 1950 – one of the first with the Standard Vanguard engine – but the same basic style is produced today. Each Morgan has a Z-section chassis frame, a hand-beaten body shell of steel or light-alloy panels on an ash framework, very hard suspension, and a neat but close-coupled cockpit. One model always evolved from the last, though the latest Plus Eight has little in common, mechanically, with the Plus Four. Over the years there have been two-seaters and four-seaters, sports, tourers or coupés, and the glassfibre hardtop Plus-Four-Plus coupés.

entrenched in the 1930s. Although the engines, the performance and the details receive regular attention, the chassis, ride, roadholding, body style and construction are old designs with old fashioned results. The modern Plus Eight Morgan, with its 155bhp Rover-made 3½-litre engine and five-speed gearbox, was good for nearly 130mph with acceleration to match. Weather protection, noise-suppression and refinement do not match this, however.

Morgan machines have been built in the same Malvern Link factory, under the direction of the Morgan family, since Edwardian times. Up to 1936, however, every Morgan was a three-wheeler, with a single, driven, rear wheel – and three-wheeler production carried on into the early 1950s. In 1936, the first four-wheel Morgan, the four-seat 4/4, was revealed in a form which would be very familiar to present-day Morgan buyers. The sliding-pillar independent suspension used today was on that first 4/4, but it had been on the 1910 three-wheeler too! The Z section side members of the chassis frame are still a feature and the bodies, erected by Morgan themselves, were of simple steel foldings on an ash wood frame. Engines of the first 4/4s were side-valve Fords. Other pre-war 4/4 engines used were overhead-inlet, side-exhaust Coventry Climax 1100s and overhead-valve-converted Standard Ten engines of 1,267cc. After the war, the standard unit was used for a time, but when Standard decided to follow a 'one-model' (or rather a 'one-engine') policy, Morgan had to think again. Because of their links with Standard they decided to upgrade the 4/4 by fitting the big and heavy Standard Vangaurd unit of 2,088cc, along with a proprietary Moss gearbox.

The Plus-Four, as the new two-seat car was named, arrived in 1950, and soon made a name for itself in competition. Compared with the little 4/4 the new car was very much faster and more rugged. Even so, once Triumph had developed their TR2 sports car, it made sense for Morgan to use the tuned-up 2-litre

Below: Chris Lawrence and Richard Shepherd-Barron used this Triumph TR3 engined Plus Four to win the 2-litre class at Le Mans in 1962, beating Porsche and several other very special sports racing cars.

engine. This, then, was the definitive Plus-Four, a car lighter and more accelerative than either the Triumph TR2 or the Austin-Healy 100. During the life of the car, Morgan made few concessions to modernisation, although they improved the body style with a cowled nose and a sleeker tail. Disc front brakes were standardised late in the 1950s and when Triumph increased their TR engine size to 2,138cc Morgan followed them. For a time too they offered a 'Competition' model with Lawrence-tune TR engine and light-alloy body panels. In the meantime, from 1955, the 4/4 was re-introduced as a Series II, powered by Ford's side valve 1,172cc engine and matching gearbox. The 4/4 continues to this day, uprated regularly with the latest Ford engines – over-head-valve units being adopted in 1960.

With Triumph dropping the four-cylinder engine completely in 1967, it was clearly only a matter of time before supplies to Morgan ran out. From the autumn of 1968, then, it was no surprise to see that the Plus-Four was equipped with the 1,600cc Ford Cortina engine, and that the exciting Plus-Eight, was added to the range. This car is powered by the ex-Buick Rover 3½-litre V8 engine. When Rover introduced a manual gearbox for their engine, this replaced the old Moss gearbox, but it has itself been dropped in favour of the 'new' Rover 3500 five-speed box. Many features of the Plus-Four are evident in the Plus-Eight models. To take account of the greatly increased performance since the first Vanguard engine was fitted in 1950 (there is more than twice the power nowadays) the wheel tracks have been increased and fatter tyres and wider wheel rims introduced, along with better and more powerful brakes. Interior appointments have been improved, but the cockpit's size is little larger than it was a quarter of a century ago. More important than anything – the car's character had been maintained. Orders exceed the ten-per-week production capability and waiting lists stretch ahead for years.

Morris 'Bullnose'

Morris Oxford and Cowley models, built from 1913 to 1926 (data for 1920s Cowley)
Built by: Morris Motors Ltd., Britain.
Engine: Four cylinders, in line, in three-bearing cast-iron block. Bore and stroke 69.5mm by 102mm, 1,548cc (2.74in × 4.02in, 94.5cu.in) Cast-iron cylinder head. Two side valves per cylinder, directly operated by cylinder-block mounted camshaft. One Smith carburettor. Maximum power 26bhp (gross) at 2,800rpm.
Transmission: Double-plate clutch, cork lined, running in oil, and three-speed, sliding-pinion manual gearbox (without synchromesh), both unit with engine. Direct-acting central gear-change. Propeller shaft in torque tube, connected to spiral-bevel 'live' rear axle.
Chassis: Separate steel chassis frame, with channel-section side members and tubular and pressed-steel cross bracings. Forged front axle beam. Front suspension by semi-elliptic leaf springs. Rear suspension by three-quarter – elliptic leaf springs. Dampers not standard until 1925. Gabriel snubbers optional (standard from 1925). Worm-and-wheel steering. Foot operated rear drum brakes; no front brakes until 1926, when they became optional. Artillery-style road wheels. Morris-built coachwork, several styles from two-seat-with-dickey tourer to closed four-door saloon.
Dimensions: Wheelbase 8ft 6in (259cm), tracks (front and rear) 4ft (122cm). Unladen weight (depending on coachwork and options fitted), from 1,750lb (794kg).

History: The 'Bullnose' Morris was the British equivalent of the Model T Ford – with one important exception. Whereas Ford made sure that he built as much of his car as possible, William Morris made sure that he purchased as many 'bought out' components as he could. That way he cut down on the capital cost of selling his cars and could make more cars from a small factory in Cowley, near Oxford. The first 'Bullnose' (so called, retrospectively, because of the shape of its distinctive radiator) was delivered in 1913 and the last – more than 150,000 examples later – in 1926. Even then it was not finished, as the then-new 'flatnose' Morris was a development of the same chassis and mechanicals. Before World War I, the cars had British White-and-Poppe engines, during it Continental Motors engines from the United States were used and from 1919 they were fitted with power plants produced by Morris Engines in Coventry.

The two basically different models (only in terms of engine size and fittings – the chassis were always the same) were the 11.9hp Cowley and the 13.9hp Oxford, but there were many sub-derivatives. Like Henry Ford in North America, Morris cut his prices aggressively and every time he did so, sales rocketed. Like Ford, too, he held on to one basic model for too long, but recovered quicker after a change of heart. The 'Bullnose' cars were lovable, reliable and cheap (the cheapest tourer's price fell from £465 in 1920 to a mere £162.50 in 1925), but they were never sporting. The British public, however, merely wanted cheap transportation. Morris gave it to them. At one time in the 1920s he held more than half of the entire British market.

Left: The 'Bullnose' Morris, surely the British equivalent of the Model T Ford. In the 1920s it outsold any other British or European car. This 'All weather' was built in 1924. There were two engines, and many optional bodies.

Morris Minor

Morris Minor family car, built in saloon, convertible and estate car types, from 1948 to 1971 (data for original model of 1948)

Built by: Morris Motors Ltd. (later BMC, even later British Leyland Motor Corporation), Britain.

Engine: Four cylinders, in line, in three-bearing cast iron cylinder block. Bore and stroke 57 × 90mm, 918cc (2.24 × 3.54in, 56cu.in). Cast iron cylinder head. Two side-valves per cylinder, operation by tappets from single camshaft mounted in the cylinder block. Single SU carburettor. Maximum power 27.5bhp (DIN) at 4,400rpm. Maximum torque 39lb.ft at 2,400rpm.

Transmission: Rear-wheel-drive, single-dry-plate clutch and four-speed synchromesh manual gearbox (no synchro on first gear), all in unit with front-mounted engine. Direct action central gearchange.

Chassis: Unitary-construction pressed-steel body-chassis unit in two-door or (later) four-door saloon, convertible and estate car styles. Independent front suspension by wishbones, longitudinal torsion bars, and lever-arm hydraulic shock absorbers. Beam axle rear suspension by half-elliptic leaf springs, and lever-arm hydraulic shock absorbers. Rack-and-pinion steering. Front and rear drum brakes. Steel 14in road wheels, 5.00–14in tyres.

Dimensions: Wheelbase 7ft 2in (218.4cm), front track 4ft 2.5in (128.3cm), rear track 4ft 2.5in (128.3cm). Overall length 12ft 4in (376cm). Unladen weight 1,708lb (775kg).

History: Although Morris Motors' founder, Lord Nuffield, was reputed to have greeted the original Minor with the remark, 'It looks like a poached egg!', the public did not agree with him. From 1948, when the original side-valve engined car was launched, to 1971, when the final 1.1-litre overhead-valve types were built, more than 1.5-million Minors of all types were sold.

Until 1939 Morris had built strictly conventional value-for-money cars, but for post-war years Vice-Chairman Sir Miles Thomas, and his chief designer Alec Issigonis, were determined to change all that. Conceived during the war, and eventually launched with an old-design 918cc side-valve engine, the Morris Minor was very different from what had gone before. Not only did it have a monocoque body shell, and rounded lines, but it had torsion-bar independent front suspension (previous Morris types all used beam axles), and rack-and-pinion steering. The paradox, therefore, was that the performance (with a top speed of a mere 60mph) might have been abysmal, but the handling was excellent.

Originally there were two-door saloons and convertibles (Tourers), but four-door saloons, an 'Olde Englishe' wood-framed estate car, a van and a pick-up version all followed. By the mid-1950s, therefore, the Minor was not only the fastest-selling Morris, but would become Britain's first million-selling model.

Changes began soon after Morris merged with Austin to form the British Motor Corporation. The Minor became 'Series II' in 1952, when the overhead-valve 803cc Austin A-Series engine was slotted into place (but there was no more performance), while the front end style was changed at the same time. From 1956 the whole design was up-graded into the Minor 1000, not only with a 37bhp/948cc engine and a better gearbox, but with a one-piece curved windscreen. Faster (it could still not exceed 70mph – just), and still as nimble as ever, the Minor 1000 was set fair for years. The millionth car (one of 350 lilac-painted saloons) was produced in December 1960, and a further upgrade, to 1,098cc and 48bhp, came in 1962.

This, the definitive Minor 1000, could reach about 75mph, and struggle up to 60mph from rest in about 24 seconds – but that was not the point. It was simple, roomy for its market sector, good value for money – and ubiquitous. Not only did it have a long-established reputation as one of the best-handling small family

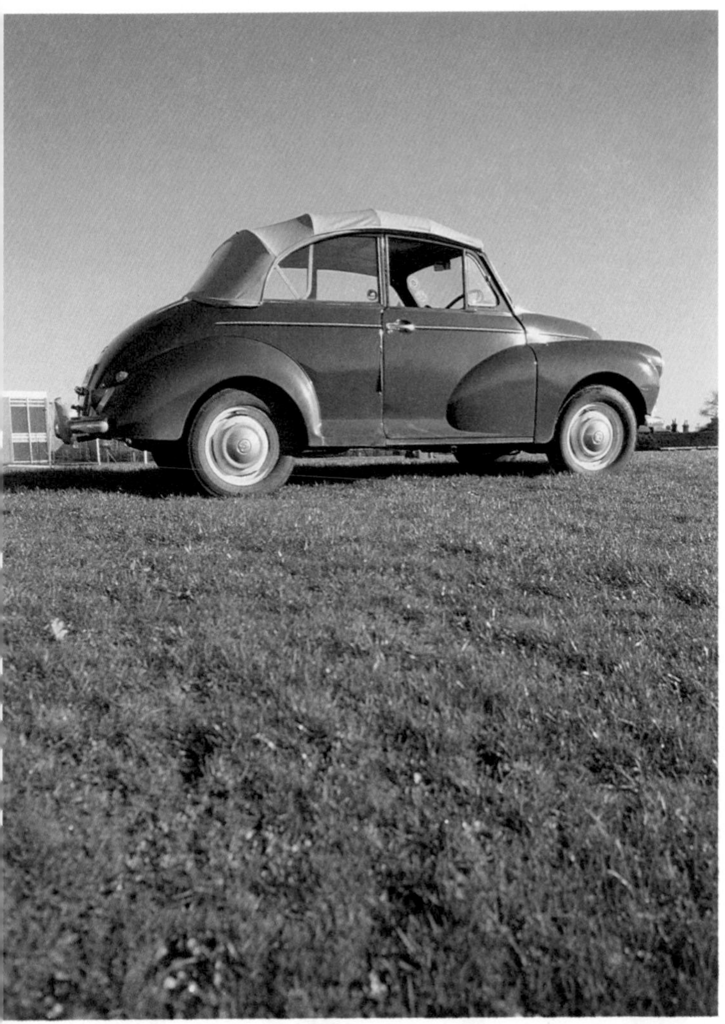

Above: The Morris Minor was amazingly successful, being built for 23 years. Saloons, estates, convertibles, vans and pick-ups were all available.

cars of all (only the front-wheel-drive Mini, from the same stable, could beat it round corners), but it was completely classless.

District nurses used Minor 1000s, so did the British police for 'Panda' patrol duty, and the Archbishop of Canterbury drove one around London as his personal transport. Yet here was a car whose mechanical specification rarely seemed to change, whose style did not alter from 1956 to 1971, and which was so reliable and simple to maintain that garages all over the UK could tackle them.

The end came in 1971, as British Leyland (which had absorbed BMC) rationalised, but enthusiasts kept the car alive, there was hand-to-mouth manufacture of a few new cars in, of all places, Ceylon/Sri Lanka, and an enthusiastic Owners' Club keeps the Minor passion alive to this day.

Napier 40/50

Napier 40/50, built from 1919 to 1924)
Built by: D. Napier and Son Ltd., Britain.
Engine: Six cylinders, in line, in seven-bearing light-alloy block/crankcase, with shrunk-in cast-iron cylinder liners. Bore and stroke 102mm by 127mm, 6,177cc (4.0 × 5.0in, 377cu.in).Light-alloy cylinder head. Two overhead valves per cylinder, operated directly by a single overhead camshaft. Single constant-vacuum Napier-SU carburettor. Maximum power 82bhp at 2,000rpm.
Transmission: Single-dry-plate clutch, in unit with engine, and four-speed manual gearbox separated from clutch by girder casting and two flexible couplings. Direct-acting central gearchange. Propeller shaft in torque tube to spiral-bevel 'live'; rear axle.
Chassis: Separate steel chassis with channel-section side members and five supporting cross members. Forged front axle beam. Front suspension by semi-elliptic leaf springs; anti-roll device on nose of torque tube. Worm-and-sector steering. Foot-operated drum brake on transmission and hand-operated drums on rear wheels (late models – 1924 – had four-wheel foot brakes). Centre-lock wire wheels (sometimes disc covered). 895 × 135mm beaded-edge tyres. Coachwork usually by Cunard, a subsidiary of Napier – many choices including limousines, cabriolets, sedancas, coupés and touring bodies.
Dimensions: Wheelbase 11ft 5in or 12ft (348 or 366cm), tracks (front and rear) 4ft 8in (142cm). Overall length from 15ft (457cm). Unladen weight (chassis only) 2,800lb (1,270kg).
History: Before World War I, Napier were one of the greatest of the British thoroughbred building companies. From 1919 to 1924, with the 40/50 model, they tried to beat Rolls-Royce once again. They failed – gallantly. Although their

Below and right: The big and stately Napier 40/50 could be supplied with a choice of bodies. The red car was the more usual formal town carriage, while the blue car (right) was built in 1920 with a sporting 'torpedo' body by Cunard. In each case the result was heavy, stable, and painstakingly engineered. The model had to compete with the Rolls-Royce Silver Ghost.

all-new engine was very advanced and effective, the rest of the chassis was Edwardian in concept. 40/50 prices were always very high and most of the bodies were supplied by Cunard, whom Napier had taken over earlier. The car, splendid and dignified though it was, could not quite match the Silver Ghost in all-round excellence, particularly as the bespoke coach-builders were rarely allowed to ply their craft. By then, in any case, Napier were very famous for their powerful and effective aero-engines and were inclined to specialise in that direction in the future. Their original enthusiastic chief, Selwyn Edge, had left the company in 1913. Incidentally, there was also a 40/50 in pre-war days, but this had a side-valve engine and different chassis.

Maximum speed of up to 70mph was clearly superior to that of the Rolls-Royce, but the suspension was hard and set more to provide stability than comfort. The engine itself, designed by A.J. Rowledge, who was also responsible for the W-formation 'Lion' aero-engine, was very advanced and effective, being light in weight wherever possible, with a single overhead camshaft and intriguing details. One interesting point is that engine roughness at low speeds was cured by having a special low-compression piston in the rear cylinder (number 6) piston only!

In addition to normal models, there was a 'Colonial' version (of which 17 were built), with increased ground clearance provided by special chassis side members and suspension parts. All up weight of the normal British limousines could be more than 5,200lb (2,358kg), which helps to explain the high price and petrol consumption. The last of the 40/50s was built in 1924, after four-wheel braking had been adopted. Only 187 of the hoped-for 500 were ever made. Strikes and very high prices had much to do with this.

Left and right: Vintage splendour in the shape of a 1921 Maythorn bodied 40/50hp Napier limousine. The 6.2-litre engine was very advanced, but the chassis still Edwardian in layout.

NSU Ro80

Ro80s Mk I, Mk II and Mk III, built from 1967 to 1978 (data for MkI)
Built by: NSU-Werke AG (since 1969, VW-Audi-NSU AG), West Germany.
Engine: Wankel-type rotary engine. Two rotors in two-chamber light-alloy housing. Engine displacement 995cc (60.7cu.in) per revolution, equivalent to 1,990cc (121.4cu.in) for four-stroke piston engine. Two-bearing eccentric crankshaft. No valves and no camshafts – ports covered and uncovered once each revolution. Three-sided trochoidal rotor forms own combustion chamber, therefore three explosions per engine revolution. Two horizontal Solex carburettors. Maximum power 115bhp (DIN) at 5,500rpm. Maximum torque 117lb.ft at 4,500rpm.
Transmission: Semi-automatic Fichtel and Sachs transmission, with torque converter and three speed all synchromesh manual gearbox, both in unit with engine. Direct-acting central gearchange, with clutch actuated by microswitch in gearchange knob. Front-wheel-drive power pack, with torque converter and engine ahead of front-wheel line and gearbox behind it. Exposed, universally jointed drive shafts to front wheels.
Chassis: Unitary-construction pressed-steel body/chassis unit four-door saloon. Engine/transmission pack in nose, driving front wheels. Independent front suspension by MacPherson struts (with built-in dampers) and anti-roll bar. Independent rear suspension by coil springs, trailing arms and telescopic dampers. Power-assisted rack-and-pinion steering. Four-wheel hydraulically operated disc brakes, inboard mounted at front, with vacuum-servo assistance. 14in pressed-steel disc road wheels and 175 × 14in tyres.
Dimensions: Wheelbase 9ft 4.6in (286cm), track (front) 4ft 10.3in (148cm),

track (rear) 4ft 8.5in (143cm). Overall length 15ft 8.2in (478cm). Unladen weight 2,670lb (1,211kg).

History: Felix Wankel spent years developing his rotary engine concept and eventually sold his ideas to NSU in West Germany. Their first pilot-production machine was the single-rotor Wankel Spider, merely a sighting shot to test commercial possibilities. The Ro80, with its 115bhp twin-rotor engine, was a much more ambitious project. Even without the revolutionary engine, the Ro80 would have been quite a car. In road manners, in response and engineering, it was a simpler equivalent of the big Citroëns; the Wankel engine merely made it technically more interesting. There was never any doubt about the engine's power potential, but NSU had many problems in achieving reliability. Tip-seal wear, later cured, was an early bugbear, and most motor traders did not like the car's complexities. The semi-automatic transmission was necessary to damp down the engine's rough low-speed characteristics. When going properly, however, an Ro80 is a delightful machine. There is no limit to the engine's revs, apart from considerations of wear, and it is one of those rare cars which seems to get quieter as speeds rise. The front-wheel-drive system is very effective, the aerodynamics good and high-speed cruising very restful.

Mazda in Japan have sold many more Wankel engines than NSU have, but the Ro80 is unquestionably the most sensuous of the breed. NSU also produced a piston-engined derivative of the chassis – the K70 (later made as the VW K70) – but the Ro80 was not further developed since the early 1970s. Production finally ended in 1978.

Left: NSU's Ro80 was the world's first Wankel-engined saloon car, and could reach 110mph. The twin-rotor engine was rated as a 2-litre.

Packard Eights

Eight-cylinder cars, built from 1923 to 1942 (data for 1930 Speedster)
Built by: Packard Motor Car Co., United States.
Engine: Eight cylinders, in line, in cast-iron block, attached to nine-bearing light-alloy crankcase. Bore and stroke 88.9mm by 127mm, 6,306cc (3.5in x 5.0in, 384.8cu.in). Detachable cylinder head. Two side valves per cylinder, operated by tappets and rocker levers from single crankcase-mounted camshaft. Single up-draught Detroit Lubricator carburettor. Maximum power 145bhp (gross) at 3,200rpm.
Transmission: Single-dry-plate clutch and four-speed manual gearbox (without synchromesh), both in unit with front-mounted engine. Direct acting central gearchange. Open propeller shaft to spiral-bevel 'live' rear axle.
Chassis: Separate pressed-steel chassis frame, with channel-section side members and fabricated and tubular cross bracings. Bijur automatic chassis lubrication. Forged front axle beam. Semi-elliptic leaf springs at front and rear with lever-type hydraulic dampers. Four-wheel, rod, shaft and cable-operated drum brakes. Wire-spoke, artillery-style or steel-disc wheels available to choice (exclusively wire disc on Speedster cars). 7.00 × 19in tyres.
Two-seater coachwork with dickey.
Dimensions: Wheelbase 11ft 8.5in (357cm), track (front) 4ft 9.5in (146cm), track (rear) 4ft 11 in (150cm). Overall length 16ft 9in (510cm). Unladen weight

3,900lb (1,769kg).
History: Packard's Single Eight was revealed in 1923 as the successor to the Twin Six and the new engine served as a backbone of Packard production until the end of the 1930s. Only in 1932, with the arrival of another exclusive (and expensive) 12-cylinder Packard, and in 1935, when the Type 120 8-cylinder engine replaced the famous unit as a modern eight, was it out of the limelight. Mechanical development in these years was steady and patient and, unlike other firms in the American industry, Packard had to pay little heed to the disasters of the Depression. By the 1930s the company was a market leader with about 50 per cent of the 'prestige car' business. At the beginning of the 1930s, the Type 734 Speedster was a very rare model, with only 150 examples built in 1930. Four-speed gearboxes were new to Packard in that year and they were given synchromesh gears in 1932. In 1933 came the addition of servo-assisted brakes and down-draught carburation. For 1937, every Packard had independent front suspension and hydraulic brakes. The pedigree was finally lost in 1939 when an entirely new straight-eight, with no light-alloy in its structure, was announced.

Below: There were Packard Eights for nearly 20 years. This Super Eight Roadster was built in 1933.

Packard Twin Six

Twin Six, built from 1915 to 1923 (data for 1920 model)
Built by: Packard Motor Car Co., United States.
Engine: 12 cylinders, in 60-degree vee-formation, in two cast-iron blocks, with three-bearing light-alloy crankcase. Bore and stroke 76.2mm by 127mm, 6,950cc (3.0in × 5.0in, 424cu.in). Detachable cast-iron cylinder heads (integral heads in original production design). Two side valves per cylinder, operated by tappets from single camshaft mounted on top of crankcase. Single up-draught Packard carburettor. Maximum power 85bhp.
Transmission: Multiple-dry-plate clutch and three-speed manual gearbox (without synchromesh), both in unit with front-mounted engine. Direct-acting central gearchange. Open propeller shaft to spiral-bevel 'live' rear axle.
Chassis: Separate pressed-steel chassis frame, with channel-section side members and pressed and tubular cross bracing. Forged front axle beam. Front and rear suspension by semi-elliptic leaf springs. Worm-and-nut steering. Rear-wheel drum brakes, mechanically operated from foot pedal. Artillery-style road wheels, with fixed centres but detachable rims. 33 × 5in tyres.
Dimensions: Wheelbase 11ft 4in (345cm), tracks (front and rear) 4ft 8in

142cm). Unladen weight depending on chosen coachwork, 3,910lb to ,415lb (1,773kg to 2,002kg).

listory: The Packard brothers bought a Winton car in 1898 and decided they ould improve on it and the result was the 1899 Packard car. The single-ylinder 12hp soon led to bigger and better fours and sixes and before 1910 ackard was established as one of North America's finest cars. However, for 915, while the rest of the industry was still debating the merits of six or ight cylinders as the best for a luxury car, Packard (with a car designed by lenry Joy) jumped straight to a 12-cylinder machine, the Twin Six, which vas the world's first such machine. The engine was neatly designed, with ll the porting concentrated in the centre of the vee (which meant that xhaust pipes were led out behind the centre of the engine, over the ransmission), and it had fixed cylinder heads. Left-hand-drive was a novelty, ut this was later abandoned. It was Packard's only model from 1916 to 920, when it was joined by a new six, and it was finally dropped in 1923.

A total of 35,046 Twin Six cars were made and Packard's reputation as a remium manufacturer was completely sealed. The cars, with their noble adiators and excellent equipment, were spirited competitors for Cadillac nd any of the exotic imported makes.

Left: Packard's Twin Six model of 1915, the world's first production vee-12. It was built until 1923.

Pegaso Z102

Z102 cars, built from 1951 to 1958 (data for 1951 Z102)
Built by: Empresa Nacional de Autocamiones SA., Spain.
Engine: Eight cylinders, in 90-degree vee-formation, in five-bearing light-allo block/crankcase. Bore and stroke 75mm by 70mm, 2,474cc (2.75in, 151cu.in). Tw over-head valves per cylinder, opposed to each other at 90-degrees in part-spherica combustion chambers and operated by twin overhead cam-shafts per cylinde head. Dry-sump lubrication. Single down-draught twin-choke. Webber carburetto Maximum power 140bhp at 6,000rpm. Maximum torque 135lb.ft at 3,900rpm Alternative engines, either with higher-compression heads and twin Webe carburettors, or bored-out to 2.8 litres and with original carburation, were available
Transmission: Single-dry-plate clutch, in unit with front-mounted engine. Ope propeller shaft to five-speed manual gearbox (without synchromesh), in unit wit spiral-bevel final drive. Remote-control central gearchange.
Chassis: Unitary-construction pressed-steel and light-alloy body/chassis structure Independent front suspension by wishbones and longitudinal torsion bars. De Dior rear suspension, with transverse torsion bars, radius arms, and sideways slide block location. Telescopic dampers. Four-wheel hydraulically operated rum brakes inboard at rear. 16in centre-lock wire wheels. 6.00 × 16in tyres.
Dimensions: Wheelbase 7ft 8in (234cm), track (front) 4ft 4in (132cm), track (rear 4ft 2.7in (128.8cm). Overall length 13ft 4in (406cm). Unladen weight 2,160lb (980kg).
History: The only post-war Spanish car to achieve international 'super car' fame ir the 1950s was the Pegaso, designed by Wilfredo Ricart (ex-Alfa Romeo) and buil in a factory once occupied by Hispano-Suiza. The Z102 was first shown in 1951 anc was a thoroughly exotic and modern design, obviously meant for small-scale production at high cost. The company was government-backed and had already

Below: Just about every Pegaso Z102 coupé was hand-built. Both these 1953 models have Touring of Milan body styles, but differ considerably in tail treatment. Hidden away is the unique Spanish twin-cam vee-8 engine, in this case of 2.8-litre capacity, along with a five-speed gearbox, and advanced De Dion rear suspension.

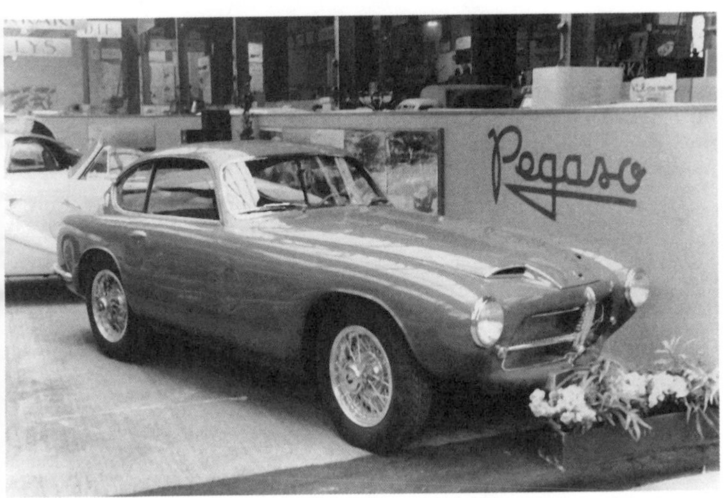

Above: The Pegaso out-ran Ferrari in many respects, even performance, and the body styles (this was from Touring) were always elegant.

made its name with unitary-construction coaches of more than 9-litres.

The original car had a 2½-litre V8 engine, with four overhead camshafts, dry-sump lubrication, a five-speed gearbox in unit with the back axle and De Dion rear suspension. Later developments, also at a very low rate of production, were the Z102B (with 2.8-litres and 210bhp), the Z102SS (with 3.2-litres and up to 280bhp) and finally the Z103 series (which had a rather different overhead valve engine of 4.0, 4.5 or 4.7-litres). The cars were supplied with a bewildering variety of engine tunes, including a few with superchargers, and one or two sprint records were taken in 1953. The cars were strikingly styled in the Italian-coupé manner. When Ricart retired in 1958, car production ceased. Only about 125 Pegasos were made in all.

Peugeot 205GTi

Peugeot 205GTi sports hatchback, built 1984 to 1994 (data for original 1.6-litre model)
Built by: Societe Anonyme des Automobiles Peugeot, France.
Engine: Four cylinders, in line, in five-main-bearing light-alloy cylinder block. Bore and stroke 83 x 73mm, 1,580cc (3.32 x 2.87in, 96.5cu.in). Light alloy cylinder head. Two valves per cylinder, in line, operation by single overhead camshaft, and inverted bucket tappets. Bosch L-Jetronic fuel injection. Maximum power 105bhp (DIN) at 6,250rpm. Maximum torque 99lb.ft at 4,000rpm.
Transmission: Front-wheel-drive, single-dry-plate diaphragm spring clutch and five-speed all-synchromesh manual gearbox, all in unit with transverse front-mounted engine. Remote-control, central gearchange.
Chassis: Unitary-construction pressed-steel body-chassis unit, in three-door hatchback style. Independent front suspension by MacPherson struts, coil springs, lower wishbones, telescopic dampers and anti-roll bar. Independent rear suspension by transverse torsion bars, trailing arms, telescopic dampers and anti-roll bar. Rack-and-pinion steering. Front disc, rear drum brakes, no ABS. Aluminium alloy 14in road wheels, 185/60-14in tyres.
Dimensions: Wheelbase 7ft 11.3in (242cm), front track 4ft 6.8in (139.3cm), rear track 4ft 4.4in (133.2cm). Overall length 12ft 1.9in (370.5cm). Unladen weight 2,004lb (909kg).
History: Other 'hot hatchbacks' were earlier, and others were faster, but the Peugeot 205GTi is the car which everyone will remember. Launched in 1984 to a shower of praise from testers, it sold in huge numbers for more than a decade. Other Peugeot GTis – 309, 106 and 306 among them – all followed, all leaning

heavily on the original for elements of their character.

So what was so appealing about the 205GTi? On paper, and in a straight line, there was nothing remarkable about it, but no driver stayed immune from its charms for long. A combination of style, of handling, and of response to the driver's commands all helped. Peugeot, surely, cannot have known, quite, what they were developing – but once the point had been made, the engineers made sure that later models did the same thing.

The original 205 of 1983 was a family hatchback, complete with five doors, a transversely mounted engine and front wheel, and a wide choice of engines, including a small diesel. Like other previous Peugeots, it was expected to sell well, to make good profits, and to be in production for many years. Because VW's own Golf GTi had made such an impact, a similar derivative of the new Peugeot was expected. When it arrived, in February 1984, it was soon seen as something different – and better. Originally with a 105bhp/1.6-litre fuel-injected engine, it was a briskly accelerating 116mph machine – but that was only part of the appeal.

Not only did it look good – compact, nicely detailed, with special styling touches including special road wheels – but it was a three-door machine, still unique to the 205 at that time. The fuel-injected engine was smooth, responsive and high-revving, but it was the kart-like handling (a touch tail-happy on the limit, but no-one seemed to mind), and the feline steering response which made all the difference.

But that was only the start, as Peugeot made haste to improve an already excellent car. First, in 1986, they launched a chic convertible with the same engine, which was a great success, not only in the cities, but in the seaside resorts. Then, before the end of that year, there was an additional model, with a 1.9-litre/130bhp engine, which not only made the GTi faster (120mph and more was possible, with 0-60mph in less than eight seconds) but more flexible. Since this car also had four-wheel disc brakes, it became an even more formidable road burner. At the same time the original 1.6-litre car's engine was uprated, to 115bhp.

From then until the early 1990s, when the larger 306GTi made its bow, the 205GTi was the Peugeot which every aspiring sportsman seemed to covet, and every rival hatchback seemed to be measured against it. Complaints about on-the-limit handling were brushed aside, for no other car seemed to offer the same ballet-like ability to change direction, to perform, or simply to charm.

The 205GTi was even more significant that it might seem, at first glance, for it ushered in a complete sea-change in the character of all Peugeots. Before the 205, they had been worthy, usually staid, and not at all trendy, but after that every succeeding model seemed to move in the 205GTi's same attractive direction. All this, and a successful rally programme by the distantly related 205 Turbo 16, changed Peugeot's image for ever.

Left: The style, the character and the performance of the 205GTi redefined the 'Hot Hatch'. 1.9-litre cars could reach more than 120mph.

Pierce-Arrow Straight-Eight

Pierce-Arrow Eight, built from 1928 to 1938 (data for 1930 6.3-litre)
Built by: Pierce-Arrow Motor Car Co., United States.
Engine: Eight cylinders, inline, in cast-iron block, with nine-bearing light-allo crankcase. Bore and stroke 88.9mm by 127mm 6,318cc (3.5in × 5.0ir 386cu.in). Detachable cast-iron cylinder head. Two side valves per cylinde operated by tappets from camshaft in crankcase. Single up-draugh Stromberg carburettor. Maximum power 125bhp at 3,000rpm.
Transmission: Single-dry-plate clutch and four-speed gearbox (withou synchromesh), both in unit with front-mounted engine. Direct-acting centra gearchange. Open propeller shaft to spiral-bevel 'live' rear axle.
Chassis: Separate pressed-steel chassis frame, with pressed and tubular cros bracing. Forged front axle beam. Front and rear suspension by semi-elliptic lea springs. Lever-arm hydraulic dampers. Worm-and-ball-tooth steering. Fou wheel, mechanically operated drum brakes. Bolt-on disc wheels.
Dimensions: Wheelbase 12ft 0in (366cm). Track (front) 4ft 10in (147cm) track (rear) 5ft 1.5in (156cm).
History: After the gargantuan Model 66, Pierce-Arrow had to make mor modest cars for a time and even though North America was prosperou during the 1920s, sales began to slide rather ominously. Like other rivals i the business, the company decided that an eight-cylinder engine could b their salvation and in 1928 they duly launched the Group A and Group straight-eights which were to carry them through the 1930s. In th meantime, the company's shareholders had voted to merge their compan with Studebaker of South Bend, Indiana, which was duly accomplished i 1928. For four years, until the V12 Pierce-Arrow car was ready as a nev flagship, the straight-eight cars did their best to keep the company afloat The car itself was excellent – and sales of 8,000 in 1929 confirmed this. Eve in 1930, when expensive cars were a drug on the market, 7,000 wer delivered. Most were delivered with factory-built bodies, in many styles, an all but a few were discreet and unadorned.

For years, of course, there was no company badging in the nose –

possible client was not thought to need that sort of ostentation to bolster up his standing in the community. In spite of the fact that Studebaker sold off Pierce-Arrow to a group of businessmen in 1933 and in spite of the announcement of the outstandingly modern Model 1601 car with the straight-eight engine, nothing seemed to go right for the cars, and sales continued to slide. Prices were too high and appeal too limited for the straitened times of 1930s North America, but Pierce-Arrow could not readily adjust without losing their cars' character altogether. The last was made in 1938, less than ten years after the new engine design and model range had been launched. It was another nail in the coffin of American car individuality. It is no more than coincidence that Studebaker also announced a straight-eight when they annexed Pierce-Arrow – the engines were of different designs, but with obvious modern similarities.

Above, left and far left: Details of the Straight-Eight Pierce-Arrow and the car itself. It was an exclusive and costly product, made in good numbers in spite of the American Depression. This car dates from 1929.

Porsche 356

Porsche 356 cars, built from 1948 to 1965 (data for 1960-type S90)
Built by: Dr. Ing.h.c. F. Porsche KG., West Germany.
Engine: Four cylinders, horizontally opposed, in three-bearing, light-alloy block/crankcase, air cooled. Bore and stroke 82.5mm by 74mm, 1,582cc (3.25in × 2.91in, 96.5cu.in). Two light-alloy cylinder heads. Two overhead valves per cylinder, operated by pushrods and rockers from single camshaft, centrally mounted in crankcase. Two downdraught Zenith carburettors. Maximum power 90bhp (net) at 5,500rpm. Maximum torque 89lb.ft at 4,300rpm.
Transmission: Single-dry-plate clutch, and four-speed, all-synchromesh manual gearbox, both in unit with rear-mounted engine. Engine behind line of rear wheels and gearbox ahead of it. Remote-control central gearchange. Spiral-bevel final drive, and exposed, universally jointed drive shafts to rear wheels.
Chassis: Pressed-steel punt-type chassis frame, topped by pressed-steel and light-alloy-panelled coupé or convertible bodyshells. Independent VW-type front suspension by trailing arms, transverse torsion bars and anti-roll bar. Independent rear suspension by swinging half-axles, radius arms and transverse torsion bars. Telescopic dampers. Worm-and-roller steering. Four-wheel, hydraulically operated drum brakes. 15in pressed-steel-disc wheels. 5.60 × 15in tyres.
Dimensions: Wheelbase 6ft 10.7in (210cm), track (front) 4ft 3.4in (130.5cm), track (rear) 4ft 2.1in (127cm). Overall length 13ft 1.9in (401cm). Unladen weight 1,985lb (900kg).
History: Dr. Porsche had been in the centre of modern motor car development since Edwardian times, but it was son Ferry who laid out the bare bones of the Porsche car project after World War II. Using VW Beetle mechanical equipment – engines, transmissions and suspensions – Porsche built their very first car in 1948 and this had the engine ahead of the rear wheel line. However, all production cars reverted to the familiar VW-style layout, with the air-cooled flat-four engine overhanging the rear wheels.
Type 356, incidentally, indicates that this was the 356th project undertaken by the Porsche design office since its formation in 1930. Early Porsches were 1100s, with very nearly standard VW engines, but they very rapidly found success in motor racing

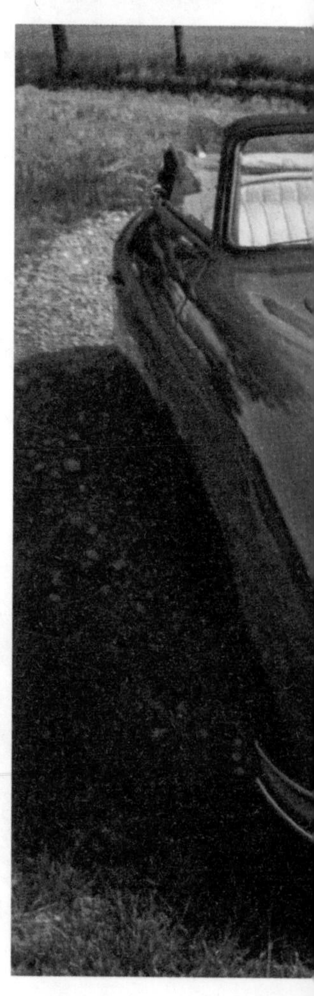

Right: Only an expert can tell the age and pedigree of a Porsche 356 from a picture. This is a 1951 Cabriolet – note the divided screen and flush-fitting headlamps. Engines from 1,100cc to 2,000cc were supplied, and the last of all 356s was built in 1964.

and proved to be surprisingly strong rally cars.

Production was well under way by 1950, when steel-bodied cars were phased in at the new Zuffenhausen works, to replace the original light-alloy. Enlargement began in 1951 when the 1,286cc car was announced, 1,488cc Porsches were revealed in 1951 and the first 1,582cc car followed in 1955. This engine, developed from its original 60bhp output to 95bhp in 1965, was standardised for the last ten years of the 356's life. In all this time there was only one significant restyling operation – in 1959 when headlamps and bumpers were raised, the windscreen enlarged and trim updated. The Porsche's shape was always aerodynamically efficient, and the last of the Super 90s was good for 115mph, with excellent fuel economy. Although the 356 carried on until 1965, it was effectively replaced by the 911 series, which went into series production in 1964.

Porsche 911

Porsche 911 and 912 models, built from 1963 to 1999 (data for 1976 3-litre Turbo)

Built by: Dr. Ing.h.c. F. Porsche KG., Germany.

Engine: Six cylinders, horizontally opposed, in detachable finned light-alloy barrels, with two-piece, eight-bearing magnesium crankcase. Air cooled. Bore and stroke 95mm by 70.4mm, 2,994cc (3.74in × 2.77in, 182.7cu.in). Detachable light-alloy cylinder heads. Two overhead valves per cylinder, inclined to each other in part-spherical combustion chambers and operated by rockers from single overhead camshafts; Bosch fuel injection and KKK turbocharger. Dry-sump lubrication. Maximum power 260bhp (DIN) at 5,500rpm. Maximum torque 253lg.ft at 4,000rpm.

Transmission: Single-dry-plate clutch and four-speed, all-synchromesh manual gearbox, in transaxle assembly. Engine behind line of rear wheels, gearbox ahead of it. Remote-control central gearchange. Hypoid-bevel final drive. Exposed universally jointed drive shafts to rear wheels.

Chassis: Unitary-construction pressed-steel body-chassis unit. Rear-mounted engine/transmission, engine overhung to rear of car. All-independent

suspension, front by lower wishbones, torsion bars and anti-roll bar, rear by semi-trailing links, transverse torsion bars and anti-roll bar. Telescopic dampers. Rack-and-pinion steering. Four-wheel hydraulically operated disc brakes. 15in forged aluminium-alloy road wheels, 205 × 15in front tyres, 225 × 15in rear tyres.
Dimensions: Wheelbase 7ft 5in (226cm), track (front) 4ft 8.5in (143cm), track (rear) 5ft 1in (155cm). Overall length 14ft 2in (432cm). Unladen weight 2,700lb (1,224kg).
History: To replace the legendary Type 356 family, Porsche embarked on an entirely new design. Although no old component was carried forward the design philosophy was not changed – the car still had a rear-mounted, horizontally opposed, air-cooled engine, a 2+2 seating arrangement and a sleek closed coupé body style. In case of the 911, the engine was a flat-six, with a single overhead cam-shaft per bank, and there was a five-speed or four-speed gearbox according to the model. Although the 911 was in a different, higher, price class than the 356 once this had been drawn a 912 model was sold with the 1,582cc Super 90's flat-four unit installed. Even in this guise the car could clock up 120mph, but 130 was quite normal for the sixes. The 911 was launched as a 2-litre in 1963, and was in production by the following summer. The 911S was a highly tuned version with 160bhp, and was immediately successful in endurance racing and rallying. Over the years the car was further developed: the 2-litre engine became 2.2-litres in 1969, 2.4-litres in 1971, and 2.7-litres in 1973. There have been 3.0-litres since 1975 and 3.3-litres since 1977.

Also introduced in the model's long life span had been the removable-roof 'Targa' body style, and the semi-automatic 'Sportomatic' transmission, but the most sensational development of all was the 3-litre Porsche Turbo. This installation, proved first in prototype racing, had an exhaust-gas-driven turbocharger to boost the inlet mixture, is very tractable, and endows the car with a maximum speed of more than 160mph. Even with twice as much power as the original 911 had, the Porsche Turbo's handling is probably safer and more predictable than ever and the aerodynamic aids (including the large engine-lid spoiler) make it very stable at high speeds. All 911s have an impressive reliability record, and recent versions use galvanised structural panels, a seven-year guarantee being offered accordingly.

Left: Announced in 1963, the Porsche 911 sold well ever since. Engines have been enlarged from 2-litre to 3.3-litre over the years. The basic two-door fastback always looks good.

Porsche 917

917 Model, built for racing from 1969 to 1971 (data for 1971 5-litre)
Built by: Dr. Ing.h.c. F. Porsche KG., West Germany.
Engine: Twelve cylinders, horizontally opposed, in detachable finned light-alloy cylinder barrels, with eight-bearing magnesium crankcase. Air cooled. Bore and stroke 86.8mm by 70.4mm, 4,998cc (3.42in × 2.77in, 305cu.in). Detachable aluminium cylinder heads. Two overhead valves per cylinder, inclined to each other in part-spherical combustion chambers and operated inverted-bucket tappets from twin overhead camshafts per bank. Bosch fuel injection. Power drive take-off from gears at centre of crankshaft, through drive shaft in base of crank-case. Dry-sump lubrication. Maximum power 630bhp (DIN) at 8,300rpm. Maximum torque 425lb.ft at 6,400rpm.
Transmission: Mid-mounted engine, driving through gearbox, behind line of back wheels, in transaxle. Triple-dry-plate clutch, and four-speed or five-speed all-synchromesh gearbox (depending on application). Spiral-bevel final drive with limited-slip differential. Exposed, universally-jointed drive shafts to rear wheels.
Chassis: Separate multi-tubular aluminium frame. Engine and transmission mounted behind seats. All independent suspension, front by coil springs, wishbones and anti-roll bar, rear by coil springs, lower wishbones, radius arms and anti-roll bar. Telescopic dampers, rack-and-pinion steering. Four-wheel, hydraulically operated disc brakes, 15in cast-magnesium road wheels of varying widths (depending on application). Tyre size according to requirements. Glassfibre two-seat racing bodywork by Porsche, short or long tail, open or closed, according to requirement.
Dimensions: Wheelbase 7ft 6in (230cm), track (front – with 12in rims) 5ft 1.7in (156cm), track (rear – with 17in rims) 5ft 2.7in (158cm). Overall length (917K short tail) 13ft 7.6in (416cm). Unladen weight 1,763lb (800kg).
History: The Type 917 sports-racing car was designed specifically to meet a new category, which allowed 5-litre cars to be raced as long as 25 identical examples had been made. This, the authorities thought, would get rid of specialised racing cars. They were wrong. Porsche developed the 917 (using 8-cyl 908 parts in the flat-12 engine) in less than a year and announced the car with a line-up of 25 examples standing in the factory ready for inspection! Only very few of these were ever sold, most being used by the factory or loaned out to

Above: Porsche 917s came in many shapes, but all shared the same flat-12 engine with more than 630bhp. For years they were fast and unbeatable.

sponsored teams. The car was the ultimate expression of Porsche's air-cooled lightweight two-seater racing car philosophy. Although it had a poor 1969 season, it was well-nigh invincible thereafter.

The 917 used the most powerful automotive air-cooled engine of all time and was one of the most rapid two-seaters ever built. 'Works' cars were run by the JW Automotive team from Britain in 1970 and 1971, winning the world sports car championship very easily from Ferrari. When the rules were again changed, banning 5-litre cars (the 917 had originally been 4.5 litres, but got its enlarged engine after the first year), some cars were converted to open sports cars and when turbocharged they could boast outputs of at least 1,000bhp. They, without doubt, are the most powerful racing cars ever built.

Left: The low and stubby short-tail 917s were aerodynamically very stable on all tracks. Most were closed coupés.

Porsche 959

Porsche 959 sports coupé, built in 1987 and 1988
Built by: Dr. Ing. h.c. F. Porsche KG, Germany.
Engine: Six cylinders, in 'boxer' horizontally opposed formation, in seven-bearing light-alloy cylinder block/crankcase. Bore and stroke 95 × 67mm, 2,851cc (3.74 × 2.64in, 174cu.in). Two light-alloy cylinder heads. Four valves per cylinder, in vee, operation by twin overhead camshafts and inverted bucket tappets. Bosch fuel injection and twin KKK turbochargers. Maximum power 450bhp (DIN) at 6,500rpm. Maximum torque 370lb.ft at 5,500rpm.
Transmission: Four-wheel-drive, single-plate-diaphragm spring clutch and six-speed all-synchromesh manual gearbox, all in unit with rear-mounted engine. Remote-control, central gearchange.
Chassis: Unitary-construction pressed-steel body-chassis unit in two-door 2+2 seater coupé layout. Independent front suspension by coil springs, wishbones, telescopic dampers, and anti-roll bar. Independent rear suspension by coil springs, wishbones, telescopic dampers, anti-roll bar. Electronic ride control at front and rear. Rack-and-pinion steering with hydraulic power assistance. Four-wheel disc brakes with power assistance and anti-lock. Cast light alloy 17in road wheels, 235/45-17in (front) and 255/45-17in (rear) tyres.
Dimensions: Wheelbase 7ft 5.4in (227.2cm), front track 4ft 11.2in (150.4cm), rear track 5ft 1.0in (155cm). Overall length 13ft 11.7in (426cm). Unladen weight 3,197lb (1,450kg).
History: Conceived in 1983 as a car with which Porsche might dominate Group B category motor racing, the 959 matured into the most complete, most sophisticated, and most capable Supercar of its period. However crude it might have been when invented, when it went on sale it was the most beguiling of any

Below: Originally shown as the 'Gruppe B' project car in 1983, the turbocharged four-wheel-drive Porsche was only a distant relative of the 911.

Above: Even before sales began, Porsche used the 959 to win the gruelling Paris-Dakar 'Raid', where long-distance durability and four-wheel-drive were essential.

rear-engined Porsche so far introduced. Although broadly based on the rear-engined/rear-drive air-cooled 911, the 959 evolved so far that it retained only the same basic body shell, yet it had precious little in common with that famous model. With four-wheel-drive instead of rear-drive, with water-cooling instead of air-cooling to the cylinder heads, it had moved on a long way.

The story began in the early 1980s when the authorities introduced Group B motorsport, demanding only that 200 cars needed to be built to qualify for homologation (while allowing manufacturers to make a further 20 'Evolution' examples of an even more special type). Most car-makers chose to go rallying, but Porsche, at least at first, had circuit motor racing in mind. The 'Gruppe B' concept car was shown in 1983, when it was not nearly ready to go out on to the tracks, let alone go on sale, and in 1984 the first normally aspirated four-wheel-drive 'Gruppe B' 911s competed in the Paris-Dakar marathon rally, winning at their first attempt. Porsche meantime, in its own methodical way, then evolved the definitive car, taking so long to do it that the first examples would not be put on sale until 1987. The wait, however, was worth it, for every possible snag had been ironed out, and every possible ability added in.

Starting on the basis of an existing 911 monocoque body shell, with the flat-six engine in its usual position, way out in the tail, but retaining no more than that, the engineers then changed, improved and upgraded everything. First of all the engine, chosen in 2,851cc form, was given four-valves-per-cylinder water-cooled twin-cam cylinder heads, a KKK turbocharger and an intercooler to each bank – and produced a rock-solid 450bhp. Much more was available in racing form, for this was a unit which had evolved from that already being used in the fabulously successful 956 racing two-seater.

Next, and integral to the entire design, was the four-wheel-drive system (the first ever to have been developed at Porsche), where there was a massive six- ▶

speed all-syncromesh manual gearbox ahead of the engine, in the usual Porsche position (under the rear seats), which was linked to the front axle casing by a propeller shaft inside a solid aluminium torque tube.

Next there was the chassis, with an ultra-wide-track coil spring/wishbone independent suspension at each corner, and with rack-and-pinion steering, naturally enough with hydraulic power-assistance. Vast ventilated disc brakes (with electronic ABS, even though some of the test drivers felt that competition-inclined drivers would not want this feature) completed the chassis set up. But there was more. Computer sensing controls helped the transmission decide what proportion of the torque should be fed to the front wheels, while the suspension ride height could be adjusted to allow for smooth or rough roads: computers, in any case, looked after ride levelling at high speeds, allowing the car to sink further towards the ground to improve the aerodynamic balance.

To complete the picture, there was the styling, at once 911-related, but all the same totally separate, and instantly recognisable. Each difference, it seemed, had a good reason to be there – the faired-headlamp nose to reduce the drag, the bulging wheelarches to cover the wide-track suspension and ultra-wide tyres, the wide sills under the doors to link those arches, and the cool air intakes to feed the brakes (front corners) and the twin intercoolers (rear). There were exhaust vents behind the rear wheels, which allowed the twin turbochargers to 'breathe', and finally there was the full-width, fixed-incidence, aerofoil, across the tail to trim the high-speed handling.

Could anything have been more beguiling? Porsche thought not, which is why they confidently put the car on sale at an ex-factory price of DM 420,000 (which was roughly equivalent to £150,000 at that time). At this point there were two road-going 959s on offer, one of them the normal car, the Sport, which came without a rear seat, and a higher-specified, higher-priced type called the 959

Comfort, which had electric window lifts, air-conditioning and central locking. With motorsport in mind, a 961 version was also planned, but since Group B motorsport had already gone past its best by 1987 such cars were not seriously marketed.

When customers took delivery of their 959s, its reputation had already been made, for a trio of fully specified 'works' cars had competed in the Paris–Dakar marathon (all the way across the Sahara desert, flat out), to a 1-2 finish, while Claude Ballot-Lena's car had won the IMSA class and taken seventh place overall at Le Mans in the same year.

The 959's straightline performance, of course, was astonishing, for its top speed was almost 200mph – and a comfortable all-day cruising speed of 170–180mph seemed to be acceptable – while, aided by the tenacious grip of the four-wheel-drive system, the 450bhp car could sprint up to 100mph in about nine seconds. That, though, could only tell half of the story, for those lucky enough to drive 959s found that they not only looked good, and sprinted well, but that they were cool and comfortable to drive, the ride was as fluid as any other Porsche, and they seemed to be as well-built as any of the world's most expensive limousines.

No other company, it was generally agreed, would have taken so much trouble to finalise such a limited-production car, and since sales were limited to 250 cars, the 959 can surely not have made a profit for Porsche. No matter. It was the best 911-based car of all, and even as the new century opened, it had still not been surpassed by a better and more complete machine.

Below: Although the 959 shared its cabin with the 911, the floor pan, four-wheel-drive running gear, engine, chassis, and front and rear-end styles were all unique.

Porsche Boxster

Porsche Boxster two-seater sports car, introduced in 1996 (data for the original model)

Built by: Dr. Ing. h.c. F. Porsche KG, Germany.

Engine: Six cylinders, in horoizontally-opposed formation, in four-bearing light-alloy cylinder block/crankcase. Bore and stroke 86 × 72mm, 2,480cc (3.39 × 2.83in, 151.4cu.in). Two light-alloy cylinder heads. Four valves per cylinder, in vee, operation by twin overhead camshafts, with variable camshaft timing. Bosch Motronic fuel injection. Maximum power 204bhp (DIN) at 6,000rpm. Maximum torque 181lb.ft at 4,500rpm.

Transmission: Rear-wheel-drive, single-dry-plate diaphragm spring clutch and five-speed all-synchromesh manual gearbox, all in unit with mid-mounted engine. Remote-control, central gearchange. Tiptronic semi-automatic transmission also available as an option.

Chassis: Unitary-construction pressed-steel body-chassis unit with some aluminium panels, as two-seater open sports car style. Independent front suspension by MacPherson struts, coil springs, wishbones, telescopic dampers, and anti-roll bar. Independent rear suspension by MacPherson struts, coil springs, trailing arms and lower wishbones, telescopic dampers, and anti-roll bar. Rack-and-pinion steering with hydraulic power assistance. Four-wheel disc brakes with power assistance and ABS. cast alloy, 16in road wheels, 205/55-16in (front) and 225/50-16in (rear) tyres.

Dimensions: Wheelbase 7ft 11in (241.5cm), front track 4ft 9.3in (145.5cm), rear track 4ft 11.4in (150.8cm). Overall length 14ft 1.9in (431.5cm). Unladen weight 2,739lb (1,242kg).

History: In the late 1980s and early 1990s, Porsche had a troubled existence. Management came and went, new models were started, then cancelled, sales peaked in 1990 then plummeted in the next few years, and for a time the company made big financial losses.

It was not until 1992 that a solid new strategy was adopted, one cornerstone of which was to develop a new 'entry-level' two-seater roadster. The reason was that Porsche prices, in general, had drifted gradually but firmly upwards in the previous decade, and many enthusiastic drivers could no longer afford to buy. It was not feasible to get down to a truly stripped-out car, but it was certainly possible to claw back to a smaller, and cheaper base. The result was the Boxster of 1996 – except for its choice of a flat-six engine layout a car with no links at all with Porsche's illustrious past.

From the windscreen forward, the Boxster was to be common with the still-secret new-generation 911 (Porsche would later claim that 35 per cent of the two cars were the same in every detail), but aft of that it was unique. Whereas the next-generation 911 would have a rear-mounted engine, the new flat-six engine of the Boxster was water-cooled (cylinder heads *and* cylinder blocks – a real novelty for Porsche), and was positioned ahead of the line of the back axle.

Above: The all-new Boxster was the first Porsche ever to have a new-generation water-cooled flat-six engine. The entire front end was shared with the new-generation 911.

By definition, this meant that the 'chassis' platform of the Boxster was unique, as was the transmission and the rear suspension which was all linked to it. The pressed-steel body style itself was rounded, and sleek, without a trace of so-called fashionable wedge, or of folded edges in it, with twin roll-over hoops behind the seats, a flat rear deck to emphasis the compact engine – and space for stowage at front and rear.

The engine itself was at once all-new (water-cooled, don't forget) yet instantly recognisably Porsche. Compact, with all its fuel injection and auxiliary drives packaged above it, it sat ahead of its transmission, and was effectively underneath where the '+2' seats might otherwise have been found. Initially it was rated at 204bhp/2,480cc, but it was clear that much more power (and enlargement) was possible – this being proved within a year when the first 300bhp/3,387cc version of the same engine appeared in the new-type 911!

Complete with all-round MacPherson strut suspension, and big four-wheel disc brakes, the first Boxster looked appealing, and capable – and so it was. Handling better than any previous Porsche had ever done, it was already capable of nearly 140mph, but by existing Porsche standards this was milk-and-water stuff, so demands for higher-powered versions were soon made. Porsche, of course, had already thought about this, and within three years they had introduced a 220bhp/2.7-litre/150mph version of the original Boxster, along with a 252bhp/3.2-litre/161mph Boxster S. All this, note, was with a still-young and normally aspirated engine – so prospects for the 2000s, when turbocharging was applied, were intriguing.

Left: The new Boxster was so carefully proportioned that it was difficult to realise that the engine was actually behind the seats, but ahead of the rear axle line.

Renault Alpine

Alpines 1955 to 1977 (data for 1600S model of 1970)
Built by: Automobiles Alpine srl., France.
Engine: Renault-manufactured, four cylinders, in line, in five-bearing light-alloy block. Bore and stroke 77mm by 84mm, 1,565cc (3.03in × 3.31in, 95.5cu.in). Light-alloy cylinder head. Two overhead valves per cylinder, operated by pushrods and rockers from single camshaft, high-mounted in cylinder block. One twin-choke Weber carburettor. Maximum power 138bhp (gross) at 6,000rpm. Maximum torque 106lb.ft at 5,000rpm.
Transmission: Engine mounted longitudinally behind line of rear wheels, driving through gearbox, ahead of rear wheels, and transaxle. Single-dry-plate clutch, and five-speed, all synchromesh manual gearbox. Central, remote-control gearchange. Drive forward over final drive to gearbox, then back to hypoid-bevel final drive. Exposed universally jointed drive shafts to rear wheels.
Chassis: Separate tubular backbone chassis frame, with square-section and circular-section built-up frames supporting suspensions and power pack. Independent front suspension by coil springs, wishbones and anti-roll bar. Independent rear suspension by swinging half axles, coil springs, radius arms and anti-roll bar. Telescopic dampers. Rack-and-pinion steering. Four-wheel disc brakes, with optional vacuum servo. Cast-alloy, 15in road wheels. 145 × 15in, or 165 × 13in tyres. Two-door, two-seat, closed glassfibre bodywork by Alpine.
Dimensions: Wheelbase 6ft 10.6in (210cm), track (front) 4ft 3in (129.5cm),

Right: Alpine-Renaults are really rally cars which can be used on the road. With a tubular chassis, light glassfibre bodies, and powerful modified Renault engines, the A110 was an outright winner for years. This was Pat Moss-Carlsson's Monte example.

track (rear) 4ft 2.2in (127.5cm). Overall length 12ft 7.5in (385cm). Unladen weight 1,400lb (635kg).

History: Jean Redélé worked in the family Renault dealership when young, and started competition motoring in the not-very-sporting 4CV saloon model. From this he progressed to building a glassfibre special using mainly 4CV parts – the very first Alpine-Renault sports car. From very small beginnings, this dumpy little machine was built in limited quantities; it was given a larger engine and refined and it gradually built up a loyal clientele. The breakthrough came in 1961, when the A108 Tour de France machine was introduced, visually very similar to the cars to be made for the next fifteen years, with a steel backbone chassis and steel platform floor, with the Renault Dauphine 956cc engine. Development thereafter was rapid, with first an 1,108cc and later a 1,255cc engine.

Alpines were very successful class and 'Index' performers on the race track and in smooth-road rallies, but it was not until the light-alloy Renault 16 unit was made available that outright victories became possible. From the end of the 1960s, the cars were also strengthened, until by the early 1970s they could win rallies through the Alps, in the dust and sand of Morocco, and continue to shine on the race tracks. As a production car the Alpine was only a compromise, for its very lightweight and flexible glassfibre body shell and tail-out handling was strictly competition-inspired. The company is now financially controlled by Renault, the French giant and operates that company's official competition programme.

Renault Grand Prix Cars

Grand Prix Renaults of 1906, 1907 and 1908 (data for 1906 model)
Built by: Renault Frères Billancourt, France.
Engine: Four cylinders, in line, in two cast-iron blocks, with light-alloy crankcase. Bore and stroke 166mm by 150mm, 12,975cc (6.54in × 5.91in, 791.7cu.in). Two fixed cylinder heads. Two side valves per cylinder, exposed at side of cylinder blocks and directly operated by single camshaft mounted in crankcase. Single Renault carburettor. Maximum power 105bhp at 1,200rpm.
Trnasmission: Leather-cone clutch, in unit with front-mounted engine and shaft drive to separate three-speed manual gearbox (without synchromesh). Remote-control right-hand gearchange. Open propeller shaft to straight-bevel final drive, without differential.
Chassis: Separate pressed-steel chassis frame, with channel-section side members and tubular cross members. Forged front axle beam. Front suspension by semi-elliptic leaf springs. Rear axle location. Rear suspension by semi-elliptic leaf springs (with torque arm between axle casing and chassis frame in gearbox area in 1907 version). Lever-arm hydraulic dampers. Hand brake to drums on rear wheels, foot brake to transmission drum behind gearbox. Wooden artillery-type wheels, with detachable rims only. 870 × 90 (front) or 870 × 120 (rear) tyres. Open two-seater bodywork.
Dimensions: Wheelbase 9ft 6.2in (209cm), tracks (front and rear) 4ft 5.2in (135cm). Overall length 14ft 1.8in (431cm). Unladen weight 2,183lb (990kg).
History: In the good old days when motor racing was not so tightly wrapped

Below and right: Colourful detail of the world's first successful Grand Prix car. The 1906 Renault, however, was a development of a 1904 machine, and the engine was new for the 1903 Paris-Madrid road race. Radiators mounted behind the engine were a feature of all Renaults – racing or production cars – built up to 1928.

Above: Szisz's winning Renault pulling away from a halt during the 1906 Grand Prix, held at Le Mans. This picture shows an unusually smooth section of the track, which was otherwise very dusty, and covered in loose pebbles. An early Grand Prix was a real test of endurance – the 1906 race occupying more than 12 hours on two days. The Renault's winning average was 63mph.

around with rules and regulations, it was much simpler for any interested manufacturer to build a competitive machine. At the beginning of the twentieth century, with motoring still in its infancy, the sport was still easy to understand. When the French decided to organise the very first Grand Prix in 1906, the only regulation applying to the cars was that they should weigh no more than 1,000kg (2,205lb) unladen. Renault had been active in motor sport from the start (Marcel Renault himself being the team's star driver), but when Renault was killed in a Paris-Madrid crash in 1903 the factory abruptly withdrew its support. In 1904, however, they built a machine for an American customer, with an enlarged version of the Paris-Madrid engine, and by 1905 they were tempted to return to the sport, with further-developed versions of this engine and its transmission in a new chassis. For 1906, for the Grand Prix to be held at Le Mans, a team of new cars was built up; this represented modern thinking about that sort of car. The chassis, of course, was simple in the extreme, with handling and braking taking a back seat to sheer power and (hopefully) strength. The nucleus of Renault's GP effort was a yet further developed version of the 1903 Paris-Madrid engine, which got its power and formidable torque from 13 litres, rather than from any particularly advanced breathing capability. It was a big, slow-revving, four-cylinder unit, with vast 6.5in pistons, and peak power of 105bhp produced at a mere 1,200rpm. It was a trend-setter in some ways, because, like every other Renault ever made, it had shaft drive. Most fast cars of the period were faithful to chain drive, which was very vulnerable to damage from dust and from the atrocious roads used, even for racing, in those days. The three-speed gearbox, right-hand gearchange and stark two-seater body were all normal to the period. The Renault was noted for its very sleek sloping nose and for its water radiators carried behind the engine and immediately in front of the passengers. A riding mechanic was compulsory and necessary, to look after the car and to deal with the inevitable punctures. In this respect, the car was originally built with non-detachable wire-spoke wheels, but after practice a set of artillery wheels was substituted, with detachable rear rims. Other oddities

were that the rear axle had no differential and that the cars (three were built) were painted bright red (national colours not then being compulsory). In 1906, only one of the three cars finished, but it won the race outright, driven by Ferenc Szisz. Its maximum speed was about 100mph and it averaged 63mph for the gruelling 769 miles. A year later, with identical but newly built cars, Szisz's car took second place, hampered by a fuel-restriction formula, six minutes behind Nazzaro's Fiat.

For 1908, the new restrictions on piston area limiting the four-cylinder bore to 155mm, Renault modified the engines with a longer (160mm) stroke. Breathing and other improvements allowed the unit to peak at 2,000rpm, and maximum power was very slightly improved. The cars were still completely competitive, but tyre troubles robbed Szisz of another high placing and the team mates were neither as experienced nor as brave.

The cars are now legendary, because they were the first of that long and continuing strain of machinery which culminated in the ultra-specialised single-seaters of today. Yet the Grand Prix car of the early 1900s was very closely related to a big fast touring car and some of the less-specialised machines were often converted for ordinary road use after their racing career was over. Looking at those narrow tyres, the complete lack of weather protection and the terrible state of the roads used, one had to marvel at the cars and the drivers who tackled the early races. The Renault, by its consistent running and fine appearance is a splendid and significant member of that rare breed of Titans. We must be thankful that one has survived, and that Renault themselves now cherish it.

Below: Tyre changes because of punctures were inevitable on the bad roads of the 1900s, and the Renault's detachable Michelin rims helped to cut down the time needed for this. In spite of the car's mechanical crudity, it could exceed 100mph, though the brakes were almost non-existent. There were two seats because a mechanic travelled with the driver.

Riley Sports Cars

Riley Nines, Lynx, Imp, MPH and Sprites, built in the 1930s (data for 1936/' Sprite two-seater)

Built by: Riley (Coventry) Ltd., Britain.

Engine: Four cylinders, in line, in three-bearing cast-iron block. Bore and strok 69mm by 100mm, 1,496cc (2.72in × 3.94in, 91.3cu.in). Detachable cast-iro cylinder head. Two over-head valves per cylinder, inclined to each other at 9 degrees in hemispherical combustion chamber and operated by pushrods an rockers from two high-mounted camshafts in cylinder block; one cam for inle mounted in 'inlet' side of block, one in 'exhaust' side for exhaust valves. Twi horizontal constant-vacuum SU carburettors. Maximum power 60bhp a 5,000rpm.

Transmission: Wilson-type preselector epi-cyclic gearbox with four forwar speeds. No clutch, drive taken up by gear friction band as it is engaged. Gearbo in unit with engine. Pre-selector quadrant control on right side of steerin column, under steering wheel. Propeller shaft enclosed in torque tube fixed t spiral-bevel 'live' rear axle.

Chassis: Separate pressed-steel chassis frame, with box and channel-sectio side members and pressed and tubular cross bracing. Forged front axle bear Semi-elliptic front and rear springs, with friction-type dampers. Worm-and whee steering. Four-wheel rod and cable-operated drum brakes. 19in centre-lock wir wheels. 5.00 × 19in tyres. Two-seat open sports coachwork by Riley, wit optional cowled or 'traditional' front.

Dimensions: Wheelbase 8ft 1.5in (248cm), tracks (front and rear) 4ft (122cm Overall length 12ft 4in (376cm). Unladen weight 2,210lb (1,002kg).

History: The true pedigree of Riley's famous sports cars of the late 1920s an the 1930s was established by the new family of engines with the still-uniqu twin-high-camshaft arrangement and inclined valves in the hemi-heade cylinder heads. The first engine was called the 'Nine' and was produced in 1927 with 1,087cc; this was followed by a 1,458cc six in 1932 and a big and lust 1,496cc four in 1934. The famous Freddie Dixon 'Brooklands' Rileys achieve their first miracles with much-tuned 'Nines', but later became ferociously fas projectiles, with 2-litre versions of the six. This engine, with its water-coole crankshaft bearing, was also the basis of the ERA racing-engine design, wher

Above: The 1934 Riley MPH, so clearly related to the later Sprite, had a tuned Riley six-cylinder engine, available in three different sizes. Only 15 were made.

in supercharged form the very best 2-litres produced well over 300bhp! Nevertheless, the 1½-litre four was the most useful, commercially, and was to be a Riley production engine until the mid 1950s. From 1933, the trio of really shapely Rileys consisted of the Imps (with 'Nine' engines), the very rare MPHs (with the six), and the Sprites (which used the 1½-litre four). MPHs were very fast and very exotic and they bore a strong resemblance to the 8C Alfas *and* to the Triumph Dolomite prototypes (not surprising, as Donald Healey was connected with both Riley and Triumph at the critical time), but they were too expensive. Only about 15 were built. The Sprite, in effect, used the MPH body and chassis with a new engine installation. The preselector gearbox was a popular proprietary fitment in British 1930s cars, being strong and versatile if heavy. In the days when gearboxes had no synchromesh it was a great advance and was very suitable for driving tests and other forms of motor sport. The Sprite was offered by Riley with alternative noses – the one style with a traditional (but sloping) exposed radiator, and the other with the radiator cowled by a semi-streamlined panel. With no fuss from its very practical engine, the 1½-litre Sprite could beat 85mph for £425, which made it a very good bargain. Production ran out in 1938 when Riley were purchased by Lord Nuffield.

Left and right: Riley's Sprite of 1936 saw the first tentative breakaway from 'classic' styling, with the option of a cowl radiator. The Sprite used a modified MPH chassis, and a 1½-litre 4-cylinder engine. A pre-selector gear change was standard. Helped by this the Sprite was a successful rally car.

Rolls-Royce Corniche (Final model)

Rolls-Royce Corniche, second/final generation, introduced in 2000
Built by: Rolls-Royce Motor Cars Ltd., Britain.
Engine: Eight cylinders, in 90-deg vee formation, in five-main-bearing light alloy cylinder block. Bore and stroke 104.1 x 99.1mm, 6,750cc (4.09 x 3.90in, 411.7cu.in). Two light-alloy cylinder heads. Two overhead valves per cylinder, operation by pushrods, rockers and hydraulic tappets from a single camshaft in the cylinder block vee. Bosch fuel injection and Garrett AiResearch turbocharger. Maximum power 325bhp (DIN) at 4,000rpm. Maximum torque 544lb.ft at 2,100rpm.
Transmission: Rear-wheel-drive, torque converter and four-speed automatic transmission, all in unit with front-mounted engine. Remote-control gearchange on steering column.
Chassis: Unitary-construction pressed-steel body-chassis unit, in two-door four-seater drop-head coupé body style, with power-operated soft-top. Independent front suspension by coil springs, wishbones, telescopic dampers, and anti-roll bar, with adaptive ride control. Independent rear suspension by coil springs, semi-trailing arms, telescopic dampers, anti-roll bar, and adaptive ride control. Rack-and-pinion steering with hydraulic power assistance. Four-wheel disc brakes. Cast-alloy 17in road wheels, 255/55-17in tyres.
Dimensions: Wheelbase 10ft 0.5in (306.1cm), front track 5ft 1in (155cm), rear track 5ft 1in (155cm). Overall length 17ft 8.8in (540.5cm). Unladen weight 6,030lb (2,735kg).
History: Nothing at Rolls-Royce is ever carried out in haste, which company policy sees as undignified, and likely to lead to errors, so it was really no surprise to see that a second-generation Corniche did not appear until 2000. This car, in fact, was based on the Bentley Azure (though with different body skin panels), which had itself been launched in 1995, and *that* car was based on the Bentley Continental R (a two-

Below: Rolls-Royce charged £250,000 for the Corniche of 2000. Part of that price was reflected in the high-quality facia, seats and equipment.

Above: Although it was based on the Bentley Azure, the Corniche's exterior style was unique. Built by craftsmen, this was a magnificent convertible.

door coupé) of 1991.

This is a story which started with the Silver Shadow of 1965, which eventually donated a developed version of its high-tech chassis platform and all-independent suspensions to the Silver Spirit of 1980. The V8 engine, much improved over the years, had first been seen in 1959.

Two-door coupés and convertibles based on the Silver Shadow had been around since 1966, and the newly styled Bentley Continental R began to take over in 1991. The Azure, on which the Corniche was to be based, followed in 1995. Which leads neatly to the birth of the second-generation Corniche, which looked likely to be the last new-from-Crewe model to use the venerable old V8, which by that time was being manufactured by Cosworth Technology in Northampton.

Like all this generation of models (which were not to be confused with the BMW V12-engined types which followed in 1998), the new Corniche rode on a steel platform of venerable lineage, power by the equally venerable alloy V8, turbocharged in this instance, and rated at 325bhp with a whopping 544lb.ft. peak torque figure. Backed by the familiar GM automatic transmission, and riding on the usual softly damped (with electronic ride control) independent suspension system, this was not so much a Supercar as a Supermagic Carpet.

The Corniche's appeal was not so much in the sheer size and presence of its open-top four-seater layout, with a colossal, totally power-operated soft top, but in the cost-no-object quality of the fixtures and fittings, most notably the leather seats, the thick pile carpets, the wooden facia/instrument panel, and the delicated crafted instruments and switchgear.

There was no point in asking a Corniche buyer why he was willing to hand over £250,000 for a car which was not too fast (at 6,030lb/2,735kg it was extremely heavy, which guaranteed that fuel consumption was rarely likely to better 15mpg), and which did not handle as much as make progress, for this would display complete ignorance. Purchase of such a Rolls-Royce said more about the owner than it did about the car's engineering, its use being more of a statement, than about the need to go far and fast. Far and fast, for sure, but only on long motorway journeys – for if one put the Corniche up into the mountains where it got its name, progress would be much slower, and more ponderous.

That did not, of course matter, for this Corniche was one of the world's most carefully crafted, carefully built, and most extensively tested and assessed machines. Fit, finish, ambience and quality were more important than acceleration figures. When BMW (scheduled to be Rolls-Royce's owners from 2003) set about building a better Corniche, it would not be easy.

Rolls-Royce Phantoms I and II

Phantom I model, built from 1925 to 1929 (data for 1925 model)
Built by: Rolls-Royce Ltd., Britain.
Engine: Six cylinders, in line, in two groups of three cast-iron blocks, with seven-bearing light-alloy crankcase. Bore and stroke 107.9mm by 139.7mm, 7,668cc (4.25in × 5.5in, 467.9cu.in). One piece detachable cast-iron cylinder head. Two overhead valves per cylinder, operated by pushrods and rockers from single crankcase-mounted camshaft. Single twin-jet Rolls-Royce carburettor, with separate carburettor on top of induction manifold. Power and torque figures never quoted by Rolls-Royce.
Transmission: Single-dry-plate clutch, in unit with engine. Separate four-speed manual gearbox, with remote-control right-hand gearchange. Propeller shaft in torque tube, to spiral-bevel 'live' rear axle.
Chassis: Separate pressed-steel chassis frame, with channel-section side members and pressed, fabricated and tubular cross bracing. Forged front axle beam. Front suspension by semi-elliptic leaf springs. Rear suspension by cantilever leaf springs. Adjustable friction-type dampers (lever arm hydraulic dampers from 1926 – front – and 1927 – rear). Worm-and-nut steering. Four-wheel rod and cable-operated drum brakes, with Rolls-Royce servo-assistance (motor driven from tail of transmission). 33in centre-lock wire wheels (disc covers often specified). 5x 33in tyres.
Dimensions: Wheelbase 12ft or 12ft 6.5in (366cm or 382cm). Short wheelbase tracks (front) 4ft 9in (144.7cm), (rear) 4ft 8in (142cm). Overall length, 15ft 10.2in or 16ft 4.7in (483cm or 499.6cm). Unladen weight, depending on coachwork, up to 6,500lb (2,948kg).
History: The New Phantom, as the Phantom I was called until it was replaced in 1929, was really only the third new production Rolls-Royce in more than 20 years – after the Silver Ghost and the Twenty. It was a direct replacement for the Ghost and retained that car's chassis, complete with Edwardian suspension design. The engine, however, was much modified, being an amalgam of the best of the Ghost (having two three-cylinder blocks on a common crankcase), and of the much more modern and sleek Twenty layouts. There was no single part of the Twenty in the Phantom's engine, but many of the details were visually similar. One great advance

(not a pioneering invention – Hispano-Suiza had seen to that) was the mechanical servo-motor assistance for the four-wheel brakes. The motor itself, a small disc-clutch device mounted to the side of the gearbox, used the momentum of the car to help brake actuation through friction in the discs. This was marvellously effective and refined, and was used by Roll-Royce for a complete generation before they came to trust the normal vacuum-type of servo assistance.

Phantom I cars were built in Britain and (from Springfield) in the United States – a total of almost 3,500 being sold. The price in Britain was £1,850 for the chassis alone and it was a lucky and parsimonious customer who got his complete car for less than £2,600. As always, Rolls attempted to build the best possible car, as refined and as dignified as any other in the world, and they succeeded in this. They gave a full three-year guarantee (much more extensive than for the Ghost) and the car's construction made this quite practical. Rolls-Royce never built bodies themselves, but Phantoms were finished off in many guises – sporting, touring, or as limousines, by the cream of coachbuilders in Britain and North America. Standards of workmanship were very high and quality control second to none. The car, however, badly needed a new chassis and suspensions, which could only be supplied by a re-design.

In 1929 the New Phantom became the Phantom II. This was achieved by giving the car a new chassis frame with better controlled (semi-elliptic) springs all round; hydraulic damping had already been adopted for later New Phantoms. The engine was given more power, with an aluminium cylinder head and revised manifolding, while the transmission was simplified, with the gearbox now in unit with the engine. Strangely enough, this advance was to be reversed for the Phantom III in 1935. The axle was quietened by having hypoid-bevel gearing and the propeller shaft was now of the exposed type. Other and later improvement included centralised chassis lubrication and the gradual adoption of synchromesh gearing. Even so, the general design began to fall behind that of the prestigious continental rivals, particularly in performance and general silence and refinement. The car, however, was still splendidly built of the very best materials and was retired in 1935 in favour of the more advanced Phantom III.

Left: The elegance of a Phantom II hides the real advances in mechanical design compared with the Phantom I.

Rolls-Royce Phantom III

Phantom III models, built from 1935 to 1939
Built by: Rolls Royce Ltd., Britain.
Engine: Twelve cylinders, in 60-degree vee-formation, in seven-bearing light-alloy block/crankcase. Bore and stroke 82.5mm by 114.3mm, 7,338cc (3,.25 × 4.5in, 447.7cu.in). Two detachable light-alloy cylinder heads. Two overhead valves per cylinder, operated by pushrods, rockers and hydraulic tappets from single camshaft mounted in centre of cylinder block 'vee'. Single down-draught twin-choke carburettor. Power and torque figures never quoted by Rolls-Royce.
Transmission: Single-dry-plate clutch, in unit with engine. Separate four-speed, synchromesh manual gearbox (no synchromesh on first gear). Remote-control right-hand gearchange. Open propeller shaft to hypoid-bevel 'live' rear axle.
Chassis: Separate pressed-steel chassis frame, with box-section side members and pressed cruciform, fabricated and tubular cross bracing. Independent front suspension by wishbones and coil springs in oil-filled casing, also containing adjustable hydraulic lever arm dampers. Rear suspension by semi-elliptic leaf springs and anti-roll bar. Hydraulic lever arm dampers. Cam-and-roller steering. Four-wheel, cable-operated brakes, with servo-assistance by motor driven from back of gearbox. Centralised chassis lubrication. 18in centre-lock wire wheels. 7.00 × 18in tyres. Coachwork not supplied by Rolls-Royce. Several approved specialist coachbuilders and a multitude of styles.
Dimensions: Wheelbase 11ft 10in (361cm), track (front) 5ft 3in (160cm), track (rear) 5ft 1in (155cm). Overall length (depending on coachwork) 16ft 10in (513cm). Unladen weight from 5,400lb (2,449kg).
History: Under Sir Henry Royce, Rolls-Royce had stuck too long to the successful traditions of the Ghosts and Phantoms. By the time of his death, in 1933, it was already obvious that the next new 'big' Rolls would have to jump

Above: 'Maharajah' styling made this late-model Phantom II distinctive – later Phantom IIIs were generally more discreetly decorated.

Below: By 1939 a typical Phantom III had become even more impressive and dignified than at first. This splendid machine had an H.J. Mulliner-built four-door body with twin side-mounted spare wheels. The Phantom III was a massive car – about 17 feet long – but the body shape usually disguised this. A complete car could cost between £2,700 and £3,000 depending on details. Most have been lovingly preserved.

forward by a complete generation. The new car, conceived before Royce died, but not revealed until the end of 1935, was a magnificent piece of engineering in all respects. At a stroke, it seemed, Rolls-Royce could once again claim to be making 'The best car in the world'. Logically enough, the new car was called a Phantom III, but there was no part of the old Phantom car carried forward. In that the new design had a separate chassis and was still clothed by the same exclusive band of coachbuilders, there was some family resemblance (and of course the radiator design was not changed), but that was all. The new car's two great innovations were that it had independent front suspension, and that it had a very advanced V12 engine. Neither was altogether unexpected. Independent suspension was well established in North America and becoming fashionable in Europe, while Rolls-Royce themselves (with aero-engines) were already noted for their V12 designs.

The engine itself was new from end to end, except that the bore and stroke were the same as the smaller six-cylinder Rolls-Royce. It leaned heavily on the R-type and Merlin aero-engine experience, with light-alloy castings and wet liners, but the hydraulically operated tappets were a British innovation, inspired from Detroit. It is interesting to know that Roll-Royce had been experimenting with new engines for many years; the most promising alternative had been a straight-eight. A V8 had also been considered,. But rejected as it was neither exclusive enough, nor smooth enough to satisfy the perfectionist engineers. The new V12, although never officially given a power output by the discreet management, was nevertheless man enough to propel cars weighing up to 6,000lb (2,721kg) at more than 90mph. Fuel consumption, on the other hand, rarely amounted to better than about 10mpg, but to a Rolls-Royce owner this was not something for him to worry about. In 1935, when announced, the Phantom III cost more than £2,500 with the cheapest of the RR-approved bodies, which made it easily the most expensive of all British cars. Only hand-built machines like the best of Hispano-Suiza, or the virtually unobtainable

Grosser Mercedes, were as costly.

It has to be said that the car was not necessarily the fastest, nor even the grandest, of all, but it had a combination of virtues quite unmatched by any other make and model of car at the time. The suspension, in fact, was very advanced for the period and exceptionally so for an enormous prestige car. It was based on a General Motors design and Rolls-Royce paid royalties for the privilege of using it. The chassis, certainly, was very stiff and the handling was better than almost any other large saloon in the world. Even so, it was as an ultra-dignified town carriage that the Phantom III sold so well and the company notched up an impressive list of titled customers.

British coachbuilders produced a variety of sumptuous bodies for the chassis, some of them surprisingly sporting, but the car was most often seen as an ultra-sophisticated town carriage or limousine. Very few Phantom IIIs were driven by their first owners, which must have been a source of great joy to their chauffeurs. There was a vast amount of space in the rear seat area where the titled or moneyed owner would normally recline and much work went into making the ride first class.

In spite of its price and in spite of the work that had gone into the design, the V12 engine was not immune from lubrication problems. The hydraulic tappets, in particular, demanded absolutely clean and well-filtered oil to work properly, which was a source of worry to second and subsequent owners. The Phantom III went out of production at the end of 1939, with the outbreak of war, and would have been much too expensive to re-introduce in 1945/46. It was, and is, the most exclusive of all pre-war production-line Rolls-Royce cars, a total of 710 being built in about four years.

Below: An owner-driver Phantom III, by the Barker coachbuilders. This was built in 1936, but the same style was shown at Olympia in 1935 as a 'non-runner'.

Rolls-Royce Phantoms V and VI

Phantom V built 1959-1968, Phantom VI 1968 to 1992 (data for original Phantom V)
Built by: Rolls-Royce Ltd., Britain.
Engine: Eight cylinders in 90-degree vee-formation, in five-bearing cast-alloy combined block/crankcase. Bore and stroke 104.1 × 91.4mm, 6,230cc (4.09 × 3.59in, 380cu.in). Detachable cast-alloy cylinder heads. Two valves per cylinder, in overhead valve layout, with operation by pushrods and rocker from single camshaft mounted in centre of 'vee'. Two semi-downdraught SU carburettors. Power output and torque figures never quoted by Rolls-Royce.
Transmission: Four-speed automatic transmission with fluid coupling, in unit with front-mounted engine. Steering-column mounted change control. Open-propeller shaft to hypoid-bevel 'live' rear axle.
Chassis: Separate pressed-steel chassis frame, with box-section side members, pressed-steel cruciform and cross-bracings. Independent front suspension by coil springs, wishbones, and anti-roll bar. Rear suspension by half-elliptic leaf springs. Lever-arm hydraulic dampers, adjustable for stiffness at rear. Cam-and-lever steering, with power assistance. Four-wheel drum brakes, with hydraulic operation, and servo assistance from friction servo mounted on transmission. 15in pressed-steel disc wheels. 8.90-15in tyres. Ceremonial four-door limousine coachwork by specialist coachbuilders, mainly by Mulliner-Park Ward, or James Young.
Dimensions: Wheelbase 12ft 1in (368cm), track (front) 5ft 0.9in (154.6cm), track (rear) 5ft 4in (163cm). Overall length 19ft 10in (624cm). Unladen weight from 5,600lb (2,540kg), depending on options fitted.
History: After the Second World War, the continuous run of Rolls-Royce 'Phantom' models was broken for some years until, between 1950 and 1956, 16 virtually hand-built Phantom IV models were supplied exclusively to royalty, and to heads of state. Until 1959, therefore, the largest series-production Rolls-Royce was the Silver Wraith.

In 1955, however, the new Rolls-Royce Silver Cloud/S-Series Bentley car had been revealed, and in 1959 this car was updated by the insertion of a brand-new light-alloy vee-8 engine, said to have been influenced by the layout of current Cadillac units. It was a stretched version of the Silver Cloud II chassis, with a lengthy (145in) wheelbase, which was chosen as the basis of a new 'standard'

Above: The Phantom V had two headlamps, while the Phantom VI had four, but both shared the same massive, but dignified, limousine body style. If needed, the car could exceed 100mph, but it was more at ease gliding gracefully through city streets. Air conditioning was standard.

Phantom – the Phantom V.

Like the majority of Rolls-Royce cars ordered for ceremonial and the highest commercial purposes, all Phantom Vs were fitted with massive, but graceful coachbuilt body shells. A few were supplied to 'approved' concerns like James Young to erect their own type of body style, but the vast majority of all Phantom Vs had the 'standard' six/seven seater limousine style by Mulliner-Park Ward of London, which was a Rolls-Royce subsidiary. Naturally these cars featured a division, to isolate the chauffeur from the rear seat occupants, and it was normal to find two foldaway 'jump' seats at the front of this compartment.

The Phantom Vs were not meant to be high-performance cars, but they could still reach 100mph. On the other hand, they were ideally built for creeping slowly and majestically through heavy traffic, aided by the GM-built automatic transmission, and by the impeccable low-speed manners of the vee-8 engine. They were big and heavy cars, but extremely dignified, with an enormous amount of space in the rear compartment, which contrasted strongly with a rather cramped driving position. Air conditioning was standard, and the scope and quality of the fittings was of the highest possible standard. Even after the Silver Cloud series was dropped in 1965, the Phantom V, complete with its drum brakes and its mechanical friction servo, carried on. By 1968, no fewer than 832 Phantom Vs had been built, at which point the Phantom VI was announced. This was mainly distinguished by the use of separate front and rear air conditioning, but unchanged styling. A further 311 were built before 1978, by which time production was down to fewer than 30 cars a year; from this time the enlarged 6,750cc engine was fitted, and the car was still being built in the early 1980s.

H.M. The Queen has been supplied with three special Phantoms of this type, all with raised roof lines and extra glass and 'perspex' rear panels to increase the crowds' visibility of her. This body style is affectionately known at Mulliner-Park Ward as the 'Canberra' style, and was never made available to any other customer.

Left: A Phantom VI was always special, but the landaulette was very rare indeed. The drop-down hood was power-operated, of course, automatic transmission was standard, and no Phantom VI owner would be without the fitted drinks box.

Rolls-Royce Silver Ghost

Silver Ghosts, built from 1906 to 1925 (data for 1907 model)
Built by: Rolls-Royce Ltd., Britain.
Engine: Six cylinders, in line, in two groups of three cast-iron blocks, bolted to seven-bearing light-alloy crankcase. Bore and stroke 114.3mm by 114.3mm, 7,036cc (4.5in × 4.5in, 429cu.in). Non-detachable cylinder heads. Two side valves per cylinder, with springs and shafts exposed, operated by rockers and anti-friction rollers from single crankcase-mounted camshaft. Single Rolls-Royce/Krebs two-jet carburettor. Power and torque figures never quoted by Rolls-Royce.
Transmission: Cone clutch, in unit with engine, and separately mounted four-speed manual gearbox (without synchromesh). Right-hand gearchange. Open propeller shaft to straight-bevel 'live' rear axle.
Chassis: Separate pressed-steel chassis frame, with channel-section side members and tubular and pressed cross braces. Forged front axle beam. Front suspension by semi-elliptic front springs. Rear suspension of 'platform' type by semi-elliptic leaf springs, with rear extremities attached to single transverse leaf spring bolted centrally to the chassis frame. From 1908, Rolls-Royce friction-type dampers. Worm-and-nut steering. Foot-operated contracting-shoe brake acting on propeller shaft drum behind gearbox. Hand-operated expanding shoe brake in rear-wheel drums. Non-detachable artillery-type wood-spoke wheels. 875 × 105 front tyres and 875 × 120 rear tyres.
Dimensions: Wheelbase 11ft 3.5in, or 11ft 11.5in (344cm or 364cm), tracks (front and rear) 4ft 8in (142cm). Overall length, depending on coachwork, from 15ft 3.8in (467cm). Unladen weight (chassis only), from about 2,646lb (1,117kg).
History: Strictly speaking there has only ever been one 'Silver Ghost' – the car built up by Rolls-Royce on the thirteenth chassis, with a silver-painted touring body and silver-plated fittings, and given that name by them in 1907. A more conventional title would be the '40/50', which denotes the engine type and power rating, but as this could be confused with later Phantoms it is never used.

The Ghost was conceived by Henry Royce in 1905 as a complete redesign of the six-cylinder Thirty which the company had been making for a short time. While the Thirty had suffered from all manner of technical problems in its engine, mainly concerned with the vibration characteristics of a long six, the Ghost was almost immediately very reliable; it was magnificently built and rightly became a legend in its own lifetime. Around 8,000 Ghosts were built in total, between 1907 and 1926, of which just over 1,700 were built by Rolls-Royce of America at Springfield, Massachusetts. In spite of the fact that the car was no more than technically up-to-date when announced and well behind the times when dropped, it always seemed to perform better and in a more refined manner than any of its contemporaries and it was with this car that the 'best car in the world' reputation was established. While the engineering, in many cases, was matched by concerns like Napier and Lanchester, the workmanship and the care taken in building were peerless.

The car was available with a variety of splendidly built bodies – Rolls-Royce never built their own bodies at this point in their development – and a really well-equipped and kitted-out limousine of the type purchased by the gentry could weigh as much as 5,000lb (2,268kg). There were two wheelbase lengths, the shorter of which measured 11ft 3.5in, and a long, low, and exquisitely riveted bonnet panel leading back from the Rolls-Royce radiator, whose shape was becoming famous, and which was scarcely to need change in the next seventy years.

The engine, although conventionally laid out, with side valves, was meticulously detailed, even to the extent of having rocking levers between the camshaft and the valve stems themselves. It had a very sturdy crankshaft,

Above: This unique Silver Ghost, built in 1907, and now owned by Rolls-Royce, has silver-plated fitting.

which defied the onset of torsional vibrations, and ran very silently indeed at all times. Despite the deliberately conventional design, and none better than Royce realised how it was slipping back in the 1920s, there were significant improvements over the years. The engine itself was 'stroked' to 7,428cc in 1909. The original gearbox had an 'overdrive' fourth gear at first, but three speeds were used between 1909 and 1913, after which a direct-top arrangement was restored. The platform-type of rear suspension soon gave way to normal semi-elliptic springs, and to cantilevers from1912. The straight-bevel axle, not silent enough for Royce, was replaced by a spiral-bevel design in 1923. A Lanchester-type engine torsional damper was added from 1911. Dynamo current generation was adopted from 1919. The footbrake operated on a transmission drum at first, but on rear wheel drums from 1913. Four-wheel brakes arrived in 1924, along with the unique RR-type of transmission-driven servo. Hartford dampers were standardised in 1924. Wire wheels became optional in 1909, and were standardised in 1913.

At no time was the Silver Ghost a design leader, but at all times it was the best built and most carefully tested car in the world. It was never ostentatious, but always most obviously dignified. It was very expensive to buy, and was invariably tended by a full-time chauffeur with a heated motor-house and workshop at his disposal. It was the best, for the best, and expected the best treatment. It would have to be replaced by a supreme design – and the Phantom I was that design.

Below: A more typical four-seater 40/50 'Ghost' with timeless and elegant styling. About 8,000 were made.

Rolls-Royce Silver Shadow and Camargue

Silver Shadow four-door, four-door long-wheelbase, and coachbuilt two-door Corniche, built from 1965 to 1994 (data for 1966 Shadow)
Built by: Rolls-Royce Ltd. (since 1971, Rolls-Royce Motors Ltd.), Britain.
Engine: Eight cylinders, in 90-degree vee-formation, in five-bearing cast-alloy cylinder block. Bore and stroke 104.4mm by 91.4mm, 6,230cc (4.1in × 3.6in, 380cu.in). Two light-alloy cylinder heads. Two overhead valves per cylinder, inclined in wedge combustion chambers and operated by pushrods, hydraulic tappets and rockers, from single camshaft mounted in cylinder block 'vee'. Two side-draught constant-vacuum SU carburettors. Neither power nor torque figures quoted by Rolls-Royce.
Transmission: General Motors/Rolls-Royce four-speed automatic transmission, with torque converter. Steering-column gearchange. No manual transmission option. One-piece open propeller shaft to subframe-mounted hypoid-bevel final-drive unit. Exposed, universally jointed drive shafts to rear wheels.

Below: The Silver Shadow style, introduced in 1965, was still appropriate in 1980. From 1977 the Shadow II was the best of the bunch, with rack-and-pinion steering.

Above: No mistaking that radiator. Although it looked completely different from the old Silver Cloud, the technically advanced Silver Shadow was unmistakeable.

Chassis: Unitary-construction pressed-steel four-door saloon body/chassis unit. Front and rear suspensions mounted on pressed-steel subframes, attached to main shell. Independent front suspension by wishbones, coil springs and anti-roll bar. Independent rear suspension by semi-tailing wishbones and coil springs. Telescopic dampers and self-levelling controls. Power-assisted recirculating-ball steering. Four-wheel disc brakes with multiple hydraulic circuits. 15in pressed-steel-disc wheels. 8.45 × 15 in tyres.
Dimensions: Wheelbase 9ft 11.5in (304cm), tracks (front and rear) 4ft 9.5in (146cm). Overall length 16ft 11.5in (417cm). Unladen weight 4,636lb (2,100kg).
History: After nearly ten years, development of systems and components,Rolls-Royce announced their new Silver Shadow in 1965. Apart from the 6.2-litre light-alloy V8 engine and the four-speed automatic transmission, carried over from the superseded Silver Cloud model, the Shadow was an all-new concept. No previous Rolls had used a unitary-construction body shell, and none had offered independent rear suspension, let alone a complex but effective self-levelling control system. Four-wheel disc brakes were new, as was the safety-conscious duplicated hydraulic circuitry which went with them. Every effort had gone into eliminating extraneous noises from the cabin and the suspensions were most carefully mounted on insulated sub-frames. There was also the Bentley T-Series, identical with the Shadow except for its radiator and badging. This badge engineering was no stigma and both cars continue to this day. Although the Shadow was in production for 16 years, it was still mechanically abreast of the times at the end. The styling was always meant to be 'timeless' and it remains so, but it is now very familiar. Production crept up over the years – the factory at Crewe built 3,347 cars in 1978 – every one of them pre-sold before being completed.

Coachbuilders had a hard time making special bodies for the Shadow. Only Mulliner-Park Ward (owned by Rolls-Royce) were supplied with rolling underbody units. Only 50 of the James Young two-door saloon were made, these being converted from complete four-door cars. The Mulliner cars – a two door coupé and a two-door convertible – were announced in 1966. In 1971, the Mulliner cars were updated and re-named Corniches, becoming official members of the Rolls-Royce Shadow family. In the late 1960s, too, a longer-wheelbase Shadow (with or without division) had been announced, although this was never badged as a Bentley. Over the years many mechanical improvements have unobtrusively been phased in. A new three-speed automatic transmission arrived in 1968 and in 1970 the engine was enlarged, by lengthening the stroke, to 6,750cc. Major suspension revisions and flared wheel arches to accommodate fatter tyres were phased in in 1974 and in 1976 a further facia revision was incorporated. Shadow II was announced in 1977. Now, as then, Rolls-Royce like to think of their car as 'The Best Car in the World'. The Corniche outlived the Shadow which was dropped in 1980.

ROLLS-ROYCE CAMARGUE

Camargue Coupé, built from 1975 to 1986
Built by: Rolls-Royce Motors Ltd., Britain.
Specification as for Rolls-Royce Silver Shadow, except for engine with single Solex carburettor. Special two-door light-alloy closed four-seater coachwork by Mulliner-Park Ward.
Dimensions: Wheelbase 10ft (305cm), track (front) 5ft (152cm), track (rear) 4ft 11.5in (151cm). Overall length 16ft 11.5in (417cm). Unladen weight 5,175lb (2,347kg).
History: The Camargue, quite simply, is the most expensive production car in the world. Roll-Royce conceived it that way. The Camargue, in Britain, is double the price of a Silver Shadow saloon. It is based on the same chassis and power train as the Silver Shadow, except that further work has taken place on the engine to reduce emissions. A feature is the automatic air-conditioning, standard to every Camargue, claimed to be the most advanced in the world. Originally the cars were painstakingly assembled by Mulliner- Park Ward, but now take shape at Crewe. No more than one

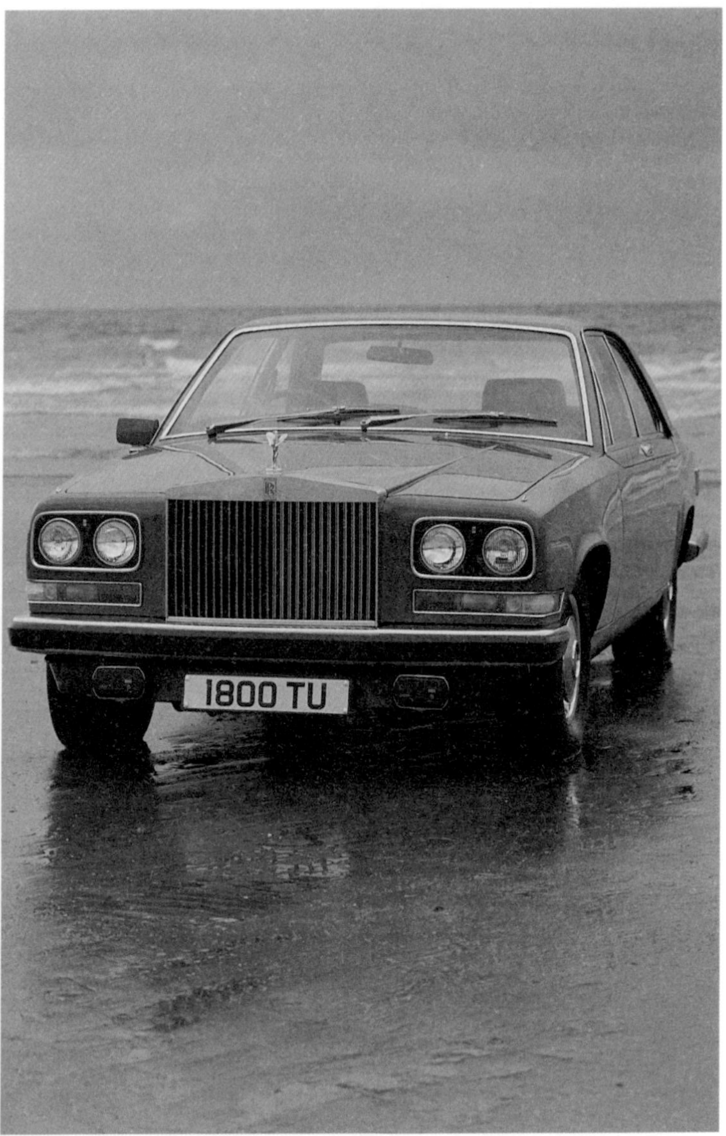

Above: The Camargue was the only Rolls-Royce ever to be styled by Pininfarina. This four-seater coupé was once one of the world's most exclusive cars. Production did not exceed 50 cars a year.

Camargue is built in a week. Styling was by Pininfarina, to a Rolls-Royce brief, and the classic radiator shell has been retained. Even so, for all that money, it is more difficult to get into the rear seats than the shadow and the performance is in no way improved. On exclusiveness alone, however, the Camargue is extremely desirable. Almost every example built is earmarked for an export market.

Rolls-Royce Silver Wraith

Silver Wraith models, built from 1947 to 1959 (data for 1947 model)
Built by: Rolls-Royce Ltd., Britain.
Engine: Six cylinders, in line, in seven-bearing cast-iron block/crankcase. Bore and stroke 88.9mm by 114.3mm, 4,257cc (3.5in × 4.5in, 259.8cu.in). Detachable aluminium cylinder head. Two valves per cylinder, overhead inlet and side exhaust, in so-called 'F-Head' layout; exhaust valve directly operated and inlet valve operated by pushrod and rocker, from single side-mounted camshaft. Single down-draught twin-choke Stromberg carburettor (downdraught Zenith on long-wheelbase models). Power and torque figures never quoted by Rolls-Royce.
Transmission: Single-dry-plate clutch and four-speed, synchromesh manual gearbox (no synchromesh on first gear), both in unit with engine. Remote-control right-hand gearchange. Two-piece open propeller shaft to hypoid-bevel 'live' rear axle.
Chassis: Separate pressed-steel chassis frame. Channel-section side members, with pressed-cruciform members and pressed and tubular cross bracing. Independent front suspension by coil springs and wishbones, with cross-coupled hydraulic lever arm dampers. Rear suspension by semi-elliptic leaf springs and controllable lever arm hydraulic dampers. Cam-and-roller steering. Four-wheel drum brakes, hydraulically operated at front, mechanically operated at rear, and assisted by gearbox-driven mechanical servo. 17in pressed-steel-disc wheels. 6.50 × 17in tyres (7.50 × 16in tyres on long-wheelbase versions).
Dimensions: Wheelbase 10ft 7in or 11ft 1in (322.5cm or 337.8cm), track (front) 4ft 10in (147.3cm), track (rear – short wheelbase) 5ft (152.4cm) track (rear – long wheelbase) 5ft 4in (162.6cm). Overall length 16ft 8in or 17ft 2in (508cm or 523cm). Unladen weight, depending on coachwork, from 4,700lb (2,131kg).
History: The Silver Wraith was purely a post war model, but it stemmed from the pedigree of both the 1939-model Wraith and the Mark V Bentley. The pre-war Wraith was a much modernised 25/30, but with a new welded-construction chassis and independent front suspension like that of the Phantom III. After the war, the Silver Wraith took on the mantle of the company's most expensive model (and was export-only for some time), along with the exposed-spring front suspension and a newly developed engine. This unit, of overhead-inlet, side-

Above: Every Silver Wraith was provided with a body erected by an independent coachbuilder. This particular car carries a particularly graceful Park Ward style.

exhaust layout, was also shared with the new Bentley models and with the Silver Dawn, which followed, and was the final derivative of the 1920s-type Twenty design. In this guise it displaced 4,257cc, but before the end of its life it was to be bored out twice more – to 4,566cc and finally to 4,887cc. The Wraith was important because it was the only Rolls-Royce model supplied to coachbuilders in chassis form specifically for their attention. Post-war Bentleys and the Silver Dawn had a standard steel saloon body shell (although chassis were also supplied to coachbuilders to special order). The Silver Wraith was in production for twelve years, during with automatic transmission, power-assisted steering and many other improvements were standardised. Even though disc brakes were fitted by many British manufacturers in the late1950s, they were never offered on the Wraith, which continued to use the famous transmission-driven servo for its drums. When the all-new Rolls-Royce V8 engine was launched in 1959, it was fitted to the Phantom V chassis, which replaced that of the Wraith and continuity with the 1920s was finally lost.

Left: Over the years Silver Wraiths were produced in many guises. This short-wheelbase model carried a semi-razor-edge style by one of the company's favoured coachbuilders, Hooper.

Simplex 50HP

Simplex 50hp, built from 1907 to 1914 (data for 1907 model)
Built by: Simplex Automobile Co. Inc., United States.
Engine: Four cylinders, in line, two cast-iron blocks, with three-bearing light-alloy crankcase. Bore and stroke 146.1mm by 146.1mm, 9,797cc (5.75in × 5.75in, 598cu.in). Non-detachable cast-iron cylinder heads. Two side valves per cylinder, in T-head layout with exposed valve stems and springs, operated by tappets from two camshafts, each in separate cast tunnel on outside of crankcase. One up-draught carburettor.
Transmission: Cone clutch, in unit with front-mounted engine, separate four-speed manual gearbox (without synchromesh). Remote-control right-hand gearchange. Straight-bevel differential in tail of gearbox and countershaft to sprockets. Final drive to rear wheels by twin side chains.
Chassis: Separate pressed-steel chassis frame, with channel-section side members and pressed and tubular cross bracings. Forged front axle beam. Front and rear suspension by semi-elliptic leaf springs. Friction-type dampers. Worm-and-sector steering. Foot brake, mechanically operated, by contracting bands on gearbox countershaft drums. Hand brake, mechanically operated, on rear wheels drums. Fixed artillery-style road wheels 35 × 5in tyres. Choice of coachwork, open or closed touring or saloon.

Dimensions: Wheelbase 10ft 6in (320cm), tracks (front and rear) 4ft 8in (142cm). Unladen weight, depending on coachwork, from 3,750lb (1,701kg).
History: The Simplex car evolved from the Smith and Mabley motor agents in New York. At first they sold Mercédès, Panhard and Renault cars, but in 1904 they began to build a Smith and Mabley Simplex car, first of 18hp and later of 30hp. The company went out of business in 1907, but the moribund concern was acquired by Herman Broesel, who had a vast new 9.8-litre 50hp car designed and called it – simply – a Simplex. The company was only to live for ten years, but the original chain-drive 50 was always part of the range. It was a big, expensive ($4,500 for the chassis alone) and exclusive car, with bodies from prestigious coachbuilders. The mechanical layout was typical of the period, but the engine had a lot of potential, as stripped models proved time and time again on the American race tracks. By 1911, there was a shaft-driven 38hp model being built alongside the 50 and in 1912, the massive 75 (still with chain drive) was introduced as a faster version of the 50 model.

A change of company ownership in 1914 spelt the end for the classic Simplex car and the big 50 disappeared. No more Simplexes were built after 1917. There were two types of radiator fitted to these cars – one a conventional Mercédès-type flat unit and the other a sharply pointed vee radiator.

Below: As suggested by its name, the Simplex was mechanically simple, but sold for a very grand price. This 50hp model was built in 1909 – the 75hp car was even faster and more massive.

Squire

Squire cars, built from 1934 to 1936 (data for 1934 1½-litre)
Built by: Squire Car Manufacturing Co. Ltd. Britain.
Engine: Anzani manufactured. Four cylinders, in line, in cast-iron block, with four-bearing light-alloy crankcase. Bore and stroke 69mm by 100mm, 1,496cc (2.72in × 3.94in, 91.3cu.in). Detachable light-alloy cylinder head. Two overhead valves per cylinder, opposed to each other at 90 degrees in hemispherical combustion chambers and operated by steel tappets from twin overhead camshafts. One horizontal constant-vacuum SU carburettor and Roots-type supercharger. Maximum power 110bhp (gross) at 5,000rpm.
Transmission: No separate clutch. Separate Wilson-type preselector gearbox, with clutch take-up by gear friction bands. Remote-control central gearchange. Open propeller shaft to spiral-bevel 'live' rear axle.
Chassis: Separate pressed-steel chassis frame, with channel-section side members, tubular and pressed cross-bracing and pressed cruciform. Forged front axle beam. Front and rear suspension by semi-elliptic leaf springs and lever-arm hydraulic dampers. Marles Weller steering. Four-wheel, hydraulically operated drum brakes. 18in centre-lock wire wheels 5.00 × 18in tyres (Short chassis); 5.25 × 18in tyres for long chassis.
Dimensions: Wheelbase 8ft 6in or 10ft 3in (259cm or 312.5cm), tracks (front and rear) 4ft 6in (137cm). Overall length 13ft or 14ft 9in (396cm or 450cm). Unladen weight (chassis only) 1,680lb or 1,740lb (762kg or 789kg).
History: The Squire sports car, as a commercial proposition, was doomed right from the start. It was one man's dream of his ideal machine, to be sold in small numbers to the public. Nothing was allowed to interfere with his dream, certainly not the questions of costs and profits. The car itself was one of the most exciting-looking and best detailed of all the British post-vintage thoroughbreds. Its two most impressive features in 1934, when it was announced, were the sleek and lovely looks (this was at a time when many body

Above: Built in 1935, the unique Squire 'featherweight' had an eye to competitions, and not to elegance. It used the short chassis, and super-tuned twin-cam Anzani engine.

Below: The 1½-litre supercharged Squire was one man's dream car – made in tiny numbers (nine in all) by Adrian Squire's little company near Henley-on-Thames. Almost everything was bought out, including the elegant and rakish bodies. This beautiful two-seater style was by Vanden Plas.

designers were still reluctant to consider sweeping lines on a sports car) and its unique twin-camshaft supercharged engine.

Adrian Squire had cherished the ambition of building his own sports car since he had been at school. An engineering apprenticeship was followed by spells of work with Bentley at Cricklewood and with MG at Abingdon, before the 21-year-old Squire moved into a cottage on Remenham Hill, near Henley. There a small garage and filling station was established, and later he also acquired showrooms in Henley-on-Thames. Design on the Squire car began in 1933 and the manufacturing company was founded in January 1934 with capital of only £6,000.

Squire were too small to make much of their own cars, so they contracted to buy engines from British Anzani, gearboxes from ENV (of the preselector Wilson type) and axles from the same source. The engine was unique in Britain in that it was a supercharged twin-cam unit. Its origins were in a special car raced by Archie Frazer-Nash in 1927/28, but the supercharging was Squire's own idea. It was a very powerful unit, but not at all refined or quiet, as the camshaft drive was by a train of gears with considerable backlash, and valve clearances were always very high. The chassis itself was conventional enough, but rather more rigid than was usual, with a stout cruciform member behind the gearbox. Suspension was entirely 'British conventional', as Squire's own aspirations had not yet experienced the latest European independent suspensions. Such was the flexibility (and small scale) of Squire's operations, that they built the first three cars with overslung rear frames and the remainder with underslung frames.

The most immediately striking aspect of the Squire apart from its engine noise, was the styling. The general layout was conventional enough – there were only two seats and the usual 'build-up' weather protection – but the vee-profile radiator was swept back to make the nose distinctly rakish and both front

and rear wings were well swept with delicately profiled skirts. The very first car, bodied by Vanden Plas, looked reminiscent of a Bugatti from some angles and of an Aston Martin from a few others, but was unmistakably a Squire. In the manner of the 1930s, a great proportion of the body was taken over by mechanical components, but on the first car there was even an enclosed tail for the spare wheel and big petrol tank.

There was no doubt that it was going to be an expensive car – at £1,220 complete with body it rivalled a 3½-litre Bentley – but, with a 100mph maximum speed, individual craftsmanship in the construction and the promise of exclusivity, Squire was confident enough. The tragedy was that although hundreds of enquiries were received after the car's first showing, they were not backed by firm orders. Within two years that part of Squire's activities had failed financially and it is a sad commentary that of only seven cars built, no fewer than four of them were first owned by Squire themselves, or by Squire directors.

Even though the asking price was slashed in 1935 to less than £1,000, there was no demand for this elegant but costly device. By then, unfortunately, SS had released the SS100 two-seater and had rendered most other people's prices obsolete. The company had to be wound up; all the spare parts were sold off and Squire himself moved to Staines where he rejoined W.O. Bentley at Lagonda. Then, during the war, Squire worked for the Bristol Aeroplane Company and was tragically killed in an air-raid. Val Zethrin, of Kent, bought up a lot of parts and managed to assemble two more Squires before the war, but total production of all Squires, including the single-seater which raced at Brooklands, was no more than nine. All but the single-seater survive to this day.

Below: The 1 1/2-litre supercharged Squire was Adrian Squire's dream car, with an Anzani engine. The open sports-car style was by Vanden Plas.

Stanley Steam Cars

Steam models, built from 1897 to 1907 (data for 1907 Ex model)
Built by: Stanley Manufacturing Co. (later Stanley Motor Carriage Co.), United States.
Engine: Two cylinders, horizontally positioned in parallel, in cast-iron casings. Bore and stroke 76.2mm by 101.6mm, 926cc (3.0in × 4.0in, 56.5cu.in). Stevenson's Link valve-gear motion, and double-acting porting. Vertical fire-tube boiler, with 450 18in tubes. Normal steam working pressure 380lb per sq.in. Furnace heated by kerosene. Power output 10bhp at 380lb per sq.in steam pressure, rising to 28bhp at 650lb per sq.in.
Transmission: By spur gear from engine crankshaft to toothed ring on differential gear of 'live' rear axle. No reverse gear, except by reversing valve motion.

Chassis: Wooden chassis frame supporting body. Tubular front axle, linked to 'live' rear axle by light tubular steel underframe. Fully elliptic leaf springs at front and rear. No dampers. Worm-and-wheel steering. Foot-operated contracting-band brake on differential housing. Hand-operated internally expanding drums on rear wheels. Emergency braking by reversing valve motion and admitting steam. Wood-spoked artillery wheels. 30 × 3in tyres.
Dimensions: Wheelbase 7ft 6in (229cm), tracks (front and rear) 4ft 8in (142cm), overall length 10ft 3in (312cm). Unladen weight 1,400lb (635kg).

Below: The Stanley steamer belongs to North American folklore, like the Curved Dash Oldsmobile and the Model T Ford. This beautiful Model EX was one of the last made. Note the high frame and full elliptic springs.

History: In the earliest days of motoring, steam engines were immeasurably more reliable and powerful than petrol engines. Their disadvantages were – then as now – that engine auxiliaries (furnace, condenser and other details) were more complex than the engine itself. Water consumption was always a big problem and the more efficient little units had intricate plumbing. The first-ever Stanley runabout was a frail little thing completed by F.E. Stanley in 1897. He was joined by his brother in 1899. By then only four cars had been sold, but hundreds of orders received. To fulfil the promise the business was sold to Locomobile.

A feature of all Stanleys of the period was the light tubular underframe connecting both axles together. Bodies had their own chassis frame (of wood) and also carried the steam engine and works. The frames were separated by elliptical leaf springs (a transverse spring on the early Stanleys). The first two-cylinder car had its engine positioned vertically under the seats, with the valve-motion open to attack by dust and mud. The boiler, placed behind the engine,

was simple, but with the drawback that the water level had to be constantly watched. Surprisingly condensers (to improve water consumption) were optional extras.

Locomobile had lost faith in steam cars by 1903 and they sold back the rights to the Stanley brothers, who celebrated this by producing the EX model in 1904. This was so successful that it remained in production until 1909. There were no fundamental changes, although the tubular frame was now sprung on fully elliptic leaf springs all round and the burner was redesigned to run on high-grade kerosene. Boiler and furnace were moved up front, under the 'bonnet', and the two-cylinder engine was horizontally placed under the floor, with its crankshaft directly geared to the back axle. Cruising speed was about 30mph, but, with judicious over pressurising of the steam engine, up to 50mph was possible. The range between stops for water, because of a big tank, was now 40 to 50 miles.

Stanley steam cars, in progressively improved form, were made until 1927.

Below: Not only the engine, but the layout of Stanley cars was unusual. Axles were connected by a frame and the body had a separate frame, with the two-cylinder engine under the floor, geared to the axle.

Stutz Bearcat

Bearcat, built from 1914 to 1917 in original design (data for 1914 model)
Built by: The Stutz Motor Car Co. of America, United States.
Engine: Wisconsin manufactured. Four cylinders, in line, in cast-iron block, with three-bearing light-alloy crankcase. Bore and stroke 120.6mm by 139.7mm, 6,388cc (4.75in × 5.5in, 390cu.in). Non-detachable cylinder head. Two side valves per cylinder, in T-head layout single up-draught carburettor. Maximum power about 60hp at 1,500rpm.
Transmission: Cone clutch, in unit with front-mounted engine, and shaft drive to three-speed manual gearbox (without synchromesh), in unit with straight-bevel 'live' rear axle. Remote-control right-hand gearchange.
Chassis: Separate pressed-steel chassis frame, with tubular and pressed cross bracing. Forged front axle beam. Front and rear suspension by semi-elliptic leaf springs. Optional friction-type dampers. Worm-type steering. Rear-brakes only. Choice of artillery-style wheels with detachable rims, or centre-lock wire wheels.
History: Harry C. Stutz's famous Bearcat sports car was also one of the very first cars his Indianapolis-based company ever designed. His first products were racing cars, from 1911 on-wards, but the Stutz Motor Car Co. was founded in 1913 and announced the Bearcat for 1914 production. The racing Stutz cars helped pave the way for the Bearcat, but this had also been obviously developed with an eye to the Mercer Raceabout, which it resembled visually and whose

Below: The stark and purposeful Stutz Bearcat of 1914, with that distinctive monocle windscreen for the driver. The engine was a 6.4-litre.

market it sought to invade. Like the Raceabout, the Bearcat was a big-engined rough-and-ready sports car, of the type where hairy-chested behaviour and performance was thought all-important. There were two seats, but no doors and certainly no windscreen. The driver had a 'monocle' screen to protect him from the flies and debris, but the passenger had nothing at all. The uncompromising bonnet hid a big and conventional 6.4-litre engine and really the only novel fitting in the chassis was the three-speed gearbox; this found itself in unit with the back axle, which had been a Stutz-built speciality for several years.

One reason behind the car's fame was that a team of racing cars, the White Squadron, performed well in 1915. These cars had special sixteen-valve overhead camshaft engines of 4.8-litres, and were far from standard, but this did not deter the customers. Cannonball Baker also used a Bearcat to break the Atlantic-Pacific record in 1916 – by an astonishing margin and without any mechanical problems.

More than any other, this one model reminds the world of Stutz, even though there were many other, more practical, products from that stable in Indianapolis before the last car of all was assembled in 1935. With a wheelbase of 120in, the Bearcat had space for only two seats and there was absolutely no weather protection - but this was a real sports car.

Seldom has a car become so indelibly etched in memory via a single model. Worth a fortune today, the original Bearcat retailed for only $2,000 in 1914, but even in those expansionist days sales were limited. When Stutz started making cars again after World War I, its clientele demanded more comfort, so this exposed-to-the-weather style faded from the scene.

Stutz DV32

DV32 models, built from 1931 to 1935 (data for 1931 model)
Built by: The Stutz Motor Car Co. of America, United States.
Engine: Eight cylinders, in line, in nine-bearing cast-iron block/crankcase. Bore and stroke 85.72mm by 114.3mm, 5,277cc (3.37in × 4.5in, 322cu.in). Detachable cast-iron cylinder head. Four overhead valves per cylinder, opposed to each other and operated by inverted pistons attached to valve stems from twin overhead camshafts. Up-draught twin-choke Schebler carburettor. Maximum power 156bhp (gross) at 3,900rpm. Maximum torque 300lb.ft at 2,400rpm.
Transmission: Single-dry-plate clutch and four-speed manual gearbox, both in unit with font-mounted engine. Direct-acting central gearchange. Open propeller shaft to underslung-worm-drive 'live' rear axle.
Chassis: Separate pressed-steel chassis frame, with channel-section side members and channel and tubular cross bracing. Forged front axle beam. Semi-elliptic leaf springs at front and rear. Hydraulic dampers. Four-wheel, hydraulically operated drum brakes. Transmission drum handbrake. 18in bolt-on wire wheels. 7.00 × 18in tyres. Variety of coachwork – open or closed styles.
Dimensions: Wheelbase 11ft 2.5in to 12ft 1in (342cm to 368cm), track (front) 4ft 10.5in (148.6cm), track (rear) 4ft 8.4in (143cm). Overall length from 16ft (488cm). Unladen weight from 3,900lb (1,769kg).
History: At a time when the opposition was busy introducing cars with V12 or even V16 engines, Stutz already knew that they had one of the very best chassis in the North American motor industry. Their engineering standards were high and because they lacked the resources – in men or in money – to produce a brand-new 'vee' engine to meet the competition, they elected to produce a splendidly conceived twin-cam version of the Vertical Eight engine, with no fewer than four valves per cylinder. This, of course, explains the new model's title of DV32. Apart from updated bodies to match the new engineering – which incidentally, endowed the car with at least a 100mph maximum speed in open

Above: There were several DV32 styles, all of which looked glorious and purposeful. Power was by a sophisticated 156bhp twin-cam straight-eight engine.

'speed model' form – the car was mechanically much as before. The snag, a very important one in Depression-hit North America, was that the DV32 retailed for nearly $5,000. In spite of being a bravely marketed car of undoubted merit, there were simply not enough customers to keep this sort of model afloat and Stutz, unlike Cadillac, did not have the backing of luckier and more viable partners. Even though the transmission reverted to three-speed (customer preference) in 1932, and the price was cut by $1,000, it meant a slow and lingering death for Stutz.

Left: This 1932-model DV32 has a close-coupled four-seater tourer body style, on a specially shortened 116in-wheelbase chassis. The top speed was more than 100mph.

Stutz Vertical Eight

Vertical Eights, built from 1926 to 1935 (data for 1928 Model BB Black Hawk)

Built by: The Stutz Motor Car Co. of America, United States.

Engine: Eight cylinders, in line, in nine-bearing cast-iron block/crankcase. Bore and stroke 82.55mm by 114.3mm, 4,894cc (3.25in × 4.5in, 298cu.in). Detachable cast-iron cylinder head. Two overhead valves per cylinder, operated by inverted pistons attached to valve shafts, from single overhead camshaft. Up-draught twin-choke Zenith carburettor. Maximum power 115bhp at 3,600rpm. Maximum torque 238lb.ft at 1,600rpm.

Transmission: Single-dry-plate clutch and three-speed manual gearbox (without synchromesh), both in unit with front-mounted engine. Direct-acting central gearchange. Open propeller shaft to underslung-worm-drive rear axle.

Chassis: Separate pressed-steel chassis frame, with channel-section side members and channel and tubular cross bracing. Forged front axle beam. Semi-elliptic leaf springs at front and rear. Hydraulic dampers. Four-wheel hydraulically operated drum brakes. Transmission drum handbrake. 32in centre-lock wire wheels. 6.20 × 32in tyres. Open two-seater sports car bodywork.

Dimensions: Wheelbase 10ft 11in (333cm), track (front) 4ft 10.5in (148.6cm), track (rear) 4ft 8.4in (143cm). Overall length 16ft (488cm). Unladen weight 3,600lb (1,633kg).

History: The original Bearcat had been closely linked with motor sport, but when road racing disappeared from the American scene its attractions too, faded. By 1925 Stutz were in trouble. To pull out of this, Charles Schwab, the new owner of Stutz, enticed Fred Moskovics away from Marmon to become Stutz's president. Under his leadership the famous Vertical Eight Stutz cars were conceived. In one form or another they ran from 1926 to 1935, but the single-cam cars were probably most famous as the Black Hawk sports cars. Cars of this type raced at Le Mans in 1928 and proved to be as fast as the victorious

Bentleys, while in 1929 supercharged versions could achieve no more than fifth place. A much modified Stutz Eight raced at Indianapolis in 1930 and finished a creditable tenth overall. After 1931 the cars were renamed SV16s, because by then the even more exciting DV32 models had been introduced. Stutz Eights looked typical of late-vintage North American cars, but were distinguished under the skin by straight-eight engines and the under-slung-worm-drive back axle.

Above and left: The Stutz Vertical Eight (so named because of the type of engine used) was built for ten years. Both the cars shown were built in 1929. The most famous derivatives were the fast sports 'Black Hawks'.

Subaru Impreza

Subaru Impreza sports saloon, built from 1992 to 2000 (data for original four-wheel-drive 2000 Turbo)

Built by: Fuji Heavy Industries Ltd., Japan.

Engine: Four cylinders, horizontally opposed in 'boxer' formation, in three-main-bearing light-alloy cylinder block. Bore and stroke 92 × 75mm, 1,994cc (3.62 × 2.95in, 121.7cu.in). Two light-alloy cylinder heads. Four valves per cylinder, in vee layout, operation by twin overhead camshafts per cylinder bank. Electronic fuel injection, plus turbocharger. Maximum power 208bhp (DIN) at 6,000rpm. Maximum torque 201lb.ft at 4,800rpm.

Transmission: Four-wheel-drive, single-dry-plate diaphragm spring clutch and five-speed all-synchromesh manual gearbox, all in unit with front-mounted engine. Remote-control, central gearchange.

Chassis: Unitary-construction pressed-steel body-chassis unit, in four-door sports saloon body style. Independent front suspension by MacPherson struts, coil springs, wishbones, telescopic dampers, anti-roll bar. Independent rear suspension by MacPherson struts, coil springs, wishbones, telescopic dampers and anti-roll bar. Rack-and-pinion steering, with hydraulic power assistance. Four-wheel disc brakes, with servo assistance and ABS as standard. Cast light-alloy 15in road wheels, 205/55-15in tyres.

Dimensions: Wheelbase 8ft 3.2in (252cm), front track 4ft 9.5in (146cm), rear track 4ft 9.1in (145cm). Overall length 14ft 2.9in (4,340cm). Unladen weight 2,675lb (1,213kg).

History: Success in motorsport can change the image of a company – completely. Subaru of Japan provides the perfect example. Until the late 1980s, the company was known for producing a series of sturdy, unexciting, but very capable four-wheel-drive cars. Then came the Legacy, then came the rally programme – and the company's reputation was transformed. Although the Legacy looked good, and sold very well all round the world, when the shorter and lighter Impreza arrived in 1993, it made a good chassis behave even better. Top of the range, the 2000 Turbo, not only had a torquey turbocharged 208bhp 2-litre engine, but four-wheel-drive to make it a very secure high-performance machine.

The Impreza was not endowed with sensational styling – although very definitely

Oriental in shape, it was otherwise anonymous – but it had exceptional performance. A developed version of the Legacy's flat-four 'boxer' engine was up front, this having four valves per cylinder, and twin cams per bank, matched to the five-speed gearbox from the same car, and the four-wheel-drive layout which was so very effective.

Even in standard form the 2000 Turbo could nudge 140mph, sprint to 100mph in 18.7 seconds, and it always felt secure on any road surface. Ford's Sierra and Escort RS Cosworths, of course, could do the same, but the new Subaru had one unassailable advantage – it was also much cheaper than its rivals. When British sales of the Impreza began in 1994 the retail price was £17,499 – some £8,000 less than that of the equivalent Ford.

Even if that obvious bargain did not seem to be attractive enough, the car's record in World Championship soon clinched the deal. After winning its first major event in 1994 (Greece), it then went on to provide Colin McRae's World Championship in 1995, and the team won the Constructors' series three years in succession – 1995, 1996 and 1997. Although competition was even more fierce thereafter, the 300bhp-plus Impreza and its development, the Impreza World Car, were still winning rallies at all levels at the start of the 2000s.

At no point was there anything magical about this performance. The engineers, on the other hand, seemed to have left little to chance, noting everything that was good about their opposition, and making sure that the Impreza was better. Outwardly, this was a conventional medium-sized machine, with a choice of four-foor or five-door (sporting estate) styles, and with normal four-seater accomodation. The secret, and the excitement, was all hidden, not only in the cluttered engine bay (no company stylist had been allowed to tidy up the compartment), but in the transmission itself.

To those who knew where to look, however, there were the much enlarged front-end air intakes, which included bigger scoops for the radiator and intercooler and a scoop in the bonnet itself, along with intakes at the corners of the front bumper to keep the disc brakes cool too.

But that was only the start, for as the 1990s progressed, more and yet more exciting limited-edition versions of this car were launched, culminating in the fire-breathing 280bhp versions which delivered 155mph top speeds, and which put almost every other maker of high-performance 'homologation specials' in the shade.

Left: The Impreza Turbo was a great rally car, the 'works' examples having more than 300bhp. This was the limited-edition 'Series McRae', which celebrated Colin's World Rally success in 1995.

Sunbeam Alpine and Tiger

Alpines I, II, III, IV and V, Tigers I and II 1959 to 1968 (data for Tiger I)
Built by: Rootes Ltd., Britain.
Engine: Ford-of-Detroit manufactured. Eight cylinders, in 90-degree vee-formation, in five-bearing cast-iron block. Bore and stroke 96.5mm by 73.0mm, 4,261cc (3.80in × 2.87in, 260cu.in). Two cast-iron cylinder heads. Two overhead valves per cylinder, operated by pushrods and rockers from single camshaft mounted in centre of cylinder block 'vee'. One down-draught twin-choke Ford carburettor. Maximum power torque 258lb.ft at 2,200rpm.
Transmission: Single-dry-plate clutch and four-speed, all-synchromesh manual gearbox, both in unit with engine. Remote-control central gearchange. Open propeller shaft to hypoid-bevel 'live' rear axle.
Chassis: Unitary-construction pressed-steel two-seat sports car body/chassis unit, heavily modified by Jensen from Sunbeam Alpine shell. Independent front suspension by coil springs, wishbones and anti-roll bar. Rear suspension by semi-elliptic leaf springs and Panhard rod. Telescopic dampers. Rack-and-pinion steering. Four-wheel hydraulically operated brakes, front discs and rear drums, vacuum-servo assisted. 13in pressed-steel-disc wheels. 5.90 × 13in tyres. Optional bolt-on steel hardtop.
Dimensions: Wheelbase 7ft 2in (218cm), track (front) 4ft 3.7in (131cm), track (rear) 4ft 0.5in (123cm). Overall length 12ft 11.2in (394cm). Unladen weight 2,640lb (1,197kg).
History: In the early 1950s, Rootes produced a stylish two-seater car, based on a Sunbeam-Talbot saloon, called the Sunbeam Alpine. This was too heavy and cumbersome to be very popular, although it did have some competition successes. In 1959, a new Sunbeam Alpine appeared, this being based on the sport-wheel-base Hillman Husky floorplan and fitted with Sunbeam Rapier engine and transmission. The fashionable finned body was Rootes' own work. In a complex commercial deal involving Rootes having an engine like that of the Armstrong-Siddeley Sapphire for their big Humbers, the Alpine was originally assembled by Armstrong-Siddeley in Coventry. At first the car had a 1½-litre engine, but this was soon enlarged to 1.6 litres. That was the Alpine II. Alpine III came along in the early 1960s, with more refinement and a smart new steel

Left: The Sunbeam Tiger was Rootes's answer to the AC Cobra, and had a similar Ford vee-8 engine squeezed into the modified Alpine body shell. The Tiger II of 1967 had 4.7 litres and 200bhp.

hardtop, but within a year this was superseded by Alpine IV which had its rear fins cropped. In the meantime, Rootes' North American importers looked at the AC Cobra, liked what they saw and engineered a similar prototype transplant of their own. The Sunbeam Tiger, announced in the spring of 1964, was really a Sunbeam Alpine with a 4.2-lite Ford V8, a Borg-Warner four-speed gearbox and a heavy-duty back axle installed, together with many other modifications to keep the engine cool and to make the handling satisfactory and the traction sound. Pressed-Steel produced the bodies (as they did for the Alpine), then Jensen made all the Tiger changes and carried out final assembly on Rootes' behalf. Soon after this, Alpine IV became Alpine V, the engine being enlarged to 1,725cc to match the already specified all-synchromesh gearbox. Both cars were smart and sold well, but unhappily they did not make profits for Rootes. Soon after Chrysler took a financial stake in Rootes they brought political pressure to bear and the rival Ford V8 engine was dropped. This was a shame, as Tiger II, announced for 1967, had been much fiercer with its more powerful 4,727cc (289cu.in) V8 engine. The Alpine V was discontinued in 1968.

Left: The Rootes Alpine had a sleek body style hiding more humble mechanical parts. The floor was from the Hillman Husky, and the power train from the Rapier. The 1959/64 version had more pronounced tail fins. Later cars had an all-synchromesh gearbox. This final version, the 1,725cc Series V, could beat 100mph. The last was built in 1968.

Sunbeam 3-litre Coupe de l'Auto

3-litre, built from 1911 to 1913 (data for 1912 type)
Built by: Sunbeam Motor Car Co. Ltd., Britain.
Engine: Four cylinders, in line, in cast-iron cylinder block, bolted to five-bearing light-alloy crankcase. Bore and stroke 80mm by 149mm, 2,996cc (3.15in × 5.87in, 182.8cu.in). Non-detachable cylinder head. Two side valves per cylinder, completely exposed and directly operated by crankcase-mounted camshaft. Single up-draught Claudel-Hobson carburettor. Maximum power 74bhp at 2,600rpm.
Transmission: Leather-faced cone clutch, in unit with engine, and separate four-speed manual gearbox (without synchromesh). Right-hand gearchange. Open propeller shaft to straight-bevel 'live' rear axle.
Chassis: Separate pressed-steel chassis frame, with channel-section side members and tubular and pressed cross bracing. Forged front axle beam. Semi-elliptic leaf springs front and rear, with Triou friction-type dampers. Worm-and-sector steering. Foot-operated drum brake, on transmission behind the gearbox. Hand-operated brake on rear-wheel-mounted drums. Detachable steel artillery-type road wheels. 815 × 105 (front) and 815 × 120 (rear) Michelin tyres. Open racing type two-seater bodywork, in light alloy. No weather protection and, normally, no wings.
Dimensions: Wheelbase 8ft 11in (272cm), tracks (front and rear) 4ft 6in (137cm), overall length 14ft (427cm). Unladen weight 2,030lb (921kg).
History: The Coupe de l'Auto Sunbeam was developed particularly for a series of races in France and was Louis Coatalen's first real triumph as a designer of very fast cars. Coatalen had worked for Hillman in Coventry before joining Sunbeam in Wolverhampton, and had already designed noted road cars before being encouraged to turn the 12-16 series of 1910 into a competition car. The Coupe de l'Auto was awarded for a race for *voiturette* machines, restricted to a

Above: There was no attempt at streamlining, even by using a radiator cowl, in 1912. A single splash guard protected the driver from the worst of the stones and road water – the passenger had no such luck. There were no front brakes, and the tyre treads were almost smooth.

Below right: Car '3' is the famous 1912 car which (driven by Victor Rigal) won the Coupe de l'Auto race at Dieppe at 65.3mph. These views show the simple construction, and the exposed back axle. Half-elliptic leaf springs were used and the exhaust pipe swept up high to the tail. The car weighed about 2,000lb but could reach more than 90mph. Two people were carried.

minimum weight of 1,764lb (800kg) and with a stroke/bore ratio not more than 2:1. The maximum stroke allowed, too, was 156mm. These restrictions came about because of the freak machines built by French manufacturers a few years previously.

Sunbeams were actually raced in three successive events, between 1911 and 1913, although they would once again have been used in 1914 if the event had not been cancelled because of the outbreak of war. Their basis, at first, was a perfectly standard 12-16 production car chassis, with the addition of friction-type dampers and a modified version of that car's engine. Twin overhead camshafts had not yet been 're-invented' by Peugeot, so Coatalen thought it normal to use side valves like the production engine. However, the 'racer' used a monobloc cylinder casting, whereas production cars had twin pairs, and the stroke was lengthened to 149mm to take full advantage of the regulations. Incidentally, it may be more than coincidence that W.O. Bentley's first 3-litre car also used identical dimensions a few years later. Another change from the production chassis was that the racing car used a straight-bevel final drive, whereas production cars had used a worm drive. In 1911 form, the four-speed gearbox had an 'overdrive' top gear ratio, although this was changed to give revised ratios and a direct top gar for the following year.

The 1911 cars, which looked rather ungainly because of the angular coachwork lines and the vestigial wings fitted to satisfy the scrutineers, were not a success. For 1912, though, everything was to be different. Coatelen had learnt much from the first race and, although the 1912 event was not scheduled until the end of June, he sent much revised cars to the circuit near Dieppe in February for practice and training. The new cars were much sleeker and more striking, as well as rather more powerful than in the year before. Although a touring-car gearbox was still used, it had closer ratios in this racing application. The cars' maximum speed was around 90mph, which was very creditable, although Coatalen had hoped for 100mph. Five cars were taken to the race, one

of them a spare. In the event, over this very gruelling two-day course, three of the four cars survived to win the *voiturette* section of the race outright (Grand Prix machines could also enter). Rigal drove the winning car, averaging 65.3mph, which compared well with the best Grand Prix car (Peugeot) speed of 68.45mph.

In 1913, the same cars were improved, and used once more, with the important (but disastrously wrong) innovation of having axles without differentials. Power was increased to about 87bhp and maximum speed was increased to between 95 and 100mph. Three cars were entered and the 1913 race was held at Boulogne. In that year, success was not as sweeping, but Guinness' car took third place overall behind two of the Peugeots. The cars also raced at Brooklands in 1912 and 1913. Touring 12-16s were improved noticeably because of the racing experience, and by 1914 sporting models with Coupe de l'Auto details were on sale, but in rather detuned form. As Sixteens these cars were also adopted by the British army as staff cars for the 1914-18 conflict – made by Rover in Coventry on Sunbeam's behalf, as the firm was too busy building aero-engines. In post-war days the cars carried on until 1924, before finally being replaced by more modern 'vintage' designs.

The Sunbeams, like the Peugeots with which they were contemporary, proved for the first time that it was often wiser to get more performance by improving engine efficiency than by increasing engine size and Coatalen's careful attention to roadholding and reliability was also significant. Sunbeam's great successes with Grand Prix cars in the 1920s stems from this experience.

Below: In almost every way the Coupe de l'Auto Sunbeams were typical of pre-Great War voiturettes. Illustrated are the three versions raced by the factory. Car '17' is the original 1911 version, with a rather humped body, as driven at Boulogne by T. Richards without success. Car '4' is the 1913 car, with a revised body and much lower seating.

Tatra

Type 77, built from 1934 to 1937
Built by: Ringhoffer-Tatra-Werke AG, Czechoslovakia.
Engine: Eight cylinders, in 90-degree vee-formation, in three-bearing cast-iron block/crankcase, cylinder block with fins and air-cooling. Bore and stroke 75mm by 84mm, 2,970cc (2.95 × 3.31in, 181.2cu.in). Two detachable cylinder heads. Two overhead valves per cylinder, and operated by pushrods and rockers from single camshaft mounted in centre of cylinder-block 'vee'. Single down-draught Zenith carburettor. Dry-sump lubrication. Maximum power 60bhp at 3,500rpm.
Transmission: Single-dry-plate clutch and four-speed manual gearbox (without synchromesh), both in transaxle and in unit with rear-mounted engine. Clutch behind line of rear wheels and gearbox ahead of that line. Remote-control central gearchange. Spiral-bevel differential. Exposed, universally jointed drive shafts to rear wheels.
Chassis: Tubular-section steel backbone chassis frame with full-width four-door saloon body shell fixed to it. Independent front suspension by transverse leaf spring and swinging half axles. Four-wheel hydraulically operated drum brakes. Pressed-steel-disc wheels. 16 × 45 tyres.
Dimensions: Wheelbase 10ft 4in (315cm), tracks (front and rear) 4ft 3in (129.5cm). Overall length 16ft 11in (515.6cm). Unladen weight 3,700lb (1.678kg).
History: The first Tatras were built in 1923, having succeeded the Nesselsdorf cars built before that time. All Tatras have been built in Koprivnice in Czechoslovakia, but as this town was called Nesselsdorf and was in Austria, before and during World War I, the connection becomes a little more clear. Tatra's distinguished designer was Hans Ledwinka, who had started his career with Nesselsdorf at the end of the 19th century. He had, however, left that concern to join Steyr during the war, and only returned to the renamed town to design the first true Tatra of 1923. Right from the start, Ledwinka's cars exhibited their pedigree and his personal likes in motor car design. The first Type 11 used an air-cooled 'vee' engine and swing-axle rear suspension. Even though its engine was at the front, these traits were to be continued forward for generation after generation. The backbone chassis frame, similarly, was a Ledwinka trademark. Things progressed in logical fashion until the 1930s, when Tatra startled the entire motor car world by announcing the brand-new Type 77 machine. Not only was it a vee-engined air-cooled car, with backbone chassis and swing-axle suspension, but the engine was at the rear, overhung behind the line of the back wheels, and the full-width body was streamlined in a more successful style than that of Chrysler's Airflow, which had preceded it. The Type 77

was the first of a whole family of Tatras.

The backbone chassis tube was forked at its rear and embraced an air-cooled 90-degree V8 engine. The power pack, unusually for its time, but familiarly today, had the engine behind the line of the transaxle and the gearbox ahead of it, so that the gear linkage could pass through the backbone tube to a lever between the front seats. The rear suspension, as in so many subsequent rear-engine designs, featured a massively wide transverse leaf spring clamped to the top of the axle case and fixed to hub carriers at each side; along with the fixed length half-shafts this gave the car swing-axle rear suspension. The Type 77 was a big car in every way. It was as long from bumper to bumper as a Rolls-Royce of the 1970s and weighed about 3,700lb (1,678kg) without passengers, so its engine had to work hard to give it a respectable performance. Maximum speed was of the order of 85mph (or more than 90mph when an enlarged 3,400cc engine was fitted). Handling was not very good – a combination of the heavy rear engine and the swing-axle suspension did not help – but there was an astonishing amount of space by conventional standards. The absence of a normal chassis frame was a great advance, of course, and the full width styling did the rest.

During the 1930s the Type 77 family was steadily improved and expanded. After the Type 77A came the Type 87, in which the engine became 2,970cc again, but with a lot of weight taken out of the car, and power output boosted to about 75bhp, maximum speeds of up to 100mph were claimed. A sister car, the Type 97, with the same basic body but with a new horizontally opposed four-cylinder 1,760cc engine, produced only 40bhp. After the German occupation I 1939, private car manufacture was discouraged, and the factory was turned over to truck production, although there were Type 87 models on sale until 1941. Tatra's factories were nationalised by the Communist Czech state in 1945 and the Type 87 rear-engined car was put back into production. The engine pedigree of the Type 77/87/97 family was lost in 1948 when the Tatraplan 600 appeared, but even this car was based on the same structure and chassis engineering. Production was transferred to Mlada Boleslav from Koprivnice, to make way for expanded truck production, and sales of cars continued to be restricted to Czechoslovakia and her immediate friendly neighbours. There was even a gap between 1954 and 1957 when no private cars were made at all, but the new Type 603, which still subscribed to the well-known Ledwinka layout was then introduced, with a 2,472cc rear-mounted air-cooled V8 engine. This car, in much restyled and much modernised form, is now known as the T613, and survives with a 3.4-litre engine. A classic, if unconventional strain.

Left: The rear-engined Type 77 Tatra, one of the most famous designs ever to come from Hans Ledwinka's drawing board. It was made in restricted numbers in Czechoslovakia, yet contained many advanced features. The engine was an air-cooled vee-8 at the rear, the style of body full-width, and there was all-independent suspension from a tubular steel backbone chassis frame. The wind-cheating qualities were good, but the car was heavy and handled rather badly.

Thomas-Flyer

K-6-70 models, built from 1907 to 1912 (data for 1908 New York-Paris racing car)

Built by: E.R. Thomas Motor Co., United States.

Engine: Four cylinders, in line, in four separate cast-iron blocks, with three-bearing light-alloy crankcase. Bore and stroke 146.1mm by 139.7mm, 9,362cc (5.75in × 5.5in, 571cu.in). Non-detachable cast-iron cylinder heads. Two side valves per cylinder, in T-head layout with valve stems and springs exposed, operated by two camshafts mounted in sides of crankcase. Single up-draught carburettor. Maximum power 72bhp.

Tansmission: Triple-dry-plate clutch, in unit with front-mounted engine, and separate four-speed manual gearbox (without synchromesh). Remote-control right-hand gearchange. Straight-bevel differential, in tail of gearbox, and countershaft drive to exposed sprockets. Final drive to rear axle by side chains.

Chassis: Separate pressed-steel chassis frame, with channel-section side members and pressed cross bracing. Forged front axle beam. Front and rear suspension by semi-elliptic leaf springs. Friction-type dampers (on New York-Paris race car). Worm-type steering. Mechanically operated foot brake by externally contracting bands on drums fixed to transmission countershaft each side of gearbox. Mechanically operated hand brake by externally contracting

bands on rear wheel drums. Fixed artillery-style wheels. 36 × 4in tyres (front) and 36 × 5in tyres (rear).
Dimensions: Wheelbase 11ft 8in (356cm), tracks (front and rear) 4ft 8in (142cm).
History: Edwin Ross Thomas was a businessman, previously interested in railways, bicycles and motor cycles, although he never learned to drive a car. The first Thomas car was built in 1902 and the name changed to Thomas-Flyer in 1905. By that year the range included four big chaindrive cars, 40hp and 50hp fours and a 60hp six, all in the best North American engineering traditions, with individually cast cylinders on an alloy crankcase, a T-head layout and fixed cylinder heads. Prices ranged from $3,000 to $7,000 – which put the cars in the Peerless/Packard bracket.

The company's high spot was in winning the New York-Paris race in 1908. A K-6-70 model driven by George Schuster (the company's chief road tester) took 170 days to complete 13,341 miles – and that car is preserved at Harrah's Collection in the United States. The car was quite typical of Thomas-Flyer engineering at the time, except that shaft-drive cars were already being offered. The famous victory, however, meant that the K-6-70 model was retained, complete with chain drive, until 1912, by which time its engine had been enlarged to 12.8-litres.

Below: There were Thomas cars from 1902 and Thomas-Flyers from 1905. At first they all featured chain drive, and big T-head pattern engines, but from 1908 conventional shaft drive was also used. The 1909 model shown had everything a wealthy North American enthusiast could need, including fine styling, a strong chassis, ample ground clearance and good effortless performance. The Thomas-Flyer which won the mammoth 170-day New York to Paris road race of 1908 (a distance of 13,341 miles) was a factory-developed version of the standard product, and was driven by the company's chief tester. This historic car has been restored, and is in Harrah's Collection, in America.

Toyota MR2

Toyota MR2, two-seater sports coupé, built from 1984 to 1989 (data for the original model)
Built by: Toyota Motor Co. Ltd., Japan.
Engine: Four cylinders, in line, in five-main-bearing cast-iron cylinder block. Bore and stroke 81 × 77mm, 1,587cc (3.19 × 3.03in, 96.9cu.in). Light-alloy cylinder head. Four-valves per cylinder, in vee, operation by twin overhead camshafts and inverted bucket tappets. Nippondenso electronic fuel injection. Maximum power 122bhp (DIN) at 6,600rpm. Maximum torque 105lb.ft at 5,000rpm.
Transmission: Rear-wheel-drive, single-dry-plate diaphragm spring clutch and five-speed all-synchromesh manual gearbox, all in unit with transverse mid-mounted engine. Remote-control, central gearchange.
Chassis: Unitary-construction pressed-steel body-chassis unit, in two-seater sports coupé style. Independent front suspension by MacPherson struts, coil springs, wishbones, telescopic dampers, and anti-roll bar. Independent rear suspension by MacPherson struts, coil springs, lower wishbones, telescopic dampers, and anti-roll bar. Rack-and-pinion steering. Four-wheel disc brakes, with vacuum servo assistance. Cast alloy 14in road wheels, 185/60-14in tyres.
Dimensions: Wheelbase 7ft 6in (232cm), front track 4ft 6in (137.2cm), rear track 4ft 6in (137.2cm). Overall length 12ft 6in (392.5cm). Unladen weight 2,319lb (1,051kg).
History: Too many cynics have branded the Japanese motor industry as no more than expert copiers – and lived to regret this. In the case of the mid-engined Toyota MR2, though, the jibe was justified. What happened seemed to be perfectly clear. Never having been in the 1.6-litre sporting coupé market

section with an appealing and well-packaged car, Toyota studied the opposition, concluded that the Fiat X1/9 was a much better car than any of the front-engine/rear-drive opposition, and designed a new car on the same lines.

Although the company boasted that it had spent a decade developing its ideas, by the time it appeared the MR2 (Toyota told us that 'MR' meant 'Midship Runabout') was a familiar layout. Inside the all-steel, monocoque steel two-seater coupé, the 1.6-litre engine and five-speed transmission was mounted behind the cabin, positioned across the car, and drove the rear wheels. In all but detail (and the fact that the steering gear was omitted!), this power pack was lifted straight out of the front-wheel-drive Corolla GT. MacPherson strut front and rear suspension, a small space for stowage up front (ahead of the toeboard) and a larger space behind the engine, in the extreme tail, were all exactly as already well-known in the Fiat X1/9. The only significant packaging differences were that the spare wheel of the MR2 was mounted up front, and the roof panel could not be removed for summer-time motoring.

The style was still in the 'Japanese origami' trend of the day, with a wedge-nose, sharply defined edges, with a sharply cut off coupé roof, and with a sizeable spoiler across the tail to trim the handling. As on other, larger Toyotas, the headlamps were normally hidden, but could be flipped up when needed. This, though, was strictly a two-seater, for the sports seats, when pushed back to the limit of their slides, were hard against the bulkhead immediately in front of the engine – not even space to stow a briefcase being left over.

Toyota, of course, had done an extremely competent development job, and had also produced a car which looked well, handled well, and was as refined as any of its saloon car counterparts. As originally sold in Europe and the USA, with a 122bhp engine, it was good for nearly 120mph. That, though, was only one of the types available, for Toyota produced a very meek-and-mild 1.5-litre/83bhp version for home consumption, balancing that eventually with a 145bhp/1.6-litre supercharged type for true extroverts. Then, to round off the range, in 1986 a removable-roof derivative was launched, this allowing two small panels to be taken out (leaving a rigid T-bar still connecting the screen rail to the rear) and either stowed up front in the front 'luggage' area, or left at home.

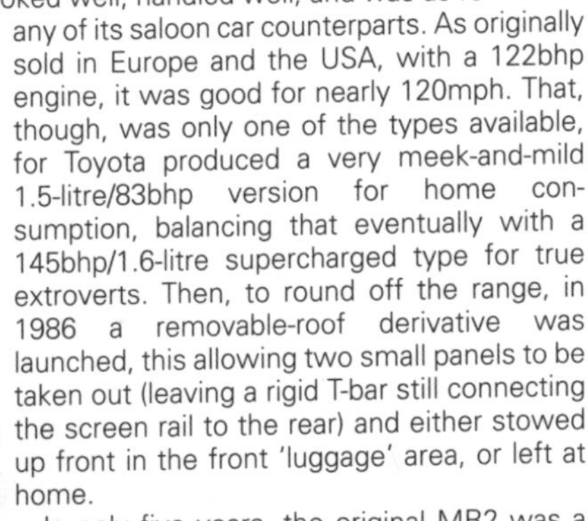

In only five years, the original MR2 was a great success, for no fewer than 166,104 such cars were sold (many of them on the West Coast of North America) before the second-generation MR2, a much larger, somehow softer-character, and more spacious model, came along. Having established itself in this market sector, however, Toyota was not about to give in lightly, and a third-generation type was put on sale before the end of the century.

Left: The original MR2 of 1984-1989 had very sharp-edge styling: the removable-panel version was an option.

Triumph TR Sports Cars

TR2, TR3, TR3A, TR3B, TR4, TR4A, TR5 and TR6 (data for TR3A)
Built by: Standard-Triumph Motor Co. Ltd., Britain – later British Leyland Motor Corporation Ltd., Britain
Engine: Four cylinders, in line, in three-bearing cast-iron block. Bore and stroke 83mm by 92mm, 1,991cc (3.27in × 3.62in, 121.5cu.in). Cast-iron cylinder head. Two overhead valves per cylinder, operated by pushrods and rockers from single side-mounted camshaft. Twin semi-downdraught SU carburettors. Maximum power 100bhp (net) at 5,000rpm. Maximum torque 118lb.ft at 3,000rpm.
Transmission: Single-dry-plate clutch and four-speed synchromesh manual gearbox (no synchromesh in first gear), with optional Laycock overdrive, all in unit with engine. Remote-control central gearchange. Open propeller shaft to hypoid-bevel 'live' rear axle.
Chassis: Separate steel chassis frame, with box-section side members, box and tubular cross bracing and cruciform centre section. Independent front suspension by coil springs and wishbones with telescopic damper. Rear suspension by semi-elliptic leaf springs and lever-type hydraulic dampers. Worm-and-peg steering. Four-wheel, hydraulically operated brakes, front discs and rear drums. 15in pressed-steel-disc wheels or centre-lock wire spoke wheels. 5.50 × 15in tyres. Open two-seat pressed-steel sports car bodywork, with optional steel hardtop.
Dimension: Wheelbase 7ft 4in (224cm), track (front) 3ft 9in (114cm), track (rear) 3ft 10in (117cm). Overall length 12ft 7in (384cm). Unladen weight 2,170lb (984kg).
History: Triumph were taken over by the Standard company in 1945. Several minor attempts were made to sell successful pre-war Triumphs in the 1940s, but it was the inspired improvisation which produced the TR2 that really provided the spark. The TR sports car was requested by managing director Sir John Black as a small-production car to compete with MG and Morgan, but using many standard parts. The prototype even used a much-modified pre-war Standard Nine chassis frame, which made it certain that the roadholding would be poor; development soon eradicated the problems, however. The TR2's design started in 1952, the car was on sale by summer 1953 and by the end of 1954 it was an acknowledged success. The formula, apart from low cost and simplicity, was to use the understressed Vanguard ▶

Right: Perhaps the most 'classic' of all Triumph TRs – the TR3A built from 1957 to 1962. This was the improved version of the TR2, with front-wheel disc brakes, and a 100bhp engine. It was the most popular British rally car of the 1950s, winning many events.

Above: Spiritual ancestor of the TR2, but with little common engineering was the TRX prototype of 1950. Only three were built (two are still in use) with this smooth two-seater touring body. The chassis and engine were Standard Vanguard, and there was electro-hydraulic operation of seats, hood, and headlamp covers. The body shell was of double-skinned alloy. Unfortunately the car was quite heavy, and could only reach about 80mph.

engine, tuned and modified (and sleeved down below the important 2-litre competition class limit), with modified versions of the Vanguard's gear-box and back axle behind it. The chassis frame was, in production form, quite new, but front suspension was from the quaintly styled Mayflower saloon. The Laycock overdrive was an important option, and before long this was arranged to operate on top, third *and* second gears. The TR2 was fast – it could nudge 110mph – and recorded more than 30mpg in everyday use. It was also very rugged and reliable, which made it an ideal prospect for European-style rallying. Private owners also found that the engine could be persuaded to give more than 120bhp and found the TR2 a worthy club-race car. The factory also raced, for publicity purposes and to prove engineering developments such as the Girling disc brakes tried successfully at Le Mans in 1955.

The TR2 became the TR3 in 1955, with more power, and a year later that car was equipped with front-wheel disc brakes – the first British car to be so offered. For 1958, the TR3 became the TR3Am, with yet more power (100bhp instead of the TR2's original 90bhp), with a revised front style, better trim and more standard fittings. The doors now had outside handles and with the hardtop the car was a cheekily effective little GT car. Before the last of the TR3As was sold in 1962 a total of 83,500 examples had been built and the United States market in particular had taken the car to its heart. MG, for all their traditions, feared the TRs very much and did everything they could to surpass them. After the TR3A, changes came thick and fast. In 1961 the TR4 arrived, really an improved TR3 chassis, with modern wind-up-window body by Michelotti. Less than four years later the TR4A was revealed, using TR4 mechanicals and the same basic body, but with a new all-independent suspension chassis (rear coil spring suspension was like that of the luxurious Triumph 2000 saloon).

That was the last of the 'traditional' four cylinder engined TRs, for the TR5 of 1967 was really a TR4A in chassis and body with the relatively new fuel-injected six-cylinder 2,498cc engine, also developed for Triumph 2000 saloon use. The last of the changes to the still-recognisable strain came at the beginning of the 1969 year, when the Karmann-styled bodyshell, adapted from that of the TR5, was announced as the TR6. The TR6, then taking on the mantle of almost a 'vintage style' British sports car, ran more or less unchanged until 1976, when it was finally phased out from the North American market. The last examples had been sold in Britain and Europe a year earlier. By then the TR6 had been superseded by the all-new TR7 which carried over absolutely none of the traditional features. The TR's attraction, whether in 1955, 1965 or 1975, was that is was a determinedly simple machine, refined enough for its purpose, but nevertheless a man's car. Well over a quarter million of all types produced – TR2 to TR6 – confirm that the formula was right.

Top: One of the very first Triumph TR2s, built in the autumn of 1953. The driver is Ken Richardson, who had much to do with the car's development and its (later) competition programme. The TR2 was simple, strong, and offered remarkable value for money. Only 8,628 TR2s were built, but well over a quarter million TRs were sold.

Middle: By 1967 the Triumph TR series had already been given one new body shell and an all-independent chassis. Then came this version, the TR5, with a 2½-litre six-cylinder engine, with fuel injection (first on a British production car), and 150bhp. It could reach 120mph, was restyled for 1969, and became the long-running TR6.

Bottom: Last in the line was the fixed-head coupé TR7, with its engine taken from the Dolomite saloon range. The TR7 was aimed particularly at the North American market, and fittings like the 'safety' bumpers are obvious on this example. The last TR7 was built in 1981.

OHP 242

LDU 158F

TVR Griffith

TVR Griffith sports car, introduced in 1992 (original specification)
Built by: TVR Engineering Ltd., Britain.
Engine: Eight cylinders, in 90-degree vee formation, in cast-alloy cylinder block/crankcase. Bore and stroke 94 × 77mm, 4,280cc (3.70 × 3.03in, 261cu.in). Two light-alloy cylinder heads. Two valves per cylinder, overhead, in line, operation by pushrods and rockers from a single camshaft mounted in the vee of the block. Lucas fuel injection. Maximum power 280bhp (DIN) at 5,500rpm. Maximum torque 305lb.ft at 4,000rpm.
Transmission: Rear-wheel-drive, single-plate diaphragm spring clutch and five-speed all-synchromesh manual gearbox, all in unit with front-mounted engine. Remote-control, central gearchange.
Chassis: Separate multi-tube chassis frame, of basic backbone profile. Glass-fibre body shell. Independent front suspension by coil springs, wishbones, telescopic dampers and anti-roll bar. Independent rear suspension by coil springs, wishbones and telescopic dampers. Rack-and-pinion steering. Four-wheel disc brakes, with vacuum-servo assistance. Cast alloy wheels, 15in at front, 16in at rear, 205/55-15in (front) and 225/50-16in (rear) tyres.
Dimensions: Wheelbase 7ft 6in (228.6cm), front track 4ft 10in (147.3cm), rear track 4ft 10.4in (148.3cm). Overall length 13ft 0in (396.2cm). Unladen weight 2,304lb (1,045kg).
History: Amazing, isn't it, how one model name can be applied to entirely different cars? The original TVR Griffith of the 1960s was a raw, crude, fast, point-and-squirt machine, whereas the beautiful 1990s-style Griffith was an extremely desirable two-seater sports car. To quote one of the British magazines which tested it at the start of its life: 'So close to greatness, it hurts . . .' – which really sums up the miracle achieved by the tiny development team in Blackpool. Yet the car they originally conceived was not the car which went on sale.

At first TVR decided to convert an V8 S chassis, with a new body style, this being what was shown at the 1990 NEC Motor Show. Second thoughts, though, bred better ideas. Having kept the same swooping, achingly sleek body style,

Below: Like all other TVRs, the Griffith had a multi-tube chassis, all-independent suspension, and very high performance. The name harked back to an earlier TVR model.

Above: The rounded lines and complete lack of stick-on features meant that the Griffith looked right from every angle. It could exceed 160mph.

this was then applied to a lightly modified version of the racing Tuscan rolling chassis instead. At a stroke, here was a much stiffer backbone frame, but one that had always been intended to deal with a lot of high-torque Rover V8 power. But the Tuscan was loud, boisterous and in-your-face, and the Griffith could be none of those. The new model, which eventually went on sale in 1993, was altogether more sophisticated.

Everyone, but everyone, raved about its looks, for there was not a straight line nor a flat plane in evidence, no bumpers to get in the way of the airflow, and not a single flaw. Instead, here was a style, designed in-house, which started with an oval grille flanked by driving lamps, flowed over faired-in headlamps, swept across the doors which had no exterior method of being opened, and reached the curvaceous rump without a hiccup, or a blemish. Hidden away inside this desirable two-seater machine, as usual for a TVR of this period, was a much-modified version of the fuel-injected light-alloy Rover V8 engine and its matching five-speed gearbox, with all-independent suspension, four-wheel disc brakes, alloy wheels, and rack-and-pinion steering.

In the beginning, Griffiths were sold as 240bhp/3.9-litre cars, or 280bhp/4.3-litre cars, the larger and faster type being capable of more than 160mph. Nor was that available at silly prices, for to get 280bhp in 1992 you only had to pay a mere £28,295 – and the unique looks came free. The big rush in sales came at once, for more than 600 cars – well over half of the number of TVRs being assembled at the time – were delivered in 1992. TVR then introduced the Chimaera, a larger, somehow softer, and subtly less sporty machine than the Griffith, and the emphasis shifted away from the Griffith.

But not for long. The Griffith 500 then appeared in 1993, a car which combined a full 5.0-litre version of the engine, but delivering 325bhp into the bargain, and demand continued. here was a car which could tear away tyre treads at every opportunity, but one which still had a well-balanced chassis. By that time power-assisted steering was an option, the claimed top speed was up to 170mph, yet neither the style nor the appeal had diminished. It was still in TVR's ever-expanding product range at the end of the century.

Unic 12/14 Taxi

12/14 model, built from 1908 to 1928 (data for 1910 model)
Built by: Sté. Des Anciens Ets. Georges Richard (later S.A. des Automobiles Unic), France.
Engine: Four cylinders, in line, in cast-iron block, with three-bearing light-alloy crankcase. Bore and stroke 75mm by 110mm, 1,944cc (2.95in × 4.33in, 118.6cu.in); stroke increased to 120mm and capacity to 2,121cc (4.72in and 129.4cu.in) from 1912. Integral cast-iron cylinder head. Two side valves per cylinder, in T-head formation with exposed valve stems and springs, operated by tappets from crankcase-mounted camshafts. Single up-draught Unic carburettor. Maximum power about 15bhp at 1,500rpm.
Transmission: Cone clutch, in unit with front-mounted engine, and shaft drive to separate three-speed manual gearbox (without synchromesh). Remote-control right-hand gearchange. Open propeller shaft to straight-bevel 'live' rear axle.
Chassis: Separate pressed-steel chassis frame, with channel-section side members and channel-section cross bracing. Forged front axle beam. Front and rear suspension by semi-elliptic leaf springs. Optional lever-arm hydraulic dampers. Worm-and-sector steering. Rear wheel drum brakes operated by foot pedal. Transmission drum brake, externally contracting, operated by hand lever. Artillery-style wheels. 810 × 90mm tyres. Taxi-cab bodywork, with no front doors.
Dimensions: Wheelbase 8ft 10.3in (270cm), tracks (front and rear) 4ft 5in (135cm). Overall length 12ft 2.1in (371cm). Unladen weight (chassis only) 1,455lb (660kg).
History: The marque name derives from Georges Richard's desire to make only a single model of car from his new factory, but this resolve lasted less than a

Above: The legendary Unic 12/14 model, only ever sold as a taxicab, and a well known sight on London streets for a generation. The driver was exposed, but the 'fare' was comfortable.

year. Richard had left the Richard-Basier business in 1905, after a policy clash, and set up again nearby. Unic products were never famous for their performance, or for their looks, but the 12/14 model, which was never sold as a private car, is now legendary as the famous London taxi for more than a generation. The taxi was simple and rugged, having that mandatory tiny turning circle, and seemed to be mechanically indestructible. All the time that the taxi was being made, other private cars were being sold, but in general they were undistinguished and Unic became more interested in selling commercial vehicles (they are now a subsidiary of Fiat). Modern taxi drivers, and enthusiasts, should look closely at the Unic, to see the spartan conditions in which the drivers had to operate. They had no doors to keep them warm, and certainly no heater, although the fare-paying passengers were somewhat better off.

Left: Early in the life of the famous taxi, Unic also built a few private cars on the same basic chassis. In 1909 there was this two-seater tourer, which looked very sporting by the style standards of the Edwardian period.

Volvo P1800

P1800, 1800S, 1800E and 1800ES, built from 1960 to 1973 (data for 1800S)
Built by: AB Volvo, Sweden.
Engine: Four cylinders, in line, in five-bearing cast-iron block. Bore and stroke 84.1mm by 80mm, 1,778cc (3.31in x 3.15in, 108.6cu.in). Cast-iron cylinder head. Two overhead valves per cylinder, operated by pushrods and rockers from single side-mounted camshaft. Twin semi-down-draught constant-vacuum SU carburettors. Maximum power 100bhp (net) at 5,800rpm. Maximum torque 110lb.ft at 4,000rpm.
Transmission: Single-dry-plate clutch and four-speed, all-synchromesh manual gearbox, with electrically operated overdrive, all in unit with engine. Remote-control, central gearchange. Open propeller shaft to hypoid-bevel 'live' rear axle.
Chassis: Unitary-construction pressed-steel body chassis unit, in closed two-seat coupé form. Bodies built by Pressed Steel in Britain. Car assembled by Jensen, but from mid 1960s assembled by Volvo in Sweden. Independent front suspension by coil springs, wishbones and anti-roll bar. Rear suspension by coil springs, radius arms and Panhard rod. Cam-and-roller steering. Front disc brakes and rear drums. 15in bolt-on pressed-steel-disc wheels. 165 x 15in tyres.
Dimensions: Wheelbase 8ft 0.5in (245cm) tracks (front and rear) 4ft 3.8in (132cm). Overall length 14ft 5.3in (440cm). Unladen weight 2,500lb (1,140kg).
History: The Volvo 1800 sports coupé made its name all over the world as the car chosen by The Saint in that well known TV series based on the Leslie Charteris

Below: Although the P1800 was originally designed as a coupé, as the 1800ES, it was finally built as a smart 'sporting estate' from 1971.

Above: The P1800 reaped world-wide publicity when used by Roger Moore as 'Simon Templar's' car in the popular 1960s TV Series 'The Saint'. Those are non-standard Minilite wheels.

novels. It was a strikingly styled closed two-seater (shaped by Volvo without outside assistance) and used a compete power train from the Amazon range of saloons which had already established Volvo's reputation for rugged, reliable and no nonsense motoring. At the end of the 1950s Volvo were short of factory space, and made a unique agreement in Britain. Pressed Steel would build the body shells, while Jensen would assemble the cars from components supplied from Sweden. The arrangement worked well for a few years, until Volvo decided to upgrade the car, improve the quality, and make it themselves. P1800s were Jensen-built, while 1800S cars were built in Sweden. The 1800 engine was enlarged to a full two litres in 1968, but from 1969 this engine was given Bosch petrol injection and developed up to 125bhp. In 1971 Volvo jumped on the three-door band-wagon by giving the car an estate car shape with a vast opening rear window. This, as the 1800ES, carried on into 1973, when it was finally discontinued. There was no sporting-car successor from Volvo until 1997.

VW Beetle

Beetles, built in various forms from 1939 to date (data for 1950s-type 1200)
Built by: Volkswagenwerk GmbH, Germany.
Engine: Four cylinders, horizontally opposed in separate light-alloy cylinder barrels, with three-bearing light-alloy crankcase. Bore and stroke 77mm by 64mm, 1,192cc (3.04in × 2.52in, 72.7cu.in). Two light-alloy cylinder heads. Two overhead valves per cylinder, operated by pushrods and rockers from single camshaft, centrally mounted in crankcase. Single down-draught. Solex carburettor. Maximum power36bhp (gross) at 3,700rpm. Maximum torque 56lb.ft at 2,000rpm.
Transmission: Single-dry-plate clutch and four-speed synchromesh manual gearbox (without synchromesh in first gear), both in unit with rear-mounted flat-four engine. Engine behind line of rear wheels and gearbox ahead of it. Remote-control central gearchange. Spiral-bevel final drive and exposed, universally jointed drive shafts to rear wheels.
Chassis: Pressed-steel punt-type platform chassis frame, topped by bolted-on pressed-steel two-door saloon or convertible coachwork, all built by VW. Independent front suspension by trailing arms and transverse torsion bars. Independent rear suspension by swinging half-axles, radius arms, and transverse torsion bars. Telescopic dampers. Worm-and-roller steering. Four-wheel,

Above: This was the original Beetle, as unveiled in 1938. Neither the basic layout, nor the style, changed thereafter, but production did not start until 1945.

Below: Over the years, every Beetle component was changed or improved. By the 1970s there was a panoramic screen, MacPherson strut front suspension and a 1.6-litre engine. In 2000 the car was still being produced, in Mexico.

hydraulically operated drum brakes. 15in bolt-on pressed-steel-disc wheels. 5.60 × 15in tyres.
Dimensions: Wheelbase 7ft 10.5in (240cm), track (front) 4ft 3in (130cm), track (rear) 4ft 2in (127cm). Overall length 13ft 4in (406cm). Unladen weight 1,610lb (731kg).
History: By every logical consideration, the VW Beetle should never have succeeded. It was uncompromisingly original, the victim of politics and a ruinous world war, and it was rejected as war preparations by the so-called sophisticated car-makers. Yet the Germans persevered with it, put it haltingly into production at the end of 1945 and made an enormous success of it. To date – it is still being built (not in Germany but in several other countries, principally in Mexico) and more than 21 *million* have been sold – which makes the Beetle the best-selling car of all time. Only the Model T Ford could approach it and that now lags around five million behind. The VW has never officially been called a 'Beetle', but was given that nickname soon after its public debut at the end of the 1930s. The general layout of the car goes back even further into history than is generally realised. At first it was the private brainchild of Dr Ferdinand Porsche, who set up his own design studios in Stuttgart at the beginning of the 1930s. For Zundapp (a five-cylinder radial engined car) and for NSU (a flat-four) he designed rear-engined prototypes, but neither could afford to tool up for mass production. In 1934 Porsche was directed by the Nazi government to design a 'people's car'. The first three prototypes, similar in many ways to the NSU designs, were built by Porsche in his own workshops, and were ready in 1936. A series of 30 pre-production cars were built n his behalf by Mercedes-Benz in 1937 and by 1938 the final version was ready. Foundations for the new factory at Wolsburg were laid in 1938. But for the preparations for war the production cars would have been ready in 1939/40.

Military machines, using VW mechanicals, were built in the 1940s, but in 1945 the factory had been bombed and was nearly derelict, and private-car production had still not really begun. However, under the direction of the occupying powers (the British in this part of Germany) the cars began to be built; the first 1,785 examples were made before the end of 1945. At first they had 1,131cc engines, un-synchronised transmission and cable brakes, but they were remarkably cheap, reliable and popular in car-starved Germany. In spite of every possible practical and financial obstacle, sales continued to rise. By the end of the 1940s the factory was already being expanded and VW was well on its way to being a formidable German car maker, with the dedicated Nordhoff in charge of the business. Exports, world-wide, began at the start of the 1950s, and with this came the gradual refinement of the early crude machine. Technically, everything was against the Beetle's success: the roadholding was always poor, performance very restricted, styling was a non-event and passenger/luggage space was restricted. On the other hand, air-cooling meant that the Beetle could be used anywhere in the world and the car's impressive quality and reliability record soon made it an essential for the developing countries.

VW stayed faithful to the machine for far too long – they were a one-product company until the beginning of the 1960s – but this meant that they could concentrate every effort on the Beetle's progressive improvement. Engines were

Top: Only two details identify this as a Beetle of the late 1960s - the enlarged, rectangular, rear window, and the more prominent tail lamps.

Middle: By the early 1970s the Beetle had become the 13093S, complete with panoramic screen, MacPherson strut front suspension, and an 80mph top speed.

Bottom: As 'classic' cars, the rather rare Cabriolets are among the most desirable Beetles. Karman assembled these cars. As expected, build-quality was rock solid.

SKO
918H

GJJ 317N

enlarged to 1,192cc in the 1950s, but it was the end of the 1960s which saw the engine pushed up first to 1,300, then 1,500, and finally to 1,600. Hydraulic brakes. Porsche-type synchromesh and very high standards of construction were developed, but nothing was ever done about the living space and very little about the roadholding. An automatic transmission became optional at the end of the 1960s and for a long time Beetles were being built with three or four different engine sizes as options. As the car slipped more and more behind the times, it was given coil-spring front suspension and major restyling, but when VW began to announce their new water-cooled cars – Passat, Golf and Polo – in the 1970s, it became clear that the Beetle would be allowed to die. Interestingly enough, it has outlived all the cars developed from it – notably the VW1500/1600 range and the rather different 411/412 cars. Sales continue from overseas factories long after German production has ceased, mainly in South America and Mexico. It is the classic case of reliability and ruggedness succeeding against all fashion. Like the Model T Ford, it had no obvious close rivals and benefited strongly because of that.

Although VW had moved on immeasurably since the air-cooled Beetle was in its hey-day, the company could never wean its clientele away from that heritage, and there were persistent demands for them to 'do another Beetle'. Accordingly, in the mid-1990s the stylists were allowed to indulge themselves with a similar-looking car – but this time they had to base it on an existing model, the Golf hatchback.

Except for the pastiche style, which was complete with two passenger doors, and a ratherhumpback profile, a new shape but with certain similarities to the old, the 'New Beetle',as it was titled, could not have been mechanically more different under the skin. Front (transversely mounted) engined, with front-wheel-drive instead of rear/rear-drive, and water-cooled instead of air-cooled, this was a car more lavishly equipped than any old-style Beetle. Instead of one type of crude, flat-four engine, there was a complete range of modern overhead-camshaft engines – stretching from a four-cylinder 90bhp diesel to a powerful 150bhp/1.8-litre petrol engined version –

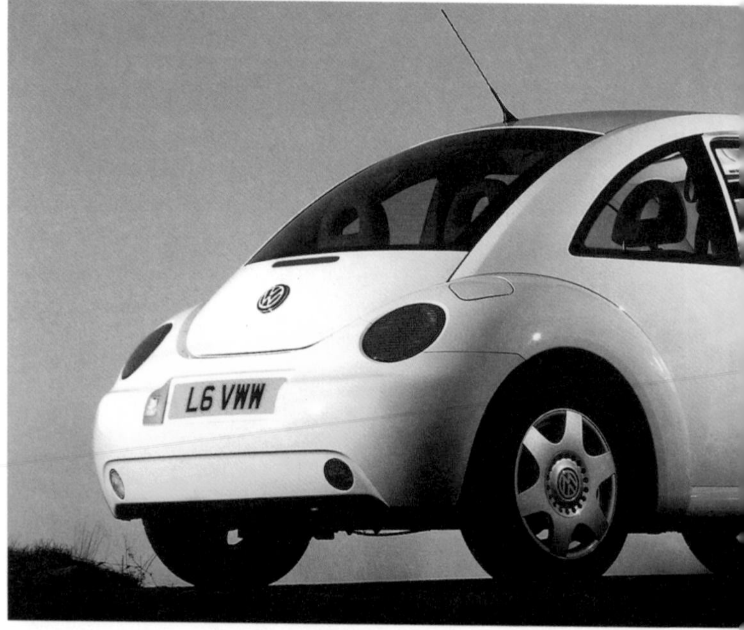

Above: Although the new Beetle of 1998 was based on the front-engined platform of the Golf, its style was a smoothed-over pastiche of the old-type Beetle.

and even the most humble model could reach 106mph, the 150bhp device being good for no less than 126mph.

Visually, for sure, there might have been a resemblance, but there was none in character, ambition, or in performance. But then, was there really any comparison with the old? That was Then. This is Now....

Left: Why build a front-engined car like this? Because the New Beetle played unashamed homage to the original type, including using its two-door layout and sloping tail.

Willys Jeep

Jeeps, built from 1942 onwards (data for 1942 military model)
Built by: Willys-Overland Co., United States.
Engine: Four cylinders, in line, in three-bearing cast-iron combined block/crankcase. Bore and stroke 79.4mm by 111.1mm, 2,199cc (3.12in × 4.37in, 134.2cu.in). Detachable cast-iron cylinder head. Two side valves per cylinder, operated, by tappets, from single camshaft mounted in side of cylinder block. One single-choke down-draught Carter carburettor. Maximum power 60bhp (gross) at 3,600rpm. Maximum torque 105lb.ft at 2,000rpm.
Transmission: Four-wheel-drive layout, with normal and emergency-low speed ranges. Single-dry-plate clutch and three-speed, synchromesh manual gearbox (without synchromesh in first gear), along with two-speed-range transfer box, all in line and in unit with front-mounted engine. Three direct-acting gearchanges, in centre of car. Optional front-wheel drive (can be locked in or out of action by one gear lever). Open propeller shaft from transfer box to front and rear hypoid-bevel 'live' axles.
Chassis: Separate pressed-steel chassis frame, with box-section side members and pressed-steel cross bracings. Live front and rear axle beams. Front and rear suspension by semi-elliptic leaf springs. Telescopic hydraulic dampers. Cam-and-lever steering. Four-wheel, hydraulically operated drum brakes, in wheel hubs. Cable operated hand brake, acting on internally expanding shoes in transmission drum behind transfer gearbox. Pressed-steel bolt-on disc wheels. 6.00 × 16in tyres. Open four-seat bodywork, cross-country type, with canvas hood.
Dimensions: Wheelbase 6ft 8in (203cm), tracks (front and rear) 4ft 0in (122cm). Overall length 11ft 1in (333cm). Unladen weight 2,315lb (1,050kg).
History: Until the beginning of World War II, Willys had led a largely

Above and below left: Two views of the legendary Willys Jeep. The vehicle's name was originally 'G.P.' – or 'General Purpose' – but was quickly modified. A Jeep could go anywhere, and do most things. It was simple, rugged and had excellent (four-wheel-drive) traction. Millions have now been made in military and civilian form.

unspectacular and often unsuccessful existence in Toledo. Indeed, as recently as 1933-1936 the company had been struggling through receivership with unpopular and dull cars. In 1939, however, Joe Frazer became president and general manager, and in 1942 he made sure that Willys got a contract to produce probably the most famous utility vehicle of all time – the four-wheel-drive Jeep. This machine was built against a US Army requirement for a general purpose (G.P.) vehicle for its forces, and although Bantam claim to have built the first such car it was Willys and Ford who reaped the benefit and produced many thousands of them. The 'Jeep' name was a natural bowdlerisation of 'G.P.', and Frazer was astute enough to register it as a Willys trade-mark, which survives to this day. Hundreds of thousands of military Jeeps were made and civilian versions are still in production. The Jeep, along with the British Land-Rover, which followed its layout closely, is probably the most universally exported and most universally appreciated, working machine in the world. The design was simple, rugged, and obvious. The 2.2-litre, four-cylinder engine had been used by Willys cars of the 1930s and there was a rugged three-speed gearbox with transfer gearing, a choice of upper or lower sets of ratios and the option of driven front-wheels or free-wheeling front wheels. The chassis had boxed main members, the tyres were 'chunkies' and the bodywork was rudimentary almost to a fault. It was meant to – and could – tackle almost anything, and during the war the Allied forces used their Jeeps as indiscriminately as they used bicycles. The Jeep might not have won the war, but victory would have been that much less attainable without it.

Wolseley Hornet Special

Wolseley Hornet Specials, built from 1932 to 1934
Built by: Wolseley Motors (1927) Ltd., Britain.
Engine: Six cylinders, in line, in four-bearing cast-iron block. Bore and stroke 57mm by 83mm, 1,271cc (2.24in × 3.27in, 77.5cu.in). Cast-iron cylinder head. Two overhead valves per cylinder, operated by single overhead camshaft. Twin-side-draught constant-vacuum SU carburettors. Power output not quoted. Maximum rpm about 5,000.
Transmission: Single-dry-plate clutch and four-speed manual gearbox, without synchromesh, but in unit with engine. Remote-control central gearchange. Open propeller shaft to spiral-bevel 'live' rear axle.
Chassis: Separate pressed-steel chassis frame, with channel-section double-drop side members and minimal pressed-section cross members. Forged front axle beam. Semi-elliptic leaf springs at front and rear, with hydraulic lever arm dampers. Worm-and-wheel steering. Four-wheel hydraulically operated drum brakes. 18in centre-lock wires wheels. 4.75 × 18in tyres. Supplied as rolling chassis to specialist coachbuilders.
Dimensions: Wheelbase 7ft 6.5in (230cm), track (front) 3ft 9in (114cm), track (rear) 3ft 6in (107cm). Overall length (depending on coachwork) from 11ft 5.2in (348cm). Unladen weight (chassis only) 1,316lb (597kg).
History: The Hornet special is a much maligned motor car. When in production, in the early 1930s, it got itself a bad name because of the flashy bodywork fitted by firms which Wolseley could not control. This was their own fault, as the Hornet

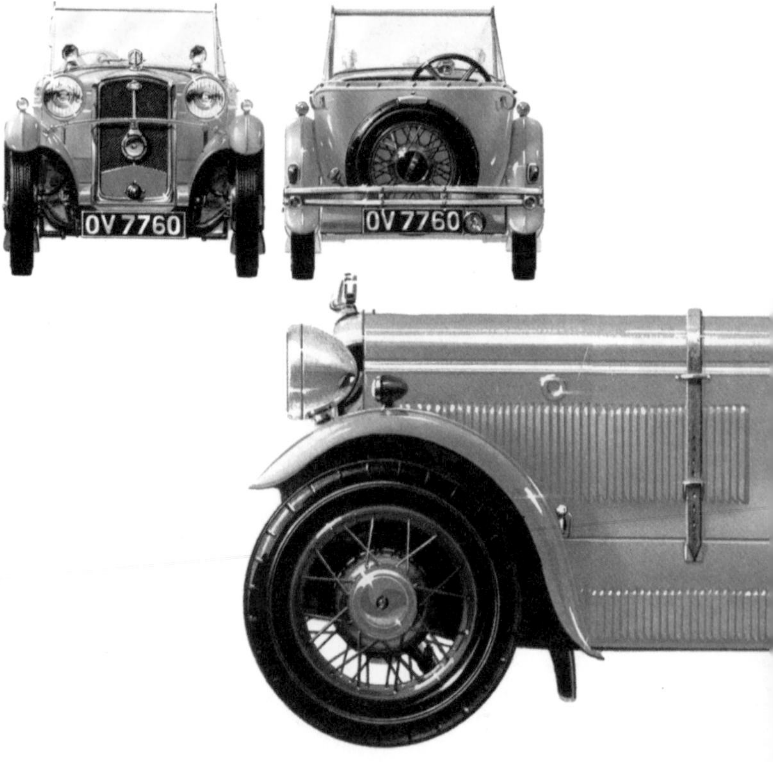

Special was sold purely as a rolling chassis. It must not be confused with Hornet saloons completely made by Wolseley in Birmingham. The Special's chassis was too flimsy, which made roadholding not as good as – say – that of an MG Magna with which it had to compete. The engine, although genealogically related to that of the six-cylinder MGs, was not as well developed, and not nearly as powerful. In particular it needed good cylinder-head breathing. The camshaft drive, note, was conventional in this version, by chain, whereas in the MG it was by vertical shaft incorporating the dynamo armature. MG and Wolseley were both personally owned by Sir William Morris at the time and eventually MG record-breaking experience with cross-flow cylinder heads led to this type being fitted to Hornet Specials.

Hornet Specials were rarely used in racing, as their engine size was well below the 1½-litre class limit, but coachbuilders like Eustace Watkins and Swallow could produce some very purposeful sports-car bodies. Cars could have two-seat or four-seat layouts to choice. Along with the cross-flow cylinder head, 1934 models also had synchromesh added to top and third gears, while the chassis frame had cross-bracing added in the shape of a distorted cruciform. Finally, in 1935, the Hornet Special's engine was enlarged to 1,604cc (once again, quite unsuitable for serious competition), with a larger bore *and* stroke of 61.5mm by 90mm (2.42in × 3.54in, 97.9cu.in). In this form it boasted 50bhp at 4,500rpm and was lively though rather under-geared. After 1935, with Nuffield rationalisation progressing apace, the Hornet Special was discontinued and MG was the group's only future sports car.

Left and below: Every Hornet Special had a coachbuilt body, as Wolseley only sold a rolling chassis. Swallow, who later evolved the SS car, built this four-seater in 1932. Hidden away is the double-drop chassis frame, and the six cylinder engine which was related to MG units of the day. At the time, the bodies were sometimes thought to be flashy. There were two- and four-seat Hornet Specials, with bolt-on or knock-off wire wheels. The louvres and the bonnet strap were typical, and looks were as important as speed.

Wolseley 'Horizontal-Engined' Models

Wolseley single, twin- and four-cylinder cars, built from 1900 to 1905 (data for 1902 10hp)
Built by: Wolseley Tool and Motor Car Co Ltd., Britain.
Engine: Two cylinder, parallel to each other, in two-bearing cast-iron block, horizontally positioned under the forward floor. Bore and stroke 114.3mm by 127mm, 2,606cc (4.5in × 5.0in, 159cu.in). Cast-iron cylinder head. Two valves per cylinder, automatic (atmospheric) inlet valve and side exhaust valve operated by single cylinder-block mounted camshaft. Leaf-spring return pressure for exhaust valve. Single Wolseley carburettor. Maximum power 10bhp at 700rpm.
Transmission: Leather-faced cone clutch and Renolds chain drive from clutch to separately mounted gearbox. Sliding-pinion gears, giving four forward speeds; differential and countershaft inside gearbox and final drive by side chain on exposed sprockets to rear wheels.
Chassis: Separate steel chassis frame, with channel-section side members and pressed-steel cross members. Forged front axle beam. Semi-elliptic leaf springs at front and rear. No dampers, Tiller steering at first, but wheel steering by 1902. Steering by worm and wheel. Footbrake operating gearbox countershaft-mounted drum. Handbrake (early series) acting on rear wheel rims (later series) or in drums in rear wheel hubs. Wooden artillery road wheels. Coachwork to choice – ash framing and hand-beaten steel panels.
Dimensions: Wheelbase 7ft (213cm), track (front) 4ft (122cm), track (rear) 4ft 1.2in (125cm). Overall length (with four-seat tonneau body) 10ft 9.8in (330cm).
History: The Wolseleys built between 1900 and 1905 are historically important because they were really the first *wholly British* machines in any sort of quantity-production. Daimler were selling cars which were mainly Benz copies and Lanchesters. The very first Wolseley (a tricycle) was built in 1896 and the second (also a tri-car) followed in 1897/98. These two cars, like all the later horizontal-engined models, were designed by Herbert Austin, General Manager of the

Above: Entrance to rear seats was from the back.

Wolesely company. Their story comes to an end when Austin's career at Wolseley ends. In effect, his directors wanted to adopt vertical engines and Austin refused to design such things. The result was that he left the company, formed his own Austin concern – then introduced a series of vertical engined Austins! His first four-wheel Wolseley voiturette was built in 1899 and examples competed in the Automobile Club's 1,000 Miles Trial of 1900. Its performance was such that the company decided to go into production with it. That first car, a single-cylinder machine, was speedily followed by others – twins or horizontal in-line fours – between 1900 and 1905. A total of 327 cars were sold in 1901 and 800 in 1903. This made Wolseley the most prolific of all British makes, a lead which they retained until the out break of World War I. ▶

Below: From 1900 to 1905 the horizontal-engined Wolseleys grew up steadily. The first cars were singles with 4½hp, but by 1905 there were twins and four-cylinder machines. This 10hp twin was built in 1902. The Wolseley-built body is a 'tonneau' and the mechanical layout is typical of the range.

Features of the layout were that the single-cylinder 4½hp engine was placε under the tow-board, with the axis of the cylinder pointing forward and the heac therefore, being at the front of the unit. Whereas the prototype slipped its primary drive belt (from engine flywheel to separately mounted gearbox) the production car had a conventional cone clutch between crank-shaft and belt pulley. The gearbox, mounted amidships, had a countershaft with the final drive teeth attached to it, and drive to the rear wheels was by chain. The 1,000 Miles Trial car had had tiller steering, but this was replaced by conventional wheel steering in 1901. Within months the first production Wolseley was joined by the 10hp twin-cylinder model, which effectively had double the original engine, but mounted essentially in the same place in a rather longer and more capacious chassis. Between 1900 and 1904 the single's power output was pushed up to 6hp, while the twin was consequently urged to give 12hp. Between 1902 and 1904 there was also a more expensive horizontal-engined 'four', with a horizontally opposed layout, which also shared the same cylinder dimensions. This engine, for obvious reasons, had two primary chain drives to the gearbox, one on each end of the engine's crankshaft, and therefore two clutches. A feature common to many other cars of the period was the 'automatic' or atmospheric inlet valve, opened by suction within the cylinder during the appropriate stroke. This was not at all efficient and one reason for the cars, improvements in power in later years was that a mechanically operated inlet valve was specified. Austin was a great believer in motor sport for publicity purposes (at least, he was at this time – later he changed his tune somewhat) and caused a whole series of vast horizontally engined race cars to be built for the Paris-Madrid, Circuit des Ardennes, and Gordon Bennett events. Called Beetles these machines never enjoyed much success.

Once the Wolseley directors had decided they preferred vertical engines (and inexorable motoring fashion all over the world suggested that they should), there was no future for the original range of cars at Wolseley. The company had already been building Siddeleys, on behalf of J.D. Siddeley, which had vertical engines, and these were satisfactory. The last 'horizontal' Wolseley was built in 1906, but it left behind a legacy of well-proven design details and a company which was already renowned in the British motor industry.

Below: In 1904 the single-cylinder 6hp Wolseley looked like this with its engine under the floor, and final drive by chain. There was no windscreen. Wheels were fixed.